"*I feel an intense pride, Robert, that I live in a country rich enough to have war and peace at the same time.*"

The Dollar

US balance of payments deficits, aggravated by the Vietnam War, resulted in the collapse of the Bretton Woods system of fixed exchange rates. US dollar devaluations, in 1971 and 1973, provoked anger among oil producers, which led them to raise oil prices.

"*Call me a sentimental fool, but I still worship the almighty dollar.*"

Take Your Partners

Orion, the Consortium Banks and the Transformation of the Euromarkets

Richard Roberts

with

Christopher Arnander

palgrave

First published 2001 by
PALGRAVE
Houndmills, Basingstoke, Hampshire RG21 6XS and
175 Fifth Avenue, New York, N.Y. 10010
Companies and representatives throughout the world

PALGRAVE is the new global academic imprint of
St. Martin's Press LLC Scholarly and Reference Division and
Palgrave Publishers Ltd (formerly Macmillan Press Ltd).

ISBN 0–333–94774–6

This book is printed on paper suitable for recycling and made from fully managed and sustained forest sources.

A catalogue record for this book is available from the British Library.

Library of Congress Cataloging-in-Publication Data

Roberts, Richard, 1952–
    Take your partners : Orion, the consortium banks and the transformation of the Euromarkets/Richard Roberts with Christopher Arnander.
        p. cm.
    Includes bibliographical references and index.
    ISBN 0–333–94774–6
    1. Orion Royal Bank. 2. Bank consortia—Europe. 3. Euro-dollar market.
4. Euro-bond market. I. Arnander, Christopher. II. Title.

    HG2998.O75 R63 2000
    332.4'94—dc21   00-049108

10   9   8   7   6   5   4   3   2   1
10   09   08   07   06   05   04   03   02   01

Printed in Great Britain by Antony Rowe Ltd,
Chippenham, Wiltshire

Contents

Foreword

by the Rt. Hon. Sir Edward George,
Governor of the Bank of England

The heyday of Orion and its fellow consortium banks in the 1970s now seems a different era in very many respects. The Euromarkets they were mostly set up to exploit, which were at that time still relatively new and in a stage of rapid growth, have now long since become an established and familiar part of the financial scene. And the consortium investment bank itself looks a strange beast from the perspective of the turn of the millennium, when international investment banking has become a theatre for fierce competition rather than co-operative endeavour between institutions. But while the *form* of financial innovation may have changed, the fact of it is ever-present, and as the impact of the Internet begins to be felt it is interesting to see that some institutions have chosen to combine with others to develop their on-line business activities when confronted with a new and unfamiliar market with high entry costs – much as their predecessors did thirty years ago.

Another theme with contemporary resonance is the impact of tax and regulation on financial institutions and markets. It is generally accepted that a large part of the reason why London became the centre of activity for the Euromarkets was that it was considered, as is mentioned in Chapter 1, 'a very warm place for doing business.' That much, I hope, has not changed over the subsequent decades, and I like to think that the Bank of England has played its part in making it so. A successful market-place must have rules of engagement however, and I note that two initiatives of the Bank of England – the 'Blunden letter' of 1974 seeking letters of comfort from the major shareholders of UK-incorporated banks, and the provisioning matrix of 1987 – are interpreted as having made life more difficult for the consortium banks. The Bank of England is still very much involved in the striking of this balance, although nowadays our concern is with the stability of the system as a whole rather than the regulation of individual institutions.

But, above all, the story of Orion and of consortium banking more broadly stands as a fascinating account of a period of innovation, growth and, periodically, of crisis in the international financial markets.

E. A. J. George

Preface and Acknowledgements

Take Your Partners: Orion, the Consortium Banks and the Transformation of the Euromarkets tells the story of Orion, setting it within the context of the development of consortium banking and the Euromarkets. Orion was the most ambitiously conceived and, in its heyday, the most successful of the consortium banks. Covering Orion, the consortium banks and the European banking clubs, this volume fills a gap in the literature on late twentieth century banks and banking.

The project to write the Orion story had its origins at a dinner to celebrate the 75th birthday of William de Gelsey, who worked for the bank in a senior capacity from 1971 to 1989. Together with Lord Swaythling, who as David Montagu led Orion at its peak and who sadly did not live to see the completion of this book, a project was launched to write the history of the bank. A group of ex-Orion executives, Patrick Browning, Rod Chamberlain, Charles Fisher, Michael Perry, Philip Hubbard and William de Gelsey, came together to push the project forward. They were joined by Christopher Arnander, a friend and retired banker, who became the project's principal *animateur*. I became involved when I was approached by him as the potential author. I welcomed the opportunity to tackle such an interesting subject and to extend my understanding of the Euromarkets. I have worked closely with him in the preparation of the text and his advice has been invaluable, particularly in relation to the appendices and the illustrations. The whole group has been very supportive and I have benefited greatly from their comments on earlier drafts. We were all delighted when Sir Edward George agreed to contribute a Foreword.

I am grateful to National Westminster Bank for allowing me access to the Orion papers in their archive, accumulated during the years in which the bank was a shareholder. My thanks, in particular, to archivists Fiona McColl and Susan Snell for their professional efficiency and cheerful hospitality. I am also indebted to Alvaro Holguin for the large collection of Orion papers he produced, many of which were not to be found at NatWest.

Euromoney, the magazine of the Euromarkets, has been a stalwart supporter of the project throughout. I am most grateful to chairman Padraic Fallon, who was editor for many of the Orion years, for his insights and for access to past editions of *Euromoney* and other assistance. I would also like to thank Kapila Monet of *Euromoney* for his help with Euromarket statistics and Howard Picton and his team at the Bank of England Library.

This book was made possible by the financial and other contributions of many former Orion employees, business partners and advisers, in addition to those mentioned, namely: John Abell, Ian Armour, Johannes Attems, Rodney Baker-Bates, David Banks, Carol Barrazone, Norman Bergel, Christian Brand, Christian Bull, John Bunting, Guy Burgun, David Burnett, Sir Christopher Chataway, Joseph Cook, Antonino Cravero, Jefferson Cunningham, Johannes de Gier, John Edwards, Julian Fane, Peter Fricker, Stewart Gager, John Gent, Sir Samuel Goldman, Sir Ronald Grierson, William Gurry, Robert Hamburger, Keith Harris, Lord Harrowby, John Haley, Jan Hasek, John Howell, Nicholas Jordan, Sven Kado, Martin Klingsick, Richard Knight, Hermann Kunisch, Colin Lambert, John Langton, Sir Andrew Large, Hans Leukers, Robin McConnachie, Philippe Manet, Anthony Marshall, Patrick Meier, Fergus Murison, Henry Mutkin, David Pritchard, Lutz Raettig, David Robertson, David Rockefeller, Joel Romines, Michael Ross, Alexander Russell, John Sanders, Paul Sauvary, Guy Scammell, Ana Soares, Peter Sterling, Julian Sturdy-Morton, Colin Sturgeon, Geoff Styles, Paul Taylor, Bill Tudor John, Jan Willem van der Velden, Nicholas Villiers, Michael Watson, Michael Webber, Sir Graham Wilkinson, Sir Philip Wilkinson, Murray Wilson, Paul Wilson, David Woods and Spike Wright.

A large number of others have provided information and ideas, namely: Yousef Al-Awadi, Abdulwahab Al-Tamar, Iain Allan, Carlos Alberto Alvarenga, Nick Anderson, Jan Ankarcrona, David Anthony, Peter Ardron, Anthony Asseily, John Baden, Brian Balderson, Neil Balfour, Lawrence Banks, Nicholas Baring, Peter Barton, Robert Bee, Peter Belmont, Simon Beloe, Sir Norman Biggs, Robert Binyon, Henrik Bjørn, Sir George Blunden, John Booker, Pascal Boris, Richard Bristow, Vivian Brown, Walter Brown, Gottfried Bruder, John Butterwick, Alan Cameron, Lord Camoys, Massimo Carello, Francis Carnwath, Michael Carter, John Champion, Jim Chesters, Clive Christiansen, Alan Clifton, Lord Cobbold, Paul Coleman, Peter Cooke, John Dare, Steven Davis, Sir Robin Dent, Marc de Guillebon, Gonzalo de las Heras, Peter de Roos, Edmund de Rothschild, Leopold de Rothschild, Richard Elliston, Anthony Enders, Alexander Ercklentz, Khodadad Farmanfarmaian, Richard Fawcett, Mohammed Fezzani, John Finch, Robin Fox, Sir Ian Fraser, Staffan Gadd, Thomas Gaffney, Rodney Galpin, François Garelli, Gavin Geekie, Kenneth Gibbs, Michael Gibbs, Martin Gordon, Jinx Grafftey-Smith, Lawrence Grand, Sir John Gray,

Edwin Green, Brian Grimmond, Henry Grunfeld, George Gunson, Peter Gwinnett, Maurice Hobson, George Hoffman, Sir John Hogg, David Hunter, Leonard Ingrams, Alexander Jablonowski, Sir Martin Jacomb, Clive Jenkins, Peter Johnson, Christopher Keen, Michael Kenyon-Slaney, David King, Lord Kingsdown, Leslie Knox, Rodney Leach, Gérard Legrain, Gunnar Ljungdahl, Ian Logie, Marcel Luckman, Euan Macdonald, Michiel Matthes, James McNeill, Kenneth Mendenhall, Maximilian Meran, Robin Monro-Davies, Alan Moore, Sir Jeremy Morse, Sean Murphy, John Nash, Junichi Nishiwaki, Bertil Norinder, John Orbell, Darius Oskoui, Sir Geoffrey Owen, John Padovan, Alan Peachey, Nigel Pearson, Uli Pendl, Dennis Phillips, Thomas Pomeroy, Brian Quinn, John Ratner, Hisham Razzuqi, Helen Redmond Cooper, Jürgen Reimnitz, Lord Richardson, Michael Robarts, Dr Duncan Ross, Stanley Ross, Kevin Ruxton, Lord Sandberg, Peter Sandringham, Rainer Schlitt, Sir David Scholey, John Sclater, Professor Brian Scott-Quinn, William Slee, Terry Smeaton, Peter Stormonth Darling, Ian Stoutzker, Graham Sunderland, David Sunray, Russell Taylor, Stephen Timewell, James Tree, Sir Anthony Tuke, Simon Udale, Simon Wathen, Martin Vander Weyer, Alberto Weissmüller, Michael Wells, David West, Richard Wheeler Bennett, Giorgio Winteler, Alan Wiseman, Michael Wood, John Woodhead, Stanislas Yassukovich, James Young, Graham Ziegler and Minos Zombanakis.

Among the organizations that have supported the book in significant ways are Allen & Overy, Bremer Landesbank, International Securities Market Association, National Westminster Bank, Österreichische Kontrollbank, Royal Bank of Canada, The Mitsubishi Centre, Westdeutsche Landesbank Girozentrale and UniCredito Italiano.

After an era of considerable success in the 1970s, the European consortium banks and banking clubs fell into abeyance by the end of the 1980s; shareholder competition, deregulation, globalization and the Third World Debt crisis changed their world. It looked as though cross-border joint ventures in banking were a passing phase. But by the beginning of the twenty-first century, a new type of association had emerged among international banks – specialized joint ventures with specific aims. So consortium banks were reappearing, in a new form appropriate to the new age.

Richard Roberts

List of Tables

List of Plates

Acknowledgements and Notes for End Papers and Plates

The author is very grateful to the following publications, artists, photographers, publishers and other sources, as the case may be, for permission to reproduce images in the end papers and in the plates section. Every effort has been made to trace copyright owners but, if any have been overlooked, the publishers will be pleased to make the necessary arrangement at the first opportunity. The author is grateful to the Centre for the Study of Cartoons and Caricature, University of Kent, Canterbury for access to its archives and for advice.

END PAPERS – PUBLICATION [ARTIST]

Front left (*upper*) © The Telegraph Group Ltd [Nicholas Garland, 1967]; (*lower*) by kind permission of Associated Newspapers plc [Gus, 1967]. **Front right** © The New Yorker Collection from cartoonbank.com. All Rights Reserved [(*upper*) J.B. Handelsman, 1968; (*lower*) Joseph Mirachi, 1980]. **Back left** © The New Yorker Collection from cartoonbank.com. All Rights Reserved [(*upper*) Ed Fisher, 1974; (*lower*) Robert Weber, 1974]. **Back right** (*upper*) © Punch Limited [Dickinson, 1982]; (*lower*) © The New Yorker Collection from cartoonbank.com. All Rights Reserved [William Hamilton, 1976].

PLATES – PUBLICATION OR OTHER SOURCE [ARTIST/PHOTOGRAPHER]

1.1 Private collection [Vincent Finnigan]. 1.2 Deutsche Bank AG/Historisches. Institut. 2.1 UBS Warburg [Raymond Skipp]. 2.2 Private collection [Nick Rogers]. 2.3 © Bank of England. 2.4 KBC Banking & Insurance Holding Company, Historical Archives. 3.1 Euromoney Institutional Investor plc. 3.2 International Financing Review [David Langdon]. 4.1 Private collection. 4.2 Private collection. 5.1 © Bank of England. 5.2 International Financing Review. 5.3 Private collection. 6.1 Citibank. 6.2 Euromoney Institutional Investor plc. 6.3 Private collection

[Tim O'Leary]. **6.4** © The Nobel Foundation. **7.1** Private collection [Tony Healy]. **7.2** Courtesy of JP Morgan & Co. Incorporated. **7.3** Private collection. **7.4** Euromoney Institutional Investor plc [Robin Laurance]. **8.1** Private collection. **8.2** Private collection. **8.3** Private collection. **9.1** © Punch Limited [David Langdon]. **9.2** Private collection [David Langdon]. **9.3** © Punch Limited [Dickinson]. **10.1** Private collection. **10.2** Euro-money Institutional Investor plc. **10.3** International Financing Review. **11.1** Euromoney Institutional Investor plc. **11.2** © Punch Limited [David Langdon]. **12.1, 12.2** Private collection. **12.3** Royal Bank of Canada. **12.4** Morgan Stanley Dean Witter. **13.1, 13.2, 13.3** © Punch Limited [David Langdon]. **14.1** Private collection. **14.2** Royal Bank of Canada. **14.3** Private collection. **15.1, 15.2** Private collection [David Langdon]. **16.1** International Financing Review [David Langdon]. **16.2** © Punch Limited [David Langdon]. **16.3** Sunflowers, 1888 by Vincent van Gogh (1853–90); National Gallery, London, UK/Bridgeman Art Library.

NOTES

1.1 David Rockefeller of Chase Manhattan Bank inspired the formation of Orion Bank which greatly benefited from Chase's strong ties in Saudi Arabia and other parts of the Middle East. Chase formed a consortium bank with Saudi partners and advised on the Saudi Industrial Development Fund [p. 97].

1.2 Deutsche Bank's Hermann Abs was very wary of US bank expansion in Europe and launched the EBIC club, as a potential Europe-wide bank. Deutsche clashed with its own consortium bank over Spain's first Eurobond issue, highlighting the contradictions inherent in consortium strategies [p. 181].

2.1 Siegmund Warburg launched the first Eurobond issue [p. 8].

2.2 Ronald Grierson was the first Chairman of Orion Bank [p. 62].

2.3 George Bolton's Bank of London and South America (BOLSA) 'resisted all entreaties' to join consortia, as did its shareholder, Lloyds Bank [p. 22].

2.4 Fernand Collin, Chairman of Kredietbank: his bank's principal 'currency cocktail' was the European unit of account [p. 7].

3.1 The Euromarkets had been greatly helped by the US Interest Equalisation Tax and it was soon to be removed. Many leading bankers felt that the market would disappear and gravitate back to New York [p. 19]. They were proved wrong.

3.2 The 'Belgian dentist' typified the Eurobond investor [p. 7]. Risk averse and tax averse, he liked to invest in companies with household names. Later, institutions became more important than individuals as investors in the Eurobond market. The ECU (European Currency Unit) was a 'currency cocktail' that was slow to take off, because it unduly favoured the investor.

4.1   After Midland Bank acquired his family merchant bank, David Montagu [p. 79] took the helm at Orion during Britain's 'gravest crisis since the war.'

4.2   Mrs Thatcher lunches at Orion, while Leader of the Opposition, with David Montagu and William de Gelsey, who was the 'heart and soul of Orion' [p. 173].

5.1   Bank of England Director George Blunden's request to international banks that they should stand by their consortium banks came as a bombshell and led to considerable rationalization in the sector [p. 85].

5.2   Orion did the first Eurobond based on a swap [p. 123]. Philip Hubbard went on to join the faculty of the Harvard Business School [p. 170].

5.3   Christopher Chataway [p. 83] appeared in the 1952 and 1956 Olympic Games and won the three-mile race at the 1954 British Commonwealth Games; fellow middle-distance runner Emil Zatopek won three Olympic gold medals in 1952.

6.1 and 6.2   Walter Wriston restructured the bank to operate throughout the USA, skilfully avoiding the inter-state banking restrictions. He also led the lending spree to developing countries; his remark that countries 'don't go bankrupt' provoked the riposte that 'the banks that lend to them do' [p. 108]. 'The world's only international bank' – from *Business World*, 1996 quoting from a book by Philip Zweig (see also note 45, page 338).

6.3   Michael von Clemm [p. 20], leading Euromarket banker, helped launch a new financial centre, Canary Wharf, in London's docklands.

6.4   Milton Friedman, Nobel Prize winning economist, encouraged the Chicago Mercantile Exchange to offer financial futures. Dismissed as a 'bunch of crapshooters in pork bellies' at the time [p. 114].

7.1   Julius Strauss of Strauss Turnbull & Co., got little support for his efforts from the London market; most early Eurobond trading was done by consortium banks, such as Western American and Orion [p. 71], or specially formed firms, such as Bondtrade.

7.2   John Meyer, with his predecessor Thomas Gates, at JP Morgan's head office, 23 Wall Street, the 'financial crossroads of America.' He helped form Euroclear, without which 'we would all have gone broke' said one Eurobond trader.

7.3   John Langton, chief executive of the International Securities Market Association, successor to the Association of International Bond Dealers.

7.4   Stanley Ross started the 'grey market' [p. 116]. Trading Eurobonds before issue, he exposed and undermined the traditional pattern of fees, which fell from 2.5 per cent to almost nothing over 25 years.

8.1   Andrew Large (*second left*) with Orion colleagues at an IMF/World Bank meeting. He was active in making ties with central banks and monetary institutions around the world – a vital outlet for Eurobond placement.

8.2   Joe Cook's departure for JP Morgan suggested a decline in Orion's investment banking commitment [p. 170]; soon Orion dropped out of Eurobonds.

8.3   Spike Wright was seconded to Orion from NatWest [p. 60]. For most of the other consortium banks funding was a perennial nightmare, as they had no natural deposit base.

9.1   The first 'Oil Shock' saw a quadrupling of oil prices in two months [p. 92].

9.2   For bankers, such as Jinx Grafftey-Smith, Jeddah's Kandara Palace Hotel will always be written on their hearts. It was here that the scramble for petrodollars often began [p. 96].

9.3   The second 'Oil Shock' (1978 80) induced a certain paranoia, with talk of oil going to $100 a barrel and the Arabs buying up the whole world. Kuwait took advantage of the 1987 stock market crash to build a 21 per cent stake in BP, which the UK government forced it to reduce.

10.1 Jeff Cunningham (*centre*): one of Orion's architects, he returned as its chief executive [p. 140]. Roy Jenkins (*right*) had given up the European Commission Presidency a few weeks previously; was he celebrating his freedom from multinational supervision? Within weeks, Orion gave up multinational ownership, when Royal Bank of Canada bought out its partners [p. 158].

10.2 *Euromoney* 'tombstone' advertisements (*Plate 11.1*) were vital for the *amour propre* of international bankers.

10.3 Many a bank's Xerox machine seized up on Monday mornings as it copied Christian Hemain's weekly Euromarkets newsletter, *AGEFI* (later *IFR*). As his advisor, Orion helped sell the business to Thomson [p. 165].

11.1 The start of 1974 saw power cuts, fuel shortages, bank failures and a falling stock market in Britain, which nearly ran out of foreign exchange. The Orion Group arranged a $2.5 billion financing for the UK Treasury (described in *Euromoney*, May 1974) and $500 million for the Greater London Council [p. 117].

11.2 In the same year, UK Chancellor Denis Healey appealed to the International Monetary Fund for support, like numerous other UK Chancellors.

12.1 Minos Zombanakis (*right*) put syndicated loans on to a new plane [p. 13]; here with Denis Healey (*left*) and Giorgio Cappon, Chairman of Istituto Mobiliare Italiano, at a loan signing. Consortium banks were market leaders in this business, until their shareholders found that they could do it themselves.

12.2 Abdlatif Al-Hamad. He chaired United Bank of Kuwait and launched the Kuwaiti Dinar bond market with loans to the World Bank [p. 99].

12.3 Royal Bank of Canada bought Tony Fell's investment bank, Dominion Securities [p. 175]. The convergence of investment and commercial banking was highlighted when Fell became Deputy Chairman of Royal Bank itself.

12.4 Evan Galbraith [p. 11] later became US Ambassador to France – 'one of the most brilliant since Benjamin Franklin,' according to Jacques Soustelle of l'académie française.

13.1   The Inter-Alpha banking club was unnerved by the fraudulent fall of
       Banco Ambrosiano, previously a sound bank, with strong Vatican links,
       but it recovered and was one of the few clubs to survive [pp. 195–6].
13.2   Petrodollars were extensively [p. 186] lent to developing countries,
       reeling from oil price rises; the money often ended up in off-shore
       units of the same banks that had made the loans.
13.3   US savings and loan associations lost $13 billion in 1988 [Appendix I].
14.1   Libra Bank executives (*from right*) Carlos Santistevan, John Finch,
       Ken Ramsay, Tom Gaffney (Managing Director), Norman Simons,
       Rick Haller and Peter Belmont. As a consortium bank dedicated to
       Latin America, it could not avoid large losses, but they were
       mitigated by profitable trading of loans [p. 191].
14.2   Jock Finlayson took over as Chairman of Orion when it was acquired
       by Royal Bank of Canada [p. 158].
14.3   Jesus Silva Herzog (*left*), with Gérard Legrain of International
       Mexican Bank. When Mexico could not pay its debts, bankers were
       reassured to learn that 'Jesus is working for us;' as Finance Minister,
       with the assistance of the International Monetary Fund, he organized
       the rescheduling of Mexico's loans [p. 186].
15.1   Consortium banks were formed to 'test the waters' of unfamiliar and
       risky markets, often with little forethought; new banks seemed to be
       formed on the spur of the moment, 'after a good lunch' as Orion
       Chairman, David Montagu, put it [p. 41]; the gestation period for
       Orion was nearly two years.
15.2   Stanislas Yassukovich peers at the consortium banking stars as they
       fall. Orion was acquired by Royal Bank of Canada; others (all even-
       tually to disappear) are Libra Bank, Banque Europeénne de Crédit,
       European Asian Bank and Yassukovich's own European Banking
       Company [banks profiled in Appendix II].
16.1   The Euromarkets thrived on innovations, such as floating rate notes;
       however, innovation could get out of hand, as happened when a glut
       of FRN 'perpetuals' cost traders and investors $800 million in two
       days [p. 173]. The 1985 FRN issue of $1.8 billion (the largest till
       then), for the European Economic Community, caused severe indi-
       gestion for market traders.
16.2   Futures, swaps and other derivatives developed very rapidly [p. 115].
16.3   Huge asset inflation took place in the Japanese stock, real estate and
       art markets [p. 171]. One van Gogh painting (similar to the one
       shown) of sunflowers went to Japan for a record $40 million, then
       another van Gogh for twice as much. The speculative fever was
       fuelled by warrants, which enabled Japanese companies to borrow at
       negligible cost; some of them made more money out of speculation
       than manufacturing. By the end of 1989, the stock market had
       quadrupled over five years; then the bubble burst.

PROLOGUE

Meeting in Manhattan

Wednesday 29 April 1970 was a fine day for founding a bank. It was spring in Manhattan, with clear skies and an unseasonably warm 78 degrees Fahrenheit.[1] The *New York Times'* lead story was President Nixon's forthcoming address to the American public on the prosperous state of the US economy, but there was also a report on the war in Vietnam spilling into Cambodia. Senator Edward Kennedy was being questioned about the Chappaquiddick episode. Black Panthers were demonstrating in New Haven. The fashion pages featured midi-skirts and gaucho pants. The New York Mets, baseball's reigning world champions, had trounced the San Francisco Giants.

Chase Manhattan Plaza, with its garden, its decorative water-pool, and its huge wafer-like black and white abstract sculptures by Jean Dubuffet, was thronged with financial district workers enjoying the sunshine and the warm weather. Many of them worked in the adjacent tall tower of steel and smoked glass, the headquarters of Chase Manhattan Bank. In a room at the top of that building, a meeting was in progress where a powerful new international banking partnership was being forged – Orion.

The host of the meeting was David Rockefeller, chairman of Chase Manhattan, the world's third biggest bank. His prospective partners were David Robarts, of National Westminster Bank, and Earle McLaughlin, of Royal Bank of Canada, chairman respectively of the seventh and twelfth largest banks. Although there had been many communications between the three chairmen over the past year-or-so, it was the first time that they had convened face-to-face to discuss their mutual enterprise – the formation of a jointly owned 'consortium bank'.

Backing up their bosses were a handful of senior executives from their respective banks, Willard Butcher and James Bergford from Chase, Jock Finlayson from Royal Bank, and Bill Davidson from NatWest. It was an

I

exclusive gathering, kept compact to avoiding drawing attention to their joint project.

With the downtown canyons of Wall Street forming the backdrop through the big plate glass windows, David Rockefeller welcomed his guests and opened the proceedings. The purpose of the gathering was to sign a partnership agreement committing them to 'co-operating in the development of multinational banking and financial enterprises.'[2] The agreement had six points:

- formation of a joint Management Service Unit for liaison and marketing purposes;
- establishment of a London-based merchant banking capability;
- establishment of an entity to undertake medium-term lending in the major money centres of the world;
- exchange of credit lines between the banks;
- recruitment of a French partner;
- exploration of joint projects in Belgium, Canada, France, Germany, the Netherlands and the USA.

David Robarts was the first to initial the paper. He passed it on to Earle McLaughlin. Finally, David Rockefeller penned his endorsement and dated the document. The outcome six months later was Orion – at the time the most ambitious strategic alliance in international investment banking ever attempted. As the first step towards the creation of Orion, the signing ceremony on 29 April 1970 was a significant moment in the development of consortium banking and the transformation of the Euromarkets.

CHAPTER 1

Origins of the Euromarkets

Consortium banks were creatures of the Euromarkets, and it is with the rise of the *Eurodollar* that their story begins. Eurodollars are deposits of US dollars with commercial banks or their branches situated outside the United States of America. At the outset, the Eurodollar market was made up of banks situated in European financial centres, mainly London, but also Paris, Brussels, Luxembourg and Switzerland. These banks, which included overseas branches of US banks, bid for US dollar deposits and offered loans in US dollars. These operations were conducted at the wholesale interbank level, in large amounts.

The origin of the prefix *Euro* – meaning offshore – is uncertain. One suggestion is that it derived from the cable address of Banque Commerciale pour l'Europe du Nord – EUROBANK – a Paris bank where the Soviet Union kept US dollar deposits. The word *Eurodollar* became well known in the early 1960s, promoted by its usage by the British financial economist and author Paul Einzig.[1] Eurodeutschemarks, Euroyen, or Eurosterling are deposit balances of those currencies held outside their respective national boundaries. The whole array of 'offshore' balances is called the *Eurocurrency* market. The *Euromarket* is a generic term that encompasses bank lending in Eurocurrencies as well as other offshore financial instruments such as Eurobonds, Euronotes, Euroequities and Eurocommercial paper. Appropriate while Europe was the focus of the Euromarkets, the *Euro* prefix became inappropriate as the market became global in scope; not to mention the scope for confusion with the European single currency – the euro. But it continues to be used.

DEVELOPMENT OF THE EURODOLLAR MARKET

Markets in offshore currencies were not an entirely new phenomenon. There were, for instance, active markets in sterling and dollar deposits in Berlin and

Vienna in the 1920s, though they disappeared following the international financial crisis of 1931. But the scale and scope of the Eurodollar markets were without precedent.

The rise of a market for US dollars in Europe in the late 1950s was the outcome of a combination of economic and political factors. The most important factor was the recurrent US balance of payments deficits, which created a pool of $17 billion externally held by the end of the decade.[2] Between 1950 and 1957, the deficits were modest and welcomed for providing dollars for international transactions and reserves. But from 1958 the deficits mushroomed, causing mounting concern in the USA. The resulting rapidly growing pool of externally held dollars fostered the growth of a short-term money market in US dollars in Europe – the Eurodollar market.

In the immediate post-war years 40 per cent of the world's trade was conducted in sterling.[3] But the sterling crisis of 1957 led the British authorities to impose curbs on the use of sterling to finance trade between non-sterling area countries. These restrictions led UK banks to seek dollar deposits for use in international trade finance, being encouraged to do so by the Bank of England as a means of benefiting the UK balance of payments. This stimulated the emergence of an active Eurodollar market in London.[4]

The use of dollar deposits was also fostered by other central banks as a supplement to domestic credit. The central banks of Germany, Italy, Japan and Switzerland furnished domestic commercial banks with dollars from their reserves through foreign currency swaps to achieve domestic monetary policy objectives. The Federal Reserve System, the US central banking organization, also played a part in promoting the development of the Eurodollar market through Regulation Q, which restricted the level of interest rates that US banks were permitted to pay on domestic deposits in the USA. The measure, introduced in the 1930s during the slump to stimulate investment, encouraged holders of dollars, including US residents, to place them offshore where they could earn higher rates of interest. This boosted the growing pool of offshore dollars.

Another factor that fostered the development of the Eurodollar market was the co-ordinated abolition of restrictions on the holding of foreign currencies by non-residents by the major members of the International Monetary Fund in December 1958.[5] The re-establishment of free currency convertibility stimulated the emergence of more active and more integrated foreign exchange markets, forging links between the market in offshore dollar deposit balances, other foreign currency deposits and the national money markets. These ties extended the scope for the use of dollars for banking activities and as a complement to the national money markets. By the beginning of the 1960s, interest rates were regularly posted for offshore dollar deposits at a range of maturities.

EURODOLLAR BUSINESS

An array of market distortions meant that banks operating in offshore dollars enjoyed both competitive advantages *and* higher profits. Being unconstrained by Regulation Q, they could pay higher rates to depositors than US domestic banks, thus attracting balances. They could also offer attractive rates to borrowers, since they were not party to the cartel agreements amongst the US domestic banks which constrained domestic interest payments, nor were they subject to official requirements regarding compensating balances, deposit insurance or reserves in relation to foreign currency liabilities.

In the USA, the relatively low rate of interest paid to depositors, because of Regulation Q, together with the relatively high rates charged to borrowers, determined by the level of the US prime rate plus institutional and administrative factors, provided a domestic market spread of 3.0–5.5 per cent.[6] These were wide margins, allowing banks operating in the Eurodollar market to offer better terms to both depositors and borrowers, and still make good returns. Similar distortions in European domestic banking markets also favoured the Eurodollar market.

The post-war system of fixed exchange rates provided a positive context for the early development of the offshore dollar market. Fixed exchange rates meant minimal currency risk, which encouraged European banks and the European branches or subsidiaries of US banks to develop dollar-based banking business. The stability of the Bretton Woods System allowed them to take advantage of the competitive advantages that they enjoyed relative to US domestic banks, both in terms of attracting dollar deposits and in dollar lending. Since Eurodollar business was focused in stable locations and confined to prime banking counterparties – leading European banks and the foreign branches or subsidiaries of major US banks – the higher returns were available without the assumption of greater market or political risk.

The Euromarkets provided energetic and innovative bankers with a playground in which they could create new products relatively free of official controls or cartel arrangements. Banks operating in the Eurodollar market were liberated from requirements to hold non-interest-bearing reserve balances against deposits, a form of domestic monetary control in the USA and Germany. In the absence of such costly constraints, banks were able to offer higher deposit rates, short-term Eurodollar rates being generally about 0.5 per cent higher than in the US domestic market. Furthermore, while it was forbidden in the USA to pay interest on demand deposits or time deposits of less than thirty days, no such restrictions applied in the Eurodollar market. As regards making loans, banks operating in the Euromarkets were free from the constraints that applied in most domestic markets. Liberation from regulatory restraints, the varied and dynamic cluster of market participants, the relative freedom of capital movements and the growing strategy of investors to internationalize their investments, all contributed to the appeal of the Eurodollar market to depositors, borrowers and bankers.[7]

A final 'exotic factor' was Soviet Cold War anxiety that dollar balances held in US banks might be seized by a hostile US administration or confiscated by creditors of Imperial Russia.[8] During and after the Korean War and following the blocking of some Chinese balances, the Soviet state banking organizations kept their dollar balances with banks outside the USA.[9] One of the institutions in which they were placed was Banque Commerciale pour l'Europe du Nord in Paris, which was jointly owned by State Bank of the USSR and Bank for Foreign Trade in Moscow; another was Moscow Narodny Bank in London. In good capitalist fashion, these communist-owned banks worked hard to maximize the return on their dollar deposits by on-lending them to other banks.

The Eurocurrency market grew rapidly in the late 1950s and the 1960s. In 1963, the Bank for International Settlements estimated the *overall* size of the Eurocurrency market to be $12.4 billion, of which $9.3 billion were US dollars. By the end of the 1960s the total was $65 billion, of which $53 billion were US dollars. That was an annual compound rate of growth of 31 per cent per annum.[10] Although remarkable for its rapid rate of increase, the volume of foreign currency lending was still small relative to national bank lending, the comparable figure for commercial bank loans in the USA in 1970 being $528 billion.

The Euromarket began as an interbank market – a market between banks for short-term deposits. An active Eurodollar interbank market existed from the end of the 1950s, allocating Eurodollar deposits to wherever they could most profitably be employed. LIBOR (London interbank offered rate) – an average of the rates at which the principal banks lend between themselves in the London Eurocurrency market – emerged as the market's reference point. Interbank trading resulted in large movements of funds between markets and currencies in response to even minor differentials in interest rates. Active arbitrage in the Eurocurrency market gave coherence to the increasingly complex Euromarket.

EUROBONDS

The establishment of the Eurobond market marked a new phase in the development of the Euromarkets. Eurobonds are long-term fixed-interest or floating-rate bonds denominated in an international currency, often other than that of the borrower, issued outside the borrower's home country and introduced to the market by an international underwriting syndicate of banks. The Eurobond market, a long-term international capital market, was complementary to the short-term Eurocurrency money market.

The early 1960s saw an extension of the maximum length of Eurodollar borrowings. At the beginning of the decade the normal maximum period was 12 months, with occasional extensions up to two years by special negotiation. By 1964, the maximum period had lengthened to three years, and attempts were being made to extend it to five.[11] Underlying this development was the growing popularity of Eurodollar deposits with Arab recipients of oil royalties. They appreciated the flexibility of the Euromarkets, as well as the time zone – more convenient than New York. They were looking for long-term investments and, as Eurodollar lending terms lengthened, borrowing by the issue of long-term bonds became more and more feasible.

After the Second World War, New York was the focus of the international capital market. Foreign borrowers, mostly European governments and corporations, had free access to the market, raising long-term funds through the issue of dollar-denominated bonds. In the late 1950s and early 1960s, foreign bond issues in New York totalled between $500 million and $1 billion per annum.[12] The 'lead managers' – syndicate organizers – of the New York issuing syndicates were always US investment banks, which received the lion's share of fees and commissions. But by the late 1950s, four-fifths or more of foreign bond issues were being sold in Europe, where the combination of a familiar borrower plus a dollar-denominated security appealed to investors.[13] Distribution in Europe was mostly undertaken by European banks, receiving only relatively paltry selling group commissions for their services.

European banks were eager to lead manage such issues themselves to earn both management and distribution fees. To do so they had to devise ways to circumvent the controls exercised by the European central banks over their national capital markets, with the aim of prioritizing domestic and other favoured borrowers. This led them to make innovative attempts to supply European investors themselves with attractive securities.

There were several notable milestones before the establishment of the Eurobond market. One of the earliest issues was the first multiple currency issue – with interest and principal payable in US dollars, Belgian francs or Dutch guilders – brought out by Banque Lambert, which raised $25 million for Belgian oil company, Petrofina, in 1957.[14] The issue was managed by an exclusively European syndicate of banks, and as bearer bonds they could not be sold in the USA. Another pioneering offering was that made by Kredietbank Luxembourgeoise, an affiliate of the leading Belgian bank Kredietbank, on behalf of Portuguese petroleum refiner, SACOR, in 1961.[15] This was denominated in European Units of Account in January 1961, one of the European currency cocktails which were forerunners of the euro. Interest was payable in seven European currencies and the securities were listed in Brussels, Luxembourg and Zurich. It was no accident that Belgian banks did well in the early Eurobond market; many Belgians were in the habit of buying bearer bonds in Luxembourg – beyond the tax man's gaze – a type of investor known as a 'Belgian dentist'. Then in May 1963, the London merchant bank Samuel Montagu arranged a $20 million private placement for the Kingdom of Belgium, mainly through the London market.[16]

AUTOSTRADE

The first fully-fledged Eurobond issue – with the full set of credentials defined as non-domestic US dollar-denominated, internationally syndicated and traded, tax-free, bearer securities – is generally held to be the $15 million issue on behalf of Autostrade, the Italian national highway authority, in July 1963. The 15-year bonds were guaranteed by the Italian state holding company, Istituto per la Ricostruzione Industriale (IRI), making them just a small fraction below sovereign risk. They were listed on the London and Luxembourg stock exchanges. The lead manager of the issue was the merchant bank S.G. Warburg, with Deutsche Bank, Banque de Bruxelles and Rotterdamsche Bank as the co-managers. An important role in placing the issue was played by the European offices of the US investment bank White Weld, a trail-blazer in the trading and distribution of Eurobonds.[17]

The Eurobond concept, that of a US dollar bond issued in London and other European financial centres, brought out by a European syndicate of banks, and sold mainly to European investors, was pioneered by London merchant bank Warburgs under the direction of Siegmund Warburg and Gert Whitman. To make it work necessitated path-breaking endeavours in relation to taxation, foreign exchange controls, legal documentation and listing requirements. In particular, there was a tussle with the UK tax authorities to obtain exemption from stamp duty, then 4 per cent.[18] They prevailed, thanks to support from the Bank of England, especially from Sir Cyril Hawker, the deputy governor, who persuaded the Inland Revenue and other government departments to make the necessary concessions. The groundwork put in by Warburgs cleared the way for the emergence of the Eurobond market in London.

To launch the Eurobond market with a fanfare, Warburgs wanted a high-profile borrower of impeccable creditworthiness. The European Coal and Steel Community (ECSC) was an ideal candidate, and it expressed interest in developing an alternative source of long-term finance to foreign bond issues in New York. But the timing was wrong, since it had no immediate requirement for funds.[19] Autostrade became the market's initiator because Warburgs director Ronald Grierson, who had extensive business contacts in Italy and later became chairman of Orion Bank, knew that its parent IRI, a borrower of similar standing to ECSC, was interested in raising capital. In fact, Autostrade was not the recipient of the funds which were diverted to another less creditworthy IRI subsidiary, the Italian steel company Finsider,

which was 'desperately' in need of foreign exchange to buy American equipment but could not issue bonds with tax-free coupons because of Italian
tax law.[20]

The level of European borrowings in the US capital market became a
matter of concern in Washington in the early 1960s because the outflows contributed to the big US balance of payments deficits. The administration's dis-
comfort was expressed publicly in February 1962 by the US Secretary of the
Treasury, Douglas Dillon, in a speech in Paris in which he advocated the
development of European capital markets to finance European economic
growth.[21] Bank of England governor, Lord Cromer, shared Dillon's view that
the time was right for the revival of an international capital market in Europe,
also recognizing that the development of an 'entrepot business in capital'
would bolster London's position as an international financial centre.[22] On
18 July 1963, two weeks after the Autostrade issue, President Kennedy made
a speech to the US Congress about the soaring US balance of payments deficit
in which he announced the imposition of an Interest Equalization Tax (IET)
effective from that moment. Hearing the news, Morgan Guaranty president
Henry Alexander told colleagues: 'This is a day that you will all remember
forever. It will change the face of American banking and force all the business
off to London.'[23] His prediction proved prescient.

The IET was levied on the purchase by US residents of securities issued
by most foreign borrowers with a maturity of more than three years. It was
designed to reduce long-term capital outflows without increasing domestic
interest rates. In following years, the US imposed further capital controls
with the same objective of moderating the balance of payments deficits. In
1965, the IET was widened to include bank loans with maturities of more
than one year and the Federal Reserve drew up new guidelines for US financial institutions, limiting their purchases of foreign securities and credit
facilities under the Voluntary Foreign Credit Restraint Program. In 1968,
the US government introduced the Foreign Direct Investment Program,
which required US corporations to finance overseas investments above a
minimum level by overseas borrowings.

The restrictions on US capital exports curtailed the level of the balance of
payments deficits, but they did not solve the problem, which was much
accentuated by the Vietnam War. But as intended, they effectively closed the
New York capital market to European borrowing for a decade, although it
later recovered, and greatly assisted the rise of the Eurobond market.
Following an improvement in the US balance of payments, the IET was
removed and the Voluntary Foreign Credit Restraint Program was brought
to an end in 1974.

The Eurobond market grew rapidly in the 1960s (see Table 1.1), demand
for funds being stimulated not only by the US capital controls but also by
rapid economic growth in Europe. Initially the principal borrowers were

Table 1.1 Eurobond new issues volume,
1963–72[24] ($ million)

1963	148	1968	3085
1964	681	1969	2876
1965	810	1970	2762
1966	1343	1971	3289
1967	1774	1972	5508

European governments and public sector agencies, but soon convertible
issues appeared, first for Japanese companies, then for US companies. The
introduction of the Voluntary Foreign Credit Restraint Program in 1968
brought a host of US multinational corporations to the Eurobond market to
meet their financing needs for overseas expansion; most of them were of
sound quality, but there were others, such as fraudster Robert Vesco's ICC
International, Levin–Townsend International, Farrington Overseas
Corporation and King Resources, 'which many investors would prefer to
forget.'[25]

EUROBOND TYPES AND TECHNIQUES

There was considerable experimentation in the forms of bond issue, in
response to shifting market conditions and to refine their appeal to borrowers and investors. The first convertible issue – bonds with an option to
exchange into equities – for Canon Camera, was made in December 1963.
The earliest debt with warrants issue was made in June 1964, the borrower
being IRI with Finsider warrants. Convertible and warrant issues accounted
for almost 20 per cent of issues in the first decade, enabling companies to
attract money at a low coupon at the expense of some equity dilution. The
first dual-currency issue was launched for the City of Turin in October 1964
and the first issues on behalf of US multinational corporations in July 1965,
for Mobil and Uniroyal.[26] As the market grew, the innovations multiplied,
in ever more complex ways.

The issuing method for new Eurobonds was largely modelled on the US
domestic bond market, and more-or-less standard practices soon emerged.[27]
The borrower appointed a bank as lead manager to organize the issue. The
lead manager's responsibilities were to advise the borrower on the size, terms
and timing of the issue, usually with the help of a small group of co-manager
banks. The whole issue was underwritten by the issuing syndicate of lead and
co-managers, and an underwriting group of some 25–40 banks. A bigger
selling group of 50–75 financial institutions helped to market the securities
to investors during a selling period of about two weeks. The fees, allowances
and commissions received by the participating banks totalled 2.5 per cent of
the issue in the market's early years, much more than in the US domestic and

foreign bond markets. The standard basis of division was 0.5 per cent to the management group, 0.5 per cent to the underwriters and 1.5 per cent to the selling group. The level of commissions was to be drastically whittled away over the years.

The Eurocurrency and Eurobond markets began as US dollar-based markets and the dollar continued to be the dominant Euromarket currency. However, the growth of pools of other offshore currencies led to the development of non-dollar Euromarket business. The growing concern about the levels of US inflation and its balance of payments deficits in the late 1960s led to the emergence of the Deutschemark, the Dutch guilder and other currencies as active Euromarket currencies.

Eurobond issues denominated in US dollars were made without controls imposed by the Federal Reserve. The same applied to issues denominated in the Australian dollar, the Canadian dollar, the European unit of account and the European currency unit.[28] However, the central banks of Germany, France, the Netherlands, the UK, Switzerland and Japan, which had charge of the other significant currencies of the 1970s, took a much more restrictive attitude to maintain control over their currencies; the most significant was the Deutschemark, which accounted for a market share of well over 20 per cent in most years, but the influential Swiss franc market was also important although not part of the Eurobond market as such. The Bundesbank required every Deutschemark-denominated issue to be approved by a committee, which considered its size, form and maturity and, if successful, allotted it a place in the queue of new issues. It also required that all Deutschemark issues should be lead managed by a German bank, a practice that assured the German banks of prominent positions in the issuing league tables.[29]

The floating rate note (FRN) was an important extension of the Euromarket's product range, bridging the gap between bank loans and the bond market. It was also an attractive instrument for investors in times of high interest rate volatility. Instead of a fixed rate of interest set for the duration of the loan at the start, FRNs had a variable interest rate tied to short-term market interest rates in the Eurocurrency market. The usual rate was six-month LIBOR, the short-term benchmark for deposits which was the conventional rate applied to bank loans with variable rates. But FRNs were negotiable securities, an early instance of the securitization of lending that became a phenomenon in the 1980s and 1990s.

FRNs and longer-term floating rate bonds came to be used particularly by banks as a means of raising medium-term to long-term funds to support their growing international operations. An issue of FRNs was slightly cheaper for borrowers than the alternative, a floating rate medium-term syndicated loan. For investors, the lure was their liquidity as a tradable security.

The first significant FRN issue is generally held to be the $125 million, ten-year notes, indexed to pay interest at 0.75 per cent above LIBOR, issued on behalf of Ente Nazionale per L'Energia Elettrica (ENEL) in May 1970.[30] The lead managers were Warburgs, which provided the client, and Bankers Trust International, the recognized pioneer of the FRN concept. The $75 million FRN issue for Pepsico, which Bankers Trust International lead managed soon after, consolidated its position as a top FRN house. Bankers Trust director Evan Galbraith joked that he came up with the FRN formula in his bath; a journalist took him seriously and the gag became a legend.[31] He later became US ambassador to France.

MEDIUM-TERM LENDING

The Eurocurrency market was a source of *short-term credit*, mostly between banks. The Eurobond market was a provider of *long-term loans* for governments, public agencies, financial institutions and major corporations. In-between the Eurocurrency and Eurobond markets lay *medium-term lending*, a term that usually applied to credits of three-to-ten years' duration. Medium-term lending in Eurodollars developed in the mid-1960s, stimulated by a worldwide rise in interest rates that discouraged both long-term bond issuing and resort to the short-term money market.[32] In the late 1960s and early 1970s, a large volume of borrowing was transacted with medium-term maturities.

Medium-term Eurocurrency loans were generally provided on a floating-rate basis tied to LIBOR. Floating rates were attractive to lenders as a means of passing on to borrowers the interest-rate risk involved in funding medium-term loans by means of short-term deposits. For borrowers, the benefits of medium-term bank credit were that it was a more flexible source of funds than a bond issue and was available for shorter periods.[33]

The issue of the first Eurodollar certificate of deposit in May 1966 was a notable milestone in the development of medium-term Eurocurrency finance. First introduced as domestic instruments in the USA in 1961, certificates of deposit (CDs) were negotiable claims issued by a bank in return for term deposits, for periods usually ranging from one month to five years. Eurodollar CDs were pioneered by the London branch of First National City Bank (Citibank) in an effort to attract Eurodollar deposits. Simultaneously, White Weld created a secondary market for trading them.[34] For Euromarket investors, Eurodollar CDs filled the gap in financial instruments between fixed-term time deposits offered by banks and long-term Eurobonds. Eurodollar CDs quickly became an integral part of the Eurocurrency deposit market and an important cash management tool for banks and corporate treasurers. The rapid growth of CD issues in the late 1960s was indicative of the increasing depth and sophistication of the Eurodollar market.[35]

Initially, medium-term loans were provided by banks to clients on a traditional relationship basis. But towards the end of the 1960s, the scale of credits required by clients became too large for individual banks and so they began to 'syndicate' such loans among groups of banks put together for the purpose. The techniques of syndication were borrowed from the new issue practices of the Eurobond market. The syndicate members either bought the credits themselves, or marketed them to other banks or financial institutions.

Syndicated loans are private arrangements between borrowers and bankers, although managers and participants expect public acknowledgement of their activities in 'tombstone' advertisements in the financial press. Thus there was no attention-grabbing public debut to the market equivalent to the Autostrade Eurobond issue of 1963. Among the claimants to the distinction of being the first syndicated Eurocurrency credit was the $15 million loan for the Hungarian Aluminium Industry lead managed in June 1968, by Bank of London and South America, an early promoter of the Euromarkets, whose chairman, Sir George Bolton, formerly of the Bank of England, was a leading foreign currency expert and a visionary of the financial markets. Another early credit was the $100 million for the Republic of Austria lead managed by Lehman Brothers and Bankers Trust International.[36] In January 1969, Manufacturers Hanover Limited was formed as the partly owned subsidiary of a major US commercial bank and soon became a big factor in the market, under the dynamic Minos Zombanakis.[37] The market grew very rapidly, from an estimated $2 billion in 1968 to almost $22 billion in 1973.[38]

At first, syndicated lending was developed by US and UK investment and merchant banks acting as lead managers or arrangers, but rarely as lenders themselves. Thus an opportunity presented itself for institutions combining the entrepreneurial instincts of an investment bank with the lending-power of a big commercial bank to take a major role in the market. Perception of this market opening boosted the formation of consortium banks and the creation of investment banking subsidiaries by US commercial banks in London.

EMERGENCE OF LONDON AS EUROMARKET CAPITAL

London was not the only European financial centre to play host to the Euromarkets, but it soon became the leading location. The expansion of the Eurocurrency market in London is reflected in the growth of the dollar-denominated external liabilities of UK-based banks (see Table 1.2). These multiplied ten-fold over the years 1957 to 1960, from $157 million to $1.6 billion. Over the decade of the 1960s they grew twenty-fold, and by 1972 amounted to $48 billion.

There were a number of reasons why it was London rather than Brussels or Paris or Luxembourg that became the Euromarkets' principal location.

Table 1.2 Dollar-denominated external liabilities of UK banks, 1957–72[39] ($ million)

1957	157	1963	3 002	1969	25 747
1958	308	1964	4 379	1970	31 406
1959	678	1965	5 300	1971	36 928
1960	1 579	1966	7 636	1972	48 228
1961	1 870	1967	9 691		
1962	2 475	1968	15 370		

First and foremost, was the liberal regulatory environment and even the sponsorship of the markets and their participants by the Bank of England; James Keogh, the Bank official with responsibility for monitoring the new banks being established to operate in the Euromarkets, jokingly told Russell Taylor, as he set up consortium bank Italian International Bank, that he could do whatever he liked, within the law, provided he didn't 'do it in the streets and frighten the horses.'[40] Keogh's *jeu d'esprit* reflected the Bank of England's view that well-established foreign banks knew what they were doing and were good for their obligations. The Bank's light touch as a regulator and its support for the new markets, made London, as the chairman of Chase Manhattan put it, 'a very warm place for doing business.'[41]

The wealth of accumulated international financial expertise in London, particularly in the indigenous merchant banks which gave a lead, but also in the markets, was a dynamic factor once international financial flows were deregulated in 1958. The legal and accountancy infrastructure, the concentration of financial information services, some of the world's leading money publications, specialist printers and other experts, and a substantial appropriately skilled labour force, made London a relatively easy place to develop international banking business. And the usage of English law and the English language was an attraction, particularly for American bankers.

The Banker estimated that 77 foreign banks were directly represented in London through a representative office, branch or subsidiary in 1960.

Table 1.3 Foreign banks in London, 1967–72[42]

	Directly represented	*Indirectly represented*	*Total*
1967	113	–	113
1968	134	–	134
1969	137	–	137
1970	161	–	161
1971	174	25	199
1972	213	28	241

A decade later, the number had doubled. In 1972, 213 foreign banks were directly represented (see Table 1.3) and a further 28, certainly an underestimate, were 'indirectly' represented through a shareholding in a joint-venture or consortium bank.

American banks led the charge in the foreign bank 'invasion' of the City in the 1960s and 1970s.[43] In fact, the establishment of a presence in London was part of a larger international expansion of US banks in these years. In 1964, 11 US banks had overseas branches, totalling 181 in number. By 1970, 79 US banks had 536 overseas branches. Over the same period, the aggregate assets of the overseas branches of US banks grew from $6.9 billion to $52.6 billion.[44] Participation in the Euromarkets was an important reason for the growth of the overseas presence of US banks, but not the only factor. Another closely related motive was to service US corporate clients, which were rapidly internationalizing in the 1960s. As more and more US corporations became multinationals, the US money centre banks followed them around the world. In the late 1960s, especially from 1968, the Euromarkets became the principal source of finance for such overseas expansion.

The establishment of a branch, subsidiary or even a representative office in London was an expensive undertaking, and most commercial banks lacked personnel with the necessary expertise in international banking. Entry to the new markets via a special sort of joint venture – a consortium bank – had the attractions of pooling costs and risks. In the late 1960s and early 1970s, more and more banks became participants in a consortium bank as a means of establishing a foothold in the booming Eurocurrency and foreign exchange markets.

CHAPTER 2

Rise of consortium banking

A *consortium bank* is a bank that is owned by a strategic alliance of other banks. In the spectrum of joint-enterprises in banking, consortium banks lie between loose associations, such as correspondent relationships or 'banking clubs' (see below), and more formal alliances cemented through share transactions or full mergers. The 1960s and 1970s saw the formation of a large number of consortium banks in the major international financial centres. In London, they even had their own club, the Association of Consortium Banks formed in 1975. Most of the members of this body were consortium banks according to the Bank of England's definition of that year – banks in which no other bank had a shareholding of over 50 per cent and which had two or more banks as shareholders, at least one of which should be a bank not incorporated in the UK.[1]

The consortium bank was not a new phenomenon, co-operation being as much a feature of the history of banking as competition. Such joint ventures between banks have been particularly associated with the development of new activities and entry into unfamiliar locations. Even Citibank, which generally pursued a go-it-alone strategy, adopted the joint venture route to enter some markets. 'When we go into an area which is large and relatively unknown,' observed chairman Walter Wriston, 'where the hazards are great and we do not have the management skills to man it, then we go into partnership.'[2]

HISTORICAL ANTECEDENTS

In the nineteenth century, British, French and German banks formed joint venture banks, often with their industrial or trading clients as partners, together with local interests to operate in their empires and other parts of the world. Such emerging markets of the day offered potentially fabulous opportunities to develop business, but they were fraught with political and market risk. Joint ventures meant a profitable participation in projects that went right, while the losses on those that went wrong were shared and sustainable. The origins of several major international banks are rooted in consortia of banks and bankers. Imperial Bank of Persia (later British Bank of the Middle East, now part of HSBC) was promoted in 1889 by City merchant bank J. Henry Schröder & Co., David Sassoon & Co. and Walpole Greenwell & Co., with bankers Geoffrey Glyn and Henry Keswick (former chairman of Hong Kong Bank) on the board. London & River Plate Bank (later Bank of London and South America, now part of Lloyds TSB) was formed in the 1860s with representatives of City Bank, Alliance Bank, Colonial Banking Company and Midland Banking Company on its board. These banks operating respectively in Persia and Latin America, exemplify the joint venture approach to risky, yet potentially lucrative markets.

Across the English Channel, none was more active in promoting joint venture banks than Paribas; among the many banks in whose early history Paribas was active were Banco Español de Crédito, Banco Nacional de México and Banca Commerciale Italiana (BCI); in 1910, BCI teamed up with its own shareholder Paribas to establish Banque Française et Italienne pour l'Amérique du Sud (Sudameris), which became one of the largest European-owned joint venture banking enterprises in South America. It was eventually acquired by BCI, its Italian founder. German banks were also active after 1870 in the founding of overseas banks. Deutsche Bank formed banks to operate in South America and Asia, while Dresdner Bank and some partners established Deutsche Südamerikanische Bank in 1906, which was the core of Dresdner Bank's large and long-standing Latin American business. At some stage, most of these joint venture banks faced difficulties and were taken over by one of their founders or disappeared altogether. For instance, Russo–Asiatic Bank was one of the biggest banks in the world in 1917, when it was swept away by the Russian Revolution. However, the value of joint ventures banking strategies in emerging markets had been demonstrated.

Consortium banks were vehicles by which many US banks made their first foray into international banking in the early years of the twentieth century. The establishment of overseas branches by US national banks was permitted for the first time by the Federal Reserve Act of 1913. This legislation also permitted them to accept foreign drafts, allowing them to develop international trade financing activities and thereby encouraging them to develop business abroad. The outbreak of the First World War, the following year, prevented the branches of European banks from servicing their overseas clients in sterling or other European currencies. This led to an upsurge in demand for US dollar credit facilities from importers and exporters in Latin America and Asia, presenting US banks with a unique opportunity to enter these markets.

A few US banks moved overseas through establishing branches, but many more joined consortium banks formed specially for the purpose of operating abroad. Six such jointly owned entities were incorporated under state banking law between 1915 and 1919. In the early 1920s, at their peak, they operated 81 overseas branches, mostly in Latin America and the Caribbean, but also in Asia and Europe.[3] For instance, American Foreign Banking Corporation, a New York bank formed in 1917 with 35 US and Canadian banks as shareholders, operated 19 overseas branches in Europe and Latin America; Asia Banking Corporation opened 11 foreign branches in the Far East; Bank of Central and South America had 22 offices in its region; and Park Union Foreign Banking Corporation operated in Japan, China and France.

But these consortium banks soon encountered a variety of problems. It proved easier to open a bank in an unfamiliar environment than to manage it successfully, especially when competition from European banks revived at the end of the war. In the unsettled post-war years, fluctuations in commodity prices and trade flows led to bad debts among merchant clients. The consortium banks also suffered from tensions inherent to the consortium concept itself, notably disputes among the shareholders and competition between shareholder banks and their own consortium entities. In every case, the US consortium banks of the early twentieth century were either purchased by one of the shareholder banks, sold to another bank or liquidated, and by 1927 they had all disappeared. Two were acquired by future Orion partners – American Foreign Banking Corporation was purchased by Chase in 1925, while Bank of Central and South America was bought by Royal Bank of Canada. The frustrations and fates of the US consortium banks in the 1920s did not augur well for their successors of the 1960s and 1970s.

CONSORTIUM BANKS OF THE 1960s AND 1970s

In the early years of the Eurodollar and Eurobond markets, as with any new financial market, there were worries about fund flows and liquidity, even about their durability – many wondering whether they were permanent features or the product of short-term US payments imbalances; Sir Charles Hambro, whose bank was a Euromarket pioneer, warned in 1966 that Eurobonds were perhaps a 'temporary phenomenon,'[4] while Dr Hermann Abs of Deutsche Bank feared that the Eurodollar market was a threat to national interests and, as he said to Citibank chief Walter Wriston, 'was evil, was transitory and would go away.'[5] It was also feared that these offshore markets might be curbed by anxious monetary authorities or gravitate back onshore to New York if US taxes were reduced and restrictions liberalized; in July 1972 the front cover of *Euromoney* featured a gravestone with the inscription 'R.I.P. Eurodollar 1958–1972'. Although, to paraphrase Mark

Twain's remark on reading his own obituary, 'the reports of their death were much exaggerated', these uncertainties suggested a cautious approach to participation in the Euromarkets. 'Consortium banks were set up to test the water,' explained Russell Taylor of Italian International Bank, 'at the prompting of the international banking divisions of major domestic banks ... If the results were promising, the shareholding banks could benefit directly later, either by buying out the other partners ... selling out and setting up a London branch, or even having both a branch and participation.'[6]

In the 1960s and early 1970s, even the largest commercial banks had little experience in international banking. 'It is quite surprising how many billion-dollar banks do not have a full-time foreign exchange dealer, let alone a multicurrency loan officer,' observed Professor Michael von Clemm in 1971, who combined an academic expertise about the Euromarkets with being one of their outstanding practitioners at White Weld and its successor firms.[7] For many banks, taking a shareholding in a consortium bank was a way of learning the international banking business. 'Consortium banks were always a small minority of London's banks,' commented Taylor, 'but their influence was out of proportion to their numbers. Hundreds of bankers would learn about international lending through their service with the consortium banks, and their "slam, bam, thank you ma'am" approach to lending business.'[8]

For small or regionally oriented banks, joining a consortium bank provided an entrée to the international financial markets that would otherwise have been impossible because of the cost and lack of management skills. At least 40 US regional banks invested in consortium banks in London. They hoped thereby to gain access to the Euromarkets for a fraction of the cost of setting up their own operation – wrongly as it turned out in most cases. This allowed them to offer international services to their domestic corporate clients, countering competition from the large US money centre banks. In the case of banks from Scandinavia, Italy, Japan and elsewhere, the consortium route provided an indirect means of participation in the Euromarkets when central bank restrictions prevented direct operations.[9]

A consortium bank with shareholders from the major developed countries was well positioned to serve the multi-currency requirements of multinational corporations. The growing scale of the financial requirements of such global corporations, but also governments and public agencies, made it more and more difficult for even the largest banks to provide the funds on their own. By enlisting the support of the consortium and its group of shareholders, banks could service major clients more effectively. Orion's John Haley told the *Wall Street Journal* about an instance when a European government wanted a $110 million loan but without the publicity arising from a syndication: 'We did it quietly in house,' he said.[10]

Speed was another advantage of a consortium over a syndicate. Haley described Orion as an 'instant syndicate', citing a $25 million loan for an

Italian enterprise in which all six shareholder banks joined the financing. Attilio Molendi, Orion's senior representative from Credito Italiano, recalled how, in July 1972, a $150 million financing for Istituto Mobiliare Italiano, the big Italian state credit organization, was put together in 48 hours – so rapidly that Molendi could not make it back from holiday quickly enough to take part.

Drawing on the joint resources of the shareholder banks, consortium banks could provide credits on a scale beyond the capacity of the individual shareholders. Particularly important was that they were also able to extend credits with longer maturities than was acceptable in commercial banking parlours. They could do this because they were assured, or so they thought, of a continuing and stable supply of funds from parent shareholders, directly, or under their implicit guarantee. The same factor meant a relatively low cost base since they did not have to maintain expensive branch outlets to generate deposits, although an offsetting factor was high personnel and travel costs.

In most countries, the banking authorities limited loan sizes, maturities and types. This was especially a problem for US banks, whose major clients were developing into multinational corporations with ever expanding horizons and requirements for funds. Offshore-based consortium banks enjoyed an easier regulatory regime that enabled shareholder banks to maintain facilities for their clients and to participate in other large loans to multinational corporations and other borrowers. Thus the consortium banks supplemented their shareholders' own balance sheets and allowed them to keep up with the requirements of multinational clients. Following the oil price rises of 1973–74, they helped raise large sums for governments for balance of payments purposes.

The 1960s saw the rapid growth of the global economy and great expansion in international trade. Some observers were sceptical about whether the world's resources, including its financial resources, were adequate to sustain the momentum, anxieties that were expressed in the influential book *The Limits to Growth* by Aurelio Peccei and other members of the Club of Rome published in 1972. Even the leading banks were domestically oriented and highly conservative in character. New international financial institutions seemed to be needed, and consortium banks with multinational shareholders appeared to fit the bill.

In Europe, the establishment of the European Economic Community in 1957 stimulated banks to work together in anticipation of closer economic and financial integration. The expansion of US banks into the major European financial centres was another stimulus. Informal 'banking clubs' (see page 27) were formed among the leading commercial banks from different European countries. They were useful for the exchange of information and the development of personal ties among senior management. Some of the European banking clubs established or joined consortium banks to expand international lending and capital markets activities.

Sometimes there were political motives behind the formation of consortium banks. For instance, in order to help mend fences with the Arab world after the war of Algerian independence, the French government encouraged the three leading state-owned banks to head Paris-based groups of international and Arab banks in which there would be a strong French influence: Crédit Lyonnais (promoter of UBAF);[11] Société Générale (Frab);[12] and Banque Nationale de Paris (BAII).[13] Political motives were also apparent on the Arab side, and profits may not always have been the paramount consideration for participants. Two of the largest consortium banks were later formed by Arab governments, Gulf International Bank[14] and Arab Banking Corporation,[15] both based in Bahrain.

Finally, the herd instinct was at work, as so often in the banking industry. Observing their rivals joining up, bankers rushed to jump aboard a consortium so as not to miss the boat. 'By joining with other banks, the general manager of the international division protected his back,' commented Russell Taylor, 'since, when many are responsible, none is accountable. As nearly all were to say in the years to come: "It looked right, and everyone else was doing it. My God, look at the partners that were in with us, and who else had done it. How can anyone possibly blame me for the fact that things went wrong?"'[16] Bank of England regulator Peter Cooke, who lent his name to the Cooke Committee of the Bank for International Settlements, had a recurring dream in which an endless procession of stretch limousines full of international bankers rolled up to a luxury conference hotel, each vehicle sporting an identical bumper sticker: 'two million lemmings can't be wrong.'[17]

SHAREHOLDERS

Over 200 banks and other investors became shareholders in the London consortium banks. In the main they were large commercial banks. Most of the world's major commercial banks became a shareholder in one or more consortium banks; some had shares in a dozen or more. In 1980, only six of the world's top-50 commercial banks had no significant consortium bank interest and four of these were not active overseas. The other two exceptions were Citibank and Lloyds Bank. Citibank, 'the cold, dazzling, inventive world money machine,' preferred to prowl the markets alone.[18] Lloyds Bank had been tempted by consortium strategies, such as the ambitious, but abortive, Intercontinental Banking Services[19] in 1967, but in the early 1970s chose to stay aloof, perhaps contributing to its later success. So did its affiliate, Euromarket pioneer Bank of London and South America, which as executive David Cobbold recalled, 'resisted all entreaties to join with others, being confident in our own expertise.'[20] Upon inheriting a shareholding in the London Interstate Bank through its acquisition of a bank in California in 1975, Lloyds withdrew from the consortium 'in line with the long established policy of the Lloyds Bank Group.'[21]

Among the London-based consortium banks, it was usual, but not universal, to have a UK clearing bank or merchant bank as a shareholder. The leading UK clearing banks, with the exception of Lloyds Bank, were shareholders, Midland Bank, in particular, playing a pioneering role in the development of the consortium banking movement.[22] A number of the City's independent merchant banks became partners in consortium banks. Some, notably Warburgs, Rothschilds and Hambros, played leading roles in the development of the Euromarkets and they had much to offer the other shareholders as regards international expertise and entrepreneurial culture. For the merchant banks, participation in a consortium bank was attractive because it allowed them to develop business from which they would otherwise have been excluded because of their relatively small capital base. They hoped also to gain access to the resources and clients of the large commercial banks that were their fellow shareholders.

To complete the round up of investors, several large insurance companies became consortium bank shareholders, including Eagle Star, Prudential Assurance and Riunione Adriatica di Sicurta.[23] A handful of miscellaneous partners included chemical giant ICI, consumer credit provider United Dominions Trust and the Crown Agents, an agency of the UK government which had a major shareholding in merchant bank E.D. Sassoon Banking Company.[24] One Middle Eastern consortium bank even had a few wealthy individuals among its shareholders.[25]

LOCATION

London played host to more consortium banks than any other financial centre, a total of 35 UK registered consortium banks being formed between 1964 and 1984, not to mention overseas consortium banks that also set up offices in London. This reflected its role as the focal point of the Euromarkets, and the factors that drew the international money and capital markets to London also counted in its favour as a location for consortium banks. For the consortium banks, as for the Euromarkets, the regulatory environment was a key consideration. The Bank of England was supportive of the consortium bank concept, taking the view that, as Peter Cooke put it: 'If the market supports their creation and they are from a fairly good family, we will give them their head ... but it was up to the players to make them work.'[26]

Although UK banks were closely regulated in relation to domestic banking business, British and foreign banks could operate in the Euromarkets with the minimum of constraints. Restricted at home, foreign commercial banks were able to leverage their London-based consortium banks as vehicles for international expansion and the enhancement of their lending power. A further attraction for some US commercial banks was the opportunity to develop expertise in investment banking activities, which was impossible at home because of the separation between deposit taking and securities underwriting imposed by the Glass–Steagall Act of 1933. However, a negative factor was that, as UK companies, they had their capital denominated in sterling, which was prone to depreciation in the 1960s and 1970s.[27]

London was the foremost European location of consortium banks, but not the only one. An analysis published in 1972 identified 21 consortium banks in London, seven in Paris, six in Brussels, five in Zurich, two in Luxembourg, two in Amsterdam, two in Vienna and one in Rome.[28] Consortium structures were also to be found in other parts of the world, such as Bahrain, Hong Kong and Singapore. Nassau was host to RoyWest,[29] a joint venture between NatWest and Royal Bank of Canada and Wobaco, controlled by Bank of America and Toronto Dominion Bank, an early Euromarket participant. Deltec, backed by several major international banks, was also Nassau-based. It was a successful and durable investment bank that specialized in Latin America, which Orion saw as a member of its peer group. In Australia, the government ban on the establishment of branches by foreign banks obliged them to enter the market by indirect means through financial and investment companies – 'consortium near banks' – formed with local partners, usually including one of the top indigenous banks.[30]

BUSINESS

Most consortium banks were formed to undertake medium-term Eurocurrency lending. They blossomed with the growth of medium-term syndicated loans in the late 1960s and early 1970s.[31] By 1973, the consortium banks were advancing 20 per cent of loans of three years or more in the London Eurocurrency market, with an increasing proportion of the funds being directed to Latin America and other less developed countries (LDC) of the Third World, particularly after the first 'oil shock' in that year.[32] Although not prime recipients of the new petrodollar surpluses, which went to the largest banks, they were beneficiaries of the increased international liquidity through the inter-bank market and developed their business rapidly.

They were also short-term lenders on a considerable scale, though their proportionate share of the much larger volume of Eurocurrency lending of less than one year was only 8 per cent.[33]

A handful of consortium banks carried out international investment banking activities, or claimed to do so, in addition to medium-term lending.

First and foremost, this meant managing, underwriting, placing and trading fixed and floating-rate Eurobonds. Some of them also provided advisory services for corporations and governments and undertook investment management, private banking, leasing and other activities. Orion and European Banking Company were the foremost consortium bank practitioners of international investment banking.

Some consortium banks specialized in lending to a specific region, such as Latin America and Scandinavia, or sector, such as energy. Others specialized in the deployment of surpluses from the Middle East. For the shareholders in such specialist consortium banks, they provided a means of extending the range of their businesses and opportunities for staff development.

The consortium banks were at the forefront of an historic shift in the nature of the business of banking. 'These banks, set up with no apparent functions other than to make money by buying business,' observed Taylor, 'first established the idea that "banking" could be divorced from underlying business reality, that "transactions" rather than "relationships" were the bankers' objective.'[34] This became more and more the norm from the 1980s.

PROBLEMS AND ISSUES

The consortium bank formula was, as Michael von Clemm put it, 'full of shoals, pitfalls and conflicts.'[35] The shareholders were one source of problems. Shareholders had a range of motives for joining consortium banks and a variety of expectations of service, performance and dividends. It was hardly surprising that they did not always see eye to eye, particularly as time went by. Furthermore, some banks became shareholders in several consortium banks, which could lead to conflicts of interest and loyalty resulting in divestitures. The ever-shifting kaleidoscope of shareholders was a significant source of instability.

But the biggest difficulty was the development of competition for business between shareholder banks and their consortium joint venture. Despite strivings for 'strategic synergy' at the chief executive level, in the marketplace credit officers tended to regard each other as rivals not allies. Moreover, as banks became more familiar with international operations and more confident about the Euromarkets, the profits from a fraction of a business looked a good deal less attractive than the full dollar. To develop these opportunities, US, European and Japanese banks expanded their London operations and some US commercial banks established merchant banking subsidiaries – there were eleven so-called 'Yankee merchant banks' by the end of 1973[36] – that undertook similar activities to the consortium banks of which many were also members.[37]

The management of consortium banks was another source of problems. There was the question of whether staff was to be seconded from the shareholders, and, if so, from which of them, or recruited directly by the consortium bank. The provenance of senior staff was closely related to the issue of the degree of operational autonomy that a consortium bank was allowed, again fertile ground for disputes among shareholders. Most of the London-based consortium banks had a 'London Committee', or similar body, composed of representatives of each of the shareholders drawn from the senior management of their London branch or subsidiary.[38] These bodies kept an eye on their joint entity and their approval was required for major credits and initiatives. The cost in management time was a matter of complaint on all sides.

The recruitment of high-calibre chief executives proved a headache for the consortium banks. Suitably qualified candidates who combined investment banking and commercial banking skills proved to be in short supply. Moreover, two of the principal activities undertaken – syndicated multi-currency medium-term lending and management of Eurobond issues – were novel and outside the experience of most commercial or investment bankers of the era. Uncertainties over the banks' future and their committee-oriented reporting structures, an inevitable consequence of joint ownership, deterred some candidates.

The activities and style of business of the consortium banks had more in common with investment banking than with traditional commercial banking. Even their lending activities were conducted in a form – the syndicated loan – adapted from investment banking. But the free-wheeling and free-spending ways of investment bankers were anathema to conservative and penny-pinching commercial bankers. Such culture clashes were a perennial source of friction between the consortium banks' parents and their offspring.

The consortium banks were born naked, with neither deposits nor clients. Without a retail deposit base they were highly dependent upon the purchase of deposits in the wholesale money market.[39] This was a mixed blessing. In the late 1960s and early 1970s when market conditions were favourable, they were able to develop business very rapidly and the absence of a costly branch network boosted profits. But it was also a source of weakness when market conditions turned against them and they were obliged to pay over the odds for inter-bank deposits or to fall back on shareholders for support. The lack of a client base made them ever eager to develop new client relationships, inevitably ruffling the feathers of their shareholders from time to time. The executives of the leading consortium banks adopted an 'unprecedentedly footloose approach to business development,' in the words of Orion's William de Gelsey.[40] This resulted from a combination of factors: their lack of a domestic client base anywhere in the world; the international nature of the Euromarkets; the advent of international jet travel; and improvements in telecommunications. The outcome was a truly international outlook – the consortium banks were among the pioneers of global banking.

EUROPEAN BANKING CLUBS[41]

Following the establishment of the European Economic Community in 1957, the expectation of European financial and economic integration led many major European banks to seek ways of fostering cross-border co-operation. The Werner Report of 1970, which presaged a European common currency, gave a further spur. To this end, five far-ranging bank associations, club-like in character, were formed between banks of different European nationalities. Some of these associations were cemented by modest share exchanges. Each club had its own secretariat and some had a management or holding company as well.

The European banking clubs were intended to stimulate a broad exchange of information between members and the joint development of marketing, technology and research. Exchanges of personnel were encouraged and they were regarded as important for training. A variety of joint business undertakings were pursued, including the formation of consortium banks and the co-financing of large projects. These joint ventures provided a means for sharing the costs and risks of developing an international presence, particularly outside Europe. They were expected to enhance services to corporate clients in each other's home markets and to resist the mounting challenge from the major US banks – *Le Défi Américain* (*The American Challenge*).[42]

Some of the clubs at times were even regarded as laying the groundwork for cross-border mergers and the formation of pan-European banks. But these visions did not bear fruit. Instead, from the mid-1970s the major European banks began to develop their own presence in each other's markets, undermining the purpose and roles of the banking clubs. Nonetheless, they were a significant collateral factor in the European consortium banking movement and, in their search for specific areas of co-operation, their members formed a number of such banks.

Three of the five European banking clubs, EBIC, Europartners and ABECOR, have disbanded; two, Inter-Alpha and Unico, survive.

EBIC

EBIC, the first of the banking clubs, was formed in 1958 by Deutsche Bank, Amsterdamsche Bank and Société Générale de Banque de Belgique, with the aim of promoting greater co-operation. It was known initially as the 'club des célibataires' (bachelors' club) emphasizing the independence of the members. A fourth member, Midland Bank, joined in 1963, the first step in Midland's 'grand design' to enhance its presence in international banking (see below). At this moment the arrangement was renamed the European Advisory Committee (EAC) and its existence was made public, the earlier body having been kept secret for fear of upsetting correspondent relationships. 'A novel but puzzling association,' commented *The Economist*.[43]

In 1967, the four EAC banks formed a joint consortium bank in Brussels, the Banque Européenne de Crédit à Moyen Terme, which quickly became a leading Eurocurrency medium-term lending bank.[44] The following year, a further consortium entity, European American Banking Corporation, was established in New York. In the 1960s, Midland resolutely vetoed the inclusion of Crédit Lyonnais as a French partner, on the grounds that 'we don't want de Gaulle in our club,'[45] UK membership of the EEC having been vetoed by France, but another French bank, Société Générale, Austria's Creditanstalt-Bankverein and Banca Commerciale Italiana joined in the early 1970s.

European Banks International Company (EBIC) itself was formed as a group management company in 1970. In addition to the Brussels and New York banks, four further consortium banking groups were formed by EBIC in the 1970s thereby extending EBIC's tentacles into Asia, Australasia, the Arab world and the City of London. One of them, European Banking Company, became successful as an investment bank in London.[46] At the peak of EBIC's co-operative activity in the late 1970s, its members financed many large projects together and, through their six consortium banking groups, had a presence in many markets and activities. They had over 10 000 branches in Europe and the largest European-owned bank in the USA.

EUROPARTNERS

In January 1971, Crédit Lyonnais, Commerzbank and Banco di Roma entered a wide-ranging 'triple bank alliance' pledging extensive co-operation and regarding this 'quasi-merger' as a preliminary step towards a full merger.[47] In the first year, fourteen working parties were established to cover every aspect of business. Full unification was complicated by the public ownership of the French and Italian banks, whereas the German bank was privately owned, and by political considerations, but the 'urge to merge' distinguished Europartners from the other banking clubs which were looser in character. Dr Danilo Ciulli of Banco di Roma described it as an *'ideale fusione.'*

A one-third interest was taken by the three banks in International Commercial Bank,[48] a London consortium bank, in 1973, and they were also associated with affiliates of the UBAF group, of which Crédit Lyonnais was a main architect, giving access to the Arab world.[49] An investment bank was established in New York and several other joint ventures and representative offices were opened around the world. Attempts were made to recruit a major UK commercial bank as a partner; both NatWest and Williams & Glyn's Bank were approached, without success, while Midland and Barclays were otherwise committed. The most suitable candidate, Lloyds Bank, had set its mind against consortium-owned banking operations, the 'bankers' clubs so frequently referred to in the press.'[50] Yet it did come to an 'informal agreement, falling short of any investment or formal association'[51] with

Crédit Lyonnais and Commerzbank for providing facilities in each others' home currencies to selected customers, but this was a long way short of joining the club. Instead, Europartners expanded in a different direction, enrolling a leading Spanish private sector bank, Banco Hispano Americano, as a member in October 1973.

INTER-ALPHA

Inter-Alpha Group of Banks was an association of medium-sized banks, which were significantly smaller than members of the other banking clubs. The club originated in 1971 out of the joint shareholdings in Kredietbank SA Luxembourgeoise, by four other banks, Kredietbank of Belgium, Banco Ambrosiano of Italy, Crédit Commercial de France and Nederlandsche Middenstandsbank. Together they had a sizeable branch network, with a strong orientation towards corporate clients and investment banking. Another strength was the pioneering role of Kredietbank and its Luxembourg affiliate in the Eurobond market. The founders were joined by the UK clearing bank Williams & Glyn's Bank in 1971, BHF Bank of Germany in 1972 and Privatbanken of Denmark in 1973.

Inter-Alpha focused on the provision of international and domestic corporate finance services to corporate clients. For larger borrowers, members organized Eurobond and syndicated loan facilities, often inviting one another to be co-managers. In 1972, the group took a 40 per cent share in London consortium bank Brown Harriman & International Banks[52] and established an Asian investment banking group. Joint representative offices were opened in São Paulo, Singapore, New York, Tokyo and Teheran.

ABECOR

Associated Banks of Europe Corporation (ABECOR) was established in 1974 by nine banks, Algemene Bank Nederland, Banque de Bruxelles, Bayerische Hypotheken- und Wechsel-Bank, Dresdner Bank, Banca Nazionale del Lavoro, Banque Nationale de Paris, Banque Internationale à Luxembourg, Barclays Bank and Österreichische Länderbank. Its origins date from 1967, with the formation of Société Financière Européenne (SFE)[53] by five of the future ABECOR members and the Bank of America. SFE was an international medium-term lending and investment consortium bank, based in Luxembourg and Paris. In 1971, ABECOR members established a joint US investment bank and later participated in consortium banks Euro–Latinamerican Bank and BAII.[54] Six of them set up a joint training institute in Bad Homburg in 1972.

The fully fledged ABECOR was a loose association with no aspirations to a full merger, which allowed it to operate with so many members, including two competitors from one country, Germany. It was focused on co-operation in Europe, members operating independently outside the continent. This was a distinguishing feature, the establishment of global joint undertakings being part of the strategy of other clubs.

UNICO

The Unico Banking Group was established in 1977 by co-operative banks from Austria, Denmark, Finland, France, Germany and the Netherlands. Besides a large retail clientele, they serviced the agricultural sector and numerous small businesses. Despite 40 000 outlets in their domestic markets, they provided little in the way of international services to their customers. The formation by some of them of their own consortium bank, London & Continental Bankers, in 1973, was intended to remedy this shortcoming and give them a UK presence, leading to the formation of Unico four years later.[55]

LONDON CONSORTIUM BANKS

The story of the formation of consortium banks in London (see Table 2.1) has two distinct phases, 1964–74 and 1975–84. In the first phase, a total of 27 banks were formed: 13 of them, including Orion, were generalists, with wide-ranging objectives and multinational bank ownership; 14 had a regional focus, in 9 cases a one-country focus. After the banking crisis arising out of the collapse of Bankhaus I D Herstatt in June 1974, consortium banks found it difficult, in varying degrees, to raise money from the inter-bank market; Herstatt was described by Gérard Legrain of International Mexican Bank as 'the wicked fairy over the bed,' which haunted consortium bank treasurers and hamstrung their business. As a result, the wide-ranging generalist consortium bank went out of fashion and, in due course, out of business; no new ones were formed in London after the 1974 crisis. The eight

Table 2.1 Formation of London-based consortium banks, 1964–84[56]

	1964	1965	1966	1967	1968	1969	1970	1971	1972	1973	1974	Total
Generalists	1		1	2	1	1	3	1		3		13
Regionals			1			1	2	1	4	4	1	14
Total	1		2	2	1	2	5	2	4	7	1	27

	1975	1976	1977	1978	1979	1980	1981	1982	1983	1984	Total
Generalists											0
Regionals	1	1		1		1		1	2	1	8
Total	1	1		1		1		1	2	1	8

consortium banks founded between 1975 and 1984 all had a regional or single-country focus.

GENERALIST CONSORTIUM BANKS

The pioneer consortium bank established in 1964 was Midland and International Banks Limited (MAIBL).[57] Midland Bank was the driving force behind MAIBL, colloquially pronounced 'Mabel', subscribing 45 per cent of the equity. It also provided the name, chairman and general manager. Its partners were Toronto Dominion Bank, 26 per cent, Standard Bank, 19 per cent and Commercial Bank of Australia, 10 per cent, providing a portfolio of contacts in Canada, Africa and Australia.[58]

In the early 1960s, Midland's senior management recognized the rapidly growing opportunities in international finance, and became uncomfortably aware of the bank's lack of expertise in Eurocurrency business, a shortcoming entirely typical of the British clearing banks of the day, and the paucity of its international presence, having traditionally relied on correspondent relationships.[59] But diagnosing the problem was easier than coming up with a quick cure, since the obvious solutions of developing in-house Eurocurrency expertise and establishing overseas branches were time-consuming and costly. The formation of a consortium bank with international partners offered a rapid and economical means of placing a footprint in a number of important overseas markets and of creating a specialist and independent vehicle for participation in the Euromarkets; it fitted in well with Midland's European banking club (the future EBIC) by adding a global dimension.

It was intended that MAIBL would specialize in offering medium-term loans on terms and conditions akin to those typical of a US bank *term loan*.[60] These were, as the Midland Bank's annual report for 1965 put it: 'for periods that would not suit the commercial banking system.' At the time, this was something of an innovation in UK banking where traditionally the borrowing options had been between short-term money market funding or long-term bonds and debentures.[61] The timing was fortunate since the worldwide rise in interest rates that got underway in 1965 discouraged long-term borrowing in the capital markets and shifted demand for financing to the medium-term sector of the market. Thus the first consortium bank made its debut in the medium-term credit sector of the Eurocurrency market, with buoyant demand for its services. It soon extended the range of its activities and by 1970 it was among the 175 largest banks in the world.[62]

Rothschild Intercontinental Bank began as National Provincial and Rothschild (London) in 1966.[63] It was the first partnership between a UK clearing bank and a merchant bank, a modest beginning to the UK clearing banks' full-scale entry into (and exit from) investment banking over the next thirty years.[64] For National Provincial, it provided a so-called 'back door bidding subsidiary' to get round the clearing banks' cartel on deposit rates, and a potentially exciting association with the legendary house of Rothschild. For Rothschilds, there was the prospect of access to National Provincial's substantial resources which would serve to 'extend Rothschild's credit network,' as the senior partner Edmund de Rothschild put it. There was also the possibility of corporate finance mandates, a hope in which Rothschilds was not disappointed.[65] In 1968, National Provincial and Rothschild became a consortium bank of European scope with the admission of the Belgian, Dutch, French and Swiss member banks of the 'Five Arrows group' with historic ties to Rothschilds. National Provincial's successor, NatWest, withdrew in 1969 and the bank changed its name. The scope was then broadened by the inclusion of three large US regional banks, from Seattle, Houston and Cleveland, the Industrial Bank of Japan and other shareholders.

One of the most active of the consortium banks of the late 1960s and early 1970s was Western American Bank (Europe), whose initial shareholders were three US regional banks and City merchant bank Hambros.[66] Formed in 1967, Western American grew particularly rapidly and by 1973 it was London's largest consortium bank, having added Bank of Tokyo as a shareholder. By then it had arranged $3 billion of loans, including a $1 billion loan to the UK's Electricity Council, was an active member of Eurobond management groups and was conducting a $750 million daily volume of trading in a range of financial instruments.

International Commercial Bank was formed in 1967 by two major banks from the USA and others from the UK, Germany and Hong Kong.[67] It was primarily a multi-currency, medium-term lending institution. The UK partner, Westminster Bank (later NatWest), dropped out for conflict-of-interest reasons after the formation of Orion; the capital was then restructured to enable the three Europartners club banks to hold, jointly, a one-third interest in the bank.[68]

These years saw the formation of two more joint ventures between City merchant banks and US and European commercial banks. Brown Harriman & International Banks was formed in 1968 by Brown Brothers Harriman & Co., the leading US private bank, City merchant bank Robert Fleming and Cie Financière de Suez of Paris.[69] For Brown Brothers Harriman it was a vehicle for securities underwriting, from which it was debarred at home under the Glass–Steagall Act, and a window on the Euromarkets. After Fleming and Suez dropped out in 1970, because they found themselves competing with their own joint venture, it was reconstituted with US regional banks and the Inter-Alpha Group of Banks as shareholders. Atlantic International Bank began in 1969 as a joint venture between four US regional banks and four European banks, including City merchant bank Charterhouse Japhet.[70]

The establishment of Orion, whose history is the subject of subsequent chapters, in October 1970 was a turning point in the development of consortium banking.[71] 'The imprimatur of respectability was given by the creation of Orion,' commented Russell Taylor, 'and the stage was set for frenetic expansion.' Orion's initial shareholders were two large North American banks, Chase Manhattan and Royal Bank of Canada, and two major European banks, NatWest and Westdeutsche Landesbank. Later Credito Italiano and Mitsubishi Bank joined the consortium. This alliance between the world's 3rd, 7th, 12th, 14th, 16th and 40th largest banks was a momentous development. Moreover, Orion was ambitiously conceived as an international investment bank, embracing a full range of merchant banking activities as well as medium-term lending and other commercial banking business.

The shareholders of United International Bank were drawn from a range of continental European countries and North America; the UK partner was Williams & Glyn's.[72] London Interstate Bank was a vehicle whereby five large US regional banks established a presence in the London markets, in conjunction with small City merchant bank Keyser Ullman.[73] London & Continental Bankers was set up as the London financial arm of the European co-operative bank movement, in a spirit of some idealism; the London merchant bank, Warburgs, was a small shareholder providing international expertise.[74] Lord Shawcross, the first chairman, stressed its 'sturdy parentage', with 40 000 outlets throughout Europe and his successor, Helmut Guthardt, referred to the 'broad commitment of its owners and not simply a commercial venture.'[75] Later, several of them formed the Unico Banking Group.[76]

London Multinational Bank was a carefully balanced US–European group of two larger and two smaller banks; the prime architect was City merchant bank Baring Brothers & Co., which needed access to US dollars to fund its multi-currency lending.[77] It was another example of a UK merchant bank matching its skills with the resources of larger commercial banks. The first chairman was Lord Cromer, former governor of the Bank of England, and chairman of Barings at the time.

European Banking Company, formed in 1973, was, like Orion, conceived as a full-range international investment bank.[78] Based in London, it was owned by the seven partners of the banking club EBIC. The managing director was Stanislas Yassukovich, a Euromarket veteran from White Weld, forerunner of Credit Suisse White Weld, the novel joint venture between a Swiss commercial bank and a US investment bank, which was a powerful presence in the Euromarkets.[79]

In a category of its own, the only London consortium bank focused on a single industrial sector was International Energy Bank; its shareholders were North American, UK and European banks with particular interests in the energy sector, such as Bank of Scotland, Banque Worms and Republic

National Bank of Dallas.[80] It was a pioneer in the finance of North Sea oil production, which began in 1975; it developed its lending activities over a wide range of energy activities and geographical areas.

MIDDLE EASTERN CONSORTIUM BANKS

Oil revenues brought considerable prosperity to Kuwait, both before and after independence in 1961. British Bank of the Middle East's monopoly in the provision of banking services in the emirate had been challenged by National Bank of Kuwait, formed in 1952, followed by several other indigenous banks. Five of them clubbed together to form United Bank of Kuwait[81] as an all-Kuwaiti international bank, there being obvious advantage in such young banks forming a joint venture rather than going it alone. UBK, which opened for business in 1966, aimed to serve the overseas banking, treasury and investment needs of Kuwaiti institutions and individuals, which it accomplished with considerable success.

Iran Overseas Investment Bank, a joint venture between Iranian, UK, French, German, US and Japanese banks, was formed to enable Iran to have a credible international banking presence and to lend to Iranian development projects being actively pushed by the Shah's ambitions; its international bank shareholders were from countries deemed likely to be involved in the development of Iran.[82] UBAF Bank was the London arm of the Franco–Arab banking group, UBAF, which specialized in intermediating financial flows between the Arab world and Europe.[83] UBAF's corporate structure was very complex, with affiliates in nine countries in which leading indigenous banks took shares; there were altogether some 50 participants, including shareholders from all Arab League countries. Midland Bank was the local partner in London, initially with a 25 per cent stake.

EUROPEAN CONSORTIUM BANKS

Scandinavian Bank, founded in 1969, was a regional consortium made up of banks from Sweden, Norway, Finland, Denmark and, later, Iceland.[84] Scandinavian countries were used to joint ventures, an example being the airline, SAS. An important motive in creating the joint bank was the very high degree of regulation at home, which inhibited banks from keeping up with the international needs of major Scandinavian corporations, such as LM Ericsson or Norsk Hydro. Naturally it specialized in Scandinavian business, though it also developed a wide international client base and eventually established a presence in 11 countries. Scandinavian Bank was followed two years later by Nordic Bank, founded by Swedish, Finnish and Norwegian banks and later joined by a Danish bank; it also specialized in Scandinavian business, particularly oil, forestry and shipping.[85]

Monte dei Paschi di Siena, founded in 1472, claims to be the oldest bank in the world; as it celebrated its 500th birthday, it joined three other old-established Italian banks to form Italian International Bank in London. Their approach was club-like in that the four banks established Anciennes Institutions de Crédit Italiennes Holding in Luxembourg so as to create joint ventures in several financial centres; IIB was the first and only such joint venture, as it happened. Severely constrained at home, they could spread their wings in relatively unregulated London, even though they were not entirely sure what they wanted to do. 'Consortium banks were defined by the nature of their ownership rather than their business,' observed Russell Taylor, the first managing director of IIB, adding somewhat cynically: 'in truth, no one really knew what they were for, except that everyone else was doing it.'[86] The bank's first chairman, Lord Cobbold, was a former governor of the Bank of England who had spent his early life in Italy; it had an orientation towards Anglo–Italian business, though it soon got into trouble through bad lending of a non-Italian character.[87] Among its non-executive directors was former UK Chancellor of the Exchequer and future prime minister, James Callaghan.

President Ceausescu's 'demonstrative flirtations with the West,' as Mikhail Gorbachev put it, such as inviting President Nixon to Romania in 1969, infuriated the Kremlin, but the Soviet leaders are unlikely to have lost any sleep over the formation of Anglo–Romanian Bank in 1973.[88] It was owned by Romanian Foreign Trade Bank (50 per cent), Barclays (30 per cent) and Manufacturers Hanover (20 per cent). Barclays found itself a member of several consortium banks and, on this occasion, was involved at the request of Leslie O'Brien, governor of the Bank of England, it then being UK policy to encourage President Ceausescu. Anglo–Romanian Bank was the first consortium bank to specialize in one of the Soviet satellites and was an agent for the promotion of Romania's ambitious and independent industrial development.[89]

Banco Urquijo Hispano Americano Limited (BUHAL) was the vehicle for the establishment of a Spanish Euromarket presence.[90] The chairman, George Moore, was a former chairman and a key architect of the modern Citibank; the directors included a former deputy prime minister and a future minister of industry. Banco Urquijo, the founding shareholder, was the dominant industrial and investment bank in Spain with unparalleled political and industrial relationships. BUHAL started life in 1973 as a wholly owned subsidiary of Banco Urquijo, becoming a consortium bank in 1976 when Banco Hispano Americano took a 50 per cent stake in it.

LATIN AMERICAN CONSORTIUM BANKS

Four of the consortium banks formed in the early 1970s specialized in Latin America. Their creation contributed to and coincided with the rise of sovereign lending in the region. European Brazilian Bank focused on lending to

Brazil;[91] International Mexican Bank did likewise for Mexico.[92] These two one-country specialist banks were controlled by the leading bank in each country, Banco do Brasil and Banco Nacional de México, respectively, and Bank of America, then the largest bank in the world and a founder of several consortium banks. Minority stakes were held by several large international banks and other investors.

Two other banks had a region-wide remit: Libra Bank,[93] Orion's sister bank, which is described elsewhere (see page 72), and Euro–Latinamerican Bank. The latter was half owned by Latin American banks and half by European banks.[94] Dresdner Bank, which already had a strong presence in South America, suggested the idea to Barclays, an ABECOR banking club partner. Alan Peachey, who was assigned the job of working out the details, recalled the thinking behind Barclays' participation as being: 'we have little experience of Latin America and membership of the proposed bank seems a small price to pay for getting our feet wet.'[95] This approach was typical of many consortium bank shareholders; in the end, most of them got wetter feet than they bargained for. Part of the rationale for these banks in London was that, being backed by major international banks, they expected to raise funds on more favourable terms than Latin American shareholding banks could themselves; depositors, hopefully, might see the risk as European or global rather than Latin American.[96]

JAPANESE CONSORTIUM BANKS

The Japanese economy had shown extraordinary export-driven growth in the 1960s; GNP per capita more than doubled during the decade – a much better performance than other industrialized countries. Japanese banks were heavily regulated at home and, in order to enable them to service their customers' growing international activities, the authorities permitted them access to the Euromarkets in stages. First came two all-Japanese consortium banks, both formed in 1970, Associated Japanese Bank (International)[97] and Japan International Bank,[98] of which Mitsubishi Bank, later an Orion shareholder, was a co-founder. A total of 8 banks and 4 securities houses contributed to the initial capital of these banks, 80 per cent coming from commercial banks in each case. Their main activity was participating in syndicated loans organized by major international banks. Soon, the Japanese banks were allowed to join Western banks in a number of consortium banks, to widen their experience;[99] an example of this approach was to be seen in the 5 per cent participation of Nikko Securities in Orion Pacific, the Hong Kong arm of Orion. Later they were permitted to form their own wholly owned investment banks to work alongside their branches. The whole process was an example of the classic Japanese method of development – first assimilating, then imitating and then outdoing the work of others.

LATER REGIONAL CONSORTIUM BANKS

After the troubled times of 1973–74, eight more regional consortium banks were formed, but no generalists; in two cases, they were but London arms of already existing international consortium bank groups.[100] In all eight cases, there was a public-sector presence in the shareholding group and the quest for profits may not have weighed so heavily as it did for the shareholders of the 13 generalist consortium banks analysed above.

Saudi International Bank was established in London to be Saudi Arabia's Euromarket outlet and 'window on the world of finance.'[101] An unusual feature was that the principal shareholder was the Saudi Arabian Monetary Agency, the Saudi central bank, with 50 per cent of the equity. Its main partner was Morgan Guaranty Trust, which had 20 per cent and supplied the management; five other major international banks, one of them NatWest, had 5 per cent each, unable to resist sitting at the same table as SAMA; and two Saudi banks, Riyad and National Commercial, 2.5 per cent each, which ensured Saudi control. Morgan Guaranty's effective partnership with the Saudi central bank was regarded as an 'inimitable coup.'[102] Among Saudi International Bank's non-executive directors were successive retired Bank of England governors, Lord O'Brien and Lord Richardson.

After extensive study and with strong government backing, Jordan International Bank was formed by the Jordanian government and a variety of local banks and finance houses to establish a Jordanian presence in the world's international financial centres.[103] The first chairman was the governor of the Central Bank of Jordan, Dr Mohamed Nabulsi.

European Arab Bank was the London arm of the Luxembourg-based consortium banking group European Arab Holding, set up in 1972 by many of the most powerful private and public sector institutions of the Arab world.[104] Its shareholders included Frab,[105] another Franco–Arab consortium bank, and the EBIC group banks.[106] BAII plc was the principal London banking subsidiary of BAII Holdings of Luxembourg, an international investment and commercial banking group with an emphasis on Arab business; it had been founded in 1973 under the prime sponsorship of French public sector bank Banque Nationale de Paris.[107]

By the mid-1970s, the leading Scandinavian and Italian banks were already members of international consortia. FennoScandia Bank and PK Christiania Bank were vehicles by which a number of other Scandinavian banks also established a presence in the Euromarkets.[108] ITAB Bank[109] did the same in 1983 for a set of late-comers amongst the Italian banks, including the powerful Istituto Mobiliare Italiano, a major public sector institution; by then, Italian International Bank had ceased to be a consortium bank, having had to be rescued by its shareholders and then acquired by one of them, the venerable Monte dei Paschi di Siena.

By the time President Tito died in 1980, Yugoslavia appeared to be politically viable, with its rotating presidency and non-aligned status. Though a
socialist country, it used decentralized and market strategies to good effect.
In the previous autumn, Belgrade had received the international accolade of
playing host to the World Bank/IMF annual meeting and the occasion was
used to establish Anglo–Yugoslav Bank in order to encourage trade between
Yugoslavia and other countries.[110] As with Anglo–Romanian Bank, the
British government encouraged a UK clearing bank to be involved. So
Barclays, again with Manufacturers Hanover, took a 50 per cent stake and
50 per cent was taken by a group of Yugoslav banks; the largest of these was
Beogradska Banka, headed by Slobodan Milosevic, future Serbian President.

HEYDAY OF CONSORTIUM BANKING

'The most important banking development for a generation,' was the judgement of *The Economist* about consortium banking in February 1976.[111] That
year, there were 29 international consortium banks operating in London,
whose share of the foreign currency assets of all UK banks reached a record
at 11.4 per cent. The top-10 consortium banks in London in 1976, ranked
by total assets, are shown in Table 2.2.

Table 2.2   Top-10 London consortium banks, 1976[112]

Bank	Assets (£ million)	Ownership	Type*
1. Orion Bank	998	Global	Gen
2. MAIBL	799	UK/Commonwealth	Gen
3. Scandinavian Bank	729	Scandinavian	Reg
4. International Commercial Bank	505	US/European/Hong Kong	Gen
5. London Multinational Bank	420	US/European	Gen
6. United Bank of Kuwait	400	Kuwaiti	Reg
7. Japan International Bank	379	Japanese	Reg
8. UBAF Bank	373	Arab/European	Reg
9. Associated Japanese Bank	338	Japanese	Reg
10. Nordic Bank	333	Scandinavian	Reg

* Gen: Generalist. Reg: Regional.

Had this table been drawn up a couple of years earlier, two other consortium banks would have featured towards the top. Western American Bank
(Europe) had been the largest of them until its balance sheet had to be drastically cut back. This was a result of losses in its bond business, notably on a
$75 million issue for the City of Glasgow lead managed by the bank, losses
in the UK property market and its inability to raise funds in the inter-bank

market during the 1973–74 secondary banking crisis. Western American continued for a few more years in consortium form, but much reduced in size and ambition.

The other missing face was Rothschild Intercontinental Bank, the consortium bank controlled by Rothschilds and its associates in the 'Five Arrows group' of European banks. At the beginning of the 1970s, RIB had been a cornerstone of Rothschilds' ambitious global strategy. But the RIB shareholders, notwithstanding their good relations with each other, had widely varying strategies, sizes and activities. The inherent difficulties of the consortium approach caused the partners to accept an offer from American Express Company in September 1975, whereupon RIB ceased to be a consortium bank and was renamed Amex Bank. It was the first of the London consortium banks to make the transition from joint to single ownership.

By the mid-1970s, consortium banks were an established and increasingly important part of the international financial scene. Most observers would have agreed with the optimistic outlook of Orion executive Alvaro Holguin, who told the *Wall Street Journal*, 'consortium banks will represent a power in the financial world.'[113] But, in fact, the mid-1970s were the high point of the phenomenon. Although petrodollar liquidity and sovereign lending helped to treble the size of London's consortium banks, over the ensuing ten years among the newer formations only Saudi International Bank achieved critical mass and durability; moreover, the new arrivals were all regionalists and no further generalists, such as Orion or MAIBL, were formed. Indeed, already the tensions and contradictions inherent to the consortium formula were manifesting themselves, while funding in the inter-bank market remained very difficult for them. Far from the anticipated tale of triumph, the story of the second phase of consortium banking from 1975 onwards was one of decline.

CHAPTER 3

Formation of Orion

'Orion wasn't formed after a good lunch,' observed David Montagu, Orion Bank chairman, 1974–79.[1] It was the outcome of more than a year's work of selecting shareholders, defining objectives and devising the new bank's strategy and structure, and the origins of the project went back considerably further. Few of the other consortium banks were prepared with anything like such thoroughness, being often put together on the basis of personal friendships or correspondent relationships. The prominence of Orion's shareholders, the reach of its ambitions and the novelty of its organization ensured that it burst upon the international banking scene with a clap of thunder. 'Business leaders around the world,' declared Michael von Clemm, 'suddenly awoke to the significance of the consortium approach to banking.'[2]

The genesis of Orion can be traced to an informal conversation at a summer school for international bankers at Queen's University, Kingston, Ontario, in 1967, between a Chase Manhattan Bank executive and Earle McLaughlin, president of Royal Bank of Canada. The American visitor, at the behest of Chase president David Rockefeller, suggested an alliance between the banks based on a mutual 10 per cent share swap. The proposal, which might have provoked a political outcry in Canada, was out of the question, but McLaughlin was intrigued by the idea of some sort of link-up with Chase. 'Both our banks were rather sizeable,' he recalled, 'and we decided that there were many deals that we could see were going to come along which would be too big for us individually. Should we get together some time?'[3] A month or so later in September 1967, McLaughlin and Rockefeller met at a gathering of bankers in Phoenix, Arizona, and began to formulate plans for a joint entity to operate in the burgeoning international financial markets.

In fact, the overture to McLaughlin was Rockefeller's second attempt to form an international consortium bank to participate in the Euromarkets. The year before, he had brought together a group of European partners comprising Banque de Bruxelles, Pierson Heldring and Pierson of the Netherlands, Stockholms Enskilda Banken and London merchant bank Rothschilds, to form a consortium bank to service European clients. But this had fallen apart at the last moment when the Swedish partner had pulled out under pressure from Hermann Abs of Deutsche Bank, who was hostile to the expansion of American banks in Continental Europe.[4]

CHASE MANHATTAN BANK[5]

At the time of the announcement of the formation of Orion in October 1970, Chase Manhattan Bank (Chase) was the third largest bank in the world with assets of $22.2 billion, surpassed only by Bank of America and Citibank. With forerunners beginning in the eighteenth century, Chase was the outcome of a merger between two medium-sized New York banks in 1955, which propelled it into the front rank. The rich and powerful Rockefeller family was closely connected with the bank, and in 1961 David Rockefeller became president and co-chief executive. Under his leadership, Chase made an energetic push overseas, increasing its foreign presence from 18 to 73 territories during the 1960s, in more than half through joint ventures. The foremost motive was to be able to service the international banking needs of rapidly expanding US multinational corporations, though Rockefeller, a 'true internationalist', also hoped to win local clients.[6]

Chase's strategy for expansion in developed countries favoured affiliations with large local banks and joint enterprises, in marked contrast to its arch rival Citibank. Although branches afforded better managerial control, they were costly to establish, required the commitment of scarce human resources, and took time to build a local deposit base. Affiliations with indigenous banks, on the other hand, provided local currency deposits, local knowledge and, it was hoped, a measure of protection from political discrimination against foreign banks. An important internal report of 1963 made a powerful case for overseas expansion via the joint venture route, recommending that Chase seek affiliations with large local banks even in countries in which it already had branches.[7] Hence the suggestion to McLaughlin of forming a joint venture to operate in the Euromarkets was entirely consistent with Chase's strategy, as well as being timely in terms of jumping on the consortium banking bandwagon.

ROYAL BANK OF CANADA[8]

Royal Bank of Canada (Royal Bank) was a carefully chosen partner. It was Canada's largest bank and 12th in the world, with assets of $9.5 billion. Headquartered in Montreal, it had a network of 1300 branches across

Canada and 24 000 staff.[9] Having been founded by a group of merchants in Halifax, Nova Scotia, it had always been the most international of the Canadian banks, with branches in New York, London and Paris and a substantial presence in the Caribbean and Latin America dating back to the 1920s, when it had acquired an earlier consortium bank, Bank of Central and South America. It had been one of the pioneers of the Eurodollar market, taking dollar deposits from the Moscow Narodny Bank that the Soviet bank would not place in New York.

Rivalry with Citibank, the leading US international bank, provided a bond between Chase and Royal Bank. Despite prodigious efforts, Chase was finding it hard to narrow Citibank's lead in international operations. Canada was a case in point. Both New York banks had ambitions to enter the Canadian market. The only way to do so was by a voluntary affiliation with a Canadian bank, because the Canadian government forbade the formation of new branches by foreign banks. A hostile bid was out of the question. Citibank moved first, buying a 50 per cent interest in Mercantile Bank of Canada, the smallest of the eleven major Canadian banks in 1962.[10] The following year, Rockefeller negotiated the purchase of a 25 per cent shareholding interest in the rather more important Toronto Dominion Bank, a considerable coup. But Canadian nationalism had been aroused by Citibank's acquisition and, to Rockefeller's chagrin, the political backlash against foreign ownership made it impossible for the Chase–Toronto Dominion link-up to proceed or for Chase to develop an affiliation by buying a shareholding in any other Canadian bank.

Royal Bank was also disconcerted by Citibank's purchase of Mercantile Bank, since it brought it into competition with the pushy US bank on its home turf. Faced by the prospect of American competition in its domestic market, Royal Bank looked to expand its international activities, both by establishing new overseas branches and by joint ventures.

NATIONAL WESTMINSTER BANK[11]

The outcome of the Rockefeller–McLaughlin discussions was a decision to explore the establishment of a joint venture to enter the rapidly growing Euromarkets. London, the focal point of the Euromarkets, was the logical location for such an entity, suggesting the inclusion of a major British bank in the consortium. National Westminster Bank (NatWest) was a strong candidate, being a correspondent of both Chase and Royal Bank. Moreover, Royal Bank and NatWest already had experience of working together. In 1965, Royal Bank and Westminster Bank (a NatWest forerunner), and some other partners, had established RoyWest Banking Corporation, in Nassau, Bahamas, a joint venture to undertake medium-term lending and trustee business. A few years earlier, they had held discussions about a joint venture in Continental Europe, though the project had been abandoned when President de Gaulle first vetoed UK membership of the EEC. When it came to choosing a London partner for Orion, Royal Bank's 'English pal' was top of the list.[12]

NatWest was the world's seventh largest bank, with assets of $10.6 billion. It was the product of a recent merger between National Provincial Bank, whose antecedents dated back to the mid-seventeenth century, and Westminster Bank, founded in 1834. Initiated in 1968, the merger was finally completed in January 1970. The combined bank had a national network of 3600 branches and was the second largest UK bank after Barclays. However, its international business was significantly smaller than its main UK competitors, Barclays, Lloyds and Midland, suggesting that it might be interested in teaming up with Chase and Royal Bank.

The merger process at NatWest involved reviewing every aspect of the combined bank's business. In January 1969, the board endorsed the conclusion of a working party report that defined NatWest's international ambitions as 'to become both big and profitable.'[13] International management consultants were commissioned to advise on an implementation strategy. But in May, several months before their report was due, the chairman, David Robarts, received an invitation from Chase and Royal Bank to join them in a 'Grand Alliance' to form 'the strongest, and first, truly international bank.'[14]

The NatWest working party that evaluated the approach from Chase and Royal Bank rejected the option of building an international business from scratch because: 'to achieve a truly international position and to match the US giants in the banking field, National Westminster cannot go it alone for reasons of: cost; time; staff; and know-how.'[15] It considered a range of potential consortium partners, and concluded that Chase and Royal Bank were the best available. It strongly recommended seizing the opportunity that was being presented, since: 'it must be borne in mind that it is Chase and Royal Bank of Canada which have taken the positive step of suggesting a joint venture ... If National Westminster turns down Chase and/or Royal Bank, there is no certainty that another bank of suitable size and international coverage would be willing to take their place.'[16]

NatWest's participation in the proposed 'Multi-International Bank Project' was approved by a resolution of the board in September 1969 that: 'by pooling their individual contributions of geographic coverage, banking and financial services, customer connections and information sources ... the three partners acting together could achieve their international objectives effectively and at acceptable cost; whereas, acting individually and competitively, the task might well prove prohibitively expensive.'[17]

The three banks appointed a set of working parties to define the objectives of their joint enterprise and to formulate proposals for implementation. Most of the work was done by the team in London – two from each bank – who spent five months over the winter of 1969–70 devising Orion's business strategy and structure.[18] They included Jeff Cunningham from Chase, Robert Paterson from Royal Bank and Philip Wilkinson from NatWest, each of whom played an important role at Orion in subsequent years. The working parties reported in March 1970: it was on the basis of their reports that the three chairmen committed themselves to the joint venture at their meeting in Chase's New York headquarters on 29 April 1970.[19]

WESTDEUTSCHE LANDESBANK GIROZENTRALE[20]

As the planning of the so-called 'Multi-International Bank Project' advanced during the spring and summer of 1970, the Anglo-Saxon make-up of the group came to be seen as a disadvantage in the European market. A German partner was deemed desirable because of the size of the German economy and the importance of the Deutschemark. Westdeutsche Landesbank Girozentrale (WestLB) was Germany's biggest bank and 14th in the world with assets of $9.35 billion. The Düsseldorf-based bank, like NatWest the product of a recent merger, was jointly owned by the state of North Rhine–Westphalia, a number of local authorities and some regional savings banks. WestLB was the preferred candidate because it was a leader in Deutschemark bond issues for domestic and foreign borrowers and renowned for its aggressive marketing of Deutschemark foreign bonds; it also had access to a wide range of corporate clients drawn from Germany's foremost industrial region. In any event, the three leading German banks, Deutsche, Dresdner and Commerzbank, were committed elsewhere.[21] For WestLB, joining the Orion partnership was a significant step towards becoming a major international bank.

David Rockefeller made an informal sounding of WestLB chairman, Ludwig Poullain, and received an encouraging response.[22] When a formal invitation was issued to become a fourth partner in the 'Multi-International Bank Project' in September 1970, WestLB accepted immediately.[23] Accordingly, the press announcement of the formation of Orion the following month was made in the name of the four partner banks.[24]

ENLARGEMENT OF THE ORION CONSORTIUM

By spring 1971, the final form of the Orion consortium required urgent resolution, partly to achieve some hoped-for benefits of enlargement but also to dispel the 'protracted uncertainty' about the membership.[25] There was general agreement on the desirability of linking up with powerful banks in France, Italy and Japan, but there were different views about how this might be achieved. The straightforward solution would have been to accord the new partners the same participations as the founding four, but each of the latter refused to accept the dilution of their interests that this would involve.

In fact, they all stipulated a minimum shareholding of 20 per cent, leaving only 20 per cent available for new partners.[26] But a one-third of a one-fifth participation in Orion was not an enticing prospect for the top-tier French, Italian and Japanese banks regarded as suitable additional participants.[27]

An alternative approach was to form a series of subsidiaries to operate in different regions of the world with different shareholding patterns. Richard 'Dickie' Knight, head of planning at Orion on secondment from NatWest, proposed the formation of an Orion Europe and an Orion Pacific to accommodate new European and Asian partners, which could be accorded larger shareholdings in these subsidiary entities. This suggestion horrified some Orion executives, particularly Ronald Grierson, chairman and chief executive of one of the principal operating companies: 'Those who believe that Orion's "thrust" is best preserved by keeping new Orion entities at arm's length are, I think, deceiving themselves,' he wrote in a memo circulated to colleagues. 'Indeed, the mind boggles at the effort – or dissipation of effort – which would be required to guide and animate say an Orion Europe and a Pacific Orion in addition to a London one ... this is a fact Orion shareholders must squarely face when contemplating the beautiful blueprints of a world-wide network of interlocking Orions.'[28]

The outcome of these strategic deliberations was mixed. Orion Europe never got beyond the drawing board, but Orion Pacific was formed to operate in Asia and Libra Bank to specialize in Latin America. Two new partners were admitted to the Orion consortium, but on different terms from those of the original shareholders. Credito Italiano of Italy and Mitsubishi Bank of Japan joined on the basis of shareholdings of 10 per cent each in the two Orion operating companies, and 16.66 per cent of the Orion management services entity, the latter interest being equal to the adjusted shareholdings of the original partners.

CREDITO ITALIANO[29]

Established in 1870, Credito Italiano (Credito) was the fourth largest Italian bank with assets of $6.1 billion, and 40th in the world. With head office in Milan, it had almost 300 branches throughout Italy and employed 10 600 staff.[30] It provided a full range of domestic banking services and had a relatively developed international business, providing trade finance and facilities for subsidiaries of foreign companies operating in Italy and Italian companies operating abroad. It was reported to be the most outward and dynamic of the Italian banks: during the 1950s and 1960s, the growth of deposits outstripped the growth rate of Italian national income and deposits abroad expanded at an even faster rate.[31] Overseas, it was represented in Buenos Aires, Frankfurt, London, New York, Paris, São Paulo and Zurich. Credito was controlled by the Italian state through IRI which had a 77 per cent shareholding, the other 23 per cent having been recently listed on the Milan Stock Exchange, in a partial privatization move.

Observing other leading Italian banks joining banking clubs and consortia, Credito's executives decided to knock loudly on Orion's door; simultaneously, they broached the subject of membership with WestLB, with David Rockefeller, who was visiting Rome, and with Orion Bank chairman Ronald Grierson through a mutual friend, Dr Franco Bobba of the Fiat group.[32] This concerted initiative led to formal discussions in June 1971, following which Orion's representatives reported that:

> *Credito Italiano is faced with the same dilemma as were the founding share-holders. Essentially, it wishes to expand its service capability beyond the Italian border ... But an individual bank cannot profitably compete on foreign soil on the same scale against the indigenous banks with their established reputation, large deposit base, developed branch network, and domestic staff. Therefore ... it must expand by acquisition or join a consortium ...*
>
> *It is felt the international objectives of Credito Italiano harmonise with those of Orion and its shareholders ... Credito Italiano is a suitable potential partner for Orion and, additionally, is the best available Italian candidate.[33]*

Orion's representatives listed ten benefits from the admission of Credito. These included, access to lire for both Orion and the Orion partners, and Credito's placing power, being Italy's leading underwriter of bonds. It also promised introductions to large Italian multinationals (Giovanni Agnelli, head of Fiat, was a member of the Credito board) and a thousand domestic corporate clients.[34] Moreover, it was a shareholder in the influential merchant bank, Mediobanca, in whose *salotto buono* – 'excellent drawing room' – Italy's top tycoons met and planned the future of their country's industries, under the eagle eye of managing director Dr Enrico Cuccia.[35]

The discussions with Credito became focused when it received overtures to join another consortium group. While expressing a preference for Orion, Credito executives explained that they did not want to find themselves in the position of rebuffing the other joint venture and then being rejected by Orion.[36] The negotiations were concluded in July 1971 and a public announcement was made in September 1971.

MITSUBISHI BANK[37]

A Japanese partner did not figure in the initial discussions about the 'Multi-International Bank Project', but at the meeting of chairmen in April 1970 Rockefeller urged it upon his colleagues.[38] The yen was becoming increasingly important as an international currency and there was a growing conviction that Japan was on the brink of becoming a major international financial force.[39] The revaluation of the yen in August 1971, following the suspension of the convertibility of the dollar into gold, marked the actual take-off. Anticipating these developments, the Orion shareholders decided to recruit a Japanese partner at a meeting in Montreal in May 1971.

A relaxation of restrictions on Japanese banks operating overseas by the Japanese authorities had led to some participations in joint ventures in Europe, Australia and elsewhere. But the Ministry of Finance was wary of granting consents for Japanese banks to participate in consortium banks, apparently seeking to protect them against 'possible exploitation by their consortium partners, in a market where they lacked a competitive level of expertise.'[40] Instead, two Ministry of Finance sponsored all-Japanese consortium banks, the Associated Japanese Bank (International) and the Japan International Bank, were formed in London in 1970.[41] Similar banks were formed elsewhere. Later the Ministry relented and Japanese banks were allowed more freedom overseas.

There were different views amongst the Orion partners as to which Japanese bank should be invited to join them. Bank of Tokyo was the choice of Orion executives and NatWest.[42] As the official bank for foreign exchange transactions and foreign trade financing, it had a close relationship with the Japanese authorities and was well-known to all the Orion shareholders. On the other hand, although well-established overseas, it had a mere 29 domestic branches and its relationships with major Japanese corporations was restricted to foreign exchange and letter of credit business.[43]

Chase's preferred candidate was Mitsubishi Bank (Mitsubishi), with which it already had several joint ventures in Japan.[44] In support of Mitsubishi's candidature, it was pointed out that it was the second largest Japanese bank and 16th in the world with assets of $9.27 billion. It had 181 domestic branches and a presence in the banking markets of Australia, Hong Kong, Korea and Singapore.[45] There were strong connections with Japanese multinational corporations and a host of other large Japanese companies. Mitsubishi furnished a full range of corporate banking services and could provide abundant short-term and medium-term yen resources for Orion and the Orion shareholders.

Mitsubishi was adopted as Orion's 'primary candidate' with the Bank of Tokyo next in line.[46] Discussions with Mitsubishi proceeded along the 'slow and circuitous route followed in Japanese negotiations' during the summer and winter of 1971.[47] A delaying factor was Mitsubishi's shareholding in Japan International Bank, the Ministry of Finance taking the view that its participation in Orion so soon after the formation of the all-Japanese consortium would cause a 'loss of face' for its consortium protégé.[48] But Mitsubishi assured Orion that eventually consent would be forthcoming.

At last in December 1971, a delegation from Mitsubishi visited the Ministry of Finance to request official sanction to join Orion. Much to their surprise, they were told that this was impossible because the Bank of Tokyo had already registered its candidature.[49] The Orion partners were even more surprised and NatWest undertook the task of explaining to its 'friends' at the Bank of Tokyo that 'other Japanese banks seemed to fit in more closely with Orion's objectives.'[50] The Ministry's assent was finally forthcoming, the first time a major Japanese bank was allowed to join an international consortium.[51] Mitsubishi's admission to the Orion partnership was announced in April 1972, thereby 'closing the books.'[52]

In fact, Mitsubishi Bank was unable to deliver in full measure the benefits anticipated by the other shareholders. An arrangement had already been made that Morgan Stanley would manage the London Eurobond issues of the Mitsubishi Group of companies, but this was not revealed at the time.[53]

QUEST FOR A FRENCH PARTNER

The recruitment of a French partner was one of the points in the founding agreement of 29 April 1970, and it received 'extensive consideration.'[54] Lazard Frères, the Suez Group and Crédit Lyonnais, in that order, were identified as the most promising partners by the study group led by Chase's man in Paris, Alvaro Holguin, who later joined Orion.[55] Exploratory conversations were held with Lazard Frères and the Suez Group, but they came to nothing. While these talks were going on, Crédit Lyonnais, then the second largest French bank, approached NatWest in July 1970 about joining a 'Common Market partnership' it was putting together with Commerzbank, which became the Europartners banking group.[56] This was incompatible with membership of Orion, ruling out both NatWest's participation and Crédit Lyonnais as a French candidate for Orion, but Harold Hitchcock, head of NatWest's International Banking Division, visited Paris to find out what they were up to. 'The talks centred around the need to provide medium-term money internationally and ways and means to provide local finance where customers were operating in other countries which was difficult to raise through branch representation etc.,' he reported to colleagues. 'It was all pretty familiar ground and, of course, they had not delved as deeply into the problems and prospects as have our teams.'[57]

Société Générale, the third biggest French bank, emerged as the 'number one choice' of a new working party that reported in February 1971.[58] David Rockefeller and John Haley were impatient to make an approach and pressed the other partners to agree.[59] Chase's 'arm-twisting' caused irritation at NatWest, where the senior executives were 'not convinced either that we need a French resources base or that, if we did, Société Générale would be our first choice.'[60] Nevertheless, a meeting was held with Société Générale in April 1971, but the French bankers proved to be 'unsettlingly neutral and non-committal.'[61] In fact, Société Générale too had other plans and had already begun talks about joining the EBIC group.[62]

Two more French banks, Crédit Industriel et Commercial and Banque Populaire were also unsuccessfully sounded out. Then Ludwig Poullain, WestLB's chairman, raised the matter with his opposite number at Banque Nationale de Paris, the largest French bank.[63] This was a decidedly last-ditch attempt to secure a French partner, since BNP was already committed to banking club ABECOR[64] and it was no surprise that the answer was: '*non*'. Later, after Credito and Mitsubishi had joined, an approach was received from the Suez Group, which had changed its mind about an association with Orion.[65] An 'exploratory dialogue' was held in January 1973, and it was concluded that Suez would make a very suitable participant in the proposed Orion Europe consortium.[66] But Orion Europe never happened, and because of the many 'roadblocks' Orion never had a French shareholder.[67]

THE TWIN-BANK CONCEPT

Most consortium banks confined their activities to medium-term lending, but Orion became a fully-fledged international investment bank, undertaking a full range of merchant banking activities – managing and underwriting bond issues, securities trading and, later, corporate advisory work and fund management – as well as lending and arranging syndicated credits. This broad concept of Orion's activities was present from the outset and was the reason why Orion (like European Banking Company) declined to join the Association of Consortium Banks when it was formed in 1975.

Having identified what the new 'Multi-International Bank' was to do, consideration turned to how to accomplish it. Chase executives argued 'strongly', and successfully, for the formation of two separate operating entities, independently capitalized and with different managements and directors, one to conduct medium-term lending and commercial banking business, the other to undertake merchant banking activities.[68] Uppermost in their minds was the threat of a divestment order from the Federal Reserve for infringing the Glass–Steagall legislation. By separating the medium-term lending function and the merchant banking activities into different entities, Chase would be able to come out of the merchant banking entity without affecting their position in the other should the Fed rule against it in the future.

Other considerations counted too. Separate entities might enable varying patterns of shareholdings, reflecting the interests of the different partners. As regards management, while the medium-term bank could be readily staffed by commercial bankers seconded from the shareholders, the merchant bank required the recruitment of new staff with the necessary skills. Also, the founders were 'acutely aware' of the differing styles of commercial and merchant banking business and the advantages of keeping them separate.[69]

But the twin-bank strategy also had drawbacks. It would be inefficient in its use of capital, especially in the early years. It was argued that whereas medium-term lending could be initiated rapidly and remuneratively, thanks to the in-house expertise of the shareholders and the nature of lending business, the development of the investment banking activities would take longer to get up and running and to turn a profit. Thus the merchant bank would have idle capital, while the medium-term bank would rapidly reach its capital capacity. Moreover, as separate organizations there was every likelihood that they would overlap in their market dealings, their forward exchange commitments and their country risk limits, not to mention the confusion in the market when confronted with two Orion banks.

Nonetheless, the twin-bank strategy was adopted and two operating companies were established. Orion Termbank Limited was formed to undertake large multi-currency medium-term lendings in the three-to-ten-year range. Orion Bank Limited was set up to perform merchant banking functions. A briefing paper explained that:

> *Orion aims to provide a comprehensive banking and financial service for its customers on the basis of complete 'packages' where required on a 'one-stop' basis. It combines Termbank's medium-term lending with Orion Bank's international issue activity. The resources of Orion's shareholders and their affiliates, in the aggregate probably surpass those of any other banking group, and Orion's clients have access through this network to a great diversity of banking and related services in more than 100 countries. Further, the Orion Group through its shareholders can meet requirements in virtually every important trading currency.*[70]

The development of 'an international merchant bank capacity to meet the requirements of big international corporations' was identified as a priority.[71] The 'most straightforward' way of achieving this was to purchase an existing merchant bank, which was what the working party recommended.[72] Chase was particularly impatient to buy into an existing firm, 'to get the capability as soon as possible.'[73] At the chairmen's summit meeting in April 1970, Rockefeller told his counterparts that 'as Chase were feeling the effects of competition through not having a merchant banking connection they would wish to pursue this matter independently if the other parties did not want to go on.'[74] McLaughlin and Robarts decided to go along with Chase.

A working party report identified four potential candidates among London's merchant banks, Baring Brothers, Robert Fleming, Lazard Brothers and Singer and Friedlander.[75] Lazards, comprising a unique combination of independent but entwined firms in London, New York and Paris, was the most international and the preferred choice. David Rockefeller approached André Meyer, head of the New York firm, who responded positively and undertook to discuss matters with Lord Poole, head of the London house.[76] Rockefeller's optimism was not shared by NatWest chairman David Robarts, who remarked that Lazard Brothers would be 'a difficult fish to catch.'[77]

Lord Poole was 'somewhat surprised' at the suggestion of an affiliation with the proposed 'Multi-International Bank Project' and sought clarification. Robarts explained to him that the object was to construct 'a large international banking organisation which would be able to serve the needs of the big multinational companies in any of the money centres of the world.'[78] Poole was attracted by the possibilities and the discussions resulted in an agreement in principle to an association between the parties.[79] But the Pearson Group, Lazard Brothers' principal owner, refused to reduce its interest and the minority shareholding available proved too small to be of interest to the Orion partners. With the end of the negotiations with Lazard Brothers in summer 1970, it was decided to build Orion's merchant banking capacity '*de novo*'.

ORION MULTINATIONAL SERVICES

A third Orion company, Orion Multinational Services (OMS), was established to provide co-ordination between the two Orion operating companies and the shareholders. There were three dimensions to its functions – group relations, planning and development, and marketing. The group relations function was to ensure communication and co-operation between executives of the shareholding banks and Orion. The planning and development role was intended to ensure that the corporate plans of the Orion operating entities conformed to the shareholders' objectives.

The marketing function was to promote Orion's services to the shareholders' multinational clients. John Haley, managing director of OMS on secondment from Chase, provided a hypothetical example to illustrate the potential synergies:

> *For example, if the general manager of one of the European branches of a shareholding bank is calling on the financial director of an important European multinational company, he can request that an Orion man join with him in making the call. Should it develop during the call that several key requirements of that company involve an international bond issue, a medium-term loan and a solution to problems involving a government contract in Indonesia and Canadian dollar financing for expansion in Canada, hence the Orion man could then act as the catalyst to bring Orion Bank and Orion Termbank into the picture with the Chase Manhattan's Jakarta branch and a corporate finance officer from the Royal Bank of Canada.*[80]

The OMS board comprised a chairman and six 'senior representatives' appointed by the shareholders, plus the top executives from the two operating companies. The senior representatives were also directors of Orion Termbank and Orion Bank. Their role was both to monitor what was happening at Orion on behalf of the shareholders and to help Orion's executives develop business. 'They act as a filter,' Haley explained, 'and they help us through the labyrinth of those huge banking institutions in getting advice and assistance.'[81] 'I wear two hats,' commented Mitsubishi's senior representative Katsuhisa Fujita. A further six junior executives, with the title 'area executive', were also seconded to OMS by the shareholders.

Shareholder involvement in Orion's development took two further forms, the 'Chairmen's Meeting' and the 'Shareholders' Forum'. The former was an annual event held during the World Bank/IMF meetings each autumn, the six chairmen convening for a general discussion of Orion's progress and activities. It was an occasion for an exchange of views, not a decision-making session.[82] Policy-making and the review of performance were undertaken by the Shareholders' Forum, which took place three times per year, usually followed by board meetings of the operating companies where the decisions of the Shareholders' Forum were adopted as board policies and directives for management. Those attending the Shareholders' Forum comprised six high-ranking executives from the shareholders, the six senior representatives and the chairman of OMS. The chief executives of Orion Termbank and Orion Bank were present in an *ex-officio* capacity. A 'supra board' for the operating companies was how the chairman of OMS described the function of the Shareholders' Forum.[83]

The Shareholders' Forum was also an occasion for lavish hospitality, each shareholder striving to surpass the others. There were outings and dinners, the social side of things being believed to be valuable for improving communications both between Orion and its shareholders and among the shareholders as well. Indeed, the 'club' dimension of Orion was more highly prized by the shareholders than many Orion executives realized.

WHAT'S IN A NAME?

The formation of the biggest and boldest of the consortium banks was announced on 29 October 1970.[84] At last the 'Multi-International Bank Project' had a proper name – Orion. Apparently, it was the brainchild of Royal Bank executive Robert Utting who had been a navigator in bombers during the war and had used the stellar constellation of the same name as a fixed position from which to navigate a route.[85]

'What is Orion?,' asked a public relations pamphlet trumpeting the tyro financial institution to the world. 'A famous hunter in Greek mythology, a constellation of stars visible in both hemispheres and, now, the name of a new international co-operation between banks.'[86]

And then, after all the planning and negotiating and company forming and recruiting, it was time to get down to the business of making some money.

CHAPTER 4

Orion gets going

Orion opened for business in December 1970. In the three years that had passed since the initial discussions between David Rockefeller and Earle McLaughlin, the post-war international financial system had become more fragile and was about to become much more volatile. The Euromarkets had grown and were continuing to grow rapidly – in 1969 and 1970 the size of the Eurocurrency market increased by about 50 per cent each year – but the increasing instability brought hazards as well as opportunities.

The late 1960s saw growing unease about the value of the US dollar. At the root were the US balance of payments deficit and, from 1965, a growing budget deficit, the outcome of President Johnson's commitment to both the Vietnam War abroad and the Great Society social program at home. The devaluation of sterling, the world's second reserve currency, in November 1967, after a three-year struggle, was one manifestation of the strains in the Bretton Woods system. 'It puts the dollar in the front line,' remarked Henry Fowler, Secretary of the US Treasury.[1] Revaluation on the part of the surplus countries, especially Germany, Switzerland and Japan, might have saved the situation, but nothing was done until it was too late.

In August 1971, President Nixon suspended the gold convertibility of the dollar in a bid to force the rest of the world to revalue, the dollar and the other major currencies floating against each other. The Smithsonian Agreement of December 1971 established a new system of fixed exchange rates that amounted to an average 8 per cent devaluation of the dollar. But these developments failed to solve basic problems and created new ones. 'The two years after the Smithsonian Agreement were the most economically turbulent of the post-war period up to that point,' observed Federal Reserve Board chairman Paul Volcker.[2] At the time of the Smithsonian Agreement, Orion was marking its first birthday, though some may have been wondering how many more happy returns there would be.

The crisis in the international financial system prompted governments around the world to stimulate their economies to counter the shock to confidence. The combined outcome was the most concentrated boom in output and trade that the world had ever experienced. Market demand compounded by substantial hedging out of currencies into commodities, sent raw material prices soaring. The increase in US inflation led to a new run on the dollar and a further 10 per cent devaluation in February 1973. The floating of all the major currencies in early 1973 marked the end of the Bretton Woods international financial system. The whole sorry story culminated with the Yom Kippur War of October 1973, which provided the occasion for a doubling in the price of oil – bringing it back in real terms to its price in the early 1950s – and then a further doubling in December 1973.

THE EUROMARKETS, 1970–73

Eurocurrency deposits grew almost three-fold over the years 1970–73, from $65 billion to $175 billion. There was speculation that the relaxation in 1970 of Regulation Q constraints on terms for depositors in the USA would diminish the Eurocurrency market's attractions, but in fact the impact was marginal. The rate of increase was fastest in 1973, fuelled by the international boom. Raw materials producers, benefiting from rising commodity prices, often denominated in dollars, increased their Eurocurrency deposits rather than send them to New York.

The counterparts to the increased earnings of primary producers were the higher prices paid by consumers, especially in the developed countries. The IMF's world index of wholesale prices increased slightly between 1971 and 1972, rising from a growth rate of 3.1 per cent to 4.1 per cent. But it leapt in 1973, up three-fold to 12.9 per cent. In many industrial countries, the level was substantially above the average, for instance, Canada 21 per cent, Italy 17 per cent and Japan 16 per cent. Increased inflation led to higher short-term interest rates, which had an impact on the behaviour of investors and borrowers in the Euromarkets. Higher short-term Eurocurrency rates caused investors to shift from longer-term assets to shorter-term assets. This made it difficult for borrowers to raise long-term funds by international bond issues and forced them to borrow more heavily in the Eurocredit market. When short-term rates fell they could re-finance in the bond market.

Rising interest rates and increased Eurocurrency deposits led to greater volumes of syndicated lending in the early 1970s. Between 1971 and 1972, the annual volume of syndicated lending grew from $4 billion to $6.8 billion; in 1973, it soared to $21.9 billion. As Eurocredits soared, the Eurobond market dived. Between 1972 and 1973, the volume of new issues fell from $5.3 billion to $3.5 billion. Bond prices fell too, inflicting losses on bond holders and bond traders, including some of the consortium banks.

ORION OPENS FOR BUSINESS

The three Orion companies held inaugural board meetings on 14 December
1970. Since Orion's own offices on the 7th and 8th floors of the new
Commercial Union building in the City were still being fitted out, the direc-
tors convened at NatWest's London headquarters opposite the Bank of
England.[3] The agendas were largely taken up with legal formalities and
senior appointments: John Haley, from Chase, became chairman of Orion
Termbank, as well as managing director of Orion Multinational Services
(OMS); Alex Dibbs, NatWest's deputy chief executive, became chairman of
OMS and a director of Orion Termbank. The chairmanship of Orion Bank
was left vacant, pending the recruitment of a chief executive.

Haley, a key figure in Orion's opening years, was close to Rockefeller and
shared his internationalist outlook. At the time of his appointment to Orion
he was head of Chase's activities in Central and Eastern Europe. Asked by
the *Wall Street Journal* to outline his strategy for Orion, he said: 'we must be
independent, we must have our own style, but we must work in concert
[with the shareholders].'[4]

Alex Dibbs joined the Westminster Bank when he was aged 16 and
worked his way up through the ranks. He was made joint general manager
in 1966 and chief executive of NatWest in 1972. He had responsibility for
Orion throughout the years of NatWest's involvement. 'A big out-door type,'
wrote a journalist. 'He is blunt and competitive, but ... he talks a lot about
being part of a team.'[5]

The boards of OMS and Orion Termbank had overlapping sets of directors drawn from the shareholders, a mixture of middle-ranking executives on
secondment and senior figures as non-executives. Geoff Styles on secondment from Royal Bank and Dickie Knight from NatWest were made joint
general managers of OMS, the latter with responsibility for planning and
projects.[6] Denis Greensmith from NatWest became managing director of
Orion Termbank, overseeing the start of business until retirement in May
1971. He was succeeded by Neil McFadyen from Royal Bank, who ran this
side of the business until autumn 1979.[7]

ORION TERMBANK

Orion Termbank's operational strategy and practices were outlined at the
first board meeting on 15 February 1971. Its purpose was defined as the provision of medium-term loans for leading multinational corporations and
'credit-worthy governmental borrowers.'[8] Initially, approaches to clients
would be through OMS, Orion's services being marketed to the shareholders'
corporate customers as an additional facility. It was anticipated that, in time,
Orion Termbank would develop its own relationships, independent of the

shareholders. To get the Orion name known in the market and take advantage of attractive lending opportunities, participations would be taken in syndicated loans arranged by non-shareholder banks, but this was expected to diminish as Orion's own operations expanded.[9]

A set of lending practices was established: medium-term lending was defined as five to seven years, with a maximum of ten years; short-term advances to clients were permitted to allow a flexible response to market conditions; the maximum ratio of loans to capital was set at 30 : 1; the minimum liquidity position was set at 10 per cent; and limits were adopted for unmatched trading positions.

Standby lines were negotiated with the shareholder banks in case of funding problems in the money markets. Chase and Royal Bank each earmarked $12.5 million, NatWest £5 million and WestLB DM40 million.[10] These standby lines were to be drawn upon only 'as an absolute last resort' if funds were unavailable from the market.[11] Drawings were to be outstanding for no more than fourteen days, and were to be repaid immediately funding became possible in the money market. In the event, the standby lines were not called upon in Orion Termbank's early years.

LENDING

The bulk of Orion's lending went onto Orion Termbank's balance sheet, but Orion Bank also made loans. Executives from both sides of the business worked together on the arrangement of syndicated loans. The data in Table 4.1 refer to the Orion companies aggregate financings. A significant proportion of the syndicated loans arranged by Orion was taken on to the balance sheets of its shareholder banks. Orion made its debut as a manager of syndicated loans in 1971, co-managing loans totalling $360 million. The largest was an 8-year $110 million floating rate loan for the Kingdom of Denmark, while $50 million each was raised for British Rail Engineering Limited, European Investment Bank and Massey–Ferguson Credit Corporation.

Table 4.1   Orion, syndicated loans lead and co-managed, 1971–73[12] ($ million)

	1971	1972	1973
Orion Termbank	360	477	1 243
Market	4 000	6 800	21 900
Orion market share (per cent)	9.0	7.0	5.7

In 1972, Orion co-managed loans that raised $477 million for borrowers, including $150 million for the Italian merchant bank Mediobanca, in which Credito was a shareholder, $90 million for ISCOR (South African Iron

& Steel Industrial Corporation) and $70 million for the Bank of Greece. In 1973 the business really took off, the total volume of business almost trebling to $1.2 billion; in that year Orion was ranked second by *Euromoney* among all syndicated loan managers, a remarkable achievement. The bulk of these funds was raised for European and US corporations and banks. Much the largest was the $500 million 10-year floating rate loan arranged for Mediobanca. For the day, this was an enormous sum, though credits of such size soon became commonplace with the onset of petrodollar recycling. Another Italian client was Istituto Mobiliare Italiano, for which Orion raised $150 million.

Even before the onset of petrodollar recycling, developing countries had voracious appetites for foreign capital. In 1973, Orion co-managed several syndicated loans for LDC clients. It syndicated a floating rate loan of $140 million for the Brazilian power company, Companhia Energética de São Paulo. The term was 14 years, in breach of the maximum ten-year lending term adopted at Orion Termbank's inaugural board meeting two years earlier and an example of the extension of payback terms that occurred in the mid-1970s. Another client was the Republic of Nicaragua, for which it raised $40 million. A mixed floating and fixed rate financing was arranged for the Banque Extérieure d'Algérie, a prime institution of an energy-producing state. This comprised a $150 million 15-year floating-rate note plus a $20 million fixed-rate loan. Mitsubishi played a key role in the Algerian issue by arranging a private placement for the entire fixed-interest portion 'which made the whole deal possible.'[13] All the shareholders contributed to the essential rollover credit, an example of the Orion concept at work that Haley 'warmly acknowledged.'[14] Hardly surprisingly, since the deal generated fees of £100 000. It also marked the beginning of Orion's business with the oil-producing countries, which was soon to become an important part of the story.

Orion Termbank's own lending grew at a smart pace, rising from almost nothing at the end of 1970 to £175 million in 1973. Staff increased as the business grew, rising from three at the end of 1970 to 34 in December 1973 (see Table 4.2).

Table 4.2 Orion Termbank, loans and staff numbers, 1971–73[15] (at 31 December)

	1971	1972	1973
Loans (£ million)	60	116	175
Staff	23	30	34

By the beginning of 1972, Orion Termbank had become the fifth largest lender amongst the consortium banks, according to a report to the board.[16] That year, interest on loans contributed two-fifths of Orion Termbank's total revenues, while money market operations, syndication fees and interest on capital generated about a fifth each (see Table 4.3).

Table 4.3   Orion Termbank, sources of revenue, 1972[17]

	£'000s	per cent
Interest on loans	916	43
Money market operations	447	21
Syndication fees	366	17
Interest on capital	351	17
Other	31	2
Total	2111	100

MONEY MARKET OPERATIONS

One of Orion's consistent strengths was its money market operations, accounting for between a fifth and a third of profits. Since, like other consortium banks, it had no retail deposit base, funding in the wholesale money market, obtaining the required funds for the needed term at the right price, was an essential complement to lending activity. To ensure reciprocity, part of Orion's assets was placed in the inter-bank market. In fact, far from paying a premium for funds, Orion attracted most of its deposits from the inter-bank market and elsewhere at prices better than LIBOR. Moreover, the money market team's successful proprietary trading in the forward foreign exchange market made a lot of money for Orion.[18]

Orion's money market operations were run by A.J. 'Spike' Wright and Alan Broughton, the chief dealer, both from NatWest, and Martin Klingsick, who joined as a junior in August 1971. Wright was a very experienced money market operator and highly regarded in the London and international markets; he was chairman of the Forex Association in London from 1967 to 1972.[19] The money markets team provided Orion with an 'absolutely rock solid funding operation which really set it apart from the other consortium banks.'[20]

ORION TERMBANK, PERFORMANCE, 1971–73

Orion Termbank began with paid-up capital of £5 million. By the end of 1973, Orion Termbank's paid-up capital was £9.4 million, the increase being due to the admission of Credito and Mitsubishi, and a further cash injection by shareholders in December 1973. The new capital was necessary because short-term lending opportunities had pushed Orion Termbank's ratio of loans to capital and reserves to a heady 47.4, considerably higher than the market norm or Orion's adopted limit. Aware that the Bank of England was monitoring the ratios of the consortium banks 'extremely closely', the directors instigated the call.[21]

Over the years 1971–73, Orion Termbank's pre-tax profits more than doubled from £822 000 to £2 million. Capital and reserves, with no dividends being paid, increased from £5.9 million to £11.8 million, a slower rate than profits. Thus Orion Termbank's pre-tax return on capital rose year by year, reaching a very respectable 17.3 per cent in 1973 (see Table 4.4).

Table 4.4   Orion Termbank, performance, 1971–73[22]
(£'000)

	1971	1972	1973
Profit (pre-tax)	822	1 174	2 043
Capital and reserves	5 850	7 598	11 781
Return (pre-tax) (per cent)	8.1	15.5	17.3

ORION BANK

While Orion Termbank could be staffed by executives from the shareholders, it was necessary to recruit an outsider with appropriate investment banking experience to run Orion Bank. A professional executive search firm was appointed in autumn 1970 to find a chief executive, someone who could 'get the merchant bank going and bring in outstanding individuals ... letting it create its own reputation.'[23] The search proved problematic. After three months' work, the head-hunter reported that all the 'name' merchant bankers he had approached had declined the job, some of them expressing reluctance to work for a set of commercial bank shareholders because they were doubtful that they would be allowed adequate freedom of action.

One of the figures approached was Ian Fraser, a former director of Warburgs and later chairman of Lazards, who at the time was director general of the Takeover Panel. One day, Fraser received a visit from a friend, Geoffrey Crowther, a former editor of *The Economist* and an influential City figure, accompanied by Sir John Prideaux, the chairman of NatWest. They enthusiastically announced that NatWest was joining up with other major international banks to form 'a huge new banking company in London to be called Orion which would by reason of its sheer financial power take over the world leadership of the Eurobond market from Warburgs.'[24] They offered him the job of chairman and chief executive, inviting him to name his terms. But Fraser had other plans, and turned them down. Younger candidates also declined the offer, expressing concern about job security. So the search went on.

The news that Ronald Grierson, a former colleague of Fraser at Warburgs, had expressed interest caused a flurry of excitement.[25] Grierson, aged 49, was a high-profile figure, with a wide range of top-level contacts all over the world. Of German origin, he was educated in Paris, London and at Balliol College, Oxford, but his undergraduate studies were interrupted by being interned as an 'enemy alien' upon the outbreak of war. After a distinguished war record and brief stints in financial journalism and at the UN, he joined Warburgs in 1948. He was, wrote Warburgs colleague Peter Stormonth Darling, Siegmund Warburg's 'confidant and jester and a consummate net-worker ... If there were *Guinness Book of Records* prizes for long distance travel, long distance telephoning or the number of people known personally, he would hold all three.'[26] 'One of the most extraordinary people that I have met,' declared Ian Fraser.[27]

At one point, Grierson was expected to be Siegmund Warburg's successor as head of the firm, but a series of outside appointments took him along a different career path. In 1964, at the invitation of Henry Kissinger, he became a visiting Fellow at Harvard University. In 1966, he accepted a request from George Brown, First Secretary of the UK's Department of Economic Affairs, to become managing director of the controversial Industrial Reorganisation Corporation, the Labour government's attempt at a public sector merchant bank that was supposed to rationalize and revital-ize British industry. He resigned the following year, after a series of disagree-ments with meddling ministers. He went back to Warburgs, also becoming vice-chairman of the General Electric Company but soon he was restless – not for nothing did he entitle his autobiography *A Truant Disposition*.[28] The invitation to build Orion Bank into a major international investment bank was the sort of major challenge he was looking for.

EXECUTIVE TEAM AND NON-EXECUTIVE DIRECTORS

Grierson took up executive responsibilities at the beginning of April 1971. His priority was to put together a management team, something at which he was 'particularly good.'[29] This was a 'highly delicate and confidential' under-taking, since all the candidates for senior positions already had important and responsible jobs.[30] Instead of appointing a City head-hunter or placing job advertisements in newspapers, he used his extensive range of personal con-tacts and introductions from friends and colleagues. He made three appoint-ments at the executive director level, Michael Bonsor, Ian Logie and William de Gelsey. Each was an established figure in his own field. Bonsor was a part-ner in City stockbroker Rowe & Pitman.[31] He was well-known in the mar-kets and had useful connections in Scandinavia. Logie was a director of Esso Petroleum with expertise in the important oil industry. A prominent figure in Orion's early days, he left in November 1972 to join Williams & Glyn's.[32]

William de Gelsey joined Orion in October 1971.[33] Of Hungarian birth, he followed in his father's footsteps at Trinity College, Cambridge, and worked at ICI for ten years before becoming a merchant banker; his combined expertise, as a chemist and as a banker, helped him and his brother build up a successful screen printing colour business. He began his City career at Samuel Montagu and then went to M. Samuel (forerunner of Hill Samuel), where he joined the main board. At Orion, he quickly became the driving force on the Eurobond side of the business, both in terms of securing mandates from issuers and in developing Orion's placing power.[34]

At the junior executive level, Grierson recruited a group of men in their early or mid-twenties as 'general assistants', a job-title that accurately reflected the expectation that they should turn their hands to whatever was required. 'It is my plan not to departmentalise the bank for the first year or two,' Grierson explained in his first report to the shareholders, 'but to build up an all-round team capable of tackling all tasks.'[35]

Top of the form among the junior executives were Michael Perry, Andrew Large and John Bunting, who were made Orion's first 'assistant directors' when this honorific title was introduced at the bank in February 1973.[36] Perry, who joined through an introduction to de Gelsey from a former colleague at Hill Samuel, was a solicitor from Linklaters & Paines. He became head of the Execution Department, which undertook the legal work on the deals brought home by de Gelsey and the marketing team. In the early days, he worked closely with Bill Tudor John, a lawyer who was 'on loan' to Orion from Allen & Overy from June 1971 to July 1972. Tudor John became a partner at Allen & Overy, and later senior partner.

Andrew Large and John Bunting both began their careers in the oil industry. Large, a graduate of Cambridge with an MBA from INSEAD, was working for BP when he met Grierson. He was astonished to be offered a job in Grierson's new bank: 'I had no training in banking, or even knowledge,' he recalled. 'I remember going to Lazards to find out what bonds are from a friend of Lord Poole.'[37] But Large was inspired by Grierson's confidence and enthusiasm and decided to give banking a try. He caught on quickly and became a key figure in marketing Orion's services, de Gelsey's 'right hand man in running after issuers and investors all over the world.'[38] Bunting, who later became Orion's chief financial officer, was recruited from Esso.

Theo Max van der Beugel was recruited by Grierson upon graduation from Leyden University. His father was a distinguished Dutch businessman and politician who Grierson had got to know through Warburgs. Van der Beugel played a crucial role in developing Orion Bank's syndication expertise. Anthony Marshall, who had been working in Switzerland, joined thanks to an introduction to Grierson by Large. An accountant by training, Marshall developed a streamlined accounts and back office function and became Orion's company secretary. Joe Cook, Orion's future capital markets' star, was another early recruit, joining as a junior in the Accounts Department.

Graham Wilkinson and Rod Chamberlain became the 'bag carriers' for the marketing efforts led by de Gelsey and Large. Wilkinson joined Orion Bank after Oxford and a brief dalliance with the travel industry, thanks to a personal introduction to Grierson.[39] Chamberlain had a degree in economics from Cambridge and an MBA from INSEAD. He worked at Hill Samuel and then at Beecham, where his boss was Ernest Saunders, later of Guinness fame. He came into Orion through an introduction by Large, whom he had met at INSEAD. He also knew de Gelsey from Hill Samuel and Wilkinson from prep school, 'so it really felt like home.'[40] 'We may have been scrabbling around a bit for business in those early days,' Chamberlain recalled, 'but my God it was fun.'

By autumn 1971 when Orion Bank got down to business, the team comprised four executive directors – Grierson, de Gelsey, Bonsor and Logie – and a supporting staff of about ten. In the course of 1972, the personnel grew to 60, twice the size of Orion Termbank. Expansion continued in 1973, though at a slower pace. By the end of that year Orion Bank's staff numbered 73, and the Orion group, including Termbank and a couple of fledgling subsidiaries, about 130.

'By far our greatest assets are our human resources and the quality of our teamwork,' Grierson told the staff in an end-of-term message in December 1972. 'Through these we have earned ourselves a reputation for real professionalism and, believe me, nothing is more vital for success in our kind of banking. One clumsily handled transaction, one unprofessional letter could all too easily set us back many months; hence my sometimes pedantic insistence on perfect work.'[41]

Some of Grierson's Warburgs-imbued professional practices exasperated colleagues at the time, though they were respected with hindsight. Every meeting and every 'phone call had to be recorded in written form, so that there was a complete record of client relationships. And woe betide anyone who was late for 'morning prayers', the daily morning meeting of executives. Whatever the reason, he would have to report to Grierson like a schoolboy. Then there was the ban on papers at meetings with clients – Grierson insisted that Orion Bank executives conduct meetings from memory – which ensured a thorough, and impressive, command of the subject. But when a client asked a junior to pass him the report in his briefcase, what was he to do?[42]

Grierson took most things in his stride, but the UK government Incomes Policy ban on salary increases of more than £250 per annum in February 1973 had him baffled. 'In a new organisation like us,' he told the directors, 'salary differentials start off somewhat arbitrarily, and it had been our intention to iron out the unwarranted differences during 1973. We are in rather a disagreeable situation, and I do not quite know how to handle it.'[43]

The Orion Bank board was made up of the executive directors, plus share-holder representatives. There were also two outside non-executive directors, John Loudon and Dr Franco Bobba.[44] Loudon, a Dutchman, was chairman of the Royal Dutch Petroleum Company. A friend of David Rockefeller, he acted informally as Chase's representative.[45] Bobba was general manager of Istituto Finanziario Industriale (IFI), Turin, the holding company that controlled Fiat. A friend of Grierson, his appointment established a 'useful' contact with Italy.[46]

GRIERSON'S 'FIRST THOUGHTS'

Soon after his appointment, Grierson circulated a confidential note among the Orion Bank directors outlining his 'first thoughts' and 'general guide-lines.'[47] 'We must try to convey a 'muscular' impression of ourselves,' he wrote, meaning that, with powerful parents, Orion Bank should adopt 'a principal's rather than an agent's approach, undertake a small number of large, significant deals instead of dabbling in everything.' All business handled by the bank should be 'utterly sound and conservative.' On no account should the bank get itself into the position where funds were immobilized in lock-up equity positions. Finally, delay, though frustrating, was preferable than yielding to the temptation to take on business that compromised the highest standards just to be seen to be active.

Grierson was particularly concerned about perceptions of Orion Bank in the market and on the part of potential clients:

> *In creative banking an aura of mystery can be a positive advantage and it will pay us to keep people somewhat guessing as to what we are likely to do next.*
>
> *We must develop originality of style; indeed we cannot afford to be 'filed away' under any existing classification, either with the conventional mer-chant banks or with the newly emergent medium-term consortia. Many of the institutions now at the height of fashion may by 1980 be as extinct as dinosaurs, and it will stand us in good stead to be seen as early innovators.*
>
> *Names are merely names, but there is one quite important reason why it would not suit us to become known as 'just another merchant bank'. There is among the London merchant banks a tacit agreement (not always observed) to refrain from poaching each others' clients, and since Orion clearly has no intention of being bound by any such understanding – indeed it would make nonsense of the whole Orion concept – the more we remain aloof from the common nomenclature the better.*[48]

EUROBONDS

The conduct of Eurobond new issues was Orion Bank's *raison d'être*. In the years 1971–73, Orion lead or co-managed Eurobond issues totalling

$690 million, the market share of the issues in which it played a manage-
ment role rising from 4.8 per cent to 7 per cent (see Table 4.5).

Table 4.5 Orion Bank, Eurobonds lead and co-managed,
1971–73[49] ($ million)

	1971	1972	1973
Orion Bank	158	274	258
Market	3289	5508	3709
Orion market share (per cent)	4.8	5.0	7.0

Establishing a presence as a Eurobond manager from scratch and with no
client base was a formidable challenge and assistance from the shareholders
was vital. Three of them, Royal Bank, WestLB and NatWest, were particularly helpful. Six of the ten issues that Orion Bank co-managed in 1971–72
were for Canadian clients, both corporate and public sector, arising from
introductions by Royal Bank. It was an introduction by Royal Bank that led
to Orion Bank's very first co-management position, a DM100 million issue
for the Quebec Hydro-Electric Commission in August 1971. Nine of the
issues were Deutschemark denominated, the German currency being
favoured by investors because of worries about the weakness of the US dollar. As Deutschemark issues, they had to be lead managed by a German
bank, which provided WestLB with opportunities to invite Orion Bank into
the management groups of its issues. There was also a French franc
Eurobond issue, equivalent to $20 million, for Ready Mixed Concrete's
French subsidiary, an introduction effected by NatWest.[50] As a French franc
issue, the lead manager had to be a French bank and Orion brought in
Crédit Commercial de France.[51]

The Eurobond primary market slumped in 1973 and Orion's activity fell
too, though not as sharply as the market as a whole. That year Orion Bank
was co-manager of eight issues. Four were Deutschemark issues, two for
North American energy entities and one for a Danish bank. The other was
a DM100 million issue on behalf of one of its own shareholders, NatWest,
that was lead managed by another, WestLB.[52]

The other four issues co-managed by Orion Bank in 1973 raised a total
of $90 million for Bristol, Coventry, Nottingham and Teesside. These were
part of a short-lived and controversial initiative by UK municipalities to tap
the Eurobond market at a time when UK credit was somewhat shaky, a total
of eight such issues being made in all. Though it was implicit, no formal UK
government guarantee was given on these bonds, which puzzled the market
and increased the cost. These issues petered out after Western American
Bank's ill-fated issue for Glasgow.[53]

Reviewing progress in July 1972, not quite a year after entering the
Eurobond business, Grierson presented an up-beat report to the board,

informing the directors that Orion Bank was already being invited to be an underwriter in almost 90 per cent of all Eurobond issues.[54] Nevertheless, some of the shareholder representatives were dissatisfied with Orion Bank's results. Chase executive Leo Martinuzzi criticized 'the prevalent view in Orion Bank that widespread travelling and calling were desirable in order to stimulate opportunities. Such policies wasted resources and dispersed effort over non-priorities.'[55] He expressed 'disappointment with the performance of what he regarded as the *main* part of Orion – Orion Bank. He recognised that Orion Bank had built up a good and talented team, but there seemed to be no real co-ordination, no market plan, and everyone dashing around in different directions ... Termbank was performing well ... it was Orion Bank and Orion Multinational Services, the "think-tank", which he felt to be the major parts and which were only giving minor performances.'[56] What Orion Bank needed to stifle such criticism and move forward was to lead manage a major Eurobond issue, but securing the right mandate was no easy matter. And then came the break Orion Bank's executives had been looking for.

AUSTRALIAN BREAKTHROUGH

The client was the Rural & Industries Bank of Western Australia, the funds being required to build a huge grain terminal at Kwinanna, south of Perth. The introduction was provided by NatWest's representative in the region and dynamically followed up by Chase's senior representative at Orion, Jeff Cunningham, who immediately jumped on a plane to Perth. The client wanted the funds fast and Orion secured the mandate by agreeing to meet this requirement.[57] To avoid having to join the Bundesbank's Deutschemark new issues queue, which would have delayed matters, Orion dreamt up a novel cocktail – an Australian dollar/Deutschemark dual-currency issue. Interest and repayment would be paid in whichever was the stronger currency. Thus the borrower received funds in Australian dollars, but investors regarded the bonds as Deutschemark securities, which were much in favour at the time because of fears of further devaluation of the US dollar.

As a Deutschemark issue, WestLB played a vital role. 'Without WestLB as a consultant and an underwriter in its own right, we couldn't have worked out the issue,' commented John Haley shortly afterwards.[58] However, as an Australian dollar/Deutschemark dual-currency issue, it had the incidental advantage for Orion that it could act as lead manager, which was not open to it for a pure Deutschemark issue. In London the execution team went without sleep for 36 hours to get the paperwork ready.[59] The A$30 million (equivalent to US$36 million) issue was successfully brought out in July 1972.

The Rural & Industries Bank issue was the first external borrowing under the guarantee of an Australian state, as opposed to the federal government, for 'many many years.'[60] It marked the introduction of the Australian dollar into the 'Eurobond scene',[61] establishing a connection between Orion and Australian dollar issues that was to be further developed in later years. Grierson exuberantly reported to the Orion Bank board that:

> We could not have been more fortunate in the circumstances of our first management responsibility. The issuer is of good standing and the timing exceptionally favourable.
>
> For those of us who have been slightly concerned that our first appearance as manager might have to involve a compromise over the quality of the issuer, this is a happy outcome; it is also significant that we are dealing with a new borrower and have not had to deflect him from an existing relationship.
>
> Moreover, this transaction exemplifies intra-Orion collaboration at its best. The borrower was introduced by NatWest, a parallel Australian dollar borrowing (vital to the procurement of the business) was arranged in a matter of hours by Chase, and there was excellent collaboration at all stages with OMS and with those shareholders who were directly concerned.[62]

Eurobond new issues often required managers and underwriters to take up part of an issue and hold the bonds until it was possible to sell them without disturbing the secondary market. During 1972, Orion Bank temporarily took up in aggregate $18 million of the $35 million Eurobonds of which it was an underwriter.[63] In the wake of the Rural & Industries Bank issue, with the assumption of the responsibilities of a lead manager, the potential scale of Orion Bank's bond warehousing expanded and the board authorized an increase in the total primary market bond portfolio limit from $5 million to $10 million.[64]

EUROBOND INVESTORS

Orion Bank's standing and its effectiveness as a Eurobond issuer depended on its exertions to develop its securities 'placing power' – an investment bank's ability to place new issues with long-term investors who will not quickly off-load them on the market, thereby depressing the price. As a 'new kid on the block', Orion itself had no existing investor base. Moreover, its shareholders were not structured to provide Orion with access to investors, even if they were so inclined. So, appeals for shareholder assistance to find those elusive Eurobond investors were a regular refrain of Grierson's reports. At one point, he boldly suggested that the shareholders should instruct their associate and subsidiary companies to apply to Orion Bank for all their bond requirements in excess of the amounts allotted to them.[65] But almost two years later, he was still lamenting the lack of support from the shareholders in this particular regard.[66] Orion Bank's home-grown efforts to increase placing power initially focused on developing relations with the Swiss banks, a high proportion of many issues being 'absorbed' into Switzerland.[67] To this end, Orion Bank executives, William de Gelsey in particular, became frequent visitors to Switzerland. The establishment of a Swiss subsidiary was discussed, as was buying into privately owned Handelsbank, but nothing was done; eventually, Handelsbank became a NatWest subsidiary.[68]

In the UK, early in 1972, Orion Bank joined with Commercial Union Assurance, Hill Samuel and IFI, to purchase control of a quoted investment trust with assets of £8 million.[69] Orion Bank's investment was £1.4 million. The Trust was re-named St Helen's Securities, after the street near where Orion and Commercial Union had their headquarters – it was only at the last moment that somebody spotted the shortcoming of naming it St Helen's Investment Trust in an era of acronyms.[70] Orion Bank took over management of the trust, Grierson becoming chairman and Bonsor a director.[71] It was hoped that control of St Helen's Securities would provide a repository for Orion-managed issues, as well as generating annual management fees of £35 000.[72]

CORPORATE ADVISORY SERVICES

To balance the ups and downs of new issue activity, Orion Bank endeavoured to develop corporate advisory services, a common strategy among the UK merchant banks. Thanks to personal connections with the chairman, Lord Melchett, British Steel Corporation was one of the first companies to retain it as an adviser.[73] A few months later, in July 1972, Melchett joined the Orion Bank board as a non-executive director. A grandson of Sir Alfred Mond, founder of British chemical giant ICI, Julian Melchett chose a City career. He went to work at the merchant bank M. Samuel (forerunner of Hill Samuel), of which he was managing director in the mid-1960s. In 1967, Melchett was made chairman of the recently nationalized British Steel, a high-profile and politically controversial job. It was a considerable coup for his friends William de Gelsey, who had worked with him at Hill Samuel, and Ronald Grierson to persuade him to join the Orion Bank board, his only major outside directorship.[74] Melchett's contribution was cut short by his early death in June 1973, aged 49.

Another advisory client was the catering company J. Lyons Group, thanks to an introduction by NatWest.[75] In September 1972, Orion Bank managed an innovative convertible preference stock issue for J. Lyons that raised £4 million. A tranche of the securities was placed internationally with Continental European institutional investors by a banking group led by Orion Bank in the form of Continental Depository Receipts. The stock was listed on the Amsterdam, Paris and London stock exchanges, and Orion undertook to make a market in it, hoping to establish a European market in the securities. 'In the past such securities have tended to find their way back into the UK after the issue,' commented the *Financial Times*. 'But in an attempt to prevent this the preference stock will carry a favourable dividend rate vis-à-vis the Lyons ordinary shares.'[76]

It was as financial adviser to engineering firm Babcock & Wilcox that Orion Bank undertook its first merger and acquisition work in autumn 1972. This was conducted jointly with Lazards, the eminent City merchant bank which was not amused to be partnered by such 'amateurs.'[77] There were two deals which proceeded more-or-less simultaneously, for General Electrical & Mechanical Systems, which went smoothly, and for Woodall Duckham. The latter became a protracted but ultimately successful struggle against a defence led by Kleinworts. It included a meeting of the full Takeover Panel, in which Grierson was represented, 'in a personal capacity,' by Prime Minister Harold Wilson's lawyer, Lord Goodman. Two rules of the Takeover Code were amended as a result of the case. 'After many false starts,' commented Grierson upon the completion of the deals, 'we now appear to be "launched" in the fee-earning sector.'[78]

Orion Bank's international network of shareholders was potentially a source of cross-border merger and acquisition business. In 1973, working with WestLB, Orion Bank became active in assisting British companies with acquisitions in Continental Europe. Clients included United Drapery Stores, Imperial Foods and J. Lyons.[79]

It was with a view to enhancing Orion Bank's corporate advisory activities that Grierson hired Sir Samuel Goldman as an executive director in October 1972.[80] Aged 60, Goldman had recently retired from the Treasury, where he had worked for most of his career and risen to the senior rank of Second Permanent Secretary.[81] Initially, Goldman was put in charge of 'planning', though he was never quite sure what the job entailed.[82] Then, happily, he got a real assignment. In December 1972, the Commonwealth Secretary General asked Orion Bank to undertake an investigation into the needs of developing countries of the Commonwealth in the field of export finance.[83] The study was conducted by Goldman, assisted by Patrick Browning and a foreign credit expert seconded from Royal Bank. Six months later, after visits to India, Singapore, Malaysia and Kenya, they produced a hefty report that was well-received by the authorities. 'Orion Bank will earn only a small fee on this transaction,' Grierson reported to the board, 'but it is already clear that the publicity which this study has given us with all Commonwealth Governments could be of considerable benefit in obtaining other business.'[84]

LENDING AND MONEY MARKET

Revenues from lending, though not Orion Bank's 'prime business', were expected to cover its operating overheads, at least in the short-term until its capital was required to back investment banking activities.[85] Besides earning interest, 'each loan hopefully contains the germ of fee-earning business in the future,' Grierson reported optimistically.[86]

The volume of Orion Bank's lending quadrupled over the years 1971–73, from £12.6 million to £58 million (see Table 4.6). This growth was facilitated by the hiring of the bank's own specialist to oversee its money market trading and funding in May 1972.[88] He was George Westbury from Chase, who later became head of Orion's Channel Islands' subsidiary. Management of the loan portfolio was put on to 'a more businesslike basis,' allowing an expansion from 2.5 times capital to 12 times.[89] The convergence of activities on the part of the two Orion banks, in 1972–73, was a pragmatic response to market conditions and commercial opportunities, but it was also a reflection of the problems Orion Bank was encountering in developing investment banking activities.[90]

Table 4.6 Orion Bank, loans and capital, 1971–73[87] (£ million)

	1971	1972	1973
Loans	12.6	36.2	58.0
Capital and reserves	5.0	5.2	4.9
Ratio of loans : capital	2.5	7.0	11.8

BOND TRADING

Orion Bank's entry into bond trading had two objectives. First, to strengthen its hand in winning lead and co-management positions by having an in-house trading capability to support its own issues. Secondly, to make money from bond trading in the secondary market. Thus there were two distinct parts to Orion Bank's bond portfolio (and two trading limits): bonds deriving from primary market operations; and bonds held on account of secondary market trading. Not that provenance made any difference when interest rates shot up and bond prices fell.

The trading operation was established in May 1972.[91] It was headed by Leslie Petts from leading bond dealer Strauss Turnbull & Co.[92] 'His task,' stated Grierson announcing the appointment, 'is to establish Orion in the primary and secondary bond markets, and this operation requires by its nature a plunge into the water nearer the deep end than is our normal custom.'[93] At the time, Eurobond trading was a risky activity because of the small number of market makers, the breadth of spreads and the general narrowness of the market; end investors, whether central banks or private individuals, such as the so-called 'Belgian dentist', tended to buy for keeps.

Petts, who joined the Orion Bank board as an executive director, recruited two dealers and a back-office staff of eight, a fifth of Orion Bank's total staff at the time. He proposed to make a market in about 250 high-quality securities. The ambition was 'to expand this operation so that it will become one of the most powerful dealing operations in the secondary market in Eurocurrency bonds.'[94] It was estimated that the trading operation would yield a profit of $800 000 in its first year.

Orion Bank's bond dealing activities became fully operational at the beginning of 1973. Initially, things went to plan – in fact better. The gross dealing profit for January was $250 000, and in the first three months the department handled 5370 deals with a total turnover of $180 million.[95] By June it ranked fifth in the Eurobond secondary market in terms of trading volume.[96] But profits were another matter. The rise in interest rates in the spring sent bond prices tumbling and soon the bond portfolio was showing heavy losses that more than wiped out earlier dealing profits.

ORION SPREADS ITS WINGS

The early 1970s saw the formation of two more consortium banks by the Orion shareholders in Latin America and Asia Pacific, regions believed to have strong potential for dynamic economic growth, and several subsidiaries by Orion itself, developing its business in new directions. Libra Bank was established in November 1972, as an independent consortium bank focused on Latin America and the Caribbean.[97] Chase was the driving force and made the largest commitment to its capital, 24 per cent.[98] The other five Orion partners jointly put up 33 per cent, and 43 per cent was subscribed by Swiss, Brazilian, Mexican and Portuguese banks.

Libra Bank was based in London with offices in five Latin American cities and New York. The management was provided by Chase, the largest share-holder. Libra regarded Latin America as its preserve and complained to the shareholders about Orion's attempts to develop business in the region. Like Orion, it offered a full range of commercial and investment banking services. Orion, for its part, refused to be excluded from one of the world's most promising regions for both Eurobond mandates and medium-term credits.[99] Matters came to a head in summer 1974, when both banks mounted a simultaneous marketing initiative in Mexico and the Caribbean. The turf war between Orion and Libra was referred by the parties to the Shareholders' Forum, and adjudicated at the meeting in Montreal in September 1974. The shareholders accepted that Orion was not to be subject to geographical lim-itations on its activities, and requested the senior management of the two firms to work out an 'intelligent solution to the problem of their overlapping marketing thrust.'[100]

Orion Pacific was established by the Orion shareholders in May 1973 as a separate but closely affiliated entity; its annual report formed part of Orion's report and accounts. The Orion shareholders were joined in this venture by Nikko Securities, which took a 5 per cent shareholding. Based in Hong Kong, in offices sub-let from NatWest, its activities encompassed medium- and long-term lending, securities underwriting, investment management, and merger and acquisition work. It was also active in the foreign exchange markets, the Asia and Eurocurrency markets and the international bond and equity markets. The senior management comprised executives seconded from the Orion shareholders. In 1974, in conjunction with Chase, Mitsubishi and a local partner, Orion Pacific formed an associated merchant bank in Malaysia.

Orion's earliest diversification was into leasing.[101] In the UK, leasing became a boom business in the 1970s, driven by the taxation benefits enjoyed by lessors from investing in new equipment to lease to industrial companies. The cost could be deducted for current tax purposes and the tax liability deferred, a practice described as a 'tax dodge' when abolished by UK chancellor Nigel Lawson in 1984.[102] In the meantime, the tax advantages made it seem a very alluring business for banks, even if these attractions were apt to blind bankers to unreliable covenants and the problematic residual values of industrial assets.

The concept underlying the formation of Orion Leasing Holdings in 1972 was to provide multinational corporations with a 'one source' leasing service to serve their requirements around the world 'no matter what the asset, how much the cost, or where it may be used.'[103] To furnish this ambitious facility, operating subsidiaries were established in Brazil, the Cayman Islands, Germany, the Netherlands, Italy, Singapore, Sweden and the UK.[104] To co-ordinate the growing number of Orion entities, John Haley was appointed Orion group chief executive in November 1972.[105]

Orion's diversification drive was regarded warily by some of the shareholders; at NatWest an internal report observed that: 'the more Orion expands geographically and in types of services, e.g. leasing and factoring, the more it means competition with shareholders.'[106]

ORION BANK, LEADERSHIP AND PERFORMANCE, 1971–73

Britain's accession to the European Economic Community in January 1973 created a need to fill a number of posts assigned to British nationals in Brussels. Grierson accepted an invitation from the government to become Director General for Industry and Technology, receiving a letter from the Prime Minister thanking him for 'allowing my arm to be twisted.'[107] His resignation as Orion Bank's chief executive took effect from 13 February 1973.[108] Grierson's achievement at Orion Bank was to establish a new international merchant bank at a time of unusual turbulence in financial markets. In particular, to bring together an outstanding collection of individuals from diverse backgrounds and to turn them into a team working to the highest standards. But as regards building Orion Bank's business, the job was only half done.

Grierson's departure triggered a reassignment of senior roles at Orion Bank. Group chief executive John Haley became acting chief executive,[109] but only temporarily; six months later he returned to New York to become an executive vice-president, and subsequently a member of Chase's top-level management committee. Haley continued to take a close interest in Orion's affairs and sometimes attended the Shareholders' Forum on behalf of Chase.

William de Gelsey and Michael Bonsor were appointed Orion Bank's joint managing directors. Lord Caccia, a NatWest non-executive director, became non-executive chairman. A distinguished career diplomat who had served as British ambassador in Washington, Harold Caccia joined the NatWest board upon his retirement as head of the Diplomatic Service. Admitting to a limited knowledge of banking, Caccia provided valuable support for John Haley and useful access to the higher levels of the UK government. In autumn 1973, Caccia also became chairman of Orion Termbank when Haley returned to New York. He was 67 at the time of his appointment to the Orion chairmanships, which he took on in the capacity of a caretaker. For how long, was anyone's guess.

Thanks to revenues from lending, Orion Bank broke even in 1971. The following year, the first year of fully-fledged operations, after deductions of £32 000 for incorporation expenses and a contribution of £94 000 to OMS, it made pre-tax profits of £352 000. The pre-tax return on capital was 6.8 per cent (see Table 4.7). 'This is not entirely unsatisfactory,' commented Grierson, comparing the actual result with the Management Plan target of £192 000.[110]

Table 4.7   Orion Bank, performance, 1971–73[111] (£'000)

	1971	1972	1973
Profit (pre-tax)	–	352	(428)
Capital and reserves	5007	5169	4851
Return (pre-tax) (per cent)	–	6.8	–

The year 1973 began well, the first four months generating net operating profits before tax of £224 000. However, by mid-year a provision of £142 000 was necessary for unrealized losses on the bond portfolio, 'a result of adverse market developments which have affected all major financial centres,' commented joint managing directors de Gelsey and Bonsor, 'something which we must expect on occasion and the risk of which was taken into account when it was decided to go ahead and introduce a bond dealing operation.'[112]

But the bond portfolio losses grew and grew, and by the end of the year the situation had become 'disastrous.'[113] Profits of nearly £1 million from underwriting commissions, management fees, advisory fees and interest on loans were more than offset by losses of £1.4 million from bond trading and the bond portfolio. 'With the benefit of hindsight,' commented an internal memo, 'it is now evident that Orion Bank built up a bond portfolio at prices which were to fall away in succeeding months and the cost of funding has been higher than the interest return on the bonds. Trading conditions have been very difficult and substantial losses have been incurred in reducing the portfolio from excessively high positions.'[114] The outcome was a loss by Orion Bank in 1973 of £428 000, which generated sensational headlines that completely eclipsed Orion Termbank's strong results.[115]

On a consolidated basis, the Orion group's financial results were profitable overall despite difficult times. In 1971, the first year of trading, the pre-tax profit of the Orion group was £840 000, a sound achievement for a start-up operation.[116] In 1972, the group pre-tax profit was £1.5 million, almost double the previous year. In 1973, the group pre-tax profit was £1.6 million and would have been £3 million but for the Eurobond losses.[117]

But Orion was not a 'happy ship'.[118] The departures of Grierson and Haley and the losses in the bond market had been unsettling and Orion had lost its sense of direction. Staff morale was flagging and the shareholders were becoming restive and disenchanted over the calls on the time and energy of senior executives that this joint venture demanded. Somehow the sum of the parts – excellent personnel, substantial achievements and strong shareholders – was falling short of its potential.

CHAPTER 5

Stormy weather: Montagu takes the helm

There was little to celebrate in 1974, the year of the consortium bank movement's tenth anniversary. Currency turmoil, recession and inflation, fuelled by the quadrupling of the oil price after the Yom Kippur War, dogged the international economy. In the Euromarkets, confidence was at a low ebb and business was bad all round. In the UK, there was confrontation between Edward Heath's Conservative government and the miners; despite the efforts of employment minister, William Whitelaw, a national emergency and a three-day working week had to be declared because of power shortages.

The banking system was in crisis and financial markets were diving. In February, chancellor Anthony Barber warned that the country faced 'our gravest situation since the end of the war.'[1]

The blues in the Euromarkets had a variety of causes. Rising interest rates led to plummeting Eurobond prices and losses on bond portfolios. A reverse yield curve depressed new issue activity. The volume of medium-term syndicated lending was more buoyant as countries borrowed to finance balance of payments deficits, but it was hard for any but the largest banks to make money because of the low spreads stemming from the abundance of deposits competing for lending opportunities. Moreover, with the abolition of the Interest Equalisation Tax in January 1974, there was even uncertainty about the continued existence of the offshore Euromarkets.

THE LIFEBOAT

In London, the adverse market conditions had already claimed a casualty among the consortium banks. In summer 1973, as described on page 38, Western American Bank (Europe) made large losses on a Eurobond issue it was managing and its problems were compounded by its exposure to the troubled UK property market; it survived by greatly curtailing its activities.[2]

It was property sector losses that led to the UK's secondary banking crisis and to the launch of the Bank of England's 'lifeboat' operation to prevent systemic damage in November 1973. Only one consortium bank share-holder, the merchant bank Keyser Ullman, a partner in London Interstate Bank, ended up in the lifeboat.[3] The Bank's prompt action successfully fore-stalled the failure of any important banks in London, though at one point there were even rumours swirling around NatWest's name as its shares fell below their par value of one pound, thereby inhibiting any possible rights issue of new shares.[4]

The summer of 1974 saw significant bank failures in the USA and Germany, which further undermined confidence. In May, the substantial Franklin National Bank collapsed, eroding trust in the US banking system and reviving memories of the widespread bank failures of the Great Depression. In fact, Franklin's problems were due only in part to the adverse market conditions but more to the frauds perpetrated by financier Michele Sindona. The stricken bank was acquired by European American Bank, part of the banking club EBIC, which thereby became one of the twenty largest banking organizations in the USA.[5]

The collapse in June 1974 of Bankhaus I.D. Herstatt, a leading German private bank with a large foreign exchange and precious metals trading busi-ness, was a traumatic event. The heavy-handed action of the German author-ities in closing-down the bank, while markets in the USA and elsewhere were still trading, left many deals outstanding and inflicted substantial losses on the counter-parties. The Herstatt failure sent a powerful shock wave through the international financial markets and for months afterwards business was subdued. There was an abrupt retrenchment in foreign exchange trading. Depositors in the Eurocurrency market shifted their funds to leading name banks. This was a problem for the consortium banks, which were heavily reliant on the Eurocurrency market for funding.[6] Some of them, such as those with Japanese and Italian ownership, suffered from 'tiering' of deposit rates and had to pay over the odds; once a bank paid over the odds, it became difficult to revert to the best rates in the market. A further factor discourag-ing deposits with the consortium banks was uncertainty about whether their shareholders would stand behind them if there were problems.[7] Many of them were obliged to turn to their shareholders for funding support in the form of deposits or subordinated loans.

The crisis of confidence among bankers had the potential of developing into a major international banking crisis, as had followed the failure of Austria's Creditanstalt in 1931. But this time, the leading central banks, led by Bank of England governor Gordon Richardson, acted promptly to stop the rot. Meeting in July 1974 at the Bank for International Settlements in Basle, they adopted the principle of 'parental responsibility' for interna-tional banking operations. This established that parent banks, and their respective central banks, had responsibility for all international branches, subsidiaries and affiliates. It was formalized in July 1975 as the Basle Concordat, whereby each central bank assumed responsibility for the supervision of foreign branches established by its domestic banks. These developments had implications for the consortium banks and their shareholders.

The adoption of the principle of parental responsibility led to institutional reforms in banking supervision. At the international level, the response was the formation of the Basle-based Committee on Banking Regulation and Supervisory Practices. Composed of representatives of the world's twelve leading central banks, it assumed responsibility for international co-operation in banking supervision and subsequently evolved into a key institution, setting international capital adequacy ratios and other international banking standards. The first chairman was Bank of England director George Blunden, who was also made head of the Bank's new Banking Supervision Division. In September 1974, all the London-based consortium banks received letters from him 'requesting' them to provide the Bank with written undertakings from their parent banks formally committing themselves to supporting their offspring.

Although the worst of the crisis was over, the doldrums in the markets continued. 'The Oxford dictionary defines the chameleon as a small long-tongued lizard with a prehensile tail and the power to change colour and of going without food for a long time,' wrote *Euromoney's* international bond market correspondent in November 1974. 'Faced with continuing hardship, the international bond market is showing most of the qualities of this small reptile especially as regards adaptability and resistance to starvation.'[8] But the bond market chameleon was about to change from red to green and the last month of the worst of years marked the beginning of 'the long and arduous journey to recovery.'[9] For Orion, it was 'just in time.'[10]

DAVID MONTAGU

Lord Caccia's appointment as chairman of Orion Bank early in 1973 was a stop-gap measure while a search was undertaken for a new chairman and chief executive. The ideal candidate was a senior international merchant banker who could not only run the merchant banking activities of Orion Bank but also act as group chief executive. But such figures proved to be in desperately short supply. For several months during the summer and autumn, there were hopes that James Wolfensohn, who at the time was building up Schroders' operations in New York and later became head of the World Bank, might be persuaded to join Orion, a prospect that generated enthusiasm among the shareholders.[11] But Wolfensohn could not be won over, informing Chase president Willard Butcher in November 1973 that he was 'categoric on the subject of his non-availability in the foreseeable future.'[12] In fact, the hiatus

while Wolfensohn was wooed proved a blessing in disguise since in the meantime another candidate emerged, 'a man of great importance ... someone who
is outstandingly suitable,' senior executives were excitedly informed.[13] This
was David Montagu.

The Hon. David Charles Samuel Montagu was born in 1928, the eldest
son and heir of the third Baron Swaythling. He was educated at Eton and
Trinity College, Cambridge, where he studied English literature, having tried
law and economics but found them too dull. Upon graduation in 1949, he
reported for work at the family firm Samuel Montagu & Co. founded by his
great-grandfather almost a century before. He was interviewed by Louis
Franck, the abrasive Belgian who ran the City merchant bank. 'His first
words to me were: "you have no future in banking",' Montagu recalled. 'He
saw this young pip-squeak who he thought had been born with a silver spoon
in his mouth. He couldn't have been more wrong. It was very cupro-nickel.'[14]

Despite, or rather because of, Franck's discouragement, Montagu joined
the firm and applied himself to mastering the business of merchant banking.
'That was the goad which made me determined to be chief executive and
then chairman of Samuel Montagu and to host his leaving party,' Montagu
said. In 1954, he was made a partner. While Franck focused on the firm's
foreign exchange and bullion trading, Montagu developed the corporate
finance and investment management sides of the business. He helped to
invent the split-level investment trust, the first vehicle to take account of the
different needs of investors seeking capital growth and income. He became
chief executive of the bank and chairman in 1970, at the early age of 41.
He fulfilled his ambition of hosting Franck's retirement party, though relations were never easy. 'Attended his funeral too. Enjoyed both,' Montagu
remarked mischievously.

Under David Montagu's leadership, Samuel Montagu was in the forefront
of new developments in merchant banking. It was an early participant in the
Euromarkets, a notable early deal being its $20 million private placement for
Belgium in 1963. It was also a pioneer of a link-up between a merchant bank
and a clearing bank, in the 1960s a radical departure. 'I think I was the first
person in the City to recognise that merchant banks were undercapitalised
for what was going to happen in the capital markets,' he told a journalist
from the *Financial Times*.[15] He helped bring in Midland Bank as a minority investor in September 1967 to boost the capital. He also hoped 'that
they would introduce a lot of their major corporate clients, and that would
lead to a dramatic increase in our corporate finance activities.'[16]

In April 1973, Midland Bank acquired full ownership of Samuel
Montagu & Co. In view of the family tie, David Montagu was offered
the non-executive chairmanship for life, a banking equivalent to allowing the
ancestral family to live on as tenants in a wing of a house acquired by
the National Trust. But it was made clear that he would have neither executive

responsibilities nor a seat on the Midland Bank board of directors. Montagu was outraged: 'I was supposed to chair a committee of managers meeting on Friday mornings,' he fulminated. 'I wanted nothing to do with it. A greater insult has never been offered.'[17] His frustration was plain to friends. 'You will never be able to work with the Midland,' Lord Carrington, a prominent Conservative politician and an old friend, told him at a lunch at the Bank of England, 'when are you going to find something else?'[18] Montagu resigned. It is intriguing to speculate how the development of British banking might have been different if he had been retained to succeed the elderly Sir Archibald Forbes as chairman of Midland. Might he have saved Midland from its catastrophic acquisition of Croker National Bank? Might Midland have been more successful at investment banking? Might its flag still be flying in British high streets rather than HSBC's?

Learning of Montagu's resignation from Samuel Montagu, Sir John Prideaux, chairman of NatWest, invited him to become chairman of County Bank, NatWest's small and domestically focused merchant banking subsidiary. He wasn't interested. Prideaux then asked him whether he would be interested in taking the helm at Orion. Running a free-standing international investment bank backed by half-a-dozen of the world's top banks was a different matter. 'I was fascinated by the purely intellectual challenge,' said Montagu. 'I was quite a well-known figure internationally, a regular attendee at the annual IMF meetings.'[19] He proved more than acceptable to David Rockefeller of Chase and Earle McLaughlin of Royal Bank and, after discussions in New York, he accepted the invitation to join Orion Bank as chairman and chief executive.

David Montagu's judgement and contacts were highly valued, leading to numerous outside directorships, including London Weekend Television, Carreras and United British Securities Trust.[20] 'As a financier, he was tenacious, imaginative and loyal to clients,' wrote an obituarist when he died in July 1998. 'When he adopted a cause he fought very hard for it. The broadcaster and friend John Freeman (whom Montagu helped to establish London Weekend Television) once described him as "someone I trust entirely, a man with whom I would go tiger shooting".'[21]

As regards personal matters, he married Ninette, daughter of Edgar Dreyfus of Paris in 1951. They had three children. His tastes were fastidious and civilized; he once described himself as 'a lobster-eating Jew.' He was an art collector, a theatre lover, a connoisseur of fine wine and cigars, a keen bridge player and an excellent shot. But his passion was racing. He kept a string of race-horses near his Newmarket home, a house called The Kremlin. The high point of his racing career was in 1979, when his horse *Zongalero* finished second in the Grand National. He was a founder member of the British Horse Racing Board, chairman of its finance committee and a member of the All-Party Racing and Blood Stock Committee.

He had a sharp wit, which was a delight for companions but did not endear him to its targets, first and foremost commercial bankers. On one occasion when asked to justify his first-class airline ticket by an Orion shareholder he replied, 'I'm afraid a private jet wasn't available.'[22] He enjoyed a joke against himself and was fond of quoting Barclays' chairman Sir Anthony Tuke's description of consortium banks as 'dog's breakfast banks.' His tongue made him a few enemies, but they were greatly outnumbered by friends. He possessed a genuine *joie de vivre* and was able to instill a sense of fun and excitement into every enterprise in which he was involved. Orion was no exception.

REFORMS

David Montagu took up the appointment of chairman and chief executive of Orion Bank on 1 March 1974. In the light of the turbulent and difficult market conditions, Montagu's short-term strategy was 'to avoid losing money as opposed to making it.'[23] This spelt the end of the ill-fated bond trading operation, and Orion ceased general market making in Eurobonds on 24 May 1974. This produced a reduction in overheads from £200 000 to £80 000 by cutting the bond trading staff from twenty to seven. Those who remained continued to make a market in issues managed by Orion and did deals for clients on a matched order basis. By October, Montagu was able to report that these activities were generating a weekly gross profit of £10 000.

Another unsatisfactory situation was Orion Bank's investment in St Helen's Securities now worth considerably less than had been paid for it, because of the slump in the UK stock market. Montagu quickly negotiated the sale of St Helen's Securities to Allied Investments, a provider of medical services and a medical management contractor with rapidly developing interests in the Middle East.[24] This transaction provided Orion with a 14 per cent shareholding in Allied Investments and a seat on the board. 'We have now exchanged our shareholding in a stagnant and eroding investment trust for a substantial minority stake in a growth-oriented commercial undertaking with extremely good management,' Montagu reported to the Orion Bank board.[25] Moreover, the link-up with Allied Investments provided promising financing opportunities and potential openings in the Middle East for Orion.

Tidying up the legacy of past mistakes was the least interesting item on Montagu's agenda for Orion. Holding the view that 'we are in a cyclical trend and that a resuscitation of the capital markets is inevitable,' he looked ahead. In fact, the trough of the cycle was exactly the point at which to position Orion for the upturn that was bound to come sooner or later. Internally, he instigated a management shake-up and a recruitment drive to put in place new executives. Externally, he endeavoured to forge new alliances and looked for paths to expansion. Despite the difficult environment, Orion's activities increased vigorously: in 1974, lending more than doubled and group pre-tax profits soared from £1.6 million to £4.9 million.

The management changes included the formation of new committees, 'designed to involve the maximum number of people in critical areas of the bank's activities,' and a broadening of the Orion Bank board.[26] Andrew Large, Anthony Marshall and Michael Perry were promoted to the board, generating a greater sense of participation among the younger executives, and three board-level appointments were made from outside, Christopher Chataway, Julian Fane and Philip Hubbard.

Christopher Chataway was a well-known public figure. He represented the UK as a medium-distance runner in the Olympic Games of 1952 and 1956. In 1959, he became a Member of Parliament and served as Minister for Industrial Development in Edward Heath's government. The defeat of the Conservatives in February 1974 cost him his ministerial position and he stood down as an MP when a second election was called later that year. Being without a job, he was delighted to receive a telephone call from David Montagu offering him a managing directorship at Orion. For Orion, Chataway's abilities and experience as well as his connections made him a useful and distinguished colleague, despite his lack of direct banking experience.

Julian Fane began his career as an army officer. Upon leaving the army in 1969, he joined the merchant bank Samuel Montagu & Co. as personnel manager. In 1975, David Montagu, a friend from those days, invited him to join Orion as executive director in charge of administration and personnel. Fane's appointment at this level was a manifestation of the importance Montagu attached to disciplined office practices and to staff training, unglamorous but vital functions that can undermine an investment bank, as Barings learnt to its cost in 1995. In the 1970s, it was unusual for ex-politicians or executives concerned with back-office functions and human resources to be made main board directors of London banks, and the appointment of Chataway and Fane was opposed by some at NatWest. However, they were welcomed by Royal Bank, particularly Chataway who, as the winner of the three-mile race in the British Empire and Commonwealth Games in Vancouver in 1954, was a sporting hero in Canada.

Philip Hubbard was appointed managing director in charge of the newly formed corporate finance department, which marshalled Orion's Eurobond new issues business. An American, he was educated at Carnegie Mellon University and then at Harvard Business School, where he took an MBA. He joined Morgan Stanley in 1964, where he was part of the original team that built up a successful Eurobond operation in the late 1960s. In the early 1970s, he moved to Paris where he became a director of Morgan & Cie International and a visiting professor at INSEAD.

ATTEMPTED ALLIANCES AND ACQUISITIONS

A tie-up rather along the lines of the looser European banking clubs was explored with Goldman Sachs in summer 1974. 'Full and exhaustive' discussions were held in New York and an informal link between the banks was agreed.[27] It was hoped that the link would generate fee-earning business and assist Orion's fledgling New York representative office, which had just opened.[28] In practice it came to nothing.

Montagu's most audacious initiative to reposition Orion Bank during the market downturn was the proposed acquisition of City merchant bank Hill Samuel. With a staff of 3000, Hill Samuel was one of the largest City merchant banks and conducted a wider range of activities than most, including shipping and insurance. In July 1974, Montagu learned privately that Hill Samuel was seeking a strong partner and could be acquired at book value with no premium for goodwill. He immediately visited each of the shareholders to appraise them of this 'unique opportunity' to create the largest international investment bank at a single stroke.[29] The development of merchant banking activities had been the 'centrepiece of the constellation' of the shareholders' original plans for Orion; attempts had been made to buy a merchant bank in 1970, but they were unsuccessful and subsequent progress had been slow. The acquisition of Hill Samuel would forestall the 'long and arduous task to build Orion into a competitive force' and overcome the 'difficulties of the *de novo* approach.'

The 'coincidence of events' that caused Hill Samuel to be for sale with a bargain-basement price tag, began with losses on account of the UK's secondary banking crisis and the slide in the stock market. The *coup de grace* was the Herstatt collapse in June 1974, which inflicted large foreign exchange losses – the initial estimate was £9 million, 15 per cent of its capital – and undermined market confidence in Hill Samuel's soundness.[30] For beleaguered Hill Samuel, acquisition by Orion backed by six of the world's top commercial banks looked like a welcome rescue.

The acquisition of Hill Samuel was supported by Jock Finlayson of Royal Bank and Sir John Prideaux of NatWest, who hailed it as 'a great chance to achieve at a stroke the ambitions of Orion.'[31] For NatWest, competition with its own merchant banking subsidiary, County Bank, was a potential reason for opposition. But County Bank's function was to service NatWest's domestic clients, and Prideaux accepted Montagu's reassurances about Orion's international orientation. However, the other shareholders were opposed to the move for a variety of reasons. Chase raised 'the obvious legal and regulatory problems.' Moreover, it disliked Hill Samuel's shipping and insurance activities, protesting that Montagu was 'contemplating the purchase of a large organisation, with a relatively small merchant banking capability.' It was suspicious that the enlarged Orion would be hungry for capital from shareholders, at a time when the US authorities were contemplating more stringent capital adequacy requirements in the wake of the Franklin Bank collapse. Finally, Chase was wary that the bigger and bolder Orion Bank/Hill Samuel entity would insist on a large measure of independence, whereas 'the original Orion concept called for considerable shareholder involvement and influence.'

Other shareholders echoed these points and added some of their own. WestLB protested that Hill Samuel's pattern of business was too UK-focused and that it lacked international reach. Furthermore, it would be 'difficult to envisage a unit described as the largest international merchant bank in the world accepting its supplementary function vis-à-vis the shareholders.' Mitsubishi agreed, declaring that Hill Samuel would be bound to absorb Orion and its development would be along lines not necessarily controlled by the shareholders. Credito concurred, adding that Italy's balance-of-payments problems made it unlikely that it would be able to come up with additional capital. At the conclusion of the special summit convened to debate the acquisition on 19 July 1974, the verdict was two in favour but four against, and 'that was the end of the matter.'[32]

The debate about the proposed acquisition of Hill Samuel in summer 1974 fostered mistrust among the shareholders. NatWest and Royal Bank became suspicious of Chase, wondering whether its commitment to Orion 'may now be only minimal – perhaps little more than paying lip service to a contract.'[33] Rightly or wrongly, it renewed their suspicions that Chase really regarded Chase Manhattan Limited, its recently formed London merchant bank, as the linchpin of its Euromarket activities. The outcome was also a personal disappointment for Montagu, though his standing among the shareholders was enhanced by his handling of the negotiations.[34] With the benefit of hindsight, Orion probably missed an important opportunity – almost simultaneously a somewhat similar joint venture between an international investment bank and a large commercial bank was being formed – Credit Suisse White Weld (forerunner of CS First Boston), one of the great success stories of the Euromarkets.

LETTERS OF COMFORT

Orion, like the other London-based consortium banks, received a letter from George Blunden, head of the Bank of England's Banking Supervision Division, in late September 1974.[35] Its purpose was to give practical effect to the principle of 'parental responsibility' agreed at the central bank meeting in Basle in July 1974 in the wake of the Herstatt collapse. The text of the letter, an important document in the story of the consortium banks, read:

> *In the context of banking supervision we have recently been reviewing the position of consortium banks like yours which are registered in this country, but whose shareholding banks come from a number of different countries. We consider that the shareholders must accept full responsibility for such banks and must stand behind them at all times. We think that, whenever a consortium bank has been established here, that position has been made*

clear to, and generally been accepted by, the banks involved; but we now
consider that it should be explicitly recorded. We should, therefore, welcome
your obtaining for us from your shareholding banks statements that they
accept ultimate responsibility for your bank.[36]

Naturally, the Orion shareholders complied with the Bank of England's
request, providing six so-called 'letters of comfort', to a formula suggested by
Blunden at Orion's request. Dibbs, who acted as Orion's ambassador to the
Bank, took the opportunity of meeting with Blunden to point out that the
shareholders had always been behind Orion and 'that none of them would
"run away" were any difficulty foreseen or encountered.'[37] Blunden replied
that the Bank was well aware of this, but nevertheless felt it necessary to have
'an indication of their recognition that a moral commitment existed.'
Although he had no doubts about Orion, he had a hunch that some other
consortium bank shareholders might try to wriggle out of their obligations.[38]

The Bank of England's letters of comfort engendered a significant change
in market sentiment towards the consortium banks. Reassured that their
shareholders stood square behind them, depositors became more relaxed
about placing their money with them and the funding problems that had
dogged them over the summer since the Herstatt failure abated. In the
longer-term, the letters of comfort led to a shake-up in the ownership pattern of the consortium banks. Smaller banks and passive shareholders pulled
out, being wary of commitments to support entities that were too large or
too remote for the risks to be acceptable. The letters prompted an exodus by
smaller banks whose capital bases were too small to sustain the exposure.
From 1974 to 1979, the London-based consortium banks lost ten merchant
banks and a number of other banks as shareholders.

ORION RESTRUCTURED

The amalgamation of Orion Bank and Orion Termbank was a long-standing
issue. As early as September 1971, Grierson had written a paper for the shareholder representatives pointing out the practical problems and confusion in
the market-place of operating through two banking entities and recommending their combination.[39] He returned to the subject in his report to the board
in February 1972, complaining that 'the artificial divisions between Orion
Bank and Orion Termbank continue to be the source of much confusion,
duplication and ineffectiveness.'[40] But at the end of the year, he was still beat-
ing the same drum, telling colleagues that '1973 must above all be the year of
Orion's integration, an objective towards which I have, as you all know, been
striving hard since the very beginning.'[41] But again, nothing happened.

The calls for the merger of Orion Bank and Orion Termbank were most
staunchly resisted by Chase, for the same regulatory reasons that had led to

the separation in the first place. But there was also a more widespread feeling among the shareholders that the expensive and mercurial investment
bankers at Orion Bank, which was struggling in its performance, were trying to bail themselves out by snaffling the earnings of Orion Termbank,
which was staffed by seconded commercial bankers and prospering. Thus the
amalgamation proposals by Grierson and other senior figures at Orion Bank
fell on deaf ears.

Three things happened in 1973 to change the shareholders' attitude. The
first was the convergence of the business being undertaken by the two entities. The study group report on the proposed merger commissioned by the
Shareholders' Forum in May 1974, observed that 'the collapse of the bond
market in 1973, and the concurrent growth of the market for medium-term
credits, has resulted in Orion Bank staff devoting further marketing effort to
the latter sector with the result that Orion Bank's major sources of income
are currently similar to those of Orion Termbank.'[42] The second was that
Chase's lawyers managed to find a solution to the regulatory problem. The
third was the arrival of David Montagu.

'When I first came,' Montagu told *Euromoney*, 'Orion was split into four
distinctly different operating entities. There was Orion Bank, which was
attempting to be an investment banking operation. There was Orion
Termbank, which was the medium and longer-term lending vehicle which,
at the time of conception, the shareholders wanted as an extension to their
own capabilities. There was Orion Pacific, which had no shareholding relationship with Orion Bank. And there was Orion Leasing. The first thing that
I felt was absolutely vital, and which I'm happy to say the shareholders supported me on and agreed to, was that we needed to get the Orion banking
group under one management.'[43]

It certainly did not help any residual sentiment in favour of the twin-bank
structure that they should find themselves inadvertently depositing funds
with each other, through money brokers, or that Orion Bank 'freely and
unhelpfully' paid a premium for some of its deposits, while Orion Termbank
funded itself at 'the proper rate.'[44] The merger of the two banks – the combined entity being known as Orion Bank – became effective on 30
December 1974. In 1975, Orion Pacific became a majority-owned subsidiary of Orion Bank through transfers of shares from the shareholders.
Early in 1976, Orion Leasing Holdings became a wholly-owned subsidiary.
These moves extended Montagu's authority and his ability to run the Orion
Group, as it was called henceforth.

SHAREHOLDER REPRESENTATIVES

The process of consolidation left two outstanding issues: the function of
Orion Multinational Services (OMS) and the position of the staff seconded

from the shareholders, the senior representatives and the more junior area executives. Regarding the former, Montagu wanted a reassessment of the function of this parallel entity now that Orion's planning stage was over. As regards the latter, he was determined that the seconded staff should report to him rather than to their own institutions. 'They were outside the reporting lines,' he explained. 'It is very difficult to run a business unless executives report to you, not to other people.'[45]

A review of the role of OMS and the shareholder representatives began in December 1975, with the objective of resolving the question at the chairmen's meeting and Shareholders' Forum scheduled for October 1976. Each of the shareholders was requested to submit their views on 'the retention or otherwise, of shareholder representation on the current basis and the need for the continuation of OMS as a separate entity responsible for marketing and co-ordination etc.'[46] Naturally, the chairman of OMS, at the time Vince Kelly from Royal Bank, had something to say about these matters, and it was his report circulated in April 1976 that became the focal point of debate.

Kelly made three key recommendations. First, the abolition of OMS, arguing that it was no longer necessary as a device by which the shareholders could steer and control Orion. He argued that it was inconsistent with 'a strong, centralised and responsible management for the Group.'[47] Secondly, the elimination of the positions of senior representative, who were now wastefully under-employed. Thirdly, the transformation of the six area executives into 'Directors – Marketing' and their appointment to the Orion Bank board. Besides simplifying reporting lines and eliminating sources of conflict, he estimated that these changes would save Orion £470 000 in overheads.

Kelly's proposals were fully supported by Royal Bank and NatWest, which were eager to allow Montagu to get on with the job of running Orion. However, the other shareholders had greater or lesser reservations, supporting the existing arrangements precisely because they kept Orion's management on a short leash. It was the same line-up of shareholder perceptions as over the Hill Samuel acquisition. The issues were thrashed out at the Shareholders' Forum held in Tokyo in October 1976, following the annual World Bank and IMF meetings held that year in Manila. The outcome was called a compromise, but this time Royal Bank, NatWest and David Montagu mostly got their way. OMS was retained, but its responsibility was limited to drawing up the agenda for the Shareholders' Forum in consultation with the chief executive of Orion Bank.[48] The seconded executives were culled from twelve to six, by combining the roles of the senior representatives and area executives. The shareholder secondees became executive directors of Orion Bank, reporting to Montagu as well as their own banks, and directors of OMS.

Overall the changes strengthened David Montagu's authority and control and he was far from displeased. To dispel any doubts among the shareholders, he undertook 'categorically to ensure that shareholders' interests remain maximum priority and that the seconded executive directors will be fully in the picture of all Orion activities.'[49]

'Two years ago, the Orion banking group bore a greater resemblance to a clumsy quadruped than the noble constellation from which it derived its name,' wrote *Euromoney* editor Padraic Fallon in May 1976. 'For all the careful planning that had gone into its formation, for all its impressive list of shareholders and for all its profitability, it was not living up to its promise.'[50] And then Montagu took the helm, providing a strong sense of direction and inspiring personal loyalty among the staff, the missing leadership elements. 'I'm not a clever man, I'm not an entrepreneur,' said Montagu many years later reflecting on his contribution. 'I'm a people's guy and I've intuitive management skills which have borne fruit for the people who've been employed by me ... I think I'm the luckiest man I know in business.'[51]

CHAPTER 6

Petrodollars

*Mary Tudor, Queen of England, declared that the word 'Calais' was writ-
ten on her heart.[1] For many bankers, the place nostalgically etched on their
hearts was Jeddah's Kandara Palace Hotel, where their scramble for
petrodollars began.*

The twentieth century was the age of oil, but for the first seven decades most
oil producers received only modest benefits from their ownership of the
world's foremost fuel. This was especially so for the countries of the Gulf,
though most of them only emerged as major producers after the Second
World War. Even Saudi Arabia, with its vast reserves, found itself with a bud-
getary crisis in 1958.[2] But the glut of oil led to an announcement by the
major oil companies in 1960 that they were cutting payments to producers.
This led to the formation of the Organization of Petroleum Exporting
Countries (OPEC) that year.

The 1960s saw some modest movements in the share of profits in favour
of the oil producers, making them ambitious for more fundamental revisions
to their position. Those years also witnessed the rise of Libya as a major producer, loosening the grip of the seven major oil companies over the international oil trade. Both consumption and production rose rapidly in the
1960s, but by the end of the decade the former was beginning to outstrip
the latter. The boom in the Western economies of 1970–71 sent spot prices
soaring and made the members of OPEC impatient for a bigger slice of the
cake – especially as the real price of oil had declined over the decade.

The collapse of the established order in the oil industry began on 3 May
1970, when a cable-laying Syrian bulldozer ruptured the pipeline carrying
crude oil from Saudi Arabia to the Mediterranean loading port of Sidon.[3]
The episode brought to a head a dispute about transit dues and the pipeline

stayed closed for nine months. Weeks later, for unconnected reasons, Colonel Gaddafi's Revolutionary Command Council, which had seized power in Libya in September 1969, began to impose production cut-backs on Western oil companies to persuade them to concede better terms. Together, these measures deprived the oil industry of 1.25 million barrels a day, almost 10 per cent of Middle East output. With winter approaching in Europe, the oil companies gave in to the Libyans, triggering higher payments to the Gulf producers too.

OPEC FLEXES ITS MUSCLES

The OPEC conference in Caracas in December 1970 decided to seek yet further increases. When they were resisted by the oil companies and Western governments at a meeting in Teheran in January 1971, the producers threatened to stop all exports and again the companies capitulated. The Libyans reached their own agreement at a meeting in Tripoli in April 1971. The overall result of these developments was an increase in the price of Saudi Arabian Light 'marker' crude from $1.84 per barrel to $2.18 per barrel.

The devaluations of the dollar, in December 1971 and February 1973, led to compensating increases in the oil price. Discussions in Vienna between OPEC and the oil companies about further rises during the summer of 1973 dragged on inconclusively into the autumn. Then on 6 October, Egypt and Syria attacked Israel; politics and the oil price became inextricably intertwined. Exasperated by Western resistance, on 17 October the Gulf states announced unilaterally that they were hiking the price of marker crude from $3.01 per barrel to $5.11 per barrel. The Arab oil exporters also announced a boycott of the US and the Netherlands because of their support for Israel. On 22 December 1973, OPEC announced a further increase in the oil price from $5.11 per barrel to $11.65 per barrel. Overall, during 1973 the price had quadrupled.

The oil price rises, plus a revolution in producer 'participation' in the exploitation of their oil reserves, led to sharply higher revenues (see Table 6.1) for the oil exporting countries.[4]

Table 6.1   Oil exporters' income, 1970–80[5] ($ billion)

1970	1971	1972	1973	1974	1975	1976	1977	1978	1979	1980
17.3	22.1	23.9	37.0	117.3	109.0	133.4	145.5	141.9	223.4	270.1

Some of the oil exporters had large populations and the increased revenues were quickly earmarked for development projects or current consumption. Algeria, Ecuador, Indonesia, Nigeria and Venezuela fitted this bill, and in the Gulf, Iran and Iraq and, on a much smaller scale, Bahrain and Oman. But there was also a group of countries for which the revenues were so vast that, in the short-term at least, they would have large financial surpluses that would have to be deployed as deposits or invested. The foremost was Saudi Arabia, whose revenues soared from $7.8 billion in 1973 to $35.6 billion in 1974; then Kuwait, up from $3.8 billion to $11 billion, and United Arab Emirates (mainly Abu Dhabi), from $1.8 billion to $6.4 billion. Libya too had large surpluses.

For the Western economies, the impact of the oil price rises was grim. In 1974, inflation soared, with steep price rises not only for petrol but also for commodities such as wheat, sugar and maize. Stock market prices plunged. There was a sharp recession and unemployment rose. And there were fears of worse to come, that problems in the international banking system would trigger a 1930s-style international slump. Most of the non-oil-producing countries of the world faced severe balance of payments problems, particularly, but not exclusively, Third World countries. For them, but also for the owners of the oil-derived surpluses, the recycling of the petrodollar balances through international Western banks operating in the Eurocurrency markets was a vital requirement.

But Western banks had their own troubles. The demise of the Bretton Woods system of fixed-exchange rates led to greater currency volatility from 1973 and many banks sustained losses as they struggled to adapt to 'foreign exchange dealing in a sea of floating rates,' as Bank of England director George Blunden put it at the time.[6] Losses from foreign exchange business were sustained in 1974 by several major international banks – Union Bank of Switzerland, Banque de Bruxelles, Lloyds Bank, through its Lugano branch, and Westdeutsche Landesbank, to name but the biggest losers. Professor Dr Helmut Lipfert, the WestLB director in charge of the bank's international and currency business, resigned. Lipfert, a well-known and highly regarded expert on the foreign exchange market both in theory and practice, was closely involved in the early development of Orion and a member of the Orion Bank board.

DEPLOYING THE SURPLUSES

Over the years 1974–80, the oil-exporting countries accumulated $383 billion in financial assets from their current account surpluses. A high proportion of these assets was owned by the group of Arab surplus countries discussed above, particularly Saudi Arabia, Kuwait, Abu Dhabi and Libya; initially, much of it was held through their governmental agencies, such as the Saudi Arabian Monetary Agency (SAMA). The disposition of these financial asset acquisitions was as shown in Table 6.2.

International commercial banks, mostly in London and New York, were recipients of a total of $154 billion of short-term bank deposits. These deposits were a boon for the international banking system, furnishing banks

Table 6.2   Oil exporters: disposition of surpluses, 1974–80[7] ($ billion)

	1974	1975	1976	1977	1978	1979	1980	1974–80
Current account								
surplus	69	35	39	29	6	63	111	352
Other transactions*	−10	4	3	10	18	1	5	31
Cash surplus available	59	39	42	39	24	64	116	383
Disposition of								
surplus								
IMF and IBRD	4	3	2	0	−1	−1	1	8
LDCs	5	7	7	8	9	9	11	56
Bank deposits	30	11	13	13	5	40	42	154
Other†	20	18	20	18	11	16	62	165

* Net borrowing and other capital flows.
† Government securities, corporate stock, real estate.

with vast new loan funds and stimulating their international activities. But they also generated new challenges and risks: on the liabilities side, weakened deposit-to-capital ratios and new patterns of risk of deposit withdrawal; on the asset side, how to lend the petrodollars at a profit but without over-exposure to loan defaults. Resolution of these problems required a range of innovations, including improved credit information, better liability and asset management techniques, and enhanced country-risk analysis.

Only a small number of the largest and most prestigious Western banks were on the Middle Eastern monetary authorities' lists of approved institutions. For the prime banks, the flood of OPEC short-term deposits became something of an *embarras de richesse*; reluctant to turn away the funds, they quoted rates below the market – Orion's Spike Wright heard (unconfirmed) reports of deposits being taken at zero, and even negative, interest rates.[8] Gradually the list of approved banks grew, but consortium banks, such as Orion, merchant banks and smaller banks, tended not to qualify. However, they did receive petrodollar deposits indirectly, though more expensively, through the wholesale interbank market, their main source of funding, which enabled them to build up a large medium-term lending business.[9]

The oil-exporting countries' investments in a variety of financial and real assets in the industrial nations totalled $165 billion (Table 6.2). The total was composed of several types of lending to a range of borrowers: debt securities, the largest part, comprised both public bond issues and private placements, for both governments and corporations; equity investments were mostly of a portfolio nature, but there were also some substantial 'direct' investments in particular companies; a significant amount went into real estate; and some was kept as cash. LDCs received $56 billion, mostly in the form of grants to Islamic countries. Finally, $8 billion was the net amount lent to the IMF and other international organizations after some OPEC countries had drawn on them. Although most of the assets were in government hands, from the mid-1970s there were also large institutional and personal private sector flows from the Middle East, much of it unrecorded in official statistics.

The scale and speed of the growth of the flow of petrodollar funds necessitated the recruitment of experienced Western bankers by the Middle East monetary agencies as expert guardians of the surpluses. Most notably and shrewdly, SAMA appointed two medium-sized banks of the highest reputation, Baring Brothers and White Weld as their advisers. Individuals seconded to SAMA included Leonard Ingrams from the UK merchant bank and David Mulford from the American firm. 'At SAMA we arranged private placements with corporates and governments, established bond and equity portfolios and managed an active foreign exchange programme,' Mulford recalled.[10] 'SAMA's tax-free status and its ability to negotiate special arrangements allowed us to buy assets from Japanese government bonds to German *Schuldscheine*. We pushed open many doors.' Mulford subsequently became Under Secretary of the US Treasury for International Affairs and, later, chairman international of CS First Boston.

THE SCRAMBLE FOR BUSINESS

The petrodollar surpluses presented vast opportunities for banks as depositories and as intermediaries with the financial markets. But how did they get business from clients with whom most of them had no prior contact? Former diplomats and others with Middle East connections or Arabic language skills found themselves being tempted by lucrative offers to act as their ambassadors, knowledge of banking being not necessarily required. So too were ex-politicians with international reputations. George Ball and Henry Fowler, senior figures in the Kennedy and Johnson administrations, and partners at that time of Lehman Brothers and Goldman Sachs, respectively, visited to promote their firms in the Gulf. Reginald Maudling, a former UK chancellor of the exchequer, spoke for London stockbrokers Messels as well as Kleinwort Benson. An additional reason to be represented by such distinguished, evidently WASP (White Anglo-Saxon Protestant) figures was to offset any conceivable risk of the firms being thought to be supporters of Israel.

From beyond the Anglo-Saxon world, an eminent visitor was Pierre-Paul Schweitzer, recently retired French managing director of the IMF, who toured the region as chairman of Bank of America's new venture, Bank of America International. At the end of a long day, he called on Christopher Arnander, one of the Western bankers recruited by Kuwaiti investment bank KFTCIC, expecting to have to do yet another marketing pitch for a bank with as yet modest international and investment banking credentials, albeit then being the largest bank in the world. He seemed immensely relieved by Arnander's opening question, enquiring whether he was related to Albert Schweitzer, the Bach scholar, organist, medical missionary and Nobel Prize winner; he was his uncle, as was Charles Munch, conductor of the Boston Symphony Orchestra, who once remarked proudly to Leonard Ingrams, adviser to SAMA, *'c'était mon neveu qui a sauvé la livre.'*[11] From saving the pound, a recurring task during his decade at the IMF, to selling the Bank of America's wares in Kuwait was a striking change of *métier* for Schweitzer.

The OPEC surpluses presented opportunities for banks to provide a range of fee-earning advisory services, such as asset management, or to launch joint ventures with the common idea of matching OPEC financial resources with Western financial expertise. From all over the world came bankers, industrialists, politicians and officials, sometimes in large delegations, hoping to secure a piece of the action. A host of entrepreneurs and dealers (not to mention con men) converged on the Gulf, promoting all manner of schemes, some of them highly questionable, to the locals. Euan Macdonald, a Warburgs director, who had been managing director of International Financial Advisers in Kuwait in the 1970s, saw many of the same 'old Gulf hands' 20 years later in Moscow, battling for hotel and plane reservations, as they scrambled for lucrative deals in the post-Soviet gold rush; it was a case of *déjà vu*.[12]

Although subsequently the Middle East had many fine hotels, modern communications and excellent airports and airlines, in the early days of petrodollar recycling the situation was very different. For Western bankers, doing business in the region was a logistical nightmare beset at every turn by malfunctioning and insufficient telecommunications, unreliable mail services, rudimentary air and road transport, and bureaucratic red tape such as entry and exit visas.

The Kandara Palace, being Jeddah's only hotel of remotely Western standard, was where every 'visiting fireman' – bankers or businessmen trying to do deals – stayed. Or so they hoped. Even 'confirmed' reservations counted for nothing. Jeremy 'Jinx' Grafftey-Smith, of London merchant bank Wallace Brothers, used to travel light and sprint in his gym shoes from the airport, then only a few hundred yards away, to the Kandara Palace. Carrying his own soap and a range of variously sized bath plugs, he hoped to beat the rest of the plane's passengers, who were waiting in line for the almost non-existent taxis, to avoid sharing a room or even a bed. He entered the Orion story by becoming resident director of Orion's affiliate, Allied Investments, in Riyadh.

In the early days, the only telex machine in town, apart from at SAMA, across the road,[13] seemed to be at the Kandara Palace and the operator was able to charge monopoly prices for sending telexes. Sharp-eyed bankers were able to read their rivals' confidential messages, casually strewn around the operator's desk, as they waited interminably for their own to be sent. Telexing was so costly that in the middle of negotiating a $100 million private placement on behalf of an AAA sovereign borrower with SAMA, Orion's Andrew Large ran out of money. He had to despatch a junior colleague, Graham Wilkinson, to fly back to London to obtain Bank of England exchange control consent for a further currency allowance because the telex operator's bill came to £12 000.[14]

Then there was the wild life. The flock of goats that devoured the sent telex messages – and sometimes the unsent ones – performing their own sort of recycling. And the flies. On being informed by a client that his bathroom was infested with flies, the desk clerk shrugged and replied 'wait until lunch time, then they will all go down to the restaurant.' These were frontier conditions, but for players with ambition and tenacity, like Orion, the opportunities were unrivalled. 'They were very good scramblers,' commented a competitor.

ORION'S OPPORTUNITY

As a new bank with no deposit or client base, Orion had to scramble harder than most to win business. But in the Middle East where there were few established relationships it was the quality of proposals, the striking of friendships and the energy of executives that made the difference. Moreover, the strength and prestige of its shareholders were an advantage.

Orion's first foray into the Middle East was an extensive investigative and marketing tour of the region by William de Gelsey and Andrew Large in spring 1974. They reported that the main financial decisions, particularly in the oil rich countries, were taken on a centralized basis by a small number of people and that the development of 'personal relationships based on a high degree of confidence' with these key individuals was of 'paramount importance.'[15] This meant frequent visits to the region by de Gelsey, Large and Chataway. By no means ignoring other countries of the region, they focused their efforts on Kuwait, Saudi Arabia, United Arab Emirates and Iran.

The report noted that most of Orion's shareholders were 'well-known and highly respected' in the region and that its own efforts should be closely co-ordinated with those of the shareholders. Arguably Orion's greatest advantage was its association with Chase, which had begun to expand its presence in the region prior to the oil revenue explosion and had already developed close links with SAMA, for which it served as a major depository both in New York and London.[16] In 1973, SAMA commissioned Chase to organize, staff and manage the Saudi Industrial Development Fund, to provide subsidized loans to Saudi industrial projects. At the same time, Chase was also permitted to take a 20 per cent interest in, and manage, a new specialized consortium bank, Saudi Investment Banking Corporation, as a joint venture with Saudi institutions, 65 per cent, and other foreign banks, 15 per cent. Set up to make medium and long-term loans, it was some consolation for Chase not being able to open a branch, while its arch rival, Citibank, already had two; this was because of a Saudi moratorium on new branching other than for joint venture banks.

David Rockefeller, who had cultivated a personal relationship with many of the region's rulers, was regarded by them as American royalty and a true friend. Rockefeller's visits to Egypt in September 1973 and January 1974 were characteristic bank chairman to head-of-state relationship-building exercises, in this case fitting neatly with President Sadat's political agenda of disengagement from the Soviet Union and his move to a more pro-Western stance. One of the matters Rockefeller and Sadat discussed was the financing of the proposed Suez–Mediterranean Oil Pipeline (SUMED). Chase committed to a $80 million syndicated loan for the Egyptian General Petroleum Corporation as its contribution to the $400 million project, bringing in Orion as co-manager. Orion itself lent $9 million and the rest was subscribed by Chase and 16 other banks in June 1974. The SUMED loan was hailed at Orion as an 'example of the co-operation between Orion and its shareholders – Orion's placing power helped Chase to syndicate the loan successfully. Completion of the agreement provided financial circles in the Middle East with a significant confirmation of Orion's potential strength in that area.'[17]

PROMOTING THE KUWAITI DINAR

The oil price rises of 1973 sent Kuwait's surplus earnings soaring, massively increasing the scale of Kuwaiti investment around the world. Through the Kuwait Investment Office (KIO) in London, Kuwait discreetly accumulated large holdings on the London Stock Exchange and similar purchases were carried out through foreign bankers in New York, Frankfurt and Zurich. In September 1974, at almost the nadir of the UK stock and property markets, Kuwait outbid the insurance company Commercial Union with a £107 million offer for 100 per cent of St Martin's Property Company, which owned prime buildings in the City of London. By 1976, Kuwait owned 5–10 per cent stakes in an array of leading UK companies. It also made a number of high-profile purchases of strategic stakes in companies, including a large, and very profitable, minority stake in Daimler Benz from the Quandt family.[18] Kuwait was luckier than the Shah of Iran, whose attempt to buy the Flick family's 29 per cent holding in the company was thwarted by Deutsche Bank. It also bought Kiawah Island in South Carolina, which it developed successfully into a major resort. Later, it acquired controversial stakes in British Petroleum, Grupo Torras, Metalgesellschaft and Santa Fe International Corporation, a large US oil exploration company.

The de Gelsey–Large report on Middle East prospects identified involvement in the development of local capital markets as offering 'significant opportunities.'[19] The most developed financial market of the region was Kuwait, and Orion became closely associated with the development of the Kuwaiti dinar (KD) bond market in the years 1974–77.

Since the 1950s, Kuwait had harboured ambitions of becoming the Gulf's regional business and financial centre, based on its oil revenues and its expected long-term surpluses. The National Bank of Kuwait, the first indigenous bank and Kuwait's first public company, was founded in 1952. The following year saw the establishment of the Kuwait Investment Board (later the KIO) in London to invest the country's oil surpluses.[20] The 1960s and early 1970s saw the establishment of six more banks, three insurance companies and three investment companies, which operated in the manner of investment banks, known as the 'three Ks': the Kuwait Investment Company, Kuwait Foreign Trading Contracting and Investment Company (KFTCIC), and Kuwait International Investment Company. In addition, there were several smaller investment companies with some international bank ownership, several foreign exchange companies, a major governmental pension fund and other institutional investors. Together, these institutions constituted the most diversified indigenous financial sector of any Gulf state.[21]

There were also industrial, property, transport and service sector public companies. About half the aggregate equity was owned by the private sector and about half by the government, state sponsorship being a key element in Kuwait's development as a financial centre. By the mid-1960s, there was an active stock market in Kuwait in the shares of these banks and companies.

The KD bond market was much the most important in the region in the 1970s.[22] It was inaugurated in 1967 by a KD15 million private placement for the World Bank, followed by three further such deals over several years. The World Bank worked in close association with the Kuwait Fund for Arab Economic Development whose director general, Abdlatif Al-Hamad, was also chairman of United Bank of Kuwait and one of the leading financial figures in the Arab world.[23] The market took off in 1974, and over the years 1974–80 there were 61 issues that raised the equivalent of $1.4 billion (see Table 6.3).

The idea underlying the creation of the KD bond market was to create KD-denominated debt securities on behalf of high-quality foreign borrowers that would appeal as investments to Kuwaiti government and private sector investors. But there was a problem persuading AAA grade borrowers to use the market because they were wary of borrowing in an unfamiliar and little used currency. A serious worry was that the KD would become a very strong currency and appreciate massively, because of the surpluses being earned by Kuwait. In fact, borrowers fared well from their KD borrowings thanks to the stability of the KD and its good management by the Central Bank of Kuwait.

Table 6.3   KD Eurobond issues, 1974–80[24] ($ equivalent, million)

	Principal amount	Number of issues
1974	51.3	3
1975	181.4	9
1976	263.9	13
1977	106.0	7
1978	443.7	15
1979	372.8	13
1980	26.5	1
Total	1445.6	61

Orion played a significant part in promoting the KD bond market's development in the mid-1970s by introducing a number of first-class borrowers who were persuaded to use it by the argument that, as a petro-currency, in reality the KD was a US dollar substitute. The first and foremost was Österreichische Kontrollbank (OKB), a bank owned by the leading Austrian banks that served as the Austrian government's agent for guaranteeing and financing Austrian exports. Its issues enjoyed an AAA rating by virtue of the Republic of Austria's guarantee.

The origin of this business was a conversation between William de Gelsey, Wolfgang Schmitz, president of the Austrian National Bank, and Dr Helmut Haschek, chief executive of OKB, at the World Bank/IMF meetings in 1972, when de Gelsey suggested an internationally syndicated issue for OKB.[25] The Austrian authorities had long resisted the use of the Austrian schilling as an international currency, but they accepted de Gelsey's proposal that the schilling was only to be used as a currency index, with all payments being made in US dollars. The cost of borrowing in US dollars was expensive and the market was becoming unreceptive to US dollar issues because of its depreciation. The demand for securities denominated in Swiss francs and DM, especially in the Middle East, suggested that schilling issues would be well received. Moreover, in the aftermath of the oil price rises, Austrian government policy changed in favour of foreign borrowing to assist the country's balance of payments position.

Thus OKB received permission to make the first note issue denominated in Austrian schillings and appointed Orion to undertake the issue. De Gelsey and Haschek then decided also to use the opportunity to tap the liquidity of the KD market. In May 1974, they paid a joint visit to Kuwait and had discussions with the indigenous investment bank KFTCIC. This initiative resulted in a four-year private placement of KD2 million ($6.8 million) in August 1974, a KD5 million public five-year issue and a five-year OS275 million ($14.8 million) issue, lead managed by KFTCIC and co-managed by Orion. These issues, the first ever public note issues in Kuwaiti dinars and Austrian schillings, were described by an in-house newsletter as 'a double first for Orion.'[26]

Orion helped manage six further KD issues. Shortly after the OKB issue, it brought out a similar sized note issue for the Republic of Ireland. In 1975, it conducted two note issues for first-class Finnish borrowers. The Finns were particularly welcome borrowers in the Arab currency markets, Finland having never defaulted. It was on such business that the deputy governor of Finland's central bank, Pentti Uursivirta, visited Abu Dhabi. Learning that his client's hotel reservation had fallen through, William de Gelsey offered him Orion's accommodation. When an exhausted Michael Perry returned to his room, he found a bulky Finnish central banker asleep in his bed. Perry tactfully spent the night in an armchair in the lobby.

The series of high-quality offerings organized by Orion helped establish the KD bond market as a significant international capital market. Orion returned to the KD market in the late 1970s, with bond issues on behalf of Algerian, Brazilian and Finnish borrowers. In fact, the 1970s proved to be the high point of the KD bond market. Neighbouring countries did little to support Kuwait as a financial centre, preferring Bahrain as an off-shore centre, while tight domestic liquidity and high interest rates discouraged KD borrowers. In 1980 only a single issue took place, though there was some recovery in 1981 and 1982. But the collapse of the Souq Al-Manakh shares market in August 1982, which ruined many investors, tarnished Kuwait as a financial centre and the development of the KD bond market was stopped in its tracks.

ORION'S PRIVATE PLACEMENTS

Saudi Arabia, unlike Kuwait, harboured no aspirations to become an international financial centre, even though it had the largest surpluses. Its international investment programme was concentrated within SAMA. SAMA's approach to the management of the surplus revenues was influenced by the country's ambitious development plans, which led it to place a substantial proportion of funds on short-term deposit with Western banks with a view to them being readily available for expenditure. The recipients of these deposits were a limited number of prime institutions, such as Orion's shareholders. This was partly for administrative simplicity and partly because such major banks were the safest repositories.

SAMA and governmental agencies of the United Arab Emirates (UAE), such as the UAE Currency Board and the Abu Dhabi Investment Authority, were important takers of 'private placements'; they were less prevalent in Kuwait, because of the influence of the three Ks, which were interested in organizing public issues. Loans by way of private placement are direct transactions between a single borrower and a particular lender, intermediated by an investment bank. They avoid much of the cost of undertaking a public issue, to the advantage of both parties. They were often for much larger sums than most Eurobond public issues and the terms could be tailored exactly to meet the requirements of borrowers and lenders. For Orion, private placements provided an opportunity to do business with sovereign and other borrowers which would not award it a mandate to do a public issue because the appointment would disrupt established relationships with its investment bankers. But a discreet private placement was another matter.

Over the years 1975–79, Orion made private placements totalling $1.68 billion with monetary authorities and central banks, mostly in the Middle East, on behalf of Western governments and corporate borrowers. Public sector borrowers included the Republic of Austria, the Province of Quebec, Autostrade and the UK Gas Council. Orion helped several banks to use the private placement route, for instance, Creditanstalt, National Bank of Denmark, Mediobanca and European Investment Bank. Among non-OECD borrowers were Banque Extérieure d'Algérie, the Central Bank of Jamaica and the Beogradska Banka of Yugoslavia. A noteworthy transaction was a Dh200 million private placement for Banco Nacional de Obras y Servicios Públicos of Mexico, a rare example of an issue denominated in dirhams, the currency of the United Arab Emirates.

Orion was active in gaining mandates for private placements, which sometimes were placed in unlikely new markets around the world. Malta, for instance, having secured independence from Britain in 1964, became very close to one of its wealthy oil-producing neighbours; by the mid-1970s it was 'awash with Libyan dollars,' its foreign exchange reserves rising from $300 million in 1973 to $900 million in 1978.[27] Even supposedly impoverished Yemen caught Orion's attention. Realizing that the Yemen Arab Republic received substantial dollar remittances from Yemenis working in Saudi Arabia, it occurred to Orion executive Ton Detrie that the central bank might be interested in buying Eurobonds. At the time, in 1977, Orion was preparing a dollar-denominated public issue in the USA for SNCF (French Railways), but the US market had recently seen a spate of French issues and was 'a bit tired of French paper.'[28] Orion advised SNCF that the funds could be raised more cheaply as a Eurobond issue and simultaneously Detrie negotiated with the Central Bank of Yemen to take a substantial portion of the $45 million five-year issue of this AAA grade borrower as a private placement. With such a significant part of the issue firmly put away, marketing the rest went very smoothly.

The annual World Bank/IMF meetings each autumn were convenient forums for promoting Orion's services to governments and central bankers, but clinching a deal usually depended on 'shoe leather', mostly William de Gelsey's or Andrew Large's. It required particular fortitude to get into Libya, let alone to get appointments. Large recalled being almost expelled for having a copy of *The Economist* containing a cartoon depicting Khrushchev that was taken to be offensive to revolutionary socialism. But that episode wasn't nearly as hair-raising as when in Luanda, endeavouring to sell bonds to the recently created central bank of Angola, he fell into the hands of the secret police who accused him of being a South African spy. It was through such initiatives that Orion managed to build up its formidable placing power that won it new mandates from borrowers and a place in so many syndicates for public bond issues.

Not that opportunities nearer to home were ignored. North Sea Oil production led to a large increase in UK reserves. Orion persuaded the Bank of England to invest some of these funds in AAA Eurobonds, which was not its custom. By consistently briefing the Bank about the market, Orion became, for a few years in the late 1970s, the main supplier of Eurobonds to the Bank, until others realized what was going on and stepped in to join the party.

IRAN

The oil price rises of 1973 provided the Shah of Iran with the resources to pursue his vastly ambitious economic development programme and military build-up. His impatience overstretched the abilities of his administration to manage the expenditures and the process proved chaotic, wasteful and corrupt. The ports were choked with shipping that was unable to unload because of inadequate harbour facilities, running up huge demurrage bills. Khodadad Farmanfarmaian, one of the administrators of the Shah's Plan and Budget Organization early in the 1970s and a former governor of Iran's central bank, Bank Markazi, recalled urging the Shah to slow down and to build up foreign exchange reserves. 'What do I need reserves for?,' he replied. 'Our reserves are the vast oil resources under the ground.'[29]

Chataway's mandate from Montagu was to develop Orion's merger and acquisition activities. Although the first to admit that he knew next-to-nothing about banking, he had extensive contacts in business and politics and was himself a famous figure. In particular, he felt that there were good opportunities in Iran which had recently purchased a 25 per cent shareholding in the Krupp steel subsidiary, in the expectation that Krupp would establish manufacturing capacity in Iran, and was keen to make similar investments. 'So I rang the chief executives of a dozen British companies that I knew,' Chataway recalled, 'and said "have you anything you want to sell to the Iranians?" Five said yes. And we pulled off one deal.'[30]

Chataway spent a year commuting between London and Teheran, making an interminable round of calls on ministers and officials during the day and attending their parties at night. Since Iran did not have indigenous investment banks to intermediate such deals, all negotiations were at the political level. In fact, one of the Shah's ambitions was that Teheran should become a major financial centre with its own investment banks and it was partly to this end that Iran Overseas Investment Bank[31] was formed in London in 1973. As ever, accommodation was a problem, there being at the time only two hotels of acceptable standard, the Hilton and the Inter Continental. That was one of the reasons that Orion, like other banks, established an unofficial office in the Iranian capital, in which a dormitory was set up for clients who had failed to secure a hotel room. Two flats were bought in Bucharest Avenue and this 'low profile' office was manned for a couple of years in alternating stints by executives, Patrick Browning and Sandy Geddes.[32]

The deal that came off was the sale by Orion's existing client, Babcock & Wilcox, of its 25 per cent shareholding in its German associate, Deutsche Babcock & Wilcox, to the government of Iran in August 1975. The Iranians paid DM178 million (£34 million) to the major British machinery and plant construction firm headed by John King,[33] for its holding in the German concern. Orion initiated the deal and advised Babcock & Wilcox on its execution, and received a substantial fee for its work. Chataway's initiatives also resulted in Orion being retained by Imperial Group to investigate opportunities in Iran for its food and tobacco companies. Mardon Packaging, a joint venture by BAT and Imperial Group, did the same.[34]

While the Babcock & Wilcox deal was proceeding, Chataway was also negotiating with the Iranian Ministry of Health for a major hospital construction and management contract. Orion's appointment as financial co-ordinator for the United British Hospitals Group (UBHG) arose from its 14 per cent shareholding in the medical services company Allied Investments, one of the members of the UBHG consortium.[35] Its operations in Europe, the Middle East, Canada and Korea included advising hospitals, owning and operating nursing homes and rehabilitation centres, medical personnel agencies, and a health insurance company.[36]

The UBHG consortium included firms with every specialism required for major 'turnkey' medical projects, the construction work being undertaken by Trafalgar House. The project for which Orion acted as adviser was the construction and management of five hospitals in north Iran. It involved not only the design and construction of the hospitals, but also the provision of all technical and medical services for 6000 beds and the management and staffing of the hospitals for five years. The total value of the contract was estimated to be more than £100 million.

Rival bids were tendered by French, German and American groups, as well as by another UK consortium advised by Warburgs. On government prompting, the Orion and Warburgs groups combined to constitute a single UK bidder. Their perseverance was rewarded in May 1975 when the UBHG proposal, bound in the Shah's favourite shade of blue, was awarded the contract for Phase I, the design and planning stage. Negotiations also began about Phase II, the implementation phase. But it never happened, since Iran never paid.

Because of 'slowness' with Middle East contracts and poor results in the UK, Allied Investments found itself in 'serious difficulties' in 1977.[37] Montagu organized a rescue, bringing in the National Enterprise Board (NEB), a Labour government body established to invest in British industries of the future. A new holding company, United Medical Enterprises, was formed, owned 70 per cent by the NEB, and 10 per cent each by Orion, Commercial Union and London Trust which acquired Allied Investments. Montagu's financial engineering not only saved Allied Investments but rescued Orion's investment. Moreover, the bank was retained to act in the disposal of Allied's UK subsidiaries. Taking everything into account, Orion's net gain was £300 000. The notoriously tough Willard Butcher of Chase was impressed and he complimented Montagu and his team on doing 'a fine job in getting Orion out of the unsatisfactory situation.'[38]

As a result of Orion's financial restructuring, Allied Investments had sufficient credibility to land the contract to manage the Military Hospital in Riyadh in December 1977. This $350 million deal, one of the largest hospital management contracts ever awarded, was supervised by Allied's resident director there, Jinx Grafftey-Smith.

As it turned out, implementation of Phase II of the Iranian project would have been rudely interrupted by events in that country. In the autumn of 1978 a popular uprising, fanned by fundamentalist mullahs, who were outraged by the Shah's modernization of the country, and supported by a populace angered by rising prices and repelled by the regime's corruption, extravagance and pervasive secret police, resulted in his downfall early in 1979; the Ayatollah Khomeini left his Parisian exile and returned to proclaim Iran an Islamic republic.

For the Shah, David Rockefeller proved a friend in need, being one of the key figures who supported the deposed Iranian leader's admission to the USA.[39] The Shah's arrival in New York was quickly followed by the seizure of 52 USA embassy hostages in Teheran and the freezing of Iranian assets in the USA. Fortunately, the UK and other clients whom Orion had been advising on Iranian projects had all decided not to proceed.

CAUGHT IN THE ARAB BOYCOTT

February 25th is Kuwait's National Day. At this time of year, schools close for a few days at half term and Kuwaiti families take to the desert. Usually, there has been some rain, bringing out flowers and grass; there is a profusion of birds and small mammals. The air is cool and clear, a welcome respite from the hurly-burly of Kuwait City, and Kuwaitis enjoy reliving the simple life of their forefathers in their tents.

One day during the holiday of 1976, there was an incongruous sight: a taxi bumping along the rough desert tracks, carrying an elegant passenger, in City suit and Gucci shoes. Every so often, he would jump out of the taxi and ask a startled Kuwaiti for directions. The passenger was Orion's William de Gelsey, *wandervogel* of the Euromarkets, for whom Monday in Kuala Lumpur, Tuesday in Kuwait and Wednesday in Caracas was a normal start to the week. He was looking for Abdulwahab Al-Tamar, chairman of KFTCIC and he had come to eat humble pie. Orion had got itself entangled in the coils of the Arab boycott.

Set up by the Arab states as part of the confrontation with Israel, the boycott was administered by a bureau of the Arab League in Damascus. It sought to debar from Arab markets companies which invested in or otherwise supported Israel. Thousands of companies were on the boycott list, including Ford and Coca-Cola; the latter's presence on the list enabled a look-alike Kaki-Kola to flourish for a few years in Saudi Arabia and boosted Pepsi-Cola's business in the Arab world. The 1973 oil price rise increased the activity of the bureau; companies eager to enter the region had to be investigated, while others demanded to be taken off the list, on the grounds that they should never have been on it in the first place.

In the financial services sector, Barclays Bank was briefly on the list. Barclays had operated successfully for generations in the Arab world and was not thought of as a supporter of Israel; however, it found itself on the list when it converted branches in Israel, which antedated the creation of the Jewish state, into a locally incorporated joint venture. After a year or two, Barclays got off the list, but the episode highlighted the dangers and difficulties for banks wanting to tap the Arab markets. NatWest had pre-empted a potential problem by selling its stake in Rothschild Intercontinental Bank in 1969.[40]

Among investment banks, there were two particularly notable boycotted institutions, Rothschilds and Warburgs. The interpretation of the boycott for Eurobond issues was that Arab banks could not be in a management or underwriting group where one of the managers was on the boycott list; nor could Arab managers offer underwriting to a boycotted bank. If they did so, they would be parties to the same contract with the issuer and they might find themselves at the signing ceremony together. One way round the problem was to use the private placement route, without publicity or management group; this was the original plan for Orion's mandate to raise Middle East funds for the UK's Electricity Council in 1976, but on this occasion the Bank of England had asked Orion not to approach SAMA, the prime taker of private placements, because of a competing UK public sector transaction. De Gelsey's market soundings in the Middle East indicated that a public Eurobond issue, including Al-Tamar's KFTCIC as a manager, might produce the best result.

Back in London, de Gelsey called on Rodney Leach of Rothschilds and Martin Gordon of Warburgs, for whom the Electricity Council was a prize client; he felt sure they would 'understand' if they were not part of the underwriting group on this occasion. 'Understand' they most emphatically did not; within minutes, Siegmund Warburg sent Warburgs director David Scholey to call on Lord Rothschild and an early meeting with the governor of the Bank of England, Gordon Richardson, was requested. Later in the day de Gelsey was summoned to the governor's office and told to call off the issue; he protested haplessly that it was too late. The governor's steely reply was: 'I think that you will find that it is not too late.'

Thus it was that de Gelsey found himself in the Kuwaiti desert, looking for Al-Tamar. Upon receipt of the bad news that the issue was off, the courteous Al-Tamar did not disguise his disappointment but some of his colleagues were vitriolic at Orion's *volte face*. But de Gelsey was already off to Venezuela to try to salvage the business without the complication of the Arab boycott. His mission was successful. Orion put together a $50 million 5-year note issue for the Electricity Council, with nine co-managers, including Fondo de Inversiones de Venezuela, but no Arab managers, and with both Rothschilds and Warburgs as underwriters.

Sensitivity over the Arab boycott even led Orion to redesign its corporate logo. The original logo was a five-pointed star, but this became inappropriate with the admission of a sixth shareholder. It was feared that a six-pointed star might be mistaken for the Star of David, implying support for Israel. In November 1973, immediately after the Yom Kippur War, the star was replaced by a six-sided horizontal lozenge shape with the word ORION in the middle.[41]

Orion logo 1970–73

Orion logo 1973–81

Relations between Orion and KFTCIC were soon mended and Orion continued to do good business with it and other Middle East firms. The boycott itself became ever more difficult to administer effectively. Western governments, particularly the USA, applied great pressure to undermine it and it was subject to evasion by companies, through the creation of new affiliates and other means. In the financial sector, Warburgs were taken off the list in 1980 and actually appeared in the Arab-led management group of an FRN issue for Bank of Tokyo in that year. From the inauguration of the peace process in 1993, the boycott, though technically extant, became moribund. Saudis could then enjoy a real Coke and Pepsi had to look to its laurels in the Arab world.

PETRODOLLAR RECYCLING

The balance of payments deficits experienced by many countries in the aftermath of the oil price rises of 1973 were bridged by all manner of public and private capital transfers, including the IMF's oil facility for less developed countries established in 1974. But the foremost source of funding was short-term petrodollar deposits with the international banks that were on-lent by the banks in the form of syndicated loans.

Of course, in principle, these funds could have been lent directly by the surplus countries to deficit countries, and this was done to some extent both directly by Arab governments and by specialized institutions such as Arlabank International,[42] Arab African Bank and others. However, mostly the funds were placed with the leading Western banks. This intrigued John Gray, British Commercial Counsellor in Jeddah, who took the opportunity of a meeting with Sheikh Mohammed Abalkhail, long-time Minister of Finance and chairman of the Saudi International Bank,[43] to ask: 'Why do you lend your money to the Western banks, not to the Latin American countries direct?' Sheikh Mohammed replied: 'Because that way, it is the Western banks, not Saudi Arabia, that take any risk involved.'[44] Some borrowers tried to take advantage of Saudi good nature. There was an occasion, for instance, when Sudan took an international bank loan, guaranteed by SAMA. Observers wondered why SAMA did not make the loan itself; the reason was probably that the borrower would think twice before defaulting on an obligation to an international bank but might feel that SAMA was more forgiving.

Prior to the oil shock, access to the syndicated loan market had been restricted to the most creditworthy borrowers, but in the 1970s it became a lifeline for countries of somewhat less than impeccable credit status. One reason was that, at the time of the oil shock of 1973–74, many commodity prices were very high, so that many developing countries qualified for loans according to the usual country risk credit yardsticks. There was also a prevailing belief that sovereign lending was inherently safe since, as Citibank's Walter Wriston famously observed, people and corporations may go broke but 'countries don't go bankrupt,' to which sceptics replied 'but banks that lend to them do.'[45]

From 1974, Orion became active in petrodollar recycling through its management of syndicated loans to LDC and other countries to meet balance-of-payments shortfalls. Latin American borrowers accounted for the highest proportion of these loans, followed by Asian and then Soviet bloc countries. Some of them, such as Algeria, Indonesia, Mexico and Venezuela, were major oil exporters, deemed especially good credit risks because of their oil revenues. There were also many others from all corners of the world, including Brazil, Guyana, Jamaica, Trinidad & Tobago, Panama, Peru, Fiji, Malaysia, Philippines, Egypt, Poland, Yugoslavia and the USSR. Although syndicated lending to OECD countries continued to constitute the majority of Orion's loans, the proportion by value of LDC and other non-OECD countries rose from an average of 21 per cent in 1973–75 to 34 per cent in 1976–79 and reached 41 per cent in 1979.[46]

Orion's involvement in syndicated lending was to earn fees for its work as syndicate manager or co-manager and interest on the portion of the loan taken on to its own balance sheet. Although most of the loans it arranged were taken by other banks, the managers of syndicated loans usually retained a part of a loan in-house. In Orion's case, the volume of syndicated loans that it managed or co-managed rose from $1.2 billion in 1974 to $6.5 billion in 1979. Thus the greater the volume of Orion's syndicated loan activity, the greater its exposure to Third World debt. This was not a problem in the 1970s. But it became one in the 1980s.

CHAPTER 7

Competition and innovation

For the world financial markets, the years 1974 to 1979 were a period of instability and adjustment following the collapse of the Bretton Woods system and the oil price rises of 1973. For Orion, it was an era of growth and progress, under the leadership of David Montagu.

The end of fixed exchange rates naturally led to greater currency fluctuations. For the world's most important currency, the US dollar, the direction was mostly downwards, falling 30 per cent against the Deutschemark and 20 per cent against the yen between 1974 and 1979. Inflation was the highest for a generation, surging to 25 per cent in the UK in 1975. In the USA, the rise in consumer prices averaged 8.8 per cent in 1974–79, compared to 5.3 per cent and 6.1 per cent in the comparable periods before and after. Interest rates yo-yoed up and down as the authorities struggled to influence the level of economic activity, or some other moving target. Deficits and surpluses waxed and waned. International financial flows, particularly short-term flows, became bigger and bigger.

For the Euromarkets, the period began and ended with a financial crisis; the collapse of Bankhaus Herstatt in June 1974 and the so-called 'Saturday Night Massacre' of 6 October 1979. The intervening years saw substantial growth in both Eurocurrency syndicated lending and Eurobond issues. Petro-currency recycling and large-scale borrowings by deficit countries for balance-of-payments purposes were the fundamental forces driving the expansion of the Euromarkets in these years.

In the immediate aftermath of the Herstatt collapse, syndicated lending fell sharply and Eurobond new issues slowed to a trickle. Syndicated lending was lower in 1975 than in 1974, but the Eurobond market rallied and issuing activity was three times higher. The years 1976 and 1977 saw substantial increases in both forms of borrowing as global economic growth resumed. Syndicated lending continued to increase in both 1978 and 1979. But

Eurobond issues declined in 1978 and early 1979 in expectation of higher US interest rates to support the dollar. There was a vigorous recovery in the second and third quarters of 1979, but then the dollar went into 'another of its all too familiar sinking spells,' as Paul Volcker, the newly appointed chairman of the Federal Reserve put it.[1] To halt the dollar's slide, but particularly to confront the threat of a renewal of soaring inflation, on Saturday 6 October 1979 Volcker announced the adoption of a radical new monetary policy. The Fed switched from a Keynesian policy of interest rate targeting, under which short-term interest rates were relatively stable but at the cost of fluctuating and excessive monetary growth, to a monetarist policy of targeting the money supply, causing volatile short-term interest rates. This policy change, one of the key turning points in post-war financial history, was accompanied by a hike in US interest rates and an increase in banks' reserve requirements. The outcome for the dollar sector of the Eurobond market was 'the worst plunge people could remember,' producing total losses from new issues during the year of $360 million.[2]

EUROMARKET STAMPEDE

The second half of the 1970s saw yet more new entrants to the Euromarkets. Virtually every major bank with international operations or aspirations became active in syndicated lending. Between 1973 and 1980, the number of foreign banks with a representative office, branch, subsidiary or joint venture in London, where the bulk of the business was done, grew from 267 to 403 (see Table 7.1).

Table 7.1 Foreign banks in London, 1973–80[3]

	Directly represented	*Indirectly represented*	*Total*
1973	232	35	267
1974	264	72	336
1975	263	72	335
1976	265	78	343
1977	300	55	355
1978	313	69	382
1979	330	59	389
1980	353	50	403

Following the oil price increases of 1973–74, balance-of-payments financing for non-OPEC countries had the effect of greatly increasing the size of individual syndicated loans, which favoured the large banks; these banks were thus doubly blessed, because the new OPEC liquidity was deployed mainly with them. The increased competition and the volume of oil revenues seeking profitable employment through the international banking system depressed arrangement fees and spreads on syndicated loans, mean spreads over LIBOR falling from 156 basis points in 1975 to 77 basis points in 1979 (see Table 7.2), when their fall was arrested by a temporary withdrawal of Japanese banks from the market.[4]

Table 7.2   Mean spreads over LIBOR, 1975–80[5] (basis points)

1975	1976	1977	1978	1979	1980
156	152	128	98	77	73

The high inflation of these years in the UK had a severe impact on costs, particularly labour costs. In combination, falling spreads and rising costs significantly eroded the profitability of international commercial banking.

The Eurobond market also attracted new participants. Some of the early pioneers, particularly the relatively small London merchant banks, pulled out of the activity during the 1973–74 downturn and did not return. They were replaced by New York-based investment banks and the investment banking operations of the major European universal banks, especially the leading German and Swiss banks. Again, competition squeezed commissions while inflation increased costs, putting pressure on profitability.

INNOVATION

Innovation has been a key characteristic of the Euromarkets, whose very creation was itself one of the salient financial innovations of the twentieth century. Innovation has been especially marked in the Eurobond market, which has seen a long list of changes in the infrastructure of the market and in issue terms and procedures.[6] By the end of the 1960s, the Eurobond market had evolved an institutional framework and effective arrangements for issuing and clearing. The 1970s saw a set of innovations that expanded the product range and the competitiveness of the market, drawing business away from the national capital markets, which were hemmed in by exchange controls and other restrictions. There were three major new developments, as well as a host of enhancements of existing products or techniques.

The first major innovation was the floating rate note (FRN) in 1970, whose introduction has been discussed earlier (page 11). The innovative dimension of the FRN was the application of a variable interest rate, typical of bank loans, to a tradable security. It was a major milestone in the development of 'securitization', the substitution of marketable debt for bank debt. FRNs appealed to borrowers as an alternative to variable-rate bank credit because the interest rate was lower. The marketability of floating rate notes, which were only issued by prime borrowers, was attractive to investors.

The second major innovation was the firm bid issue or 'bought deal'. The first bought deal was a $200 million issue for Mobil Oil in January 1977, which was purchased outright by Union Bank of Switzerland.[7] Prior to the bought deal, Eurobond issues featured a two-week selling period, at the end of which the terms of the issue were finalized according to demand and market conditions. Issuers found this system unsatisfactory, since the final cost of borrowing was uncertain and they bore the risk of changes in market conditions. With a firm bid issue, the lead manager agreed a fixed price and other terms prior to syndication. Thus the risk of adverse developments in market conditions shifted from the issuer to the lead manager. This provided banks willing to assume such risks with an important addition to their competitive armoury. Again, the technique enhanced the attractions of the Eurobond market vis-à-vis the domestic capital markets. It also allowed more straightforward linkages of such issues to other financial market products, notably swaps.

The development of the swaps market in the late 1970s and early 1980s, was the third major innovation. Swaps were a dimension of the rapidly expanding financial derivatives market, a development almost as important as the Euromarket itself. In autumn 1967, Professor Milton Friedman of the University of Chicago correctly estimated that sterling was overvalued – it was soon to be devalued by 14.3 per cent – and tried to get Chicago banks to allow him to sell it short.[8] The bankers threw up their hands in horror, leading to Friedman's influential espousal of financial futures and derivatives. After the end of fixed exchange rates, increased currency volatility led to demand for an instrument that would allow corporations, banks and others to hedge their exchange rate risk and to undertake legitimate speculation. The financial derivatives markets began in May 1972, when the Chicago Mercantile Exchange (CME), a long-established commodities exchange, launched a currency futures contract with Friedman's encouragement and assistance. The contract, the first financial derivatives contract, was met with ridicule by bankers. 'New Game in Town' ran the headline to an article in the *Wall Street Journal* in which a foreign exchange dealer greeted the new market with the words: 'I'm amazed that a bunch of crapshooters in pork bellies have the temerity to think that they can beat some of the world's most sophisticated traders at their own game.'[9] Edmund de Rothschild, of the London merchant bank, declined an invitation to attend a launch conference, pointing out that there already existed 'a very highly sophisticated international market for foreign exchange operations in which the major banks of the world participate.'[10]

As well as currencies, interest rates and prices also became much more volatile than hitherto in the early 1970s, as a result of the oil price rises of

1973–74 and other destabilizing factors. Intellectual underpinning for the rise of financial derivatives was provided by the work on option pricing theory of Fischer Black and Myron Scholes, published in 1973.[11] In 1975, the Chicago Board of Trade (CBOT), Chicago's other great commodities exchange and the CME's arch rival, launched the first interest rate futures contract (see Table 7.3). The business really took off after the introduction of the Federal Reserve's new monetary policy in 1979. Chicago soon had new competition from the London International Financial Futures Exchange, founded in London in 1982, and futures exchanges in other financial centres around the world.

Table 7.3 Chicago financial futures, annual volume, 1972–80[12] ('000)

	1972	1973	1974	1975	1976	1977	1978	1979	1980
CME	134	285	128	150	250	888	2313	4131	9838
CBOT	–	–	–	20	128	438	1531	3600	8845

Swaps are contracts in which two parties exchange liabilities. They are used to change an existing exposure on account of a loan, security, currency or interest rate to a different exposure. For instance, from one currency to another, or from a fixed interest rate to a floating rate or vice versa. A capital market swap is a contract which provides for an exchange of liabilities between two or more parties that stretches several years into the future.[13] Currency swapped Eurobond issues and interest rate swapped Eurobond issues began in 1979 and 1981 respectively. These were major innovations in financing techniques that allowed issues to be undertaken in one market sector and swapped into another currency or form. Thereby, borrowers could raise funds in the market in which they had the highest credit rating and then convert them into the currency or form required at that moment. Thus they reduced the cost of borrowing. Crucially, swaps allowed arbitrage between different sectors of the market and between the Euromarkets and the national capital markets. They established important linkages between markets and allowed more effective liability management on the part of borrowers. The dynamic expansion of swaps and other financial derivatives was a key element in the globalization of finance; by the end of the 1980s, the CME and other exchanges were handling 250 million financial derivatives contracts a year and the total of interest rate and currency swaps was nearly $2 trillion. It had the incidental effect of dismantling the distinctions between different sorts of financial institutions, as commercial banks, investment banks and insurance companies all fished in the same pool.

Floaters, bought deals and derivatives were the most important of Euromarket innovations, but there was also a constant stream of relatively minor refinements – 'bells and whistles' – to the greater glory of the investment banks and the bedazzlement of clients. The market's infatuation with ever-more complicated structures was satirized by the *IFR* in a spoof announcement of an issue of Y50 billion triple currency 9.75 per cent perpetual notes for the imaginary Tokyo Fugu Fish Co. (Curacao) NV, named after the potentially deadly Japanese delicacy. Despite distinctly fishy features, such as 'money back if dissatisfied warrants' and a 'select group of Swiss "undertakers",' editor John Evans, recalled how: 'when the *IFR* hit the desks that Monday, Japanese bond houses throughout the world started to call around feverishly asking for allocations of Fugu bonds. Talk about taking candy from a baby.'[14]

There were also significant institutional developments, notably the creation of two clearing systems, Euroclear in 1968 and Cedel in 1971, which saved the aftermarket from collapse. Another was the introduction of the 'grey market' in 1978 by Stanley Ross, which transformed the nature of Eurobond investment banking syndicates and their commission structure through dealing before issue. Innovation helped transform the experimental market of the early 1960s into the largest capital market in the world, bigger than any national market.

ORION'S LENDING BUSINESS

In the second half of the 1970s, as in the first, syndicated lending was Orion's largest and most stable source of earnings (see Table 7.4). Between 1974 and 1979, the scale of Orion's syndicated lending activity as a lead or co-manager grew five-fold, from $1.3 billion to $6.6 billion. This rate of increase was faster than the market, and Orion's appearance in management groups was 10.6 per cent of all transactions in 1978.

Table 7.4   Orion Bank, lead and co-managed syndicated loans, 1974–79[15] ($ billion)

	1974	1975	1976	1977	1978	1979
Orion Bank	1.3	1.3	1.7	2.6	6.9	6.6
Market	19.4	19.6	27.4	38.9	64.8	77.6
Orion market share (per cent)	6.7	6.4	6.3	6.6	10.6	8.5

This growth in transaction volume was necessary to sustain income from syndicated lending on account of the fall in spreads already discussed (Table 7.2) and the declining level of arrangement fees, which fell by half between 1976 and 1979 (see Table 7.5).

Table 7.5   Orion Bank, syndicated loan arrangement fees, 1976–79[16] (per cent)

	1976	1977	1978	1979
Fees as proportion of loans arranged	0.109	0.074	0.046	0.053

The mid-1970s saw two significant shifts in the way that Orion conducted syndicated lending. In the early years, Orion derived most of its lead or co-management positions in lending syndicates from introductions made by one of its shareholder banks. Moreover, it placed a substantial proportion of its syndicated loan participations with the shareholders. In fact, the general perception in the market was that Orion was a 'captive' loan syndication unit for the shareholders. From the mid-1970s, while sustaining a special relationship with the shareholders, Orion conducted syndicated lending with an ever lengthening list of other banks and Orion-originated deals predominated. From 1971 to 1976, the shareholders took 24 per cent of loans in which Orion played a management role, but by 1977 the proportion had dropped to 10 per cent.[17]

Orion's growing independence in the conduct of syndicated lending was the outcome of the exertions of its executives, but also the expansion of the shareholders' own Eurolending activities. As leading international banks, the shareholders became major participants in syndicated lending in the second half of the 1970s. They developed Euromarket syndicated lending to support and strengthen client relationships, diversify their activities, utilize increased domestic liquidity and enhance their standing as leading international banks. As their Euromarket operations expanded, the shareholders became keen to be seen leading transactions in their own name and not through an affiliate.

Three large syndicated loans led by Orion warrant special mention. Two of them were 10-year multi-currency syndicated loans for UK borrowers in 1974. The first was $500 million raised for the Greater London Council; a transaction that took place against a very bleak background for the UK, with the chancellor negotiating massive loans from the IMF. At this critical juncture, the Orion's shareholders acting in concert put up a $2.5 billion bank loan for the UK government – a deal initiated over lunch at Orion's office. The second, rather less happy, large loan arranged by Orion was $420 million for Burmah Oil Company, for the purchase of US oil company Signal Oil and Gas. Burmah's historic shareholdings, 21.5 per cent of BP and 2 per cent of Shell, tended to overshadow the rest of its business. Thus the company made energetic efforts to diversify through the Signal acquisition and otherwise, but the falling share price of BP, collapsing tanker revenues and high interest rates brought the threat of default at the end of 1974. The Bank of England stepped in and guaranteed Burmah's borrowings, controversially taking control of Burmah's shareholding in BP as security. Burmah's own shareholders were disenchanted at the loss of this prime asset at a knock-down price, but the company was thereby saved from having to default on its loans.[18] The banks eventually received repayment through the sale of Burmah's North American assets.[19]

The third transaction was the earliest Eurocurrency syndicated loan raised by the European Economic Community in its own name, in 1976.

Two Community entities, EIB and ECSC, had already been borrowers, but the oil shock of 1973–74 made it desirable to increase recycling options through the Community itself, so as to facilitate loans to countries with balance of payments difficulties. John Nash, a former banking colleague of David Montagu, had become Director of Monetary Affairs at the European Commission. Nash felt that an effective way of raising a $300 million loan would be to mandate Orion and European Banking Company jointly to do the job, having in mind that the two consortium banks were owned by 13 of the largest banks in the world; it looked like a ready-made syndicate. The deal was successful, though not without a certain tension arising between EBC and Deutsche Bank, one of its shareholders, which was hoping to arrange its own financings for the EEC; this was not the only occasion on which EBC and Deutsche Bank clashed, an example of the problems that could arise when consortium banks and their shareholders were engaged in chasing the same clients.[20] Later, in the same year, the EEC made large Eurobond issues, choosing as lead managers the foremost Eurobond bank of each member country; this formula caused mandates to be awarded to Deutsche Bank in Germany and Warburgs in the UK, but excluded both EBC and Orion.

Orion's management endeavoured to build on relationships established through lending operations to promote its investment banking and other services. They enjoyed some success, and by mid-1978 there were 30 clients for which Orion had managed both loans and bond issues, including Alcan, Canadian Pacific, Comisión Federal de Electricidad, International Telephone & Telegraph and Svenska Varv. At the time, the provision of an integrated commercial and investment banking service under one roof was relatively unusual, providing Orion with a competitive advantage in serving some clients. It also assisted with the promotion of Orion's investment banking business.

Table 7.6   Orion Bank, geographical distribution of the loan portfolio, June 1978[21] (per cent)

Region	
Western Europe	51
Central and South America	15
North America	11
Eastern Europe	9
Far East/Australasia	6
Africa	5
Middle East	2
Caribbean	1
	100

Orion's own loan portfolio continued to be oriented towards Western European or North American borrowers. However, an internal analysis in June 1978 (see Table 7.6), revealed that 39 per cent of the bank's lending was to other countries, including 15 per cent to Latin America; this exposure carried the seeds of the bank's future difficulties.

EUROBONDS: ORION JOINS THE TOP TEN

Orion made only modest headway in developing securities origination business in its first five years. Although the credibility conferred by its shareholders facilitated early entry into the underwriting and selling groups of international issues, it proved difficult to win mandates to lead manage issues or secure co-manager positions.

The second half of the 1970s was Orion's heyday as a Eurobond lead manager. Between 1974 and 1979, the volume of issues lead or co-managed by Orion grew from $192 million to $1.9 billion (see Table 7.7). Its appearance in management groups rose to 13.1 per cent of all issues in 1979.

Table 7.7   Orion Bank, Eurobonds lead and co-managed, 1974–79[22] ($ million)

	1974	1975	1976	1977	1978	1979
Orion Bank	192	391	1 128	1 752	1 444	1 897
Market	1 937	7 282	12 915	15 742	12 254	14 487
Orion market share (per cent)	9.9	5.3	8.7	11.1	11.7	13.1

In the latter 1970s, Orion was one of the top-ten lead managers of all Eurobond issues (see Table 7.8). It was the only consortium bank and the only *de novo* creation to achieve this success. All the others were established

Table 7.8   Lead managers, Eurobonds, 1976–78[25]

	US$ equivalent (millions)	Number of issues
Deutsche Bank	7003	84
Westdeutsche Landesbank	2842	70
Credit Suisse First Boston/White Weld	2876	64
S.G. Warburg	2340	57
Morgan Stanley	2008	42
Union Bank of Switzerland	1970	23
Dresdner Bank	1944	61
Commerzbank	1228	27
Orion Bank	*1044*	*27*
Hambros Bank	832	18

entities, or affiliates thereof, and in six cases enjoyed the benefit of a strong domestic currency (the Deutschemark or Swiss franc) and protection from their governments to achieve a place in the top-ten league table.[23] Becoming a member of this club was, in the words of Orion's William de Gelsey, 'a truly staggering achievement' for an upstart institution with no established client or investor relationships and no government support.[24]

ORION'S PLACING POWER

How did Orion rise from nothing to being one of the world's top international investment banks in the second half of the 1970s?

There were two principal reasons: its energetic exertions to secure new issue mandates from borrowers; and the successful placement of securities with end investors. The latter factor became important from the middle of the decade. In the aftermath of the oil price rises of 1973–74, Orion developed significant placement power with the central banks and other institutions of Middle East oil surplus countries. Inspired by their success with Middle East central banks, Orion executives thought laterally and developed placement capacity with a wider group of central banks and other institutional investors.

Most of the banks that originated the early Eurobond issues, from 1963 onwards, such as Warburgs, Hambros, Rothschilds, Deutsche Bank and Morgan Stanley, did not have a tradition of marketing securities outside their own client base; they would have considered it rather below their dignity. They saw themselves as merchant or investment bankers, not bond salesmen. They relied on brokers to sell the securities they issued or placed them with a traditional range of domestic investors, such as 'captive' insurance companies for US investment banks or the legendary 'Belgian dentist'. White Weld, building on its strong Swiss connections, was one of the early participants to understand the need for a network of international investors to be 'good' buyers and firm holders of Eurobonds; Orion a decade later followed the same route. As William de Gelsey explained: 'Necessity made us concentrate on placing as we realised that unless we had something special to offer to potential borrowers we would not be able to break into the major league of issuing banks.'[26] For both, it was a policy which brought considerable success in obtaining Eurobond management roles.

Orion was resourceful at finding untapped markets for placement, such as Yemen and Malta, discussed above (page 102). In Europe, for example, it worked frequently with Bank Leu, which, although one of the Big Five Swiss banks, had negligible international exposure, to provide major, confidential financings for Orion's top-rated government clients. One such was the Kingdom of Sweden, which agreed to a major private placement in Switzerland through Orion on the strict understanding that Sweden must not previously have borrowed from the then unnamed bank. In due course, the Swedish authorities confirmed, as expected, that they had no relationship with the venerable Bank Leu. The Swedes and Orion alike were horrified when the chairman of Bank Leu opened the signing ceremony by welcoming back their old client – three centuries earlier the bank had financed the wars of King Gustavus Adolphus.[27]

Placing power was one of the strengths that Orion could offer to borrowers when it bid for lead management mandates, and was an important reason why other banks invited it to become a co-manager of the issues they were lead managing. Orion's placing and new issue origination work explains its remarkable record in the US dollar sector of the market, the largest and most competitive sector, in which, according to an internal report, it ranked fifth largest by number of issues lead managed in 1976 and 1977, after Warburgs, Credit Suisse White Weld, Morgan Stanley and Deutsche Bank.[28]

The energy, enterprise and professionalism of the team of capital markets executives was a vital human factor. As already related, the advent of petrodollar recycling provided them with a once-in-a-lifetime opportunity to develop new business in the Middle East and beyond, and they pursued it relentlessly. They were equally vigorous in marketing Orion's services to new corporate clients and brought a host of first-time borrowers to the Eurobond market.[29]

They exploited opportunities in markets where the indigenous investment banks – if any – had little international clout. For example, they arranged private placements in the Middle East for Swedish shipyards Götaverken and Kokkums, to the consternation of the Swedish banks. Another example was Orion's first Eurobond issue on behalf of Canada's Export Development Corporation, at which the Canadian securities houses 'went bananas.'[30] However, it wasn't long before other investment banks began distributing and trading Eurobonds, operating in the Middle East and marketing to central banks, eroding the niche opportunities that Orion had been quick to exploit. Nor did it take much time for Swedish and Canadian banks to begin to fight back to retain 'their' clients. Thus, Orion's advantages were eaten away and it was unable to maintain a position among the top-tier Eurobond houses, despite a large increase in its business.

ORGANIZATIONAL STRENGTHS

Orion's innovative form of internal organization was a hidden strength. The normal practice in UK merchant banks in the 1970s was for each senior figure to have a team of junior executives who worked exclusively for him. Philip Hubbard, who was brought in by David Montagu and John Haley to run the corporate finance department, radically reorganized it along the lines of Morgan Stanley where he had worked previously.[31] He established a pool of juniors who worked for all the seniors, being assigned to new projects as they finished other ones. This system, which was administered through a monthly assignment list, benefited the firm because it created a set of junior executives with a broad range of experience and it curtailed internal empire building. It also allowed juniors to work for a range of seniors and was helpful in considering annual promotion reviews and career development. This organizational form became the norm in London investment banks in the 1980s, but in the 1970s it was a noteworthy strength.

The depth and rigour of Orion's market research were again an innovation in the 1970s. Under Hubbard's supervision, Orion's junior executives produced occasional papers and technical data, notably the *Funds Reflows into the Eurobond Market Report*, published annually in the late 1970s.[32] Such reports helped with appraisal of the market and gave Orion's marketing executives an edge over the competition; for instance, the quality of Orion's research reports was a factor that persuaded the Bank of England to make its first Eurobond purchases through Orion. Orion's influence with a wider circle of central banks grew through these reports, which became, in due course, the *Orion Royal Guide to International Capital Markets*, published by Euromoney Publications.

TAPS AND SWAPS

Innovation was a factor in Orion's success. Orion introduced a number of key Eurobond innovations, which besides providing original and effective solutions for clients, enhanced the bank's reputation in the market. The first was the 'multiple tranche' or 'tapstock' issue, which allowed a delayed drawdown of funds. The original financing of this kind, modelled on the UK Treasury's Tap Stock issues, was proposed by William de Gelsey and Michael Perry to Dr Helmut Haschek of OKB in 1977.[33] It provided for the authorization of a total amount of $200 million of bonds, of which only $100 million was offered initially. The remainder was to be purchased from the issuer and placed with investors as market conditions permitted. The price of subsequent tranches would be fixed by negotiation between the issuer and the lead manager at the time.

Orion also made a significant contribution to the development of the swaps market, pioneering the first currency swapped Eurobond issue in September 1979.[34] The borrower was Roylease, Royal Bank's leasing subsidiary, which awarded Orion the mandate on the basis that the cost of funds would be less than 11 per cent. 'We decided that we could use some money for the leasing company,' explained Royal Bank executive Robert Paterson, who had worked with Orion on Royal Bank's international funding for several years.[35] 'We said to Orion: see what you can get. We'll borrow anywhere provided there's no currency risk and provided the cost is less than borrowing in the Canadian market.' It was a challenging mandate for Orion,

since the US and Canadian currencies were sliding against the Deutschemark and the other hard currencies despite rising North American interest
rates, a double disincentive for European investors to buy Canadian or US
dollar bonds. Philip Hubbard's solution was to arrange a DM60 million
issue lead managed by WestLB and co-managed by Orion, and he then
swapped the proceeds two-thirds into Canadian dollars and one-third into
US dollars. The Deutschemark issue had a cost of borrowing of 6.9 per cent,
to which the swaps added 3.5 per cent in US dollars and 4.05 per cent in
Canadian dollars, resulting in total costs of 10.4 per cent in US dollars and
10.95 per cent in Canadian dollars. Paterson estimated that the novel swap
technique saved Roylease 0.5 per cent over alternative forms of financing.
This financing featured as one of *Institutional Investor* magazine's 'Deals of
the Year'; the technique subsequently became widely used.

A perceived lack of shareholder backing for Orion's efforts to develop
Eurobond business became a matter of dissatisfaction in the latter years of
the 1970s, as discussed in the next chapter. Royal Bank and WestLB were
largely exempt from Orion's complaints. With assistance from Royal Bank,
Orion was one of the three houses that developed the Canadian dollar sector of the Eurobond market, which began in mid-1974. Orion soon
emerged as the market leader in the Canadian dollar sector, lead or co-
managing 20 issues in the years 1975–79. The four issues it lead managed
for Royal Bank became the sector's benchmark bonds, one being the longest
Canadian dollar issue, another the lowest coupon issue.[36]

INTERNATIONAL MERGERS AND ACQUISITIONS

A corporate advisory capacity, focusing on cross-border merger and acquisition work for multinational corporations, was established under the leadership of Christopher Chataway in 1974. This was part of the strategy of
extending the range of services offered by Orion, enhancing its capability as
a one-stop international investment bank for clients who would avail themselves of a number of Orion's services. It was also expected to be a profitable
activity in its own right. However, as with the early Eurobond business, the
absence of a client base presented 'formidable difficulties' for the development of merger and acquisition work.[37]

The connections of the shareholders conferred scant advantage, since
most European and North American corporations had long-standing ties
with established investment banks that handled 'this particularly sensitive
area of work.'[38] The most tangible act of support given by the shareholders
was the entrusting to Orion of the sale of the shareholdings of NatWest and
Chase in Standard Chartered Bank in May 1975. These had been acquired
in 1965, when Standard had acquired another bank in which NatWest's
forerunners had shareholdings and Chase had made a friendly strategic

investment.[39] When Chase was obliged to dispose of its shareholding by the US regulatory authorities, NatWest followed its lead. These transactions and Orion's role in them attracted considerable attention, prompting the *Daily Telegraph* to comment that 'David Montagu is starting to take Orion Bank into the big league of merchant banks.'[40]

The merger and acquisition team targeted newly oil-rich clients without established investment bank relationships. Among the deals they brokered was the sale of the Dorchester Hotel on two occasions: it finally ended up in the hands of the Sultan of Brunei. They also focused on assisting European corporations with acquisitions in North America. Chataway spent much time in the USA and Canada, particularly the latter where he worked closely with Royal Bank, developing merger and acquisition opportunities, but also marketing Orion's services in general to Canadian clients.[41]

THE ORION GROUP

The various entities that comprised the Orion Group became firmly established, and mostly profitable, in the second half of the 1970s. Faced by losses of £100 000 at Orion Pacific at the end of the first year of operations, the shareholders became eager for closer control over management.[42] Prompted by the Bank of England's questioning of Orion about the $100 million advance it had on its books to Orion Pacific, it was decided to change the ownership structure and bring the Hong Kong entity under the ownership and overall control of Orion, London.[43] This was accomplished by exchanging Orion Pacific shares for Orion shares in February 1976.[44] At the time, Orion Pacific had a staff of 24 and total assets were £96 million, compared to Orion Bank's total assets of £715 million. It was already established as a leading Eurocurrency loan manager in the Pacific Basin region. Some early milestones were its co-management of a $400 million syndicated loan for the Mass Transit Railway Corporation of Hong Kong, and loans for the Federation of Malaysia and the Indonesian National Telecommunications project. Orion Pacific moved into the black in 1976, and by 1979 profits after tax were $1.5 million.[45] The Nikko Securities 5 per cent minority interest was bought out in 1981.

The other dimension to Orion's international presence was the representative office it opened in New York in spring 1974, at 70 Pine Street in the heart of the financial district. Described at the time as 'a natural development of the Orion network,' its functions were to act as a liaison channel to the important North American capital markets and to contribute to Orion's marketing efforts.[46] The office was placed under the control of the chairman of Orion Pacific, Robert Hall, an American investment executive who had worked on Wall Street for many years.[47] By 1978, some of the shareholders had become sceptical of the value of this 'expensive outpost' in the context of mounting discontent about Orion's financial performance.[48] Montagu mounted a robust defence of the New York representative office at the Shareholders' Forum in February 1979, receiving support from Chase, and Orion's Wall Street outpost survived the challenge.[49]

Orion Leasing Holdings did not initially live up to expectations and it was not until 1977 that the operations became profitable.[50] The scale of activity increased substantially from 1976 and by 1978 profits were reported to be running at $2 million per annum.[51] On the basis of this track record, the strategic review of July 1978 identified the expansion of leasing as second only to increasing Orion's own capital markets activity as the way forward for the firm.[52] But this approach was called into question only a few months later when a substantial loss was made on a leasing transaction with the German B.A.W. Group.[53] Although Orion continued to increase its leasing business, the scale of the ambitions was curtailed.

Orion Bank (Guernsey) Limited, a wholly owned subsidiary, began operations in September 1973.[54] The Guernsey operation was a useful source of deposits, in both sterling and foreign currencies from Channel Island residents and further afield. It offered a range of international banking services, but most of its business was medium-term lending. Located in the building occupied by Royal Bank, it was run by George Westbury, a former manager of Chase's branch in Belfast. The Guernsey operation was consistently profitable, profits after tax rising from £100 000 in 1974 to £467 000 in 1979.

PERFORMANCE, 1974–79

Orion's pre-tax profits more than doubled between 1974 and 1977, from £4.9 million to £10.2 million. In 1975 and 1976, it achieved a handsome 27 per cent pre-tax rate of return, its best ever performance. The rate of return slipped slightly in 1977 because capital and reserves grew more rapidly owing to large retentions, but it was still a very respectable 25 per cent. In 1978 and 1979, profits declined, despite increased contributions from Orion Pacific, the Guernsey operations and leasing. The combination of declining profits and rising capital and reserves led to a steady fall in the pre-tax rate of return, which by 1979 was down to 16.1 per cent (see Table 7.9).

Table 7.9   Orion Bank, performance, 1974–79[55] (£ million)

	1974	1975	1976	1977	1978	1979
Profit (pre-tax)	4.9	7.4	9.7	10.2	10.1	8.5
Capital and reserves	23.7	27.3	35.9	39.9	46.8	52.9
Return (pre-tax) (per cent)	20.7	27.1	27.0	25.6	21.6	16.1

Orion's strong performance in 1974–77 was mainly due to the pick-up in its Eurobond business, to its sizeable syndicated lending activities and to a substantial increase in the scale of lending activities, loans outstanding growing from £489 million to £824 million. The decline in 1978 and 1979 was the outcome of a combination of factors, which an internal analysis divided into 'market risks' and 'avoidable risks.'[56] The adverse market risk factors have already been discussed: increased competition from new entrants, falling lending spreads and fees, the vicissitudes of the Eurobond market, and cost inflation. A further factor beyond the control of Orion's management was the shifting sterling–dollar exchange rate. The appreciation of sterling, by now being seen as a petro-currency, which between December 1976 and December 1980 rose from $1.70 to the pound to $2.39, reduced the sterling value of Orion's profits, which consisted of predominantly dollar-denominated income and sterling costs and substantially reduced reported profits.[57]

Orion's performance in the second half of the 1970s was also blighted by a pair of 'avoidable risks,' both of these unfortunate decisions being taken in the period between the departure of Grierson and the arrival of Montagu. The first was Orion's smart new premises at 1 London Wall, which were purchased in October 1973 at the peak of a commercial property boom. With the onset of recession, the following year, property values and rents plummeted. A review conducted in 1980 estimated that Orion was paying £400 000 per year in excess of the market rental and that the capital value of the building was still less than had been paid seven years earlier.[58]

The second avoidable risk was Orion's involvement in shipping finance. In spring 1973, Orion took a 20 per cent shareholding participation in the Liquimarine Consortium that was formed to provide equity and debt finance for the construction of two Liquid Petroleum Gas (LPG) carriers at $30 million each and a Liquid Natural Gas (LNG) carrier for $100 million.[59] Orion's investment was held by a specially created wholly-owned subsidiary, Orion Shipping Holdings Limited. Other members of the consortium included the leading banks Marine Midland, Continental Illinois, Union Bank of Switzerland and Guinness Mahon, and the operator was the highly regarded Norwegian shipping company Leif Hoegh. At the time of commissioning, charter rates were buoyant and Orion looked forward to above average rates of return on its funds and a profit on the building contracts.[60] But the outcome was very different.

By the time the vessels were delivered in 1977, demand for energy had dropped because of the oil price rises, and all three went straight into lay-up in Norwegian fjords. Instead of generating handsome returns, Orion Shipping was a millstone round Orion's neck, costing hundreds of thousands of pounds per annum in lay-up charges and interest. At the end of 1978, Orion's exposure to the Liquimarine Consortium was calculated to be $37.9 million, which was around 40 per cent of Orion's capital and reserves.

It was not until 1979 that the situation began to be resolved. That year saw the sale of one of the LPG carriers, the *Hoegh Swallow*, which cut Orion's exposure to $29.5 million and slightly reduced the on-going losses.[61] Negotiations to sell the other LPG carrier, the *Hoegh Swift*, dragged on through 1980 and it was eventually disposed of in 1981. Even more important was the chartering of the LNG carrier *Hoegh Gandria* to the Abu Dhabi Gas Liquefaction Consortium in spring 1981. It was estimated that together these transactions would save Orion $1.7 million per annum in carrying charges.[62]

Orion's declining profits and rate of return made David Montagu pessimistic about business conditions in the Euromarkets in general and about Orion's prospects in particular. In the chairman's statement in Orion's report and accounts for 1978, he publicly voiced his concerns: 'It becomes increasingly difficult to forecast future earnings in a business which is so dependent upon currency stability and interest rate movements, coupled with the fact that political uncertainty in various areas may inevitably be reflected in the behaviour of the markets,' he declared. 'It is difficult to imagine a more depressing background to international business.'[63]

CHAPTER 8

Shareholders and management

'Question – what is the difference between a child and a robot? Answer – a child grows up': an Orion executive.[1]

CHILDREN AND PARENTS

Most of the London consortium banks, including Orion, were established in the late 1960s or early 1970s. The objective of the shareholder parents, mostly large commercial banks, in this formative 'childhood' phase, was to test the water in international banking in a prudent and modest way by sharing risks and costs. Joining a consortium enabled them to provide Eurocurrency services for their clients and for their executives to gain experience in international banking. It was also hoped that participation in the booming Euromarkets would be a profitable investment, but this was not always the primary motivation.

In the second half of the 1970s, the relationship between the 'grown-up' consortium banks and their commercial bank parents entered a new and more problematic phase. The massive increase in the size of the international financial markets, in the wake of the oil price rises, had dispelled doubts that the Euromarkets were there to stay, and any bank with international ambitions had to have a presence in them. Thus shareholders put their experience as participants in consortium banks to good use developing their own international banking capabilities. This made them less reliant for services on the consortium banks in which they were participants, and even brought them into competition. It made the parents less willing to commit further capital to their offspring, and less prepared to channel Euromarket business to them. Once a bank had the capability to do international business, why not handle deals in-house? Why split the proceeds with a set of other banks, which increasingly were rivals in the international arena?

On the other hand, as ever in international banking, it was useful to have special friends to be able to turn to for commercial information or when reliable overseas partners were needed. The participants in a consortium bank constituted the membership of an exclusive international banking club, an aspect that was highly valued by some consortium bank shareholders. But the 'club factor' complicated the already problematic task of managing the offspring.

The management of the consortium banks began with two principal objectives. First, to service the Eurocurrency requirements of their shareholders, in so doing allowing the owners to gain insight and experience into the international financial markets. Second, to make profits. By the mid-1970s, the managements of many of the consortium banks were having difficulties fulfilling either objective. As the parents themselves developed international banking capabilities, the service function became more and more redundant. But at the same time, profits became harder to achieve, initially because of the Herstatt crisis and its aftermath, and then because of increasing competition, rising costs and falling fees and spreads. Poor profitability led to criticism from the parents. This prompted the managements of the offspring to demand greater independence of parental controls, to be better able to pursue profitable opportunities as and when they occurred. But the more independent the offspring became, the less they met the service requirements of their parents. They evolved into mere 'trade investments', whose value was to be judged by their return on capital. However, the club factor compromised this performance yardstick. For both parties, it was a situation fraught with potential for friction and frustration.

FRICTION WITH SHAREHOLDERS

As Orion's shareholders developed their own international capabilities, their objectives for owning a part share in a consortium bank became less coherent and less consistent. What they did see eye-to-eye about was that they liked being members of the Orion 'club'; it was viewed as such by the chairmen and chief executives, although it was not formalized like the European banking clubs, such as EBIC or ABECOR.[2] In fact, what they wanted was Orion club membership plus the freedom to develop their international and investment banking activities as they saw fit. That these things were contradictory wasn't their problem. But it was David Montagu's.

Montagu's ambition was to make Orion not just the most successful consortium bank, but the leading international investment bank. Naturally he was also concerned about profitability, but believed that being top of the league was the best way to generate a good return on capital. Moreover, the value to the shareholders of their stake in a 'strategic investment' such as Orion ought to be more than simply financial.[3] But his endeavours to build the business in the second half of the 1970s were frustrated by what Orion's executives perceived to be a lack of shareholder support. This grievance had several dimensions.

Competition

Orion faced mounting competition not only from other international banks, but also from its own shareholders as they developed their syndicated lending and investment banking activities. This could place Orion in an awkward and disadvantageous position: 'On the rare occasions when we find ourselves in the same swing door for the same piece of business,' said Montagu, 'we make very sure that we get out of the swing door first.'[4]

In the mid-1970s, consortium banks quickly lost out to the big multinational banks in the syndicated Euroloan market. While Orion's position slipped from 2nd in 1973 to 39th in 1976, its shareholders maintained or enhanced their rankings (see Table 8.1).

Table 8.1 Position of consortium banks in the syndicated Euroloan market, 1973–76[5] (rank by number of syndicated loans lead and co-managed)

	1973	1974	1975	1976
Consortium banks				
Orion Bank	2	5	8	39
Libra Bank	10	10	15	29
European Brazilian Bank	11	15	22 =	66
UBAF	12 =	15	18	23
Western American Bank (Europe)	12 =	15	26	75
Banque Européenne de Crédit	14	17	22 =	64
European Banking Company	14	14	24	67
Orion shareholders				
Chase Manhattan	5	3	1	1
Royal Bank of Canada	11	13	8	14
Westdeutsche Landesbank	13 =	11	10	10

Among the shareholders, it was Chase that presented the biggest competitive challenge. Chase's merchant bank, Chase Manhattan Limited, opened in London in April 1973 and quickly became the engine room of Chase's syndicated loan activities. It also developed Eurobond underwriting and trading business and corporate advisory work.[6] At the Shareholders' Forum in Venice a couple of months later, Chase somewhat misleadingly assured its Orion partners that Chase Manhattan Limited 'was not a new departure and that it merely centralised and emphasised their activities in the Eurocurrency markets.'[7] Since Chase had never channelled much capital markets business to Orion, the development of its own investment banking entity did not deprive Orion of business that it had come to expect. But the banks soon found themselves competing for other business. 'Orion clashed heavily with Chase's merchant bank on occasions,' commented a shareholder representative. 'We got a bit bitter with each other at times,' admitted one of the Chase Manhattan Limited executives.[8]

County Bank, NatWest's merchant banking arm, was formed in September 1969. Focusing on UK corporate finance work, mostly domestic mergers and acquisitions, there was little overlap with Orion's activities and initially limited rivalry.[9] Nonetheless, the formation of Orion caused anxiety at County and NatWest's chief executive sought reassurance that Orion Bank 'knows where its role starts and County Bank's stops.'[10] Orion's entry into corporate finance for UK corporations was eyed warily by County, and Orion was just as suspicious about County's efforts to get into the Eurobond business, particularly for NatWest's own issues which Orion regarded as its own territory. Moreover, from the mid-1970s County Bank developed international activities, in line with the requirements of their UK clients. In April 1975, County moved into its own prestigious City premises, 11 Old Broad Street in the City of London, the former headquarters of Lazard Brothers – an appropriate address for a merchant bank with serious aspirations. With the appointment of John Padovan as chief executive the following year, as regards Orion: 'the gloves were off.'[11]

The competition with County Bank was but one aspect of an increasingly difficult relationship between Orion and NatWest in the last couple of years of David Montagu's chairmanship. The 'final straw' came in July 1978 when Montagu learned that, without consulting him, NatWest had reassigned their shareholder representative, who had become Orion's executive responsible for Scandinavia, to another job and that he would be leaving Orion in a few weeks.[12] Montagu despatched an angry letter containing a catalogue of complaints about NatWest's lack of support for Orion, which 'leave in my mind the most distressing feeling about the importance, or lack of importance, you attach to Orion – a lack of importance which is not reflected in the manner in which the other shareholders have acted in similar circumstances.'[13] Although addressed to NatWest deputy chairman, Alex Dibbs, the letter was copied to the chairman, a move that didn't endear Montagu to Dibbs. Oil was poured on the troubled waters at a meeting at which the Orion chairman apologized for the 'emotional tone' of his letter and NatWest executives were at pains to explain away his 'ridiculous misinterpretations,' but relations between Montagu and NatWest were soured. At the time of Montagu's departure, a year later, *Euromoney* reported Orion executives speaking scathingly about NatWest, one of them remarking that 'there are two good things about NatWest, its offices and its food.'[14]

Orion's executives regarded WestLB and Royal Bank as the most supportive of the shareholders. WestLB regularly included Orion as a co-manager in
its Eurobond issues, though Orion was not allowed to market its services
directly to German companies in Germany. However, WestLB's London
subsidiary, established in 1973, was becoming increasingly effective and the
potential for clashes was growing. Royal Bank directed more business to
Orion than any other shareholder, promoting Orion's services to Canadian
borrowers in the Euromarkets.[15] In Orion's early days, Royal Bank's Robert
Utting told Orion executive Ian Logic, unofficially, that Orion could count
on a $40 million participation by Royal Bank in any large syndicated loan it
arranged, sight unseen; things did not work out quite that way, but the will
was there. Royal Bank vitally assisted Orion's emergence as the leading firm
in the Canadian dollar Eurobond market. Thus the establishment of its own
merchant banking subsidiary in London in 1978, suggesting less support in
future, was yet another cloud on the horizon.

Mitsubishi Bank and Credito Italiano were slow to develop their own
investment banking subsidiaries in London, but they did not do much to
support Orion either, though the Credito connection led to some important
business with Italian borrowers such as Mediobanca and IMI. They came
bottom of the class in the analysis (see Table 8.2) of a sample of shareholder
participations in syndicated loans managed by Orion, totalling $1.9 billion,
conducted in August 1978, although Italian regulations may have made it
difficult for Credito to participate.

Table 8.2   Participations in sample of syndicated loans managed by Orion[17] ($ million)

Orion Bank	177
Chase Manhattan Bank	125
Royal Bank of Canada	103
National Westminster Bank	58
Westdeutsche Landesbank	53
Mitsubishi Bank	48
Credito Italiano	nil

Commenting on the figures, the head of Orion's commercial banking
operations, Neil McFadyen, declared that he saw 'no real validity in their
continuance as shareholders, although he accepted that any withdrawal
would have to come from them (and in the case of Mitsubishi this was very
improbable indeed).'[16]

Shareholder fund raising

In practical terms, shareholder support for Orion meant taking part in
Orion-managed syndicated loans and assisting the development of merchant

banking activities by client introductions or referrals. It also meant giving Orion a prominent part in the shareholders' own capital-raising activities in the international financial markets. Montagu demanded that Orion should lead manage every such issue, except if there was a wholly-owned investment banking subsidiary, in which event Orion should co-lead manage. For issues in yen, Deutschemark or Swiss francs, which had to be lead managed by a domestic bank, Orion should be a prominent co-manager: 'It is quite simply,' stated an Orion report in July 1978, 'that the reaction in the market place to any shareholder transaction in which Orion does not play a major role is that if its own shareholders do not consider Orion to be sufficiently competent then nobody else will. It is ironic that this support is less in evidence now that Orion's competence is proved and recognised.'[18]

Seconded personnel

In the early years, the executives seconded to Orion from the shareholders had been very able high-flyers in their own banks. But by the late 1970s, there were complaints from Orion executives about the quality of some of the later secondees. One unfortunate was described by an Orion executive as being 'incapable of running more than a suburban branch.'[19] The alleged downgrading of seconded personnel was regarded at Orion as further evidence of dwindling shareholder support.

Expansion

Growth, capital and diversification were key issues. 'Fast growth is essential,' Montagu told the shareholders in February 1979:[20] 'I owe it to them [his colleagues] to lead a bank with great expansion possibilities, or not at all.'[21] But a bigger bank required the shareholders to subscribe additional capital, and every time the subject was raised the owners procrastinated or refused. Montagu and his colleagues also had ideas for taking Orion in new directions. 'We wanted to develop other products or to buy into other businesses because we're wholly a Euromarket bank,' he told *Euromoney*. 'We have no counter-cyclical income.'[22] A move into insurance broking was one of the ideas given serious consideration. A more radical suggestion was an association with auction house Christie's. 'Kleinwort Benson and Rothschilds gained tremendously from their involvement with Sotheby's,' observed one of the Orion managing directors. But Montagu had left Orion before the proposal could be put to the shareholders.

Orion's 'irrelevance'

Finally, there was the 'irrelevance' dimension. Montagu and Orion's managing directors became convinced that Orion had become simply 'irrelevant' to its shareholders; no more than a 'useful appendage', as a shareholder executive described it at the Shareholders' Forum in October 1978.[23] For instance, by 1980 County Bank was making profits of the same order as Orion, but whereas NatWest received 100 per cent of the former it got only 20 per cent of the latter. As an Orion executive told *Euromoney*: 'NatWest makes £450 million a year. Orion in a good year will make £10 million or £12 million. What does 20 per cent of that mean to NatWest?'[24]

THE GUCCI SHOE FACTOR

There was another intangible blight on the relationship between Orion and its shareholders. Banking text-books do not have an index entry 'Gucci shoe factor' but the phrase sums up the cultural clashes which have so often poisoned relationships between commercial banks and their investment bank subsidiaries. On one side was the international investment banker, with his Gucci loafers, jetting into the Corviglia Club at St Moritz for a *tête-à-tête* with Stavros Niarchos or the Shah of Iran. On the other side, there was the commercial banker, with his lace-up rubber-soled shoes, trudging through the rainy streets of Tunbridge Wells to catch the train to London Bridge for a desk-bound day. 'I regard commercial bankers rather as toothbrush salesmen,' an Arab banker put it: 'the investment bankers are more like dentists.'[25] Some might reverse the characterizations.

Strained relationships invariably arose when commercial banks bought or formed investment banks, and the cultural chasm between the two breeds of banker might be accentuated by differences of nationality, religion and social milieu. Investment bankers earned vastly more money than most commercial bankers, and they enjoyed the status of a partner or a director. They saw commercial banks as sleepy, cosy and bureaucratic oligopolies. Commercial bankers regarded investment bankers as over-paid *prima donnas*, producing erratic and inadequate profits. Although exaggerated, there was a kernel of truth in both points of view.

Such mutual suspicions were not new or unremarked on. Lord Brand, a partner of Lazard Brothers and also a non-executive director of Lloyds Bank, once remarked: 'we merchant bankers live off our wits, while you clearing bankers live off your deposits.'[26]

Author Anthony Sampson has characterized the big UK commercial banks of the 1970s as akin to armies, commanded by 'a conservative grandee at the top of an obedient infantry of clerks and managers,' while investment bankers, lacking the 'ultimate power' conferred by billions in deposits, were mere 'temporary brokers and fixers.'[27]

Orion was not immune from such cultural clashes and recriminations. There was a feeling among Orion's investment bankers that some of the shareholders did not understand investment banking and its reliance on deal makers rather than deposits. 'If the chairmen of the five British clearing banks took a year's holiday,' observed an Orion managing director, 'it wouldn't put a tiny dent in their profits.'[28] On the other hand, a characteristic comment from NatWest, on being offered a participation in one of Orion's syndicated loans for Mexico, was that 'the margins are very slender but the fees would, of course, be substantial and it is this aspect which interests Orion Bank ... this is a typical merchant banking approach to obtain fees without regard to risk and market credibility ... It is contrary to NatWest's own policy.'[29] Sensitive management by Orion and by its consortium shareholders prevented such antagonisms from getting out of hand. Moreover, most of the individuals seconded by the shareholders caught on quickly and thrived in their new environment.

MONTAGU'S SINGLE SHAREHOLDER PROPOSAL

In October 1977, partly to satisfy Montagu's demands for greater support and partly because of shareholder concerns about Orion's future profitability, the shareholders commissioned the management to write a five-year plan for the bank for discussion at the Shareholders' Forum a year later.[30] The strategic review exercise itself, before any discussion with the shareholders took place, convinced Montagu that Orion's ownership structure was incapable of delivering the level of support which the firm required to achieve his ambitions. In fact, he concluded that joint ownership was itself Orion's foremost strategic problem. Montagu's solution was that one of the shareholders, or an outside bank, should acquire complete control. 'My wish was for them either to support Orion far more significantly,' he said, 'or – and this was my stronger wish – that they should grasp the nettle and sell it to one shareholder.'[31] Orion would then be sufficiently 'relevant' to the interests of a single shareholder to receive the level of support required. There were two recent precedents for this solution to a consortium bank's strategic dilemmas, namely American Express's acquisition of Rothschild Intercontinental Bank[32] and Chemical Bank's of London Multinational Bank.[33]

The opening shot of Montagu's campaign to recast Orion's ownership structure was a letter to the chairmen of the six shareholders, dated 7 September 1978, raising the issue of each one's continued participation in the consortium. 'I am sure we would all agree,' he wrote, 'that if Orion did not exist in its present form today, it would not be started ... You are all the heads of enormous banks and I wonder sometimes whether the 20 per cent and 10 per cent interests that you have in Orion are really of such significance in your affairs that you would not all be happier and feel more relaxed if Orion did not exist at all. Let me tell you that it would not shock me if the conclusion from some or all of you was that a participation in Orion no longer made sense.'[34]

Montagu's letter to the chairmen was a carefully calculated move. It was timed so as to put the question of the continued participation of the shareholders in the Orion consortium on the agenda of their forthcoming get together in Washington on 26 September 1978 during the World Bank/IMF meetings, in advance of the discussion of the outcome of the strategic review. The latter document, entitled *Review of the Concepts and Objectives of Orion*, was scheduled for discussion at the Shareholders' Forum that was to be held in Cambridge, England, four weeks later.[35] By writing to the chairmen, Montagu was raising the issue of the ownership structure of Orion at the highest level, over the heads of the senior executives who would be representing their banks at the Shareholders' Forum and pre-empting their deliberations.

This was not the first time that Montagu had used this tactic to present the Shareholders' Forum with a *fait accompli*. This caused considerable irritation to the senior shareholder executives who attended the Forum. In a briefing note for NatWest's chairman, Robin Leigh-Pemberton, deputy chairman Alex Dibbs commented that 'the [chairmen's] meetings originated in the thought that it would be nice for the partner banks at chairman level annually to endorse their continuing support for the Orion concept ... no-one in the management of the bank, including myself in past years, has felt that the chairmen's meeting is the appropriate forum for detailed discussion on the future policy of Orion, but there is a distinct possibility that you and your chairmen colleagues will be drawn into issues of policy which were to have been discussed in October.'[36]

In Washington, the assembled chairmen duly deliberated on Montagu's letter, but none shared his anxieties. David Rockefeller opened the discussion, expressing the Chase view that 'they were not unhappy with the present position and felt that Orion gave a closer relationship between the shareholding banks than would be otherwise possible.'[37] The other chairmen also expressed contentment with Orion's progress and Montagu's performance as chairman. All expressed a wish to remain a shareholder. Summing up, Rockefeller pronounced unanimous support among the chairmen for the Orion consortium for the next five years. They left it to the senior executives meeting at the Shareholders' Forum to discuss in detail the implications of Montagu's letter and the strategic objectives and recommendations of the *Review of the Concepts and Objectives of Orion*.

STRATEGIC REVIEW, 1978

As ever, the Shareholders' Forum in Cambridge over the weekend 28–30 October 1978 was a social as well as a working occasion for the shareholder executives. They and their wives stayed at the Garden House Hotel, on the bank of the river Cam in the historic centre, and convivial moments included black-tie dinners in the Fitzwilliam Museum and the old kitchens at Trinity College and a visit to the racing stables at Newmarket by arrangement of David Montagu, who kept his horses there. Montagu was the only Orion executive who was not also a shareholder representative in attendance.

The principal item on the agenda was the *Review of the Concepts and Objectives of Orion*. This strategic review identified four objectives and made four recommendations for their achievement:

Strategic objectives

- To consolidate and improve Orion's position as a leading investment bank in the international capital markets.
- To maintain and develop a prudent and profitable commercial banking operation.
- To develop Orion's leasing activity into a significant profit-earner for the bank.
- To enhance Orion's international reputation by increasing its share of advisory work in relation to cross-frontier mergers and acquisitions.

Recommendations

- That the shareholders should demonstrate continually and overtly their support for Orion.
- That a further injection of capital will be necessary for the proposed development of Orion.
- That Orion's balance sheet should be used to a greater extent in order to develop the growth of its investment banking business.
- Changes in the activities of Orion Pacific and its relationship with Orion Bank.

The 'objectives' were unremarkable, given that Orion was already engaged in each activity. The key 'recommendations' were the first two. What was meant by 'support' was spelt out in practical detail, with the warning that 'there is now a risk that reduced commitment by the shareholders may effectively destroy what they themselves have made possible by their efforts on Orion's behalf in the early and difficult years.'[38] The looked-for increase in capital was earmarked for 1980.

SHAREHOLDER RESPONSES TO THE STRATEGIC REVIEW

The reactions of the shareholders' representatives to the *Review* were much as Montagu must have expected, but a long way from what he would have wished. Although they all pledged 'continuing support' for Orion and undertook to 'work with Orion as an ally to the fullest possible extent,' they refused to give the concrete commitments to include Orion automatically in the management group of their own fund-raising exercises or of their international loans.[39] In fact, the shareholders responded that the Orion management was asking for more than they could deliver since, as WestLB's Dr Walter Seipp pointed out, on many occasions it was the client who dictated who was in the management group.[40] In reality, on the business generation front, as Jock Finlayson of Royal Bank put it, Orion was 'pretty much on its own.'[41]

The *Review's* recommendation of an increase in Orion's capital and its emphasis on expansion were not sympathetically received – 'No!!!' scrawled Alex Dibbs as a margin note in his copy.[42] 'Orion is an organisation run by very experienced status conscious salesmen,' observed a NatWest report on the *Review*. 'They all have the word 'Director' incorporated in their job-title and regard themselves very much as individualists, reacting very sharply to any discipline which they feel to be unimportant. Most of them work extremely hard and are seemingly untiring in their efforts to expand Orion's business … there is a general atmosphere of "onward ever onward".'[43] In contrast to the *Review's* focus on expansion, the shareholder executives placed 'great emphasis' on the concept of Orion as 'a profitable "quality" bank rather than one dedicated to balance sheet size.'[44] The message was that Orion should restrain its expansionary impulses and could expect no more capital.

Orion's profitability was the key concern of the shareholders, since the pre-tax return on equity had been drifting down from the high level of 27 per cent achieved in 1975 and 1976.[45] There was much anxiety that revenues were being hit by narrower margins in commercial lending and lower fees from Eurobonds. Dr Seipp pointed out that pursuit of the *Review's* 'expansionary objectives' would saddle Orion with a high-cost operation at a time of 'a more difficult earnings atmosphere.'[46] There was general resistance to Montagu's arguments for additional hirings of senior staff and enhanced remuneration for executives. 'Conditions have changed since the origin … and Orion will have to succeed largely on a "stand alone" basis,' wrote Royal Bank executive Jock Finlayson. 'In short, Orion will have to earn its way if it is to become as large and important as Mr Montagu and his team wish it to be.'[47]

Since all the shareholders declared that they wanted to retain their investment in Orion, the single shareholder solution to Orion's strategic dilemma was simply ignored at the Shareholders' Forum in Cambridge. So Montagu raised it again at the next Shareholders' Forum in London in February 1979. 'I told the shareholders "either we resolve this, or you ought to think of replacing me. I can't go on running it with a clear conscience vis-à-vis my team".'[48] But again, the shareholders stated that they were content with Orion's existing ownership structure. So Montagu submitted his resignation, offering to stay on until a successor could be appointed. This dramatic and potentially devastating development was kept a closely guarded secret, being unknown to both Orion's management and the market.

POSSIBLE MERGER WITH COUNTY BANK

The other significant development at the Shareholders' Forum of February 1979 was NatWest's announcement to its Orion partners that henceforth County Bank would serve as its 'primary international merchant/investment banking vehicle.'[49] But at the same time, NatWest affirmed its 'continuing commitment to Orion and to the enduring importance of a special relationship between the six major world banks which are Orion's shareholders.' These distinctly mixed messages meant that while NatWest wanted to remain a member of the Orion club, it would be channelling all its international investment banking business through County Bank in future.

NatWest's decision to develop County Bank as an international investment bank prompted Montagu to initiate talks about NatWest acquiring Orion and merging it with County Bank. He told Dibbs that the combined entity would be the world's number one international merchant bank.[50] Under this scenario, Montagu would be prepared to stay on as chairman of the merged entity on appropriate terms. To be able to run NatWest's investment banking subsidiary with sufficient independence would require a main board directorship, and probably a deputy chairmanship.[51] NatWest took the idea seriously and a meeting was scheduled at chairman level between Montagu and Robin Leigh-Pemberton. But in the meantime after internal deliberations, NatWest decided against purchasing Orion because it might precipitate a falling-out among the shareholders, it being known that Mitsubishi and Credito were opposed to selling and Royal Bank 'might be difficult.'[52] The possibility of a joint purchase of Orion by NatWest and Royal Bank was discussed by Alex Dibbs and Jock Finlayson, but nothing came of it.[53] Enthusiasm for the acquisition of Orion was by no means universal within NatWest. 'If Orion had not been established, it would not be a very attractive institution either in terms of return on investment or range of skills,' commented an internal review of Orion as an investment: 'NatWest has grown up enough to operate in all the major markets covered by Orion ... disengagement would be an entirely logical step.'[54] In fact, NatWest, like the other shareholders, had decided to maintain the status quo and was taking steps, in conjunction with Chase, to arrange Montagu's succession.

MONTAGU'S REPLACEMENT BY CUNNINGHAM AND SANDON

The meeting with Leigh-Pemberton on 18 September 1979 did not go as Montagu had hoped or expected. Much to his disappointment, the NatWest chairman informed him that the bank had decided against buying Orion and affirmed its commitment to the consortium concept.[55] That was a blow, but there was worse to come. Expecting reassurance, Montagu mentioned that there was a rumour in the market that a new chief executive had been

secretly appointed to succeed him. Put on the spot, Leigh-Pemberton confirmed that commitments had been recently entered into appointing Jeff
Cunningham as chief executive, and Lord Sandon, chairman of International
Westminster Bank, chairman in succession to Montagu. It had been the intention to discuss the succession with Montagu at the chairmen's meeting during
World Bank/IMF meetings, which that year were being held in Belgrade. The
plan, as John Haley explained somewhat incoherently, was that 'the chairmen
would sort of meet and say "This is a good idea" and say "Yes, David you've
done a splendid job" and ... David would come and report to us on whatever
tidying up needed to be done.'[56] Montagu was dumbfounded that the
appointments had been made behind his back and without consultation. He
returned to Orion's office in a daze. 'I'm out,' he told an aide: 'the shareholders have appointed Cunningham and Sandon to succeed me.' It was, according to a close friend, the worst day of his life.

END OF AN ERA

Montagu's departure from Orion hit the financial world like a bolt from the
blue, astonishing the City and provoking a sensation in the financial press.
Although the press release on 11 October 1979 attempted to dispel any idea
of a rift, stating that David Montagu 'now wishes to develop his other interests elsewhere' and featured eulogies from David Rockefeller and Robin
Leigh-Pemberton, it was widely suspected that the brilliant but unbeholden
merchant banker had been sacked by his commercial bank shareholders. His
departure was hailed as signifying the end of an era, both for Orion and for
consortium banking. 'The trouble with these joint-venture consortium bank
is that beyond a certain degree of success, they start to compete with their
parents,' wrote City commentator Christopher Fildes. 'At that point, their
scope for further development becomes limited and for disputes enormous.
If that has happened at a success story like Orion, it must call the future of
consortium banking into question.'[57]

Critics of the shareholders accused them of ineptitude at losing the cre-
ator of the most successful of the consortium banks and 'one of the few institutions that is based in London that could be termed a universal bank.'[58]
There was also censure of the high-handed manner in which they had managed the succession. 'I couldn't be more critical of the way the shareholders
have handled this,' an angry Orion managing director was reported as say-
ing: 'Dibbs and Haley have hatched this up between them. Its their way of
slitting Orion's throat.'

Stung by the barrage of criticism in the press and in the City, the shareholders defended their conduct. 'The way we do that sort of thing in our
bank,' said a shareholder executive: 'is to appoint first and tell people after. We
don't sit around and discuss it with his colleagues first.' 'The shareholders

themselves are not shrinking violets, we have a few opinions of our own,' commented John Haley. 'The City's treatment of him [Montagu] has been unfair to us,' protested a spokesman for Mitsubishi in Tokyo: 'He was not blamed at all. But they don't know the real situation. It was he who got himself fired.'

The breach between Montagu and the shareholders was about the role and development of Orion. Montagu wanted Orion to grow and build the business. The shareholders were happy with the status quo, developing their own international operations while enjoying the special relationship between them conferred by membership of the Orion club. 'What they wanted from us now seems very different from what we thought they wanted,' said an Orion managing director in the aftermath of Montagu's departure. 'We thought they wanted an institution that could compete with the Morgan Stanleys and Deutsche Banks. Now I'm confused: if they just wanted a club, why did they ask us to build a major investment bank?' 'It wouldn't be the first time that a chief executive has disagreed with his proprietors on the way ahead, and it won't be the last,' Lord Sandon, Orion's new chairman, declared philosophically.[59]

Montagu's replacement in September 1979 was the outcome of the tendering of his resignation the previous February. That the appointment of Cunningham and Sandon came as a shock, suggests that he did not believe that his offer would be accepted. It was, in Philip Hubbard's view, another move to try to force the shareholders to accept his single shareholder proposal. The demands for more capital and greater shareholder support for Orion had the same objective. The former was not only 'knowingly provocative' it was unnecessary, Orion's existing capital of £52 million being at the top end of investment banks of the day, and other Orion executives were puzzled about how the funds were to be deployed.[60] The latter demand was unrealistic, since most of the shareholders were already developing their own international investment banking operations. Trying to force the shareholders to change their minds by these tactics was a high-risk piece of brinkmanship, and ultimately he was unable to pull it off.

Following his departure from Orion, David Montagu worked briefly and unhappily for the American brokerage house Merrill Lynch. Then he joined J. Rothschild Holdings and became a member of the Board of Banking Supervision of the Bank of England. A third and distinct chapter in his career opened in 1988, when he was appointed chairman of Rothmans International, a post he held until a few months before his death in 1998.

Montagu's downfall was a milestone in the story of the consortium banks. 'To many,' wrote *Euromoney* editor Padraic Fallon: 'Montagu's unseemly departure from Orion Bank signified the defeat of a concept, the death of a belief that a group of large commercial banks could establish a major investment bank that could simultaneously serve its shareholders' needs and be independent, and compete on its own with the great universal banks in the

Euromarkets. To many, Orion Bank was the living refutation to the argument that consortium banks don't work, that they inevitably wither through shareholder interference, or from the growth of the shareholder banks' ability to do the things that they had set up a consortium bank to do. Inevitably, Montagu's departure strengthened that argument in the minds of the international financial community.'[61]

CHAPTER 9

Swimming against the tide

'The most difficult job in the Euromarkets' was *Euromoney* editor Padraic Fallon's description of the task that faced chief executive Jeff Cunningham and chairman Lord Sandon, Orion's new top management team.[1] Under their leadership, Orion continued as a consortium bank for a further 18 months until Royal Bank bought out the other shareholders. It was not an easy time for anyone involved, because of difficult external economic and market conditions, and internal tensions and strategic dilemmas.

The period from autumn 1979 to spring 1981 was one of the most volatile eras in post-war financial history. A second round of oil price rises was underway, driven by unrest and revolution in Iran followed by the outbreak of the Iran–Iraq war in September 1980, which drove the official price of oil up from $13 per barrel to $34 in 1981. Inflation took off again in the Western economies, reaching 15 per cent in the USA in February 1980 and 22 per cent in the UK in May 1980. The outlook was further blighted by the Soviet invasion of Afghanistan in December 1979. In the following three weeks, the price of gold, the traditional hedge against uncertainty, soared from $475 per ounce to its all-time high of $850 per ounce, though it was back to $481 within two months. But this time, politicians and central bankers were determined to fight inflation. In the UK, the newly elected government led by Margaret Thatcher introduced a budget in June 1979 that imposed an anti-inflationary squeeze and raised interest rates from 12 per cent to 14 per cent. In November, UK interest rates were hiked again to a record 17 per cent. Recession, rising unemployment and reeling stock market prices were the headlines of the year 1980. But by spring 1981, as interest rates returned to 12 per cent, the corner had been turned.

In the USA, short-term interest rates soared in the months following the Federal Reserve's adoption of the new policy of targeting the money supply in October 1979, the prime rate reaching 20 per cent in April 1980, a doubling in two years. Interest rates were also much more volatile, stimulating the development of interest rate derivatives to hedge against interest rate risk. The anti-inflation US budget of March 1980 tipped the US economy into recession, which led to a sharp easing of US rates in the summer, but this was followed by another tightening at the end of the year. The high interest rate policy also had, within it, the seeds of the LDC debt crisis which was to erupt two years later.

Currencies also fluctuated wildly. The dollar first rose against the Deutschemark, but then declined. It slumped against the yen. It even fell against sterling, despite the bold abolition of exchange controls by the new Conservative administration soon after taking office; the pound's sharp ascent was due to its new status as a petro-currency and as a beneficiary of a flight to quality, a phenomenon unknown for a generation. All in all, managing an international investment bank in such markets was like riding a bucking bronco.

RETURN OF JEFF CUNNINGHAM

The appointment of Thomas Jefferson 'Jeff' Cunningham III as chief executive was suggested by John Haley and met with universal enthusiasm among the shareholders.[2] Cunningham was a uniquely suitable candidate, being both an Orion old hand and at the time of his appointment an independent outsider. Banking was in Cunningham's blood, his family being important shareholders in the Fishgill National Bank, near Poughkeepsie in upstate New York.[3] After taking an MBA at Stanford Business School, he had joined Chase. His 'meteoric career' began in 1967, when Chase sent him to London to run the large Berkeley Square branch at the age of 25.[4] In 1969, he was appointed one of the six-man study group responsible for planning the creation of Orion and also Libra Bank. He then acted as Chase's senior representative and an executive director at Orion for three and a half years, playing an important role in early business development.

Cunningham left Orion in February 1974, to become Chase's area director for Northern Europe, a promotion described by *Euromoney* as 'an extraordinary achievement for one so young.'[5] Then, three years later, for family reasons, he retired as a full-time banker, though he kept a toe-hold in the banking business as a consultant. He was lured out of retirement by the challenge of running the bank that he had helped to create a decade earlier. 'Philosophically,' he told a journalist, 'I have never left the place.'[6]

Cunningham was a close and long-standing friend of John Haley of Chase and, to a lesser extent, of Alex Dibbs of NatWest. All were sensitive to the suggestion that Cunningham was the shareholders' placeman in contrast to the independent Montagu. 'He's not a Chase person, he really isn't,' Haley protested. Indeed, anyone who had met Cunningham would have agreed that he was nobody's stooge and was abundantly endowed with the strength of personality, drive, imagination and intellect that was going to be necessary to revive Orion's fortunes.

Orion's new non-executive chairman was Lord Sandon, a deputy chairman of NatWest. Sandon, whose family name was Coutts Ryder, had long-standing family connections with Coutts & Co, the private bank, where his great grandfather and grandfather had been chairmen.[7] He joined Coutts after wartime military service and became a director of National Provincial Bank, which had acquired the family firm in 1919 but left it to run autonomously. Upon the merger with Westminster Bank, he became a director of NatWest and deputy chairman in 1971. Besides his banking career, he was active in local politics and in a number of medical charities. He worked closely with Jeff Cunningham, defining his role as 'to guide the board and serve as a sounding board for the senior executives.'[8]

A third newcomer was Antonino 'Tony' Cravero from Royal Bank, who replaced Neil McFadyen as head of Orion's banking operations in November 1979. The almost simultaneous timing of this hand-over with Montagu's departure was co-incidental, but it provided Cunningham with a robust and like-minded ally from Royal Bank. Cravero, who was born in Turin, began his career in banking with Banca Nazionale del Lavoro.[9] After a lengthy posting in Canada, he decided against returning to Italy on account of his children's schooling and was hired by Royal Bank to work on the European Desk in 1970. He was made a vice-president in 1979, and almost immediately was asked to go to Orion to head up the syndicated loan side of the business. He stayed with Orion for seven years and himself became chief executive, before returning to Royal Bank as a senior vice-president in 1986.

CUNNINGHAM'S CHALLENGES

Cunningham faced three principal challenges. The first was to manage the bank as a day-to-day business, the immediate task being to limit the damage to Orion's staff morale and reputation in the market from the controversial change of chief executives. 'My brief is to keep on going,' he told a journalist. 'We are going to be as aggressive and imaginative as in the past. Clearly we have a cutting edge in the international capital markets, and we are not intending to moderate our position in any way.'[10]

The second challenge was to develop a commercial strategy and drive the business forward, improving profitability and the return on capital.

The third task was to improve relations with the shareholders. Whereas Montagu had seen it as his role to keep the shareholders off the backs of the executives, Cunningham tried to bring them together. For instance, for the first time Orion's managing directors were invited to attend the Shareholders'

Forum. Eventually the outcome was better dialogue and more, not less, operational freedom for Orion.[11]

But in the meantime, even before he had his feet under the chief executive's desk, Cunningham faced problems with Orion's senior executives. They surfaced at the Orion Bank board meeting on 29 October 1979, the last one chaired by David Montagu. By arrangement among the shareholder directors, Geoff Styles of Royal Bank read a resolution offering their thanks and appreciation. This was seconded by Credito Italiano's representative and 'unanimously applauded.'[12] But then, 'at an otherwise very tidy and straightforward board meeting,' as Alex Dibbs put it, Christopher Chataway requested permission to depart from the agenda to read a statement to which he and two more of the five managing directors, William de Gelsey and Andrew Large, had put their signatures.[13] All eyes turned to Dibbs, the senior shareholder representative present, who warily assented. After a preamble praising Montagu's 'leadership, inspiration and sheer hard work,' Chataway said:

> We feel we must voice our concern and feelings of frustration at the manner in which the new chairman and chief executive have been selected. There is, of course, nothing personal in this – both are experienced bankers. But the shareholders and Board ought to be aware that what has happened and the way in which it has happened has dealt a shattering blow to the morale of their company.
>
> They had a successful investment bank, headed by one of the leaders of London's financial community, and they have imposed a new chairman and chief executive from among their own without consultation with him or any member of top management ...
>
> The shareholders are of course entitled to do what they will with Orion; but they would also, I am sure, wish to know the views – however unpalatable – of some of their managing directors. In short, our view is that what has been done and the way it has been done will make it very difficult for this bank to recover and to progress.[14]

The discontent among Orion's executives was quickly known in the market, and became common knowledge when a blow-by-blow account of the crisis at Orion appeared as the lead story in the December 1979 edition of *Euromoney*. Immediately, City head-hunters began to circle to pick off star staff. Tony Cravero recalled Jeff Cunningham bursting into his office a few weeks later in high dudgeon.[15] 'Who died?,' said Cravero. 'Andrew Large and others are leaving,' Cunningham replied. 'Did you try to buy them?,' asked Cravero. 'No,' said Cunningham, 'they just don't want to work with us.'

Andrew Large and four other senior executives, including the head of syndications and the chief Eurobond dealer, moved *en bloc* to Swiss Bank Corporation's (SBC) recently established London-based investment bank. They constituted the core of a ready-made Eurobond team, which put SBC's investment banking operations on the map and enabled SBC to catch up with their rivals Union Bank of Switzerland and Crédit Suisse, which were well ahead of SBC in the Euromarkets. It also overnight created a new competitor for Orion. Andrew Large became the first non-Swiss member of the board of a major Swiss bank, and subsequently chairman of the Securities and Investment Board, the UK regulator. Hans de Gier, another of their number, later became chairman of SBC Warburg, following the purchase of the London merchant bank by SBC in 1995.

The resignations of Large and the others was a profound shock for Orion's management. In fact, it brought the old guard and the new appointees together, working with the common purpose of minimizing the damage and revitalising the firm. 'The reconciliation,' mused Cunningham subsequently, 'was an unexpected side-effect benefit.'[16]

But even if top management was now pulling together, defections continued at more junior levels. In April 1980, six months after becoming chief executive, Cunningham reported that Orion had lost 17 executives, including a managing director and four executive directors out of a total executive cadre of about 90.[17] This was a debilitating attrition of talent that undermined Orion's effectiveness in key areas – especially Eurobond execution and Eurobond trading – and devoured the time and energy of senior executives in crisis management and staff recruitment, distracting attention from developing the business.

When it was learned that SBC's London investment bank had made job offers to two more executives on the Eurobond side, Orion's management and the shareholders' representatives were livid.[18] Within hours, Franz Lutolf, SBC's general manager in Zurich, received strongly worded messages from John Haley at Chase, Alex Dibbs at NatWest and Jock Finlayson at Royal Bank, who 'made known their displeasure in no uncertain terms ... we pointed out that SBC now has six unhappy correspondent banks and that we felt that SBC personnel practices should recognise this fact.'[19] 'Pardon the candour,' Haley telexed Lutolf, 'but perhaps a word from you [with SBC London] that "enough is enough" would be in order.'[20]

Cunningham moved quickly to fill the vacancies. Internal promotions were preferred, both for speed and to reward loyal staff, but some outside appointments were also made. Michael Perry was promoted to managing director and Guy Burgun became head of the bond syndication department. To cement the loyalty of the other managing directors, and to signal their importance to Orion to the outside world, William de Gelsey was made deputy chairman, and Christopher Chataway and Philip Hubbard were appointed vice-chairmen. To defuse internal criticism that Orion was becoming too much under the thumb of the shareholders, Cunningham created a new management committee composed of the six senior executives, to which the board delegated 'substantial operating authority reflecting the proven record of the management in successfully establishing Orion as a leading international investment bank.'[21]

NEW PROPOSALS

At the same time as struggling with personnel problems, Orion's top management was working on proposals for turning 'the "success story" of the '70s into a leader of the '80s.'[22] 'Orion is in a state of uncertainty today,' began a report by Jeff Cunningham entitled *New Proposals for the Conduct of Business*: 'It is unsure of the shareholders' *objectives* for Orion. It is unsure of the shareholders' understanding of the *success criteria* for Orion's business. It is unsure of the philosophy and therefore the mechanisms for the *shareholders' relationship* with Orion.' Lord Sandon prepared his own complementary *Aide-Memoire re: New Proposals for the Conduct of Business*, addressing the same points. These papers were discussed at the Shareholders' Forum in London in February 1980.

The papers proposed a radical reform of the nature of Orion's relationship with the shareholders. 'Orion started for good reason as something special in the eyes of its parents,' stated Sandon. 'It is now time, for its own health, for it to be "de-specialised".'[23] NatWest's Harold Hitchcock expressed the proposed change in more adroit language, describing it as a shift from a 'strategic investment' to a 'trade investment.'[24]

Orion's traditional relationship with the shareholders was that of a 'strategic investment.' The essence of this relationship was that Orion provided significant services that the shareholders were unable or unwilling to furnish in-house, preferring to undertake them jointly with other banks through the consortium bank. But by the beginning of the 1980s, as all parties were well aware, the shareholders were able to provide a full range of investment and international banking activities themselves, which rendered the 'strategic investment' concept largely redundant. However, there were still 'the "club" advantages of the association' with the other shareholders through the consortium entity; hence the quest for, as Sandon put it, 'a "New Look" Orion.'[25]

The redefinition of Orion as a 'trade investment' implied a much more independent entity. For Orion, it meant freedom to develop new activities and to establish its own independent presence in new markets. It meant liberty to negotiate the compensation packages senior management felt necessary to recruit and retain key staff, a consideration prominent in Cunningham's mind at the time because of the high turnover of executives. It also inevitably meant greater competition with the shareholders, although Cunningham optimistically expressed the hope that: ' "competitive" situations can be channelled into "co-operative" situations.'[26] Cunningham identified Orion's principal rivals as: 'the truly independent investment banks – SG Warburg, Morgan Stanley, Salomon Brothers etc. To compete successfully, Orion must present itself to both clients and markets with the same attributes of independence and impartiality which these competitors presently do so persuasively.'[27] While arguing the benefits of greater independence, Cunningham was at pains to remind the shareholders about the magnitude of the challenge facing the bank: 'Orion operates at a disadvantage to about every competitive institution. It is virtually unique (save EBC) in having no home base. It is totally dependent on markets which are extremely cyclical. Thus Orion's profit performance must be evaluated in terms of both the magnitude of the challenge which it faces, and over time – the good years with the bad.'[28]

For the shareholders, the redefinition of Orion as a 'trade investment' simplified the relationship. It allowed them to apply the financial yardsticks by which they judged the performance of other minority holdings, particularly return on capital, and to insist upon more rigorous cost control and management accounting.[29] Another advantage was that it allowed them to develop business relationships with other banks beyond the Orion club, which some shareholder executives believed was inhibiting new initiatives. On the other hand, reservations were expressed about allowing management too much free rein, mention being made of the losses at Western American Bank and the 'trauma' of Orion's Eurobond trading losses in 1973.[30] Nevertheless, in February 1980 the shareholder executives formally ratified Orion's transformation into a 'trade investment.'[31] As an independent arms'-length entity, the role of the full-time shareholder representatives at Orion was no longer appropriate and they were abolished, although the shareholder banks were expressly encouraged to continue to send executives on secondment to Orion. Now Orion had not only grown up, it had left home.

PATTERN OF ACTIVITIES

Cunningham presented the Shareholders' Forum of February 1980 with an analysis of Orion's financial results for 1979 (see Table 9.1), which besides reviewing the previous year's performance provided a complete picture of the business. He presented a financial breakdown of each activity, details that David Montagu had repeatedly declined to provide to the shareholders. Montagu argued that he 'did not believe it was possible or desirable to identify the costs and income deriving from various aspects of Orion's activities,' and that an investment bank such as Orion had to be regarded as a whole.[32] This and the issue of costs were running irritations to the shareholder executives, causing friction between them and Montagu. The shareholder executives were delighted with the new data, congratulating management on the improvement.[33]

Syndicated lending was still much the most important income generator, producing 61 per cent of the total, three-quarters from interest and a quarter from fees. Next was money market operations, which contributed

Table 9.1   Orion Bank, analysis of income for 1979[34]

	£('000)	per cent
Syndicated and participated loans		
Commercial loan mark-up	5 559	46
Commitment fees	451	4
Loan arrangement fees	1 331	11
Money market operations	2 300	19
Securities income		
New issues	740	6
Private placements	250	2
Secondary trading	785	6
Agency business	170	1
Advisory fees		
Mergers and acquisitions	407	3
Financial advisory services	110	1
Sundry income	80	1
Total	12 183	100

19 per cent, a remarkable achievement for the handful of traders and, as Cunningham put it: 'clearly attributable to the skill of the money market team.'[35]

Securities income contributed only 15 per cent of Orion's income in 1979, the largest parts coming from new issues and secondary market trading. Advisory fees, mostly from mergers and acquisitions services, made a useful but minor contribution of 4 per cent. Thus in total, Orion's investment banking activities generated only 19 per cent of the firm's income. Given the effort that had been devoted to building up the investment banking side of the business, this was a considerable disappointment. It was also a reflection of the difficult state of the market, as well as the fierce competition and the pressure on fees and other forms of remuneration.

COMMERCIAL BANKING

Over the years 1979–81, the volume of syndicated loans lead and co-managed by Orion grew from $6.6 billion to $20.5 billion (see Table 9.2). Orion's appearance in management groups increased from 8.5 per cent of all loans to 15.6 per cent. After a dip in 1979, the business expanded rapidly in 1980 and 1981, under the direction of Tony Cravero. The bulk of Orion's loan portfolio continued to be high-grade and focused on OECD countries, an outside audit in summer 1980 commenting favourably on the 'good geographical spread.'[36]

Table 9.2 Orion Bank, syndicated loans lead and co-managed, 1979–81[37] ($ billion)

	1979	1980	1981
Orion Bank	6.6	15.3	20.5
Market	77.5	82.8	131.4
Orion share (per cent)	8.5	18.4	15.6

The drawback to Orion's conservative lending profile was the low and declining margins earned by such prime business. So Orion's executives were always on the lookout for special situations which offered better yields without commensurably enhanced risk. Two such opportunities were identified in spring 1980: Taiwan and South Africa, neither of which was on the lending list of Orion's parents for political reasons. While the People's Republic of China would have been highly displeased if one of Orion's prominent shareholders had been active in Taiwan, it turned a blind eye to recondite entities such as Orion Pacific.[38] Thus it was able to develop private sector lending on the island without upsetting the mainland and even manage public Eurobond issues, beginning in 1982 with a $100 million FRN for Taiwan Power Corp.

Orion had arranged several loans for South African borrowers in 1970–71, including a $90 million loan for ISCOR, though these transactions were omitted from the published lists of financings. But Orion soon came under pressure from the shareholders, especially Royal Bank, to have no further contact. In 1980, there seemed to be a lull in anti-apartheid activism and Orion decided to explore the development of 'good, non-political business commencing with lines to banks.'[39] Gordon Hall was recruited from the Bank of England as Orion's specialist in the region and made several marketing trips with Patrick Browning. They encountered a cool reception, with pointed remarks like 'we haven't seen you for some time.'[40] These visits agitated the shareholder executives who told Orion to keep 'a very low profile in this market.'[41] When Orion was acquired by Royal Bank, 'the shutters came down again.'[42]

INVESTMENT BANKING

Eurobond new issue activity was subdued in the second half of 1979, as might be expected given rising short-term interest rates. In 1980, as the US prime rate yo-yoed from 20 per cent in April to 10.75 per cent in the summer, and then up to 21.5 per cent by December, the market encountered 'some of the greatest strains in its history.'[43] In the first quarter of 1980 the market was 'totally demoralised,' with losses running into hundreds of millions.[44] Then after Easter, falling interest rates triggered one of the sharpest rallies in history, but this upswing ran out of steam in the summer as rates firmed and the market became flooded with paper. From summer 1980 it was 'back into the abyss' with wildly fluctuating levels of activity until summer 1982 when a sustained upsurge got underway.[45]

Despite the difficult and hazardous market conditions, the overall market volume of Eurobond issues advanced year upon year during the period 1979–81 (see Table 9.3). This was because of intense bouts of activity during market windows, such as spring 1980. It was during this window that the bought deal became a regular feature of the market. To attract investors into the market, offerings were more and more tailored to meet their requirements.[46] Floating rate notes constituted about a quarter of all Eurobond issues in these years, a much greater proportion than in previous years. Convertibles were back in fashion, constituting around 10 per cent of total new issues and warrants issues reappeared in 1981, turning into a flood in subsequent years, mainly from Japan.

Table 9.3 Orion Bank, Eurobonds lead and co-managed, 1979–81[47] ($ billion)

	1979	1980	1981
Orion Bank	2.1	1.9	6.1
Market	14.4	18.8	26.1
Orion share (per cent)	11.9	9.5	23.3

Orion's lead and co-management of Eurobond new issues slipped from $2.1 billion in 1979 to $1.9 billion in 1980. Its appearance in management groups declined from 11.9 per cent of all issues to 9.5 per cent and its position in the league tables from ninth in 1976–78 to eleventh in 1979–81.[48] However, new issue activity soared in 1981 to $6.1 billion, though much of the increase came after the purchase by Royal Bank. Four-fifths of the new issues lead and co-managed by Orion in 1979–81 were denominated in US dollars. Some 30 per cent were FRNs, a somewhat higher proportion than the market as a whole. Borrowers were approximately evenly balanced between public sector entities and private sector corporations, a considerable shift towards the latter compared to earlier years.

Orion attracted considerable attention in the industry for introducing an intriguing innovation – the partly convertible bond. In October 1980, Orion introduced a US$25 million offering of 12.5 per cent debentures for the Canadian corporation Turbo Resources, of which 25 per cent of the nominal value could be converted into Turbo Resources ordinary shares. The novel issue was not well received, partly because the coupon was too low but also because the 25 per cent conversion feature made the bonds hard to value and trade. Moreover, Turbo Resources was not in a strong financial position and within two years the company defaulted on interest payments. Perhaps because of this ill-fated debut, the partly convertible formula did not catch on and Orion never managed to become a major force in equity-linked issues.

Fees from merger and acquisition (M&A) work varied considerably from year to year, depending on the number and size of deals. In 1979, quite a good year, Orion's successful transactions included arranging for the purchase of a cement company in Canada, a ski resort in France and a hotel in England.[49] 'The key to success in Orion's type of M&A business lies in securing exclusive access to good for-sale propositions,' Cunningham told the shareholders: 'Since Orion has no corporate clients in the sense enjoyed by established merchant and investment banks, these for-sale situations are hard to find and are never brought through the door. They are secured only by continual search and by fostering close personal relationships and a reputation for professionalism over a number of years.'[50]

PERFORMANCE, 1979–81

The decline in profitability continued in 1979 and 1980, the Orion Group's consolidated pre-tax profits, which included contributions from Orion Pacific, Orion Guernsey and the leasing subsidiaries, falling to £7.2 million in the latter year. Profits were down again in 1981 to £4.2 million, though this figure was only for nine months trading because of the shift to a September year-end after the acquisition by Royal Bank. Lower profits and high retentions meant a declining return on capital employed; it fell from 16.1 per cent in 1979 to 9.2 per cent in 1981 (see Table 9.4).

Table 9.4   Orion Bank, performance, 1979–81[51] (£ million)

	1979	1980	1981*
Profit (pre-tax)	8.5	7.2	4.2
Capital and reserves	52.9	57.6	60.8
Return (pre-tax) (per cent)	16.1	12.5	9.2*

*9 months to 30 September; rate of return is annualized.

The disruption to business stemming from the fallout from Montagu's resignation was part of the explanation of the falling profits, but, in fact, the decline was underway well before the 'traumatic events' of autumn 1979.[52] To get a better grasp of Orion's situation, in summer 1980 Cunningham instigated a new strategic review of Orion's problems and prospects.

STRATEGIC REVIEW, 1980

By summer 1980, Orion had been operational for nearly ten years. Cunningham's new strategic review divided the decade into two eras of roughly five years apiece. In the first period, the Euromarkets were still quite a new source of finance and as an early entrant Orion had relatively little competition from other banks and the benefit of a substantial potential demand for its services. In the second half of the decade, the Euromarkets became much more widely used by borrowers throughout the world, but a much larger number of banks and financial institutions were competing for the business. In fact, the expansion of the supply of funds outstripped the growth of demand for funds by creditworthy borrowers, so 'opportunities for earning scarcity profits fell sharply.'[53]

As well as this analysis of the underlying reasons for the decline in Orion's profitability, the strategic review of 1980 identified a variety of Orion specific difficulties. It was a generally familiar catalogue, similar to Montagu's list in the strategic review of 1978: the high inflation rate in the UK, where most of Orion's operating costs were incurred; the appreciation of sterling against the US dollar, reducing the reported value of Orion's predominantly US dollar-denominated revenues; increasing restrictions by the UK authorities on the operations of consortium banks; and the decline in the volume of 'shareholder reinforced' business as the shareholders developed their own Eurocurrency lending capacity. A further problem identified by Cunningham's review was the inefficient operating and transaction processing system, which had become hopelessly inadequate for the volume of operations now being conducted.

This catalogue of adversities made pretty dismal reading. The problems facing Orion had not changed since David Montagu's departure, save that some of them had become more acute. A renewed attack on costs was part of the solution, and one heartily endorsed by the shareholders. An analysis of Orion's cost structure revealed the spiralling cost of clerical staff to operate Orion's outmoded settlements function. This cost had doubled since 1976, a much faster rate of growth than any other expenditure posing 'an increasingly heavy burden on the profitability of each income earning transaction undertaken.'[54] The solution was a crash programme of computerization, but in the short-term this required more not less expenditure.

BOND TRADING AGAIN

Having investigated all possible options, Cunningham and his colleagues came to the conclusion that a major expansion of Orion's Eurobond secondary market trading in sovereign risk securities offered the best prospects for developing Orion's business. A report advocating this course of action was submitted to the Shareholders' Forum in Montreal in October 1980. A major increase in activity was advocated, raising the maximum exposure limit from $7.5 million to $30 million. Having been Chase's shareholder representative at Orion at the time of the Eurobond secondary trading losses in 1973, Cunningham was only too aware of the shareholders' worries about this side of Orion's activities. 'The lessons of 1973 are deeply ingrained,' he told them, trying to be reassuring.[55]

The expansion of Orion's Eurobond trading was intended both to generate dealing profits and to defend and enhance its position in the Eurobond primary market. The report argued that an increase in secondary market Eurobond trading would 'give invaluable help to Orion to maintain its position with its special clients.' Reinforcing its position with clients was a particular concern of Orion's management at the time, because of fears that they would be poached by the team that had left to join Swiss Bank Corporation.

In the Eurobond market, Orion's strong-point had traditionally been issues for public sector clients, both in securing management mandates and especially in placing the paper of prime sovereign credits. But the late 1970s saw a shift, many of the lead management positions Orion obtained being for corporate issuers. These clients expected market-making as part of the package of services offered by an investment bank. An expansion of Orion's market-making capabilities would also allow the bank to compete for new issue mandates from smaller corporations. Although modest corporate offerings sometimes posed problems of liquidity, they offered better margins than bulky wholesale public sector issues.

The proposal to expand Orion's bond trading activity was also a response to developments on the 'buy side'. Institutional investors had become increasingly important purchasers of Eurobonds, but shortcomings on the bond trading side meant that Orion 'was not able to do much business with large institutional buyers at present.'[56] One reason was that institutional purchases of new Eurobonds were often affected by switching out of existing investments, the lead manager being expected to offer for these securities. Moreover, institutional investors expected a broadly based Eurobond service, including recommendation and execution of bonds in which Orion had not been part of the management group. For both reasons, servicing institutional buyers required an expanded bond trading operation.

It was proposed to extend FRN trading activities to all issues by prime borrowers. Several arguments were advanced for this: that it would increase turnover and generate income when the straight Eurobond market was inactive; that FRNs were an important and growing sector of the Eurobond market; that it would enable Orion to offer a comprehensive range of floating rate instruments to investors; and that it was relatively risk-free because of lower price volatility of FRNs (an assessment that proved to be misconceived). Moreover, there were as yet relatively few FRN market makers and the market was 'not yet an "efficient market" with the opportunities for profit which that implies.'

The report recommending the expansion of Orion's Eurobond trading activities was well-informed and closely argued and it impressed the shareholder executives. Moreover, they were not minded to undermine Orion's new chief executive, with whom they enjoyed generally very good relations, by rejecting his business development proposal. The Shareholders' Forum in October 1980 gave the go-ahead for the quadrupling of Orion's secondary market trading limits and the build up began right away.

NEW CAPITAL RESOURCES

Cunningham's other achievement at the Shareholders' Forum in October 1980 was to win the shareholders' consent to a new $32 million subordinated loan for Orion. Earlier in the year, the Bank of England had introduced new prudential banking controls – the 'risk asset ratio' system – for assessing a bank's capital adequacy. Orion's substantial foreign currency positions led to an unfavourable risk asset score. Applying the Bank of England's new measure would require a significant restructuring of the bank's loan portfolio from higher yielding loans to lower risk-weighted and less profitable loan types. Such a restructuring of the loan portfolio could only make Orion's financial results even worse, which Cunningham argued was 'contrary to the shareholder objectives for the business of the bank.'[57]

For Orion to meet the new risk asset ratio without significant restructuring of the loan portfolio, additional capital was necessary. There were three alternatives: more equity; third party debt; or a subordinated loan from the shareholders. Besides side-stepping a variety of problems posed by the equity and market debt options, a subordinated loan from the shareholders signalled to both the market and Orion's staff the shareholders' continued support for Orion and their confidence in the 'on-going viability of consortium banks.' The shareholders agreed to the management's request that they should subscribe a $32 million subordinated loan (in addition to $18 million already outstanding). 'I got the feeling that the shareholders recognised our need and that they also would rather keep the "capital" in the family,' Sandon wrote to Cunningham afterwards. 'I got the feeling too that the shareholders have faith in us, in that we are doing the very best of which we are capable.'[58]

ORION BOUGHT BY ROYAL BANK

As agreed at the Montreal Shareholders' Forum of October 1980, in the following months Cunningham visited every shareholder at their head office to review the prospects for Orion and the shareholders' strategic options. He recalled that:

> It was clear from these meetings that although certain shareholders wished
> to carry on, valuing the strategic partnership concept of Orion more highly
> than its financial performance, and others wished to 'resolve' Orion's future
> in one way or another, no one wanted either a public sale or a merger; the

former because of obvious public presentation difficulties and the latter
because the resulting enterprise would be even more complex and share-
holder competitive with less strategic relevance. Finally, and without excep-
tion, they all wished Orion's future to be resolved in a way which respected
and would build upon the extraordinary skills and accomplishments of its
executive management. This left us with a clear preference for a sale to an
existing shareholder.[59]

Not all the shareholders were in the running as buyers. Chase was not a
contender, principally because of the overlap of activities with its own international investment bank, Chase Manhattan Limited. Nor were Credito and
Mitsubishi which lacked the capability of running Orion.

NatWest had been David Montagu's preferred purchaser, arguing that it
would fit well with County Bank's predominantly UK-oriented activities.
Funding the acquisition would certainly not have been a problem for
NatWest. In 1980, it was the second most profitable bank in the world and
it was the eleventh largest. In fact, many outside observers were surprised
that it did not buy Orion, particularly as it had just paid $432 million – 1.7
times book value – for National Bank of North America, a New York state
retail bank described by a Wall Street banking analyst as 'sickly and poorly
managed.'[60] There was some internal support for acquiring Orion, even at
County Bank. 'Personally,' Jonathan Cohen, County Bank's director for
Europe told *Euromoney*, 'I would have liked to have seen us merge with
Orion.'[61] But there was also internal opposition as well as 'long standing cultural differences' that did not dispose Orion's management to this option. In
the event, NatWest recoiled because it 'did not wish to add to its management control problems.'

That left WestLB and Royal Bank. Cunningham had several meetings on
the subject with WestLB chairman Walter Seipp, but eventually the German
bank decided against acquiring Orion because of the problems of integrat-
ing it with their large capital markets operation in Düsseldorf.

Royal Bank had 'hinted that they might be buyers' of Orion when David
Montagu had promoted purchase by one of the shareholders in 1978.[62] Its
existing investment banking operation in London was small and 'going
nowhere,' and the acquisition of Orion provided a ready-made international capability.[63] Orion had lead managed ten funding issues for Royal Bank
and was the leader in the Canadian dollar sector of the Eurobond market.
Not only were there business synergies, there were established personal ties
with Royal Bank executives. And from Orion's side, the Canadian bank was
regarded as having a constructive attitude and the prospect of Royal Bank
ownership enjoyed broad support among management, a crucial factor.

Cunningham held discussions with Robert Paterson, Royal Bank's senior
European executive, a close friend since the original Orion working party in

1969–70, and vice chairman Robert Utting. Early in 1981, they indicated that they were willing to proceed if a deal could be done that did not result in a substantial increase in financial risk to Royal Bank. A solution was negotiated at a special meeting of shareholders in London in April 1981. It was agreed that after the acquisition by Royal Bank, Orion's non-performing assets – some LDC loans, ship loans and the office building – would stay on Orion's books and be administered by Orion, but they would remain at the original shareholders' risk in proportion to their pre-sale interest in Orion. The sale was announced the same day and completed in June.

There was an existing understanding among the shareholders that, if any of them wanted to increase or reduce their interest in Orion by buying or selling the interest of another shareholder, the fair value would be 'book value' (net asset value) since Orion was a partnership and not a strictly commercial enterprise. 'It was a natural extension of this concept that Royal Bank be allowed to acquire the other shareholders' interests at book,' Cunningham explained, 'particularly given the "graceful" exit Royal Bank was providing to the other shareholders and Orion's declining profitability.'[64] Nonetheless, *Euromoney* commented that the price was low compared to other bank purchases of the time and called it 'a steal.'[65] 'A consortium bank has "recycled" itself,' quipped *Newsweek*.[66]

CHAPTER 10

Orion Royal Bank

In the 1970s, under the leadership of Earle McLaughlin, Royal Bank rapidly expanded its international activities. At the time of his retirement in 1980, McLaughlin estimated that as head of the bank he had clocked up 2.4 million kilometres of air travel with 2456 takeoffs and landings.[1] In that year, Royal Bank's international presence comprised 200 branches and other operating units in 45 countries. McLaughlin's successor, Rowland Frazee, was also an internationalist, declaring that his mission was to make Royal Bank a 'global-minded institution.'[2] There was a sound commercial logic to the thrust overseas – overseas operations offered greater scope for growth and profits than the crowded domestic market; at the time Royal Bank acquired Orion, international banking contributed 51 per cent of the bank's profits but comprised only 38 per cent of its assets. Both Royal Bank's participation in Orion as a consortium bank in 1970 and the buy-out of the other consortium participants in 1981 were part of a broader internationalization of Royal Bank's business.

After the purchase, Orion Bank was merged with Royal Bank of Canada (London), Royal Bank's tyro London merchant bank. The combined entity was renamed Orion Royal Bank; legend has it that an early proposal to call it Royal Orion Bank was dropped because of the unfortunate acronym – 'ROB'. With a capital base of around £90 million, comprising £60 million capital and reserves and £30 million subordinated debt, total assets of £1.8 billion and a staff of 420 people, Orion Royal was set to be 'Royal Bank's flagship in its merchant and investment banking activities worldwide.'[3]

LEADERSHIP

Royal Bank was eager to establish firm control over its new investment banking subsidiary and installed its own people in senior executive and non-executive positions. The new chief executive was Lord Hardinge, a career Royal Bank commercial banker who was head of Royal Bank of Canada (London). Tony Cravero, who had served as the right hand man to Orion's chief executive since 1979, continued in the number two role with the title executive vice-president. Jeff Cunningham stayed on as deputy chairman of Orion Royal and president of OMS until 1984, by which time the non-performing LDC loans were 'on a recovery path' and the Liquid Petroleum Gas carrier *Hoegh Gandria* had been sold.[4] Later he became a director of Henry Kissinger Associates.

Jock Finlayson, Royal Bank's president and chief executive, who had been a non-executive director of Orion since 1973 and was one of the key share-holder figures, was appointed chairman of Orion Royal. Three more senior Royal Bank executives, all of whom had previously worked at Orion, joined the Orion Royal board: Geoff Styles, head of world trade and merchant banking; Allan Taylor, head of international banking; and Robert Paterson, chairman of RBC Holdings.

The change of ownership could have created a crisis of staff morale, as happened at other consortium banks when acquired by a single shareholder.[5] As well as the inevitable worries about redundancies, there were concerns about the integration of lending policy with the parent and potential friction over the investment banker's free-wheeling ways. On the other hand, it soon became apparent that it was distinctly simpler to market Orion as a Royal Bank subsidiary than as a consortium bank. 'We suddenly discovered that we did not have to spend half of each meeting explaining what a consortium bank was, why we were creditworthy and what we were about,' said Rod Chamberlain. 'The business took off, partly no doubt through market con-ditions, but significantly also through this clarification and strengthening of the fundamental credit.'[6] So spirits remained high. There were no resigna-tions among the senior executives and the established team led Orion Royal into the new era: William de Gelsey, deputy chairman, with responsibility for global marketing; Philip Hubbard and Christopher Chataway, vice-chair-men, with responsibility, respectively, for capital markets and for mergers and acquisitions; and Michael Perry and Alan Broughton as managing directors.

Lord Hardinge did not measure up to the job of chief executive of a major international investment bank. Soon, there were rumblings of discontent about his leadership and about the tight rein being exercised by Royal Bank, some executives grumbling, reported the *Financial Times*, 'that Orion was becoming a mere puppet of the group's Toronto head office.'[7] Royal Bank decided that Orion Royal would be a happier place if it was run by a career investment banker, but it had to be their man, someone they trusted to keep costs under control.

John Abell was a promising candidate. He had been born in England and educated at Oxford University, but had developed his career in Canada and become a Canadian national. He had strong family ties with the City, his father having been a director of the Bank of England and a brother was a managing director of merchant bank Baring Brothers.[8] Aged 51, Abell was vice chairman of the leading Canadian securities house Wood Gundy, Royal Bank's closest domestic investment banking friend. He had three decades of experience in the securities industry and had recently been much praised for the financial restructuring of debt-laden Massey Ferguson which he had undertaken at the behest of the Canadian government. His extensive contacts among Canada's leading corporations were expected to strengthen Orion Royal's ties with Canadian business, enhancing its usefulness to Royal Bank. Abell took over as chief executive in November 1982, and was subsequently made chairman too. But Royal Bank was wary of allowing the investment bankers too much leeway, so in a parallel development, Geoff Styles became chairman of a new executive committee of the Orion Royal board which kept a close eye on their activities.

INVESTMENT BANKING

The 1980s saw a substantial growth in Eurobond primary market activity, the volume of new issues rising from $25 billion in 1981 to $182 billion in 1988.[9] A substantial part of the increase was attributable to a particularly rapid rise in floating rate notes (FRN), which grew from 25 per cent of total volume in 1980 to 57 per cent in 1985. But the onset of liquidity problems in the FRN secondary market in late 1986 led to a slump in the volume of FRN issues, which largely explains the fall in the volume of Eurobond new issues in 1987 to $144 billion. The recovery in 1988 was driven by another great engine of growth of the 1980s – Japanese convertible and warrant issues (see Table 10.1).

Table 10.1 Orion Royal Bank, Eurobonds lead and co-managed, 1981–88[10] ($ billion)

	1981	1982	1983	1984	1985	1986	1987	1988
Orion Royal	6.4	14.5	19.8	39.4	76.4	58.2	25.9	0.7
Market	27	48	48	86	133	185	144	182
Orion Royal market share (per cent)	24	30	41	46	57	31	18	–

Orion Royal was a very active participant in the Eurobond new issues boom of the early and mid-1980s. By the bank's own calculations, the volume of issues in which it acted as lead or co-manager rose from $6.4 billion in 1981 to $76.4 billion in 1985.[11] In the league table of leading Eurobond houses calculated by the *IFR*, Orion was in the top-20 in each of the years

1982–85, and in 1983 ranked seventh, its highest position. Its 'market share' as a lead manager and co-manager also soared, reaching 57 per cent in 1985, though this was largely the result of the statistical practice of attributing full amount apportionments to co-managers and the increased number of co-managers in many issues.

Although active in a range of currencies in the international Eurobond market, most of Orion Royal's management positions in the 1980s were in the US dollar (mainly FRNs), Canadian dollar and Australian dollar sectors. As discussed in an earlier chapter, in 1975–79, Orion lead or co-managed 20 Canadian dollar Eurobond issues totalling US$664 million. Orion's position as a lead manager in the Canadian dollar Eurobond market was reinforced by its acquisition by Royal Bank and it rose higher in the league tables for this market sector: it was second in 1983; first in 1985; and third in 1986. In 1985, Orion Royal lead or co-managed 24 Canadian dollar Eurobond issues, 45 per cent of the total, and was book runner for 14 of them.[12] Its principal rivals in that year, and others, were Wood Gundy, book runner in 1985 for nine issues, Société Générale, five issues, Merrill Lynch, three issues, and Union Bank of Switzerland, three issues. Another milestone, in 1985, was Orion Royal's co-lead management of the then largest ever Canadian dollar Eurobond issue, a swap-driven Can$200 million issue for Marubeni Corporation.

Orion lead or co-managed three Australian dollar Eurobond issues in the 1970s, which established its name in the Australian dollar sector: its pioneering financing for Rural & Industries Bank of Western Australia in 1972; Australian Industry Development Corporation in 1976; and Rank Overseas Holdings in 1978. The Australian dollar sector was dormant in the early 1980s, but in 1983 Orion perceived that conditions were right for a revival. The borrower was Primary Industry Bank of Australia (PIBA), a prime client that made loans to Australian farmers but because of domestic conditions was having to pay over 17 per cent for funds. Joe Cook, who led the development of the Australian dollar sector business, did not have much difficulty in interesting managing director, John Frierson, in 5-year funds at 13 per cent. Orion also knew where to sell the bonds, thanks to its extensive experience of feeding Canadian dollar bonds to Benelux investors. 'In his typically down to earth way,' recalled William de Gelsey, 'Joe assured us that investors in Benelux would not know the difference between the two types of dollars, and our Australian dollar issue business was born.'[13] The Aus$20 million issue on behalf of PIBA, brought out by Orion in March 1983, revived investors' interest in the sector through its successful placement and strong secondary market performance.

Having re-launched the Australian dollar Eurobond market, Orion Royal was sector leader, coming first in the league tables each year from 1983 to 1986.[14] Over the years 1983–85 it was book runner on 37 issues, which raised a total of Aus$1.8 billion. Its nearest, but not very near, rivals in this market were Bankers Trust, book runner in 1983–85 on eleven issues, Hambros, nine issues, Morgan Stanley, six issues, and Swiss Bank Corporation, three issues.[15]

Orion Royal's secondary market Eurobond trading activities grew rapidly in the early 1980s, following the decision to expand this activity taken in October 1980.[16] In 1981, Orion Royal made markets in about 200 issues for prime sovereign and corporate fixed-rate issuers and FRN issues for prime banks; In 1984, It traded around 900 issues and 1000 in 1905. It was the foremost secondary market maker in Australian dollar Eurobond issues and a leading market maker in Canadian dollar Eurobond issues. From 1984 to 1987, it was also very active in trading FRN issues to support its new issue activities and as a service to investor clients.[17] The expansion of Orion Royal's Eurobond trading stemmed in part from the increased scale of its primary market activity, since it was usual and necessary for managers to make a market in the bonds for which they were book runners. But trading was also undertaken to generate revenues from the secondary market side of the Eurobond business, in the face of the downward pressures on fees in the highly competitive primary market.

The volume of corporate advisory work, particularly merger and acquisition work, undertaken by the group led by Christopher Chataway grew year by year. In 1985, they advised General Electric on the divestiture of Simplex GE to its management, the largest ever management buy-out in the UK at the time.[18] A good deal of work came their way as a result of Royal Bank ownership, such as advising the parent bank on the sale of its stake in Western Trust and similar consumer credit interests in Germany and Hong Kong. 'Not very glamorous,' commented Henry Mutkin, one of the corporate finance team, about such in-house business, 'but it made a useful contribution to the bottom line.'[19]

Orion Royal was engaged by publisher Christian Hemain, a friend of Philip Hubbard, to advise on the sale of *IFR* (*International Financing Review*), the Euromarkets' weekly journal, to Canadian publishing magnate Lord Thomson. Instead of the £3 million Thomson had originally offered, he was eventually forced to pay £6 million, causing him to complain to the Royal Bank's chairman about Orion Royal's 'twisting my tail' and forcing up the price.[20] But Christopher Chataway and Nicholas Villiers, who had joined in 1982, were delighted since their fee was based on a percentage of the excess over the starting £3 million.

Another notable episode concerned Laker Airways, for which Orion had arranged a $131 million loan in 1981. Laker Airways chairman, Sir Freddie Laker, was a people's hero, who took on the powerful cartelized airlines, such as British Airways, by offering a 'no frills' cut price service across the Atlantic under the brand name 'Skytrain'.

When his airline got into difficulties, Orion became involved in the campaign to save Laker Airways from collapse, earning newspaper headlines that Orion's corporate financiers had put together a rescue package.[21] Unfortunately, they were unable to prevent the airline's demise, though Sir Freddie lived to fight another day, successfully suing British Airways and founding another independent airline. His example spawned a number of imitators.

Orion prided itself on the professionalism of its executives. In the 1970s, Orion trainees were sent on the highly-regarded Chase credit training course. After the acquisition by Royal Bank, Orion Royal developed its own training course with an investment banking slant. It was soon sufficiently well-established to be able to sell its services to other smaller banks.[22]

COMMERCIAL BANKING

Orion Royal became the loan syndication arm of the whole Royal Bank of Canada group. The volume of syndicated lending declined in the early 1980s and Royal Bank's activity fell too: in 1981 it lead and co-managed $16.2 billion syndicated loans; in 1983, $10.8 billion. But the market revived in 1984 and in 1985 Royal Bank lead and co-managed syndicated loans totalling a record $19.7 billion. That year it ranked seventh in the league table of syndicated loan lead and co-managers, its highest position in the 1980s (see Table 10.2).

Table 10.2   Royal Bank of Canada, syndicated loans lead and co-managed, 1981–88[24] ($ billion)

	1981	1982	1983	1984	1985	1986	1987	1988
Royal Bank	16.2	16.7	10.8	13.2	19.7	8.4	10.9	6.2
Total market	78.7	61.1	41.0	68.4	91.3	85.0	122.3	205.4
RBC market share (per cent)	21	27	26	19	22	10	9	3

Orion Royal's prominence in *both* the Eurobond market and the Eurodollar syndicated loan market was a notable achievement – in 1982, the *Financial Times* identified it as one of only three international institutions that ranked among the top-15 lead managers in both activities.[23]

Unfortunately, from 1985 syndicated lending became a less profitable business as competition between lenders led to smaller spreads, which fell from 100 basis points in 1984 to 41 basis points in 1986 (see Table 10.3), a far cry from 152 basis points a decade earlier.

It was 'a borrower's market,' commented an Orion Royal publication, 'where not only spreads but also front-end and commitment fees continue to

Table 10.3 Mean spreads over LIBOR, 1981–88[25] (basis points)

1981	1982	1983	1984	1985	1986	1987	1988
89	84	86	100	65	41	44	60

contract.'[26] In response, Royal Bank drastically cut back the level of its syndicated lending activity, which by 1988 was down to $6.2 billion. As a result, Royal Bank's rank in the league table of syndicated loan lead and co-managers slumped to number 37.

The early 1980s saw the further development of the swaps market with the introduction of interest rate swaps in addition to currency swaps. Such transactions involved counter-parties exchanging liabilities denominated on a floating-rate basis for fixed-rate, or vice versa. The first interest rate swapped Eurobond issue was made in 1981.[27] The interest rate swaps market 'came of age' in 1983, during which it was estimated that interest rate swaps totalling $10 billion were transacted, as well as $20 billion of currency swaps.[28] By 1985, the total swaps market had grown to more than $100 billion. Orion Royal established a full-time swaps team in 1983, which acted as the Royal Bank group's principal swaps capability. In 1985, it managed swaps totalling $3 billion.[29]

As ever, Orion Royal's treasury and money market team traded profitably in the currency markets. It specialized in forward foreign exchange transactions, especially Deutschemarks, yen, Swiss francs, sterling and Canadian dollars, in which Orion Royal was a market maker. It was also active in the inter-bank deposit market, dealing in all major currencies. Orion Royal began trading in financial futures in 1982, both in Chicago and in London, the London International Financial Futures Exchange having just been founded; it was soon established as one of the leading banks trading currency options.[30]

BIG BANG IN LONDON

John Abell, like many other bankers, was enthusiastic about the opportunities created by the deregulation and reform of the UK securities markets initiated in 1983 – London's so-called 'Big Bang'. Following the herd, Orion Royal bought a mainly equities broker, Kitcat & Aitken, and applied to become a market-maker in the UK government debt market. Kitcat & Aitken, founded in 1900, was a well-known and well-regarded second-tier stock broker with top-rated research teams in the mining, transportation, shipping, leisure and textile sectors.[31] Kitcat had long-standing ties with Canada, and with Royal Bank in particular; they had a fund management joint venture in Guernsey. If Orion Royal was going to buy a London broker, Kitcat & Aitken was the firm with which Royal Bank was most familiar and most comfortable. 'From Royal Bank's perspective,' observed Kitcat partner Alan Clifton, 'the acquisition was for sentimental reasons as much as business reasons.'[32]

The trouble was that the business logic of the tie-up was far from obvious. Orion Royal had no need for an equities broker and there was zero synergy with its Eurobond business. 'It chewed up a lot of management time trying to find things to do together,' recalled Clifton. However, Royal Bank was happy with the acquisition, believing that it would enable the bank to acquire experience in securities business which it was unable to do at home because of the Canadian equivalent of Glass–Steagall. 'London is the only stock market we can get into,' explained Geoff Styles, 'so we will use our experience with Kitcat to help build up expertise in other markets. The equity markets will become internationalised, and we want to be part of that as they open up.'[33]

Royal Bank of Canada Gilts was formed to participate in the UK government debt market. Orion Royal had been unsuccessful (fortunately, as it turned out) in its attempt to buy leading gilts broker Pember & Boyle; it went for a much higher price to Morgan Grenfell, which later had to close it down. Royal Bank's gilts subsidiary was one of 27 successful applicants to become a market-maker in the reformed gilts market that opened in October 1986, a market that had hitherto been serviced by a handful of jobbing firms. As with equities, the strategic rationale underlying the move into gilts was that it provided a stepping stone to international securities activity. 'Gilts will become an integral part of the internationalisation of the financial markets,' said Styles. 'They'll be another international investment to sell around the world, and to be used in swaps like US Treasuries.'

By the end of the Big Bang process, the deregulated UK equity and gilt markets both had far too much capital and capacity for the scale of business. At first the over-capacity was disguised by the worldwide bull market and the euphoria that accompanied Big Bang, but soon the operational losses became more preoccupying for management than grand strategic visions. It was little comfort that a large number of other banks had made similar misjudgments.

PERFORMANCE, 1981–85

The five years following Royal Bank's acquisition saw rising and record profits at Orion Royal, peaking in 1985 at £17.7 million pre-tax. Royal Bank was more demanding of its subsidiary than the consortium partners in terms of dividends, and over the years 1981–85 Orion Royal paid a total of £21.4 million in dividends, compared to just £4 million returned in dividends to the consortium partners over the years 1971–80. Despite the dividend pay-outs, Orion Royal's capital and reserves increased from retained earnings each year, rising from £60.8 million in 1981 to £93.6 million in 1985 (see Table 10.4).

Table 10.4   Orion Royal Bank, performance, 1981–85[34] (£ million)

	1981*	1982	1983	1984	1985
Profits (pre-tax)	4.2	10.2	15.5	10.5	17.7
Capital and reserves	60.8	73.0	79.8	85.0	93.6
Return (pre tax) (per cent)	9.2*	13.4	20.6	12.4	19.0

*Years ending 30 September, 9 months 1981; rate of return is annualized.

Orion Royal's return on capital rose under Royal Bank ownership, averaging 16.3 per cent pre-tax in the years 1982–85. This was an improvement on the problematic years 1979–81, when the rate of return averaged 12.8 per cent, but considerably lower than in Orion's heyday under David Montagu's leadership in the years 1974–78, when the average pre-tax return was 24.4 per cent. The lower rate of return in the 1980s reflected the increased competition in the Euromarkets. It also had to do with Orion Royal's high cost base which, as ever, was a cause of anxiety to the proprietor and its representatives. Cravero and Styles, in particular, fought to contain costs, which meant perennial battles to hold the line on hirings and salaries, particularly in the recruitment frenzy in the City in the run-up to Big Bang. The constant struggle was exhausting and dispiriting for the Royal Bank executives involved with Orion. By the mid-1980s, in Toronto 'the "O" word' was being uttered through gritted teeth.[35]

MORE MANAGEMENT TURMOIL

John Abell's moves into the UK equities and gilts markets caused disaffection among Orion's globally minded deal-makers, although few at the time objected to participating in the largest UK equity issue of all – the British Telecom privatization of November 1984. The perception spread among the key mandate winners, syndication organizers, swaps engineers and traders, that Abell and the Royal Bank were not interested in the Eurobond side of Orion Royal's business. 'We have to fight tooth and nail against the bureaucracy for everything – for staff, for salaries, for a bonus scheme, for technology,' one complained.[36] His protest was the counterpoint to the efforts of Cravero and Styles to control costs and improve the return on capital.

The different work methods of the chairman and the senior Eurobond executives also became a source of friction. The latter were driven and demanding, put in long hours and were forever on the move – the characteristic investment banker lifestyle. But the amiable Abell was of the old school, as *Euromoney* explained: 'some Orion staff resented his relatively short working hours and his outside directorships … Abell seldom walked about the bank, and became known as the invisible chairman.'[37] Despite Orion Royal's dynamic expansion and the marked improvement in the profits of the bank under his chairmanship, there was mounting alienation among the senior executives. 'We've done well because about 20 of us worked our bottoms off,' one of them told *Euromoney*, 'while people in the other bits of the bank write memos to each other and reports to the Royal Bank.'[38]

In September 1985, John Langton head of Eurobond trading and sales and a key figure at Orion Royal, walked out with the three-man dollar Eurobond trading team to join Security Pacific. Asked why he left, Langton said: 'Because I was made an offer I couldn't refuse, and because SecPac is seriously committed to investment banking.' Langton, a member of the board of the Association of International Bond Dealers and later chief executive of its successor, the International Securities Market Association, was one of the Euromarket's most experienced and highly regarded Eurobond traders; in the 'Euromarket super-bank 1984 vintage' fantasy investment bank devised by *IFR* magazine, Langton was the chief Eurobond trader.[39] His departure was a serious blow.

Despite record profits and a record volume of business – in 1985 Orion lead managed 50 issues, one per week – complaints about John Abell's leadership from other senior executives and the loss of Langton caused alarm at Royal Bank. When Abell's three-year contract came up for review shortly after, it was not renewed. 'His views on the way ahead were not as near to those at the roots of the bank as we felt appropriate,' Geoff Styles told *Euromoney*, 'he was the odd man out.'[40]

Abell's departure in November 1985 had not been foreseen and there was no contingency plan for a replacement. While the head-hunters went to work to find a suitable candidate, a task that took nine months, Geoff Styles served as chairman and Tony Cravero as acting chief executive. They were immediately faced with a new crisis when three more executives from the Eurobond side left the following month: Michael Webber, head of syndication, left for County Bank; Joe Cook, head of capital markets, joined Morgan Guaranty; and Simon Canning went to Swiss Bank Corporation. Cook's departure was a particularly grave loss, since he was one of Orion's top money-makers, 'the key guy,' as a colleague put it, who had been the main architect of Orion's success in the Australian and Canadian sectors of the market. The departures undermined Orion Royal's competence and credibility as a Eurobond house.

The handling of Abell was the last straw for Philip Hubbard, who left in August 1986 to take up a professorship at Harvard Business School where he co-authored a notable study of investment banking.[41] Hubbard was appalled that, after all the effort that had been made to rebuild the business after the debacle of David Montagu's departure, history was repeating itself before his eyes: that once again Orion was foundering because of shareholder–management tensions; that nobody had learned the lesson that another 'bust-up' would mean a loss of hard-earned reputation, a haemorrhaging of talent and a squandering of value.[42] Hubbard, like John Langton and Andrew Large, was a member of the *IFR*'s investment banking 'dream team', in his case for his fixed-income research skills, and his departure did further damage.[43]

It was the best part of a year before Orion Royal's new permanent head took office. The appointment of John Sanders as chairman and chief executive of Orion Royal in October 1986 spelt, as the *Financial Times* put it, 'the end to one of the longest running guessing games in the Euromarkets.'[44] Sanders was a promising catch. After Oxford University, he had begun his career in banking at Midland Bank, spent seven years at Credit Suisse First Boston (or forerunner firms) and then seven at Warburgs, where he was head of the international capital markets team. He was a well-known figure in the investment banking industry, being elected as the first chairman of the International Primary Market Association and a member of the executive committee of the International Securities Regulatory Organization. At Warburgs there were plenty of other able and ambitious colleagues and it was obvious that not all of them could make it to the top. 'I accepted the offer from Orion because I thought it was time I ran something,' he explained. 'I didn't realise how great the problems were. Nobody did.'[45]

With the appointment of Sanders, Styles and Cravero returned to Canada to resume their careers with Royal Bank. Paul Taylor, a high flyer at Royal Bank who had worked at Orion as senior representative in 1974–78, and had subsequently become senior vice president in international corporate banking in Toronto, was dispatched to London as deputy chairman. Sanders pulled off a notable coup by recruiting David Pritchard as vice chairman with responsibility for Orion Royal's capital markets, treasury and trading activities. Pritchard, an expert in derivatives who pioneered both the first currency swap and the first interest rate swap, joined in November 1986. Christopher Chataway continued to have responsibility for corporate finance. William de Gelsey, who had reached retirement age in London, was asked to stay on with the specific task of marketing the group's services in the booming Japanese financial markets. He moved to Tokyo in April 1987, retaining his deputy chairmanship. Once again, Orion Royal had a first-rate leadership team, but in the meantime the business had been wasting away and junior talent departing for other firms.

GETTING OUT OF EUROBONDS

Sanders, Taylor and Pritchard introduced improved management accounting practices to monitor the business and undertook a fundamental review of

Orion Royal's activities. This exercise during the winter of 1986 and spring
of 1987 revealed that Orion Royal's Eurobond operations were unprofitable –
despite its lofty positions in the league tables, the business was losing money.
An underlying market factor was the increasing importance of distribution
in the Eurobond business.[46] Orion Royal's lack of a direct distribution base
in the USA, Switzerland or Germany was a significant weakness. Moreover,
as swaps became more important there was a growing de-linkage between
the currency preferences of investors and borrowers. To run a successful
swaps business, intermediaries had to have a multi-currency capability and
for this they needed a presence in the principal financial centres of the world,
which would have required a massive commitment of capital by Royal Bank
that was simply out of the question. And, as ever, competition was intensi-
fying as more and more banks piled into the business (see Table 10.5).

Table 10.5 Number of lead managing investment
banks, 1980–87[47]

	At least 1 issue	At least 5 issues	At least 10 issues	At least 20 issues
1980	76	24	4	2
1981	76	27	13	2
1982	83	33	19	6
1983	75	35	15	4
1984	81	42	25	11
1985	94	57	35	20
1986	112	54	38	22
1987	117	60	39	18

The growth of competition led to falling commissions. FRNs, a sector
of the market of great importance for Orion, were particularly hard hit,
commissions slumping by two-thirds between the early and mid-1980s
(see Table 10.6).

Table 10.6 Indicative commissions on floating rate note issues, 1980–86[48] (basis points)

	1980–83	1983–86
Management fee	25	10
Underwriting fee	25	10
Selling concession	100	30
Total fees	150	50

The review of Orion Royal's business indicated that its Eurobond operations had been losing money throughout the 1980s, but that the losses had been hidden by inadequate accounting procedures, particularly in relation to swaps.[49] This was a devastating discovery, since Eurobond business was Orion Royal's core activity, not to mention Sanders' personal area of expertise. Orion was still a leader in the Australian dollar and Canadian dollar sectors and an analysis was made as to whether a slimmed-down Eurobond business focusing on these niche positions would be profitable. But other banks were pushing their services in these sectors and winning mandates. Indeed, Pritchard was amazed to learn that Canadian corporate treasurers had become so spoilt for choice that they expected Orion to pay *them* for choosing to use its services. Reluctantly, Sanders, Taylor and Pritchard concluded that, as Pritchard put it, 'the business had run out of road.'

While the future of Orion's Eurobond operations as a whole was being reviewed, retrenchment began in certain sectors. In November 1986, the perpetual sector of the FRN market suffered a massive loss of confidence. Perpetuals are FRNs without a final redemption date, which were expected to trade at about par by virtue of the six-monthly setting of interest coupons; many of them were issued by AAA banks and were supposed to have virtually the liquidity and security of deposits. However, it did not work out thus and they became almost unsellable because of over-supply. Prime UK bank perpetuals fell to 90 and below; some stocks went to 70. In a couple of days, the slump in prices wiped out a 'staggering' $800 million in value across the market.[50] Moreover, since many traders ran their positions on borrowed money, they found themselves paying more for their funds than they earned on their FRNs, which were only sellable at a large loss.

Orion Royal stopped market-making markets in FRNs, as did many other banks. 'The nature of the FRN market has changed,' stated the press announcement in March 1987. 'FRN market making does not meet Orion Royal's internal requirements for an adequate return.'[51] The following month saw a 'reorganization' of staff, involving shifting people from marketing to product areas, and the first redundancies – 12 jobs.

By summer 1987, senior management had secretly decided to shut down all of Orion Royal's Eurobond activities. Before proceeding, John Sanders consulted William de Gelsey, 'who represented the heart and soul of Orion,' and by then was the firm's resident representative in Tokyo; de Gelsey agreed that there was no alternative.[52] Implementation of the withdrawal from Eurobonds – known as 'Project Phoenix', a singularly inappropriate codename – was scheduled for the end of October. But on 19 October 1987 there was an international stock market crash. Although the crash had no direct impact on Orion Royal, 'we just watched the screens turn red,' recalled Pritchard, it cast a pall over the banking and securities industry. Thus it made the public announcement of Orion Royal's withdrawal from

Eurobonds on 2 November appear to be a hasty knee-jerk reaction to a market correction, rather than a decision about which management had painstakingly considered every angle, taking almost a year.[53] At the same time as Orion Royal withdrew from Eurobonds, it also closed down its UK gilts primary dealership which was losing money. These cutbacks led to 150 redundancies, more than a third of the staff. Not long after, Orion moved out of its London Wall head office into the new Royal Bank of Canada Centre in Queen Victoria Street; its days as an autonomous entity were clearly numbered.

Orion was by no means alone in sustaining losses from its Eurobond operations or from new activities embarked upon in the euphoric build-up to Big Bang. Estimates at the time suggested that probably only four of the 27 gilts market-makers were operating profitably. Lloyds Bank was the first to grasp the nettle, closing down its Eurobond and gilts operations in June 1987. In following months, Chemical Bank, Dean Witter and Hill Samuel withdrew from Eurobonds and L.F. Rothschild and Shearson Lehman scaled back their activities.[54] After Orion Royal, there were plenty of further retrenchments in both the gilts market and on the equities side.

PERFORMANCE, 1986–89

In the years 1986–88, Orion Royal posted losses totalling £34.3 million (see Table 10.7). These unsatisfactory results were due to large-scale provisioning against losses on Orion Royal's loan book, mostly for syndicated loans made in the 1970s and early 1980s to LDC borrowers.

Table 10.7 Orion Royal Bank, performance, 1986–89[55] (£ million)

	1986	1987	1988	1989
Profits (pre-tax)	(3.4)	(16.7)	(14.2)	8.9
Capital and reserves	84.3	48.5	33.4	55.6
Return (pre-tax) (per cent)	–	–	–	16.0

Orion Royal began provisioning modestly in 1986, but drastic write-downs became necessary after Citibank's unprecedented $3 billion provision – 25 per cent of its total doubtful loans – in May 1987, which was followed by even more demanding standards from the Bank of England.[56] At the same time, Orion Royal's loan book was reduced, enabling capital to be withdrawn from the business in line with a lower level of activity. The outcome was a reduction in capital and reserves by more than half from £84.3 million in 1986 to £33.4 million in 1988. The following year, pre-tax profits returned to the black, but it was the bank's final year under the Orion Royal banner.

BIG BANG IN CANADA

While Orion Royal was cutting back in London, Royal Bank was contemplating a major new move on the investment banking side. The mid-1980s saw a push into Canada by the big Wall Street brokerage houses and the Canadian government became concerned that the domestic securities houses were, in Paul Taylor's words: 'going to get creamed by the Americans, who were coming in with 10 or 15 times the capital of the Canadians. The government said, if we're going to keep any of this business for Canadians, we had better let them be bought by the Canadian banks, which would be able to play the capital game against the Americans.'[57] Hence in December 1986, the Canadian administration announced that the regulatory impediment to commercial banks owning securities houses was to be abolished from June 1987. Thus, for the first time, Canadian banks could undertake securities business at home and a frenzied scramble ensued as banks and securities houses measured each other up.

Traditionally, Royal Bank had been closest to Wood Gundy, Canada's second largest securities house, and discussions about a merger got underway immediately.[58] But terms could not be agreed and by summer 1987 the negotiations had reached an impasse. Dominion Securities, the largest and leading Canadian securities house, with 60 offices and 640 registered representatives across Canada, initially decided that it would remain independent, like Cazenove in London, and rebuffed advances. But following the breakdown of the negotiations with Wood Gundy, Royal Bank and Dominion Securities got talking. Initially, the price demanded by the Dominion Securities partners was too high for Royal Bank, but when the securities house sustained substantial losses from its participation in the ill-fated British Petroleum underwriting that ran foul of the stock market crash of October 1987, they modified their terms. Royal Bank's acquisition of Dominion Securities was announced in December 1987. Renamed RBC Dominion Securities, but continuing as an autonomous entity, it became the Royal Bank group's investment banking powerhouse.

The advent of RBC Dominion Securities spelt the end of Orion Royal as an independent entity. A new London-based subsidiary, RBC Dominion Securities International, was created to act as the international arm of RBC Dominion Securities. It was formed by combining Dominion Securities' London entity, which specialized in brokerage services for North American securities and was a participant in the Canadian dollar sector of the Eurobond market, with Kitcat & Aitken as well as Orion Royal's government bond trading, and corporate finance teams. John Sanders became the new chairman and chief executive.[59]

The 'first priority' of RBC Dominion Securities International was to service the global investment banking requirements of the Canadian corporate clients of Royal Bank and RBC Dominion Securities.[60] 'Our vision is to become the leading Canadian investment dealer in the international marketplace,' declared Sanders. In this context, Kitcat & Aitken's business focused on UK equities was 'just irrelevant' to RBC Dominion Securities International.[61] This might not have mattered had Kitcat & Aitken been profitable, but, like most securities broking firms in the wake of the October 1987 crash, it was loss-making. Despite trimming the payroll from 210 at the time of the crash to 160 a year later, Kitcat & Aitken continued to lose money and in 1990 it was closed down. 'When the going got tough, they got out,' reflected Alan Clifton sadly.

The next stage in the dismantling of Orion Royal was the transfer of the leasing activity and the treasury and money market operations to Royal Bank's London branch in November 1987. The arrival of Orion's highly skilled team, the bank's most consistent money-spinners, boosted the profits of the London branch.[62] Those who remained on the bond origination side were also dispatched to this new home, being reassigned to client relation roles. All that then remained of Orion Royal was the banking operation, the legacy of its lending activities in the syndicated loan market. In November 1989 this was renamed RBC Europe.

And thus, not quite two decades after it first rose in the Euromarket firmament, Orion's star ceased to shine.[63]

1.1 US Secretary of State Dean Rusk presents David Rockefeller to King Faisal of Saudi Arabia.

1.2 Hermann Abs of Deutsche Bank and King Juan Carlos of Spain.

Acknowledgements and more detailed descriptions can be found on pages xii–xvi.

2.1   Siegmund Warburg, father of the
Eurobond.

2.2   Ronald Grierson, animator of
Orion's investment banking thrust.

2.3   George Bolton, Euromarket
visionary, shunned the consortium
fashion as BOLSA Chairman.

2.4   Fernand Collin of Kredietbank,
whose currency cocktail
foreshadowed the euro.

Acknowledgements and more detailed descriptions can be found on pages xii–xvi.

3.1 *Euromoney* speculates on the demise of the Euromarkets.

EUROMONEY

JULY 1972

RIP EURODOLLAR 1958~19

COULD THE EURODOLLAR MARKET DIE?

"Colgate-Palmolive in ECU is a perfect match — Toothpaste paper for the Belgian dentist!"

3.2 The 'Belgian dentist', as usual, goes for a familiar name.

Acknowledgements and more detailed descriptions can be found on pages xii–xvi.

4.1   David Montagu led Orion's thoroughbreds in the heyday of consortium banking.

4.2   Mrs Thatcher comes to lunch at Orion with David Montagu and William de Gelsey.

Acknowledgements and more detailed descriptions can be found on pages xii–xvi.

5.1 (Left) Bank of England Director George Blunden lobbed a bombshell at the consortium banks.

5.2 (Right) Orion's Philip Hubbard pioneered the use of swaps in Eurobond issues.

5.3 Reunion of Olympic athletes – Orion's Christopher Chataway and Emil Zatopek.

Acknowledgements and more detailed descriptions can be found on pages xii–xvi.

6.1, 6.2   Walter Wriston's Citicorp, 'the world's only international bank', spreads across America and conquers the world. 'Countries don't go bankrupt,' but 'the banks that lend to them do.'

6.3   Michael von Clemm: as 'uncrowned King of the FRN Market,' he sometimes seemed to walk on water. He launched Canary Wharf.

6.4   Milton Friedman encouraged Chicago 'crapshooters' to offer financial futures.

Acknowledgements and more detailed descriptions can be found on pages xii–xvi.

7.1 Julius Strauss, first London stockbroker to specialize in Eurobonds.

7.2 John Meyer (right), JP Morgan Chairman, architect of Euroclear, with Thomas Gates.

7.3 John Langton – head of Eurobond trading at Orion; he went on to lead the International Securities Market Association.

7.4 Stanley Ross unleashed the 'grey market' in Eurobonds.

Acknowledgements and more detailed descriptions can be found on pages xii–xvi.

8.1 (Above, from left) Orion's Patrick Browning, Andrew Large, David Montagu and William de Gelsey at an International Monetary Fund annual meeting.

8.2 Joe Cook, Orion's 'key guy' in the capital markets.

8.3 Spike Wright, who ensured Orion's funding at the finest rates.

Acknowledgements and more detailed descriptions can be found on pages xii–xvi.

"We give them the know-how, they go home and quadruple the oil prices."

9.1 OPEC countries developed an elite of their own citizens to manage their petrodollars.

9.2 Jinx Grafftey-Smith races to the Kandara Palace Hotel.

"It's fool-proof. We use the money from the price increase to buy up all the BP shares."

9.3 Signs of paranoia after the Iranian revolution – oil at $100 and a BP takeover?

Acknowledgements and more detailed descriptions can be found on pages xii–xvi.

10.1   Orion's Jeff Cunningham (centre)
        and William de Gelsey enjoy a
        chat with Roy Jenkins.

10.2   Patrick Sergeant made
        Euromoney the authoritative
        voice of the Euromarkets.

10.3   Christian Hemain (with César),
        founder of *AGEFI* (later *IFR*).

Acknowledgements and more detailed descriptions can be found on pages xii–xvi.

The Greater London Council

U.S. $500,000,000

Eurocurrency Loan

N.M. Rothschild & Sons Limited
European Banking Company Limited

National Westminster Bank Limited
Manufacturers Hanover Limited

Orion Banking Group

11.1 Orion helps lend $500 million to London; the group also organized a $2.5 billion loan to the UK Treasury during the first 'oil shock'

"What worries us is, for this enormous loan all you can offer as security is Britain."

11.2 UK Chancellor Denis Healey appeals to the IMF for support.

Acknowledgements and more detailed descriptions can be found on pages xii–xvi.

12.1 Minos Zombanakis (above right) launches another 'jumbo' syndicated loan.

12.2 Abdlatif Al-Hamad, Chairman of United Bank of Kuwait, most durable of London's consortium banks.

12.3 Royal Bank's Tony Fell exemplified the convergence of investment and commercial banking.

12.4 Evan Galbraith of Bankers Trust is said to have dreamt up the idea of floating rate notes in his bath.

Acknowledgements and more detailed descriptions can be found on pages xii–xvi.

13.1 The fall of Vatican-linked Banco Ambrosiano unnerved the Inter-Alpha banking club.

"Just wondering how many Hail Marys for moving my account from the Vatican Bank . . ."

13.2 The money from LDC loans all too often ended up in off-shore bank accounts.

"But, General, if we do let the world's banking system collapse, bang goes everything we've managed to salt away abroad."

"But I bet if I were a Third World country I'd never get a letter like this about my overdraft."

13.3 Banks lost heavily on consumer and mortgage loans; US savings and loan associations lost $13 billion in one year.

Acknowledgements and more detailed descriptions can be found on pages xii–xvi.

14.1   Executives of Libra Bank – Latin American
        specialist and pioneer in loan trading.

14.2   Royal Bank's Jock Finlayson steered
        Orion when it gave up consortium status.

14.3   'Jesus is working for us;' Mexico's Jesus
        Silva Herzog and Gérard Legrain of
        Intermex.

Acknowledgements and more detailed descriptions can be found on pages xii–xvi.

15.1 Consortium banks sometimes seemed to be formed 'after a good lunch.'

15.2 Stanislas Yassukovich peers at the night sky and watches the consortium banking stars as they fall.

Acknowledgements and more detailed descriptions can be found on pages xii–xvi.

16.1 Periodic excesses in the FRN market cost traders dear.

"And we've just opened our brand new Gold Futures department."

16.2 Clients were often baffled by futures and swaps (with 'bells and whistles').

16.3 The Japanese took centre stage and seemed to be buying everything in sight, until the bubble burst.

Acknowledgements and more detailed descriptions can be found on pages xii–xvi.

CHAPTER 11

Decline of consortium banking

'Consortium banking is no far-fetched concept,' observed Gérard Legrain, managing director of International Mexican Bank in a letter to the *Financial Times* in 1983. 'All we are is jointly owned banks. In many lines of business, joint ventures are created, modified, undone as a matter of course. Banking is no exception.'[1]

The first signs of the waning of the consortium banking movement began to be seen in the later 1970s, not long after it had been hailed in the press as a dynamic and permanent feature of international finance. One indicator of the significance of the consortium banks is their share of total foreign currency loans of all British and overseas banks operating in the UK (see Table 11.1). By this yardstick of Eurocurrency market share, the consortium banks as a group peaked in 1976–77 and declined thereafter, notwithstanding considerable growth on the part of many individual consortium banks.

Table 11.1   Consortium banks' foreign currency loans as a proportion of total UK banks' foreign currency loans, 1975–87[2] (per cent)

1975	1976	1977	1978	1979	1980	1981	1982	1983	1984	1985	1986	1987
10.7	11.4	11.4	10.7	10.3	9.3	9.8	7.5	6.5	6.3	5.1	4.6	4.0

Between 1975 and 1992, 29 of the 35 London consortium banks (as defined by the Bank of England's criteria of 1975), 'disappeared': 19 were bought by one of the shareholding banks; two were acquired by an unconnected bank; and eight were liquidated. Other consortium banks, outside the Bank of England's definition and control, suffered a similar rate of attrition, mostly being acquired by one of the shareholders or wound up. Six regional specialists survived, one of them ceasing to be a consortium bank in 1998.[3]

The annual number of consortium bank 'disappearances' – liquidations or acquisitions by a shareholder or other bank – between 1975 and 1992 was as shown in Table 11.2.

Table 11.2   'Disappearances' of consortium banks,
1975–92 (number of banks)

1975	1	1981	1	1987	–
1976	–	1982	–	1988	3
1977	1	1983	3	1989	3
1978	–	1984	2	1990	8
1979	1	1985	1	1991	1
1980	2	1986	1	1992	1

There are two distinct phases to the story of the decline of the London consortium banks – before and after the onset of the LDC debt crisis in 1982. The years 1975–82 saw the 'disappearance' of six consortium banks, all through acquisition, yet the overall population hardly changed, since five new ones were formed. Between 1983 and 1992, however, there were 23 'disappearances' and only three new creations. By the early 1990s, consortium banking had ceased to be a significant phenomenon of the Euromarkets, in London at least.

The 'disappearances' of 1975–82 were as shown in Table 11.3.

Table 11.3   'Disappearances' of consortium banks, 1975–82[4]

Bank	Date	Type	Method*
Rothschild Intercontinental Bank	1975	Generalist	AOB
London Multinational Bank	1977	Generalist	ACIS
United International Bank	1979	Generalist	ACIS
Italian International Bank	1980	Regional	ACIS
Western American Bank (Europe)	1980	Generalist	ACIS
Orion Bank	1981	Generalist	ACIS

*AOB: Acquisition by other bank. ACIS: Acquisition of controlling interest by shareholder.

BLUNDEN'S BOMBSHELL

The first substantial stumbling block in the development of the consortium banking movement was the letter from the Bank of England in September 1974, in the wake of the secondary banking crisis and the Herstatt failure. It was a bolt from the blue, requiring each shareholder to provide the Bank with a 'letter of comfort' pledging support for their consortium bank (see page 79). While these undertakings could be readily, if reluctantly, furnished by the major commercial banks, the creation of such contingent liabilities was a problem for the small merchant and private banks. Thus the letter from the Bank of England's George Blunden led to a general withdrawal of smaller bank shareholders in the second half of the 1970s. It also raised doubts among larger banks, which seemed to run the risk of standing bail for their weaker fellow shareholders.

These concerns featured among the reasons for the willingness of Rothschilds, its partners in the 'Five Arrows' group and the other shareholders to sell Rothschild Intercontinental Bank[5] to American Express Company in 1975; it was the first consortium bank to 'disappear'. Barings achieved a similar exit from London Multinational Bank[6] with its sale to Chemical Bank in 1977. Other merchant banks which divested their shareholdings were Hambros in 1975 from Western American Bank (Europe),[7] Charterhouse Japhet from Atlantic International Bank[8] in 1977 and Warburgs from London & Continental Bankers[9] in 1979. The withdrawal of minor City merchant bank Keyser Ullman from London Interstate Bank[10] followed its failure after bad property loans in the secondary banking crisis of 1973–74.

No bank took a clearer line than the French *banque d'affaires*, Paribas, during the chairmanship of Jacques de Fouchier from 1969 to 1978. Although it had a long history of founding joint venture banks, it swiftly pulled out of its consortium interests, including European Brazilian Bank,[11] Banque Ameribas[12] and International Mexican Bank,[13] a severance that was especially regretted since its principal consortium partner, Banco Nacional de México, had been founded by Paribas nearly a century before. Nonetheless, de Fouchier astutely foresaw that a French bank might have problems furnishing US dollars to these consortium affiliates in a cost-effective manner.

Ownership instability was a fact of life for the consortium banks, Blunden's letter being but one factor that prompted changes among the shareholders. In some cases, there were fundamental shifts every few years. London Interstate Bank,[14] for instance, started off controlled by five US regional banks, then acquired and lost a big German shareholder, then subsequently two Scandinavian banks, one of which, Sparekassen SDS of Denmark, eventually bought out all the other shareholders. Control of Brown Harriman & International Banks[15] passed from its merchant bank and investment bank founders into the hands of a group of European and US regional banks, and was then acquired by two French banks, one of which bought out the other. In only 15 years, it went through five different names before being liquidated. Such changes in ownership were unsettling for management and bad for performance, the stability conferred by a single proprietor providing a superior operating context.

COMPETITION WITH SHAREHOLDERS

Competition with shareholders was a common problem for virtually all the consortium banks, as has been seen in the case of Orion (see page 131).

The critical point of departure, in the development of competition between consortium banks and their parents, was the establishment by the latter of their own wholly owned subsidiary in London. Invariably, the purpose of so doing was to develop the parent's own Euromarket business, creating a rival focus to its consortium bank. One way of resolving this conflict of interest was to buy out the other shareholders, turning the consortium bank into a ready-made Euromarket entity. The first instance of many was Chemical Bank's purchase of London Multinational Bank[16] in 1977. Renamed, it became Chemical Bank's London investment bank, with the aim of playing 'a leading role in Chemical's world-wide merchant banking activities.'[17]

Some banks withdrew from consortium banks upon forming a London branch or subsidiary. When National Bank of Kuwait, the largest Kuwaiti bank, opened its own investment company and branch, it bowed out of United Bank of Kuwait, though it was a gradual process, over several years; like UBK, National Bank provided services for Kuwaiti individuals and institutions in London. Skandinaviska Enskilda Banken, of Sweden, reduced its stake in Scandinavian Bank[18] from 32 per cent to 14 per cent when it was planning to set up a branch in the City in 1987.

But for the most part, as in the case of Orion up to its acquisition by Royal Bank of Canada, consortium bank shareholders chose to live with the contradiction of participation in a joint venture while establishing and promoting their own subsidiary's similar activities. As time went by, the jointly owned entities increasingly suffered from competition, neglect and even obstruction from the very banks that had set them up.

Allied Bank International,[19] a New York bank with an active London branch, provides an example of rivalry and tension between shareholders and management. Allied was set up in 1969 by 18 US regional banks, each a leader in its locality, to act as their joint international arm. The aim was to serve the international requirements of their larger corporate clients, and even attract business from foreign inward investors, to counter the incursion of the New York and other 'money centre' banks into their regional markets. It was envisaged that Allied and the shareholders would generate mutually valuable business, being 'an ideal conduit for the shareholder banks in both directions.'[20] But it did not work out that way. Instead, the shareholders soon became the source of Allied's 'worst competition, roaming the world offering credit lines at rates Allied could not compete with.'[21] The inevitable result – losses and liquidation.

Neglect was the fate of the two all-Japanese consortium banks, Associated Japanese Bank (International)[22] and Japan International Bank,[23] whose shareholders became increasingly active themselves in London from the early 1970s. Since the Japanese consortium banks received insufficient referrals of business from their owners, they depended on building up their assets through participations offered to them by the major multinational banks, which often kept the best deals for themselves. Although the Japanese consortium banks did increase the quantity of their Eurocurrency lending in the second half of the 1970s, the quality of business left much to be desired. In the late 1980s, each one became loss-making and had to be rescued by one of its shareholders.

DEUTSCHE BANK'S STRONG-ARM TACTICS

Shareholder rivalry at its most destructive is illustrated by the story of European Banking Company (EBC)[24] and its abortive Kingdom of Spain Eurobond issue. In the late 1970s, EBC had become the second largest issuer of floating rate notes, a considerable achievement. EBC was owned by the seven EBIC[25] banks; one of the shareholders, Deutsche Bank, was dismissive of EBC's FRN pre-eminence, and its chairman, Wilfried Guth, chided EBC executive director Neil Balfour that 'as the child of the most prestigious banking group in the world, it is now time for EBC to come into the real world of fixed-rate dollar bonds – to handle new issue business for AAA clients.'[26]

EBC found a way of rising to Deutsche Bank's challenge. Thanks to its track-record of raising funds for Spanish clients and to Balfour's high-level personal contacts, EBC won the mandate to make the first ever fixed-rate dollar Eurobond issue for the Kingdom of Spain. EBC managing director Stanislas Yassukovich immediately contacted all the shareholder directors, expecting them to be delighted and mightily impressed. Balfour recounts what happened next:

> As the responses came in, Stani positively glowed. Then, out of the blue, came the response from Deutsche Bank, that it could not support EBC's taking on this mandate. The issuer was too important and prestigious for EBC. We had little experience of this market and Deutsche had to think of its reputation. Besides, Deutsche Bank had itself been talking to the Spanish authorities about launching a Deutsche Mark loan. EBC had strayed onto AAA territory, onto Deutsche Bank's turf.

Yassukovich called a board meeting for the next day. All the other shareholder representatives spoke in support and praise of EBC's initiative and condemned Deutsche Bank's stance. One of them was particularly outspoken: 'I can find no honourable reason or commercial logic to justify our German friend's position. In my opinion, this is driven by sheer arrogance and probably jealousy… If the efforts of our colleagues in London are blocked by the self-serving act of a single shareholder, there can be no future for this young and ambitious organization.'[27]

But Deutsche Bank was unmoved and unrepentant: 'Deutsche Bank considers EBC to be, as yet, unfit to lead manage the Kingdom of Spain's first foray into the international capital markets,' declared its shareholder representative. 'We have communicated this position to the Spanish authorities. We are within our rights to insist on this and we do insist on it.'

Balfour commented:

> We all knew what he meant. EBC was dead meat. Had we been too successful, or not successful enough? It didn't matter. From that moment onwards, even despite some further spectacular successes, like the lead management of the EEC's first $1 billion syndicated loan, the writing was on the wall.

In the event, shortly afterwards, Deutsche Bank lead managed the first Eurobond issue for Spain – a Deutschemark-denominated issue, the currency of greatest relevance to the bank's strategy. Deutsche Bank's remorseless pursuit of its own interest was a brutal reminder of which party ultimately had the upper hand in disputes between consortium banks and their shareholders.

EARNINGS AND EXTRAVAGANCE

In 1970, under official pressure, the UK clearing banks published their true profits and reserves for the first time. Previously, they had been able to show merely the trend of profits and reserves, the results being smoothed by transfers to and from undisclosed 'inner reserves'. Now, at last, the banks themselves could make meaningful comparisons with their peers. Midland Bank, for instance, was shocked to find that it earned 29 per cent less from an average branch than its big three competitors, and that Lloyds Bank, supposedly the smallest, had shareholders funds 37 per cent larger than its own.[28] Now, too, independent analysts could pore over the details of a bank's results and make share recommendations based on facts rather than guesswork.

The new disclosure requirements prompted the beginnings of a sea change in thinking on the part of UK bank managements – the idea of shareholder value very gradually started to take root among them (leading eventually to some splendid stock option deals for the fortunate few). Naturally, the value of tying up capital in minority consortium bank stakes came into question, as there was no obvious benefit to the bottom line. As banks came to regard themselves as businesses rather than providers of a public service, participations entered into without a clear profit motive, for defensive or relationship reasons, were increasingly questioned. Similar attitudes towards bank profitability were already apparent in North America and, later on, were to spread to Continental Europe and the Far East.

As the idea of shareholder value took hold, the financial performance of many consortium banks came to be more critically scrutinized, particularly the quality of earnings and balance sheets. Two related weaknesses of the

London consortium banks were that they funded themselves in foreign currencies and that they had higher costs of deposits than other international banks, because they had no retail deposit base and because major wholesale depositors, such as SAMA, confined their direct relationships to relatively few prime names. In fact, the consortium banks were more dependent on the inter-bank market for funding than any other type of bank operating in London (see Table 11.4).

Table 11.4   Use of inter-bank market for foreign currency funding[29] (average per cent)

	1978–80
American banks	46
British banks	58
Other overseas banks	65
Japanese banks	70
Consortium banks	*81*

Another weakness was the consortium banks' leverage, which resulted in frequent requests for more capital and subordinated loans, though they generally paid little in the way of dividends. All banks borrow short and lend long, but for the consortium banks there was a bold, and probably unsustainable, pattern of maturity transformation in their foreign currency business, which was more than twice the level of the UK banking sector in general and which rose in the early 1980s with the onset of LDC reschedulings (see Table 11.5).

Table 11.5   Maturity transformation in foreign currency, 1975–83[30] (per cent)

	1975	1976	1977	1978	1979	1980	1981	1982	1983
All UK banks	17	17	17	17	17	18	16	15	19
Consortium banks	39	41	39	37	39	39	40	44	51

A further structural flaw was their insufficient access to good-quality corporate business and this resulted in the relatively high proportion of lending to LDCs, which came home to roost in the later 1980s; however, in the meantime, inadequate provisioning flattered the published figures.

The profitability of the consortium banks, although apparently satisfactory in the 1970s and early 1980s, was constrained by inflated, often extravagant, operating expenses. George Moore, former Citibank chairman, recalled: '... the board was always too big – we might get 50 people at a meeting, which meant that the meeting became an excuse to go to an exotic place and eat in good restaurants and see exotic things.'[31] Consortium bank meetings drew directors, managers and, in George Moore's words, 'professional meeting-goers' to locations all over the world where the host bank would strive to out-shine the other shareholders in a hospitality contest. Many consortium bank gatherings 'just happened to coincide' with Wimbledon week, Siena's Palio or the Carnival in Rio. At Orion's Shareholders' Forum in Venice in the summer of 1973, hosted by Credito Italiano, everyone had their own gondola and the lavishness of the hospitality made a lasting impression.

There was no stinting when it came to travel, entertainment, accommo-dation or perks; legend has it that one Middle Eastern consortium bank director used to insist on being met by two stretch limousines at the airport, one for his party and one for the luggage. Directors of Western American Bank had customized car number plates – WAB1, WAB2, WAB3 and so on. While regular meetings of shareholders and directors were necessary, both legally and operationally, and were of great importance for cementing the club spirit among the partners, the gatherings had to be paid for; ultimately the expenditures fell on the consortium banks, as Orion ruefully discovered over the Venice Forum, or their shareholders. Moreover, such ostentatious and extravagant conduct generated jealousies within the shareholder banks and the disappointing results made them increasingly difficult to justify 'at home after the candles on the dinner table had gone out.'[32]

All in all, there were many causes for shareholder concern about both the quality and quantity of consortium bank earnings, not to mention the level of extravagant expenditure.

THE SLIPPING POUND

As UK banks, the capital of the London consortium banks was denomi-nated in sterling. This was a constant headache for foreign shareholders, who saw the continual decline in the value of sterling causing book losses on their investment when converted back into their own currency, offset by occa-sional periods when sterling appreciated, which had the effect of depleting reported profits; a *Catch 22* situation. The weakness of sterling was par-ticularly hard on Japanese banks, because of the appreciation of the yen. A Japanese bank subscribing £100 000 of capital to one of the two all-Japanese consortium banks formed in London in 1970 had to find Y83.5 million; when these banks folded in 1990–91, the theoretical worth of the £100 000 sterling investment was just Y23 million. Moreover, to add insult to injury, LDC provisions had by then rendered their investment worthless. Banks from other strong currency countries, such as Germany, Switzerland and Austria, had similar experiences.

However, it was not only book losses that irked the shareholders; when, for example, sterling fell from $2.40 to $1.70 to the pound between June 1974 and December 1976, it meant that a London consortium bank needed at least 40 per cent more capital to sustain the same volume of dollar assets (the predominant currency of their balance sheets), let alone increase the business. This was a recurrent problem for London's consortium banks. International Mexican Bank's solution was the formation of a sister bank, with dollar capital, in Nassau to carry out much of the business, with the shareholders participating through a holding company which owned all the shares of both the London bank and the Nassau bank.

The abolition of exchange controls in the UK, in 1979, allowed London consortium banks to denominate their capital in dollars, though initially none of them did, and to invest their capital freely in dollars, of which many took advantage. Scandinavian Bank,[33] owned by five banks from the Nordic region, devised an ingenious and unique scheme to mitigate the problem. Its sterling shares were divided into units of a basket of four currencies that reflected the overall mix of its activities; to raise £27 million new capital to support the bank's expansion, a third of the shares were offered to the public at 210 pence, early in 1987, to considerable acclaim.[34] The share price soon rose to 288, but was then hit by, as the *Investors Chronicle* put it, 'the double whammy of the October 1987 crash and third world debt write offs' and by December 1989, the shares had fallen to 133.[35] Embarrassed, the five shareholder banks bailed out the public investors with an offer of 225 a share. Scandinavian Bank's inspired double innovation of floating multi-currency shares on the London Stock Exchange was not imitated by other consortium banks and soon the bank came under the single ownership of Sweden's premier bank.

Sterling's decline led to a somewhat surreal confrontation between the consortium banks and the Inland Revenue in the mid-1970s. This concerned the tax treatment of dollar subordinated loans, which had been put up by shareholders as capital backing for their consortium banks' predominantly non-sterling activities. The consortium banks were astonished to learn about a proposal by the UK tax authorities to 'tax as conceptual profit the increase in value in sterling terms of the foreign currency assets which the subordinated loans had been used to fund, without allowing as offset the increase in sterling terms of the subordinated loans themselves.'[36]

The struggle against the Revenue's bizarre proposal was led by London Multinational Bank,[37] whose chairman was former governor of the Bank of England, Lord Cromer, and whose managing director, John Hyde, was chairman of the recently formed Association of Consortium Banks. Cromer protested that he 'in no way accepted the validity or justice' of the Revenue's contention, pointing out that the Revenue would be the loser if, as later happened, sterling were to appreciate.

Although eventually the Inland Revenue backed down, the crass attitude of the UK tax authorities infuriated overseas shareholders that had invested in London consortium banks, expecting more enlightened treatment. It was one factor that increasingly inclined banks to establish any new consortium undertakings in tax-free and little-regulated offshore centres, rather than in London.

'AROUND HERE, IT'S JAKARTA THAT PAYS THE CHECK'[38]

So said Citibank chairman Walter Wriston in 1975, epitomizing the euphoric lending to developing countries after the first oil price rise of 1973–74; and he could just as well have named Mexico City, São Paulo or Buenos Aires. 'Citibank led the pack and off we went to the races,' recalled merchant banker Geoffrey Bell.[39] A second lending frenzy followed the second OPEC oil price hike in 1979; LDC external debt rose from $336 billion in 1978 to $662 billion in 1982.[40] In both re-cycling booms, the rush to lend was fuelled by seductive spreads over LIBOR, on occasion twice those on industrialized country loans, and attractive front-end fees. It was left to others down the road to pick up the pieces when debt service problems necessitated massive provisions.

The consortium banks played a significant part in the organization of the syndicated loans that constituted the bulk of these LDC borrowings, though the lion's share of the business went to the major international commercial banks. Nonetheless, these years saw substantial increases in lending to LDCs by the consortium banks, seeking higher yielding assets and front-end fees to boost their earnings, at the same time being denied direct access to the big corporate borrowers which their shareholders tended to keep to themselves.

By 1982, most LDCs, particularly in Latin America, found themselves with record and unsustainable levels of debt service payments, as a result of both the increases in indebtedness and increases in US dollar interest rates resulting from the Federal Reserve's fight against inflation. An additional factor was that oil-producing LDCs, such as Mexico and Venezuela, were hit by the precipitous fall, after their dramatic rise, in oil prices, from 1981 onwards. Following Poland's rescheduling in September 1981, Mexico's balance of payments crisis in February 1982 and the freezing, in April 1982, of Argentina's assets in London, after the Falklands invasion, the debt crisis proper arrived in August 1982; Mexico's Finance Minister, Jesus Silva Herzog, announced a moratorium on debt payments pending an arrangement with creditors. This was followed by similar moves by most other Latin American countries and some others. The IMF rode to the rescue and, by the end of 1983, had helped reschedule the debt of 24 countries, doubling its own exposure to them in the process. Rescheduling was a wonderful solution for the bankers; it produced negotiation fees, permitted the avoidance of default and provided a breathing space to the poorest countries. As Gérard Legrain of International Mexican Bank put it: 'the bankers could get rich and go to paradise.'[41]

A new phenomenon of the LDC debt crisis years was the development of an active secondary market in bank loans. Sellers were driven by a desire to reduce exposure to high-risk non-performing LDC loans, or by balance sheet necessity as a result of constraints on country or capital limits. Buyers were motivated by the prospect of picking up assets at a big discount to their face value on which they would make substantial profits when, or rather if, payments were resumed. Controversially, purchasers included LDC debtors themselves, thereby paying off their debts on the cheap. Trading bank loans soon became established as a regular bank activity in its own right.

There was an upsurge of consortium bank 'disappearances' in 1983–86, most of which were at least partly related to the LDC debt problem (see Table 11.6).

Table 11.6 'Disappearances' of consortium banks, 1983–86[12]

Bank	Year	Type	Method*
Midland and International Banks	1983	Generalist	ACIS
Banco Urquijo Hispano Americano	1983	Regional	ACIS
Brown Harriman & International Banks	1983	Generalist	LIQ
London Interstate Bank	1984	Generalist	ACIS
Nordic Bank	1984	Regional	ACIS
European Banking Company	1985	Generalist	ACIS
PK Christiania	1986	Regional	ACIS

*ACIS: Acquisition of controlling interest by shareholder. LIQ: Liquidation or cessation.

Some consortium banks immediately made bad debt provisions, adversely affecting their results for 1982. Concern about Midland and International Bank's[43] LDC exposure led the other shareholders to accept Standard Chartered's offer to buy them out and, in February 1983, it was absorbed into Standard Chartered Merchant Bank. In the same year, Banco Urquijo Hispano Americano,[44] which had considerable exposure to Latin America, was acquired by one of the shareholders, Banco Hispano Americano, when the other, Banco Urquijo, Spain's leading industrial bank, got into serious difficulties because of ailing industrial and property holdings and over-rapid expansion abroad. The purchase of Banque Française de Crédit Industriel (previously Brown Harriman & International Banks)[45] by Banque Internationale pour l'Afrique Occidentale, also in 1983, was motivated by the consortium bank's need for more capital for growth and provisions. BFCI was liquidated and its business taken over by a BIAO branch in London.

Venture capital and LDC loan provisions led to a £2.9 million loss by European Banking Company in 1984. Shareholder dissatisfaction caused the bank to face the indignity of being put up for sale; as a result, AMRO Bank bought out the other partners in 1985.[46] It also bought EBC's associated consortium bank, European American Bank, the largest European bank in North America. These moves gave a big boost to the development of the Dutch bank's international activities.

It was regional competition and consolidation in Scandinavia, as much as debt provisioning, that led to the disappearance of three consortium banks in the mid-1980s. Sparekassen SDS of Denmark bought out the other shareholders in London Interstate Bank in 1984.[47] PK Christiania Bank (UK) was acquired by Christiania Bank of Norway and transformed into a branch in 1986.[48] In both cases, the transaction was driven by the acquiring bank's ambition to enhance its presence in London.

The announcement in August 1983 that Nordic Bank, then London's second largest consortium bank, was to be bought by Den norske Creditbank, which needed its own London operation, was interpreted by the *Financial Times* to be:

> ...*firm evidence that the era of consortium banking is coming to a close... The Nordic deal confirms a trend away from the 1970s notion of consortium banking. Most international banks now prefer to establish and operate their own banks so as to tighten control and avoid conflicts of interest. The case of Nordic Bank is a perfect example of how the idea has faded in recent years. Ten years ago, when the Eurocurrency market was still evolving, it was logical for banks to band together, share knowledge and spread the risk. The packaging of medium-term credits was a risky business and yet an exciting one – every foreign bank wanted a presence in the London market. But as the Eurocurrency market has matured, the business of medium-term lending has become more competitive and banks have been striking out on their own.*[49]

Nordic Bank managing director, John Sclater, told the *Financial Times*: 'What made sense 10 years ago no longer makes sense today. I regard this as evolutionary, not revolutionary.' But another banker interviewed for the same article made the point more harshly, remarking that: 'The only reason some consortium banks are still around is that nobody wants to buy them.'[50] The article provoked a letter to the editor from the then chairman of the Association of Consortium Banks, Gérard Legrain, who robustly took issue with its proposition that 'the concept of consortium banking is now clearly on the way out,' pointing out that a number of large new consortium banks had recently been formed in the UK and elsewhere.[51]

REED PUTS THE CAT AMONG THE PIGEONS

International co-ordination of banking supervision and standards began with the Basle Concordat of 1975, an understanding between the monetary authorities of the major countries about responsibility for the supervision of banks' foreign branches and affiliates, of which the Bank of England's request for letters of comfort in September 1974 was a forerunner. A new Basle Concordat, drawn up by the Banking Regulations and Supervisory

Practices Committee – known, successively, as the Blunden Committee and the Cooke Committee, after the Bank of England directors who chaired it – of the Bank for International Settlements, was announced in June 1983. This tightened international banking supervision by drawing holding companies into the net for the first time.[52] The Committee then turned its attention to the formulation of common capital adequacy rules. An agreement setting a capital ratio of 8 per cent was announced in June 1988. It was to come fully into force on 1 January 1993.

While these moves towards common international capital adequacy standards were being finalized, John Reed, the 'young and rather brash'[53] new chairman of Citibank, which had profited handsomely from the LDC lending business, suddenly announced, in May 1987, that his bank was making a provision of 25 per cent – $3 billion – against LDC debts. Reed explained to Federal Reserve chairman Paul Volcker and other bankers that this massive and unprecedented blow to the bank's bottom line would demonstrate that it could absorb the losses and relieve market worries about the potential impact of the LDC debt overhang on the international banking system. No-one could object to this 'refreshing realism,' though it was plain that his motives were 'commercial not charitable.'[54] 'It was hard to avoid the impression,' commented Volcker, 'that it was also his way of putting his stamp of leadership on American banking.'[55] It was also a way of drawing a line between his chairmanship and that of his predecessor, Walter Wriston, conduct not uncommon among incoming chairmen. 'Walt's loans' – the LDC lending debacle – were consigned to history.[56] Reed's initiative, generously described by Wriston as 'brilliant,' put other banks on the spot. Feeling obliged to follow Citibank's example, the major international commercial banks made similar levels of provisions, thereby inflicting on their management the humiliation of reporting large losses to disenchanted shareholders.

BANK OF ENGLAND'S 'MATRIX', 1987

The London consortium banks were affected not only by market pressures, but by the introduction of formal provisioning guidelines by the Bank of England in August 1987. The Bank's 'Matrix of Debt Recoverability' introduced a checklist for calculating the level of provisions to be made by banks. It weighted a number of factors, such as interest arrears and the number of reschedulings, to arrive at a score for each rescheduling country, producing a provision level of about 30 per cent on average for Third World loans. The average level for the consortium banks was 32 per cent, at the top end of the range.[57] The *Financial Times* predicted: 'tough interviews next time the Bank of England calls for a prudential chat.'[58]

The introduction of the 'matrix' led to increased provisioning; as a result, 18 of the 22 consortium banks still operating in London reported a loss in the years 1987–89.[59] The losses usually necessitated the immediate putting up of new capital by the shareholders, quite apart from the need to plan for capital ratios of 8 per cent by 1993, in accordance with the new Basle Committee rules; thus many of them were led to re-consider their commitment to their consortium bank which resulted in the 'disappearance' of a further 16 consortium banks in 1988–92 (see Table 11.7). Some were bought by shareholders, others liquidated.

Table 11.7   'Disappearances' of consortium banks, 1988–92[60]

Bank	Year	Type	Method*
Atlantic International Bank	1988	Generalist	LIQ
European Brazilian Bank	1988	Regional	LIQ
ITAB Bank	1988	Regional	ACIS
Anglo–Yugoslav Bank	1989	Regional	ACIS
European Arab Bank	1989	Regional	LIQ
International Energy Bank	1989	Generalist	ANB
Associated Japanese Bank (International)	1990	Regional	ACIS
BAII	1990	Regional	ACIS
Euro–Latinamerican Bank	1990	Regional	LIQ
FennoScandia Bank	1990	Regional	ACIS
International Commercial Bank	1990	Generalist	LIQ
Libra Bank	1990	Regional	LIQ
London & Continental Bankers	1990	Generalist	ACIS
Scandinavian Bank	1990	Regional	ACIS
Japan International Bank	1991	Regional	ACIS
International Mexican Bank	1992	Regional	ACIS

*ACIS: Acquisition of controlling interest by shareholder. ANB: Acquired by non-shareholder bank. LIQ: Liquidation or cessation.

Among the consortium banks that 'disappeared' in 1988–92, two were bought by Italian banks to expand their operations in London. The other Italian bank shareholders were delighted to sell ITAB Bank to one of its shareholders, Banca CRT, Cassa di Risparmio di Torino, in June 1988. It became a wholly owned subsidiary of CRT, trading as London Italian Bank. International Energy Bank had been acquired by SFE Group in 1983 and, having suffered LDC as well as energy loan losses, was acquired by Banca Popolare di Novara, giving a London presence to this Italian regional bank.

In the case of European Brazilian Bank, after making a massive £247 million loss in 1987, the second largest ever in the history of the consortium banks, the partners pulled the plug, handing back its banking licence and initiating liquidation.[61] Atlantic International Bank also closed its doors in 1988 after making provisions of £34.8 million, a sum in excess of the bank's capital and reserves. Control of Anglo–Yugoslav Bank was bought by one of the partners, Beogradska Bank, the leading Serbian Banka. Its structure was complicated by the Yugoslav turmoil, with several minority shareholders remaining from new states which had broken away from the Federal Republic of Yugoslavia; the bank's name was changed to AY Bank. European Arab Bank, the London subsidiary of European Arab Holding, was liquidated by the owners, the members of the EBIC group and Arab banks, as a casualty of LDC loan losses.

BANK OF ENGLAND'S 'NEW MATRIX', 1989

It had been anticipated that the provisioning initiated in 1987 would bolster confidence in the international banking system and stabilize the price at which LDC debt traded in the secondary market. In fact, secondary market prices went down, the logic in the market being that if the banks themselves believed that loans to LDCs were only worth 50–70 cents on the dollar, they would not make any new loans. And if the banks stopped lending, the debtors would not be able or willing to pay the interest due, so the value of LDC debt fell still further.

The Bank of England came to the conclusion that a further round of provisioning was necessary. Executive director Brian Quinn took the opportunity of an invitation to address the annual dinner of the Association of Consortium Banks in November 1989 to inform them that the authorities were looking for a further 'substantial increase.'[62] The Bank's 'new matrix' had additional factors and also indicated provisions to be made for non-rescheduling countries in certain circumstances. The result was a rise in the average level of provisioning of Third World loans to around 50 per cent.[63] The further injection of capital required to meet this level of provisioning was the last straw for many of the shareholders, which had supported their consortium bank creations through the first round of provisioning. Moreover, a number of large banks obtained considerable benefits by taking over impaired loans and setting them against their own tax obligations. So in the following two years, a further 10 consortium banks 'disappeared'.

The remaining Latin American consortium banks were seriously affected by the Bank of England's new matrix. In the aftermath of the 1982 debt crisis, Libra Bank played a leading role in the development of trading LDC debt, a market whose turnover reached $20 billion in 1987 and $40 billion in 1988.[64] As a result, Libra was able to build up loan loss reserves of £193 million out of profits by 1989, but it wasn't enough to save the bank. In 1989, it posted losses of £560 million, much the largest loss of any consortium bank. Faced by the prospect of having to provide a further substantial capital injection to Libra to meet the Bank of England's new matrix requirements, the shareholders decided to wind up the bank, taking the outstanding loans on to their own books.[65] 'Libra, which employs 200 people,' commented executive director Carlos Santistevan at the time of closure, 'is the latest of several consortium banks to fall victim to the problems of Third World debt.'[66]

In order to enable it to meet the Bank of England's first matrix requirement, Euro–Latinamerican Bank's twenty two shareholder banks subscribed, in amounts proportional to their shareholdings, $205 million in market rate interest bearing perpetual subordinated loan notes.[67] It had built up a substantial book of short-term trade finance with Latin America, between 1986 and 1989, in order to get away from medium-term lending, but when in 1989 the shareholders were faced with the prospect of having to provide a further $200 million in fresh capital to meet the new matrix, they decided to buy its outstanding loans, in proportion to their shareholdings, and to liquidate. 'They took a long hard look at the situation,' said managing director George Gunson, 'and concluded that this was the best course of action.'[68]

International Mexican Bank (Intermex), whose owners were a group of Mexican, European, Japanese and US banks, was restructured in 1989 to meet the Bank of England's first matrix requirements. To provide a 'permanent solution' to the LDC problem, the shareholders purchased over half the loan portfolio, making the bank 'smaller but sounder,' as managing director Gérard Legrain put it.[69] Like Libra, Intermex enterprisingly developed LDC debt trading and other activities, particularly trade finance and corporate finance, and returned to profit in 1991.[70] But again, the Bank of England's new matrix requirements caused the shareholders to throw in the towel. In 1992, control of Intermex was acquired by its principal shareholder, Banco Nacional de México, and became its in-house investment bank.

The two Japanese consortium banks and the pair of remaining Scandinavian ones 'disappeared' in the wake of the new matrix. Each of the Japanese banks was taken over by one of its shareholders after further LDC provisioning losses, which wiped out their capital resources. Associated Japanese Bank[71] was acquired by Sanwa Bank in 1990 and folded into its UK investment bank. Japan International Bank was bought by Tokai Bank in 1991 and merged with its London investment bank. Scandinavian Bank[72] was hit not only by the need to make provisions for LDC loan losses, but also to cover possible losses on controversial swap contracts entered into with the London borough of Hammersmith and Fulham.[73] Following a loss of £3.2 million for 1989, it was announced in June 1990 that Skandinaviska Enskilda Banken, of Sweden, was buying out the other four shareholders to enhance its investment banking activities; the buy-out of its partners took place also in the wake of a general rationalization among Scandinavian banks, affecting two of the other partners. 'A further illustration,' commented the *Financial Times*, 'of the trend for consortium banks to be bought out by one of their member companies.'[74] FennoScandia Bank, which was not beset by provisioning problems, was bought by Skopbank, of Finland, to augment its international capabilities.

The parent of London consortium bank BAII plc, BAII Holding, transferred $400 million of potentially problematic loans to a specially created Panama holding company to 'rid itself of the festering problem of LDC debt' in 1989.[75] In May 1990, the Banque Nationale de Paris bought out the other BAII shareholders, as did DG Bank, of Germany, in the case of London & Continental Bankers, integrating it into its London operations; in each case, the buying shareholders, BNP and DG, had very much been the 'guiding' shareholders of the consortium bank concerned and had been the principal founder. International Commercial Bank was liquidated in 1990, after making substantial provisions for LDC loan losses. 'Our shareholders,' managing director Michael Wells told the press laconically, 'reached the conclusion that ICB was no longer of strategic value.'[76]

THE LONG VIEW

The consolidated profitability of London's 35 consortium banks over the years 1966–90 is shown in Table 11.8. Pre-tax profit is the measure of return, because of the distorting effect of leasing on after-tax profit.

Table 11.8 Performance of UK consortium banks, 1966–90[77] (pre-tax return on capital and reserves, per cent)

1966	3.6	1975	15.9	1984	20.8
1967	4.3	1976	20.2	1985	17.9
1968	13.1	1977	17.0	1986	12.9
1969	13.2	1978	18.2	1987	−59.6
1970	15.2	1979	19.0	1988	2.1
1971	13.4	1980	21.3	1989	−218.0
1972	18.0	1981	21.9	1990	−6.6
1973	16.4	1982	21.8		
1974	14.8	1983	18.5		

After a modest start in 1966–67, the consortium banks as a group achieved acceptable returns and a rising trend in the late 1960s and 1970s, averaging 15 per cent per annum in 1968–75 and 18.6 per cent in 1976–79. The years 1980–82, the era of the second petrodollar recycling boom, saw the peak returns, averaging 21.6 per cent. Returns declined thereafter, but still averaged 17.5 per cent between 1983 and 1986, being boosted by higher loan spreads and fees from rescheduling LDC debt; only modest loan loss provisions were made in those years, despite the small likelihood that the debt could be serviced without more 'new money' arrangements, in which nearly all the banks participated and which ensured the avoidance, or post-ponement, of default.

In the years 1987–90, the accounts of the London consortium banks showed losses totalling £1.1 billion, probably a substantial underestimate of the true losses because, in some instances, the shareholders acquired doubtful loans as a way of avoiding the stigma of heavy provisioning by their consortium bank and for tax advantage. But even this underestimate was equivalent to the aggregate profits of the consortium banks between 1980 and 1986. In reality, if proper provisioning had been made, even the record performance of 1980–82 would have disappeared. But, eventually, the day of reckoning arrived and the UK consortium banks were virtually wiped out.

BANKING CLUBS WITHER ON THE VINE[78]

The European banking clubs were on the wane from the late 1970s. But being mutual associations to promote relationships and professionalism among their members, decisions to close were long-postponed. The three largest were eventually disbanded in the 1990s, while two survived.

European Banks International Company (EBIC), with its seven members and six associated consortium banking groups, was the oldest and most prominent of the European banking clubs. In its heyday in the late 1970s, the EBIC members were financing many large projects together and had a joint presence in many markets and businesses. But as the individual EBIC members expanded overseas in their own names and into each others' domestic markets, the joint-venture approach became increasingly difficult to sustain. One by one, from the mid-1980s, the EBIC consortium banks, some having made large losses on LDC lending, were wound up or sold to one of the members. By the time it was formally terminated in 1992, EBIC had been withering on the vine for several years.

The visionary fervour that had imbued the members of Europartners in the early 1970s had dissipated by the end of the decade, little progress having been made towards the original vision of a pan-European bank.[79] The joint ventures were closed down, with large losses in the case of International Commercial Bank, or taken over by one of the member banks. Moreover, the expansion of members into each others' territories, particularly by an aggressive Crédit Lyonnais from 1988, undermined the *raison d'être* of the co-operative alliance. By mutual agreement, the Europartners club was dissolved between 1991 and 1993.

ABECOR in the early 1980s advertized itself as 'the biggest banking association of its kind in the world.' ABECOR members were participants in a number of consortium banks, all of which ceased operations or came under single bank control in the late 1980s or early 1990s. A major part of ABECOR's work was devoted to enhancing the business effectiveness of members through co-operation and the provision of mutual services in areas such as economic forecasting, country and company risk analysis, sovereign debt rescheduling, computing, cash management, fraud prevention and training. With a secretariat based in Brussels, ABECOR also took on a lobbying role for members with the European Commission. These useful, but unquantifiable, benefits proved insufficient to justify the continuation of ABECOR, which was dissolved in 1997.

ABECOR's lasting legacy was the ABIN training institute for bankers in Bad Homburg, which survived the demise of its founder. Indeed, ABIN won new contracts from beyond the ranks of the former ABECOR members, including playing a role in training a new generation of Russian bankers.

Some of the factors that led to the demise of these banking clubs were similar to those already discussed in relation to consortium banks. Competition between associated consortium banks and member banks was widespread, not to mention their generally disappointing results and, specifically, the LDC losses. The unmeasurable nature of the advantages of membership, especially as banks became more concerned about profitability, was another problem.

Other factors were particular to the European banking clubs. The idealistic co-operative vision of the founding fathers was especially susceptible to disillusion by commercial reality and to dilution as those founders retired, to be replaced by younger men with more interest in the bottom line; the cost and, often, irrelevance of plenary sessions and working parties were palpable. Business rivalry between club members undermined trust and the ethos of mutuality. Progress towards European economic and political integration was slow, while incompatible legal, accounting and political environments made any thought of cross-border banking mergers very remote. Individual members were affected by unforeseen events, which weakened their relationship to the club and each other, such as the financial crisis at Crédit Lyonnais of Europartners. The nationalization of Crédit Commercial de France and the bankruptcy of Vatican-linked Banco Ambrosiano, both in 1982, were setbacks for the Inter-Alpha Group of Banks, though it recovered in due course.

Finally, as it turned out, industry-wide technological co-operation, such as Eurocheque or SWIFT, proved to be much more important than restricted club-based solutions.

SURVIVORS

At the turn of the twenty first century, the consortium banking entities discussed in this and previous chapters had all 'disappeared' save for two of the European banking clubs and six London consortium banks. Which were the survivors?

Inter-Alpha was a large but loose association of 12 banks, which provided a useful forum for chief executives and others to meet to discuss opportunities and exchange information. In addition, several members co-operated in the IBOS cash management club. Mainly because of mergers, what started as a club of middle-ranking banks acquired a number of mega-sized members, both absolutely and in relation to their home markets. Yet it survived, thanks to its informality, modest ambitions and high-level personal relations. Significant shareholding relationships, such as the near 20 per cent shareholdings of ING and KBC in the privatized Crédit Commercial de France, and ING's 39 per cent of BHF Bank, grew naturally out of more than a quarter of a century of co-operation in the club. These stakes constituted the seeds of potential cross-border mergers, but when ING made an unsuccessful attempt to buy control of CCF at the end of 1999, it was trumped by HSBC; KBC was also left on the sidelines. However, ING was able to acquire control of BHF Bank. Royal Bank of Scotland, moreover, received considerable help from its Spanish partner, BSCH, in acquiring NatWest in February 2000.

The other surviving club, Unico Banking Group, composed of 11 co-operative banks, sought joint solutions to the challenges facing its members. The mutual philosophy underlying its origins and the outlook of its members proved singularly well-suited to success as a banking club. With outlets throughout Europe and a combined market share of 15 per cent, the low-profile group continued to serve a useful purpose; it introduced its own cash management system, Unicash, to coincide with the launch of the euro in 1999.

The six surviving London consortium banks were all strongly rooted in a particular region, mostly the Arab world, or country – Kuwait, Saudi Arabia, Jordan, Iran and Romania. They faced similar problems to the other consortium banks, but regional governmental support may have helped to keep them alive beyond their natural life expectancy. In addition, the international bank partners were ready to help the banks for relationship reasons or were unable to secure an exit, even if they wanted one.

United Bank of Kuwait, founded in 1966 to provide services to Kuwaiti institutions and individuals in London, was the longest serving of them.[80] Despite some changes in the shareholding mix, it remained owned by Kuwaiti institutions, but it successfully spread its wings into non-Kuwaiti business; for example, it was one of the first banks to offer UK residential mortgages, traditionally seen as a building society function, developing a mortgage business that was sold off at a considerable profit after a few years. It was almost the only consortium bank to be unaffected by the LDC debt crisis and played a notable part in the Gulf War of 1990–91 by providing a lifeline for many thousands of Kuwaitis stranded in London.

British Arab Commercial Bank (formerly UBAF Bank) suffered large LDC losses in the 1980s and was recapitalized; as a result, HSBC became a large minority shareholder, with governmental banks from Algeria, Egypt, Iraq and Morocco as fellow shareholders. Its new name reflected its independence from its founder, UBAF.[81] Jordan International Bank[82] suffered from loan losses in its early years, but switched the emphasis of its business to treasury and investment activities, thus providing an important service for its Jordanian bank shareholders.

Saudi International Bank,[83] which played a major role in financing petrochemical and other industries in Saudi Arabia, was acquired by Gulf International Bank in 1999. It remained in consortium control, since the newly merged bank was itself owned 72.5 per cent by Gulf Investment Corporation, which was jointly owned by six Gulf Co-operation Council countries; the remaining shares were held by SAMA and JP Morgan. Gulf International Bank and Saudi International Bank had complementary strengths in investment and wholesale banking, which underpinned the logic of the merger.

Iran Overseas Investment Bank's business was stunted by the Iranian revolution.[84] The bank played a key role in the negotiations which led to the release of the 52 US diplomats taken hostage in November 1979 and in the subsequent Algiers Accords, which involved the repayment of Iran's international debts and the release of assets frozen under US influence. So, the bank's business was much reduced, and its international shareholders (Barclays and Manufacturers Hanover) bowed out. As a consortium bank owned by four of the leading local banks, it recovered in the 1990s with the gradual liberalization of Iran and the expansion of its trade.

Anglo–Romanian Bank had a somewhat similar experience.[85] After running up Romania's international debts to $10 billion in the 1970s, in furtherance of industrial development, President Ceausescu reversed the policy in the 1980s, as part of his independence strategy; international loans were paid off and economic development was stifled, inflicting great hardship on the people. With most of its lending business being related to Romanian trade or industry, Anglo–Romanian Bank had the ground cut from under its feet, but it regained momentum with the advent of the market economy after the fall of the Ceausescu regime in 1989. It ceased to be a consortium bank when its international shareholders (again, Barclays and Manufacturers Hanover) sold their shareholding to their Romanian partner, Bancorex, in 1997–98.

THE VERDICT

'The sad lesson is that "consortium" banking is not viable,' wrote George Moore: 'big boards of directors and diffuse authority make losses worse and prevent timely profit-taking. Everybody's business is nobody's business.'[86] This was a common verdict, shared by many leading banks. Barclays, for example, had long suspected that it was suffering erosion of shareholder value through its consortium participations. In 1987, the bank seconded senior executive, John Champion, to head SFE, one of the most complex of them, and he soon came to the conclusion that it was 'not viable and out of control.'[87] Yet it took five years for Barclays to extricate itself from SFE and nearly a decade to dispose of other unwanted consortium bank participations.

But there are other sides to the story. Participation in a consortium bank was the route by which most big commercial banks entered international banking. It was these so-called 'dog's breakfast banks' that introduced their lumbering domestically oriented parents to the Euromarkets and to the innovative and imaginative techniques, often derived from investment banking practices, being pioneered in this dynamic and lightly regulated environment. The consortium banks were the first bridge between the large commercial banks' domestic client base and the lending capabilities of the Euromarkets, forging links between national financial markets and the international markets. Thereby, they were in the forefront of the agents transforming the scale and scope of banking business and the Euromarkets.

The consortium banks attracted managerial talent from the commercial and merchant banks that was looking for new challenges. These executives were given their head by foreign banks operating in an unfamiliar location. They were trusted to build up a bank, develop new business methods, introduce sophisticated control systems and, on many occasions, to take the lead in arranging and structuring complicated loans.

Reflecting on the consortium banking movement, in which he had spent much of his career, George Gunson of Euro–Latinamerican Bank observed that:

> A consortium bank is a microcosm of a major bank. Whether it is a question of compliance, running a foreign exchange position or an unmatched asset/liability book, devising computer systems for ever-increasingly complicated financial operations, claiming tax allowance on written down sovereign loans, claiming tax credits on tax paid in other countries, keeping costs under control in a search for profit – it has to be as good or better than the biggest bank in the world. Management has to be fast on its feet and on many occasions it could teach lessons to their shareholders, particularly the foreign shareholders that thereby gain insights into innovative banking practice.[88]

The consortium banks made important contributions to the development of international banking and to London as a financial centre. They broke new ground, dismantled barriers and contributed to the intensification of international competition in banking. Moreover, it is perhaps arguable that had the consortium banks not existed as a conduit for LDC lending, the major banks themselves would have taken even more LDC loans on to their own balance sheets, exacerbating the threat from the LDC debt crisis to the stability of the international banking system.

'A sensible interim step,' was the verdict of Deutsche Bank's historians on its participation in EBIC.[89] A similar judgement might be made about both the European banking clubs and the London consortium banks – that they were appropriate arrangements for the formative phase of the development of the Euromarkets. However, as international finance moved on, they were unable to adapt as readily as their individual corporate members and, save for the handful of exceptions, went the way of the dinosaurs.

CHAPTER 12

Consortia and strategic alliances in finance

The formation of consortia – 'strategic alliances' as they are usually called in the literature of management science – between firms is a widespread phenomenon in international business. Such alliances are entered into when a joint approach enables firms to attain strategic objectives that they are unable to achieve individually. Through such 'competitive collaboration', firms are able to learn new skills, access new markets, acquire new technologies, or achieve economies of scale or scope.[1]

However, strategic alliances are characterized by *reluctance* on the part of participants and intrinsic *impermanence*: *reluctance*, because most managers would prefer not to enter into such arrangements with actual or potential competitors; *impermanence*, because the strategic problems they are formed to address are continually changing in a dynamic economy. Thus the demise of strategic alliances in business is as normal as their formation.

Usually in business, success and survival are linked concepts, as are failure and demise. But with strategic alliances the situation is less straightforward. Suppose, for instance, that the strategic objective of participants is to learn new skills; the sooner they are successful, the quicker the demise of the joint venture. In this light, the rapid development of competition between the consortium banks and their shareholders was a mark of success, the achievement by the parents of the strategic objective of learning to operate in the Euromarkets. Likewise, longevity may indicate failure to achieve a strategic objective. Given the reluctance of participants and the intrinsic impermanence of strategic alliances, survival requires more explanation than demise.

There is a range of possible forms of strategic alliance, depending on the motives of participants and their degree of commitment.[2] At one end of the spectrum are loose *ad hoc* arrangements, at the other formal full-blown joint ventures. Among financial institutions, four levels of strategic alliance may be identified:

- *Ad Hoc* and Informal Arrangements – syndicates and cartels.
- Formal Associations – exchanges and clubs.
- Limited-Purpose Joint Ventures – insurance pools and trade finance entities.
- Full-Blown Joint Ventures – consortium banks and regional development banks.

AD HOC AND INFORMAL ARRANGEMENTS

Many financial operations involve forms of temporary association. For centuries, merchants banded together to jointly finance ship cargoes. A more elaborate form of *ad hoc* financial arrangement is the issuing syndicate, formed for the purpose of organizing, underwriting and marketing bond issues, originally in domestic bond markets and later in the Eurobond market.[3]

Cartels are an informal form of strategic alliance. Cartelized arrangements among commercial banks were common in Western countries until the 1970s, having official backing as a means of shoring-up the banking system and exercising monetary control. Cartels also operated in investment banking. The China Consortium was an arrangement between five British banks to bid jointly for Chinese government loan mandates, which ran from 1895 to the 1920s. So was the informal issuing syndicate operated by Barings, Rothschilds and Schroders in the 1920s and 1930s, by which each offered the others reciprocal participations in the loans it issued. In the early Eurobond era, similar arrangements prevailed, for example, involving Warburgs with Kuhn Loeb, then with Paribas, but they did not survive.

EXCHANGES

Exchanges and clubs are more formal and longer-lasting forms of association in finance. Exchanges are usually *inclusive* associations, membership being open to all reputable and solvent market participants. Stock exchanges and derivatives exchanges are cases in point. So are common settlement systems, for example, for settling bankers' cheques and payments, for credit card processing and for Eurobond settlements; in the latter case, the two companies, Euroclear and Cedel, were indispensable factors in the growth and stability of the Eurobond market.

Co-operation allows participants to achieve external economies that are not available to them as individual firms. External economies accrue to firms when a positive relationship exists between efficiency and the size or form of the market or industry in which they operate. However, membership of an exchange imposes rules and regulations, which inhibit innovation on the part of individual participants. It may be that new developments, particularly technology advances, make it advantageous for an individual firm to by-pass the organized exchange, turning adherence to its rule book from an external economy into an external diseconomy. Reform of the rule book might be a solution to the problem, but there may be political or institutional impediments to this happening. If the exchange fails to adapt, it may wither or collapse as a market-place. Alternatively, it may assume a new institutional form, forsaking the practitioner prioritizing mutual form for a profit-driven and perhaps more service oriented corporate form.

The historical development of the London Stock Exchange illustrates the push and pull between external economies and diseconomies as technology developed. In the early eighteenth century, a properly regulated stock market had many advantages over the curb-market activities of traders in the coffee houses. The advent of the telegraph, but particularly the telephone around the turn of the twentieth century, led to a loss of business due to cut-price competition from non-members, abetted by members, and to a blurring in the traditional distinction between broker and market-maker. Reforms to the Stock Exchange rule book in 1908 and 1912 protected the market, in its traditional form, by strictly enforcing fixed commissions and the single capacity of firms. As a result, some of the more dynamic firms, such as Helbert Wagg, which later merged with Schroders, found conformity to the revised rule book to be an undue restraint – an external diseconomy – and resigned their membership, henceforth developing more broadly based securities business as both agents and principals.[4]

The Stock Exchange reforms of the Edwardian era proved effective until the 1970s. By then, the internationalization of the London market and developments in computing and communications technology once again led to a rapid growth of off-exchange business. Now, however, the rules were also perceived as a restrictive practice protecting the vested interests of members against the interests of clients and the general public. The Stock Exchange rule book had become not just an external diseconomy for firms, but a political liability as well. With its arm twisted by the government, the London Stock Exchange dismantled the Edwardian reforms in the process known as Big Bang (1983–86), giving the market a new lease of life.

The 1990s saw a wave of mergers among financial exchanges, with further consolidation on a global basis on the horizon. Increasingly exchanges de-mutualized, to allow them to act decisively to provide a better service for all users. Stockholm in 1993 was the first to convert from a mutual basis to corporate form, run to maximize shareholder value rather than to protect vested interests. Then Amsterdam and Sydney took the plunge. 'For a mutual it is very hard to make any decision – you get an awful lot of lobbying from your members,' observed George Möller, president of the Amsterdam Stock Exchange. 'Now, once we have consulted the market users, we can make a decision'.[5] In derivatives, the growth of over-the-counter transactions considerably exceeded the increase in exchange-based business. The Internet facilitated the matching of buyers and sellers of securities or almost anything else, by-passing exchanges. At the turn of the twenty-first century, some observers were pessimistic about the survival of organized exchanges in any form.

CLUBS

Traditional networks of bank correspondent relationships are *exclusive* associations. The European banking clubs discussed in Chapters 2 and 11 were more formally constituted bodies. Pan-European clubs similar to the banking clubs are also found in the insurance industry. These are groups of like-minded, middle-ranking insurers that have clubbed together to share operational best practice and the risks of cross-border expansion through general co-operation. Industry experts forecast a 'dramatic increase' in the number, size and influence of co-operative groupings in Europe 'as several thousand small-to-mid-sized (often mutual) European insurers club together to confront the challenges of an increasingly genuine, increasingly competitive "Single Market".'[6]

The largest such grouping in the insurance industry, Eureko, took the concept a stage further through the creation of a joint-venture down-stream holding company in order to make acquisitions on behalf of its shareholders. Founded in 1992 with the slogan 'Enabling Progress by Sharing Success', Eureko grew rapidly and even mounted an unsuccessful bid for AGF, the second largest French insurance company, in 1998. There were some similarities in its development from club to joint venture with the evolution of EBIC and Europartners. But whereas these banking clubs were long departed, at the beginning of the twenty-first century Eureko saw itself as a cohesive entity and described itself as Europe's fifth largest insurance group.[7] The announcement of its flotation in 2000 seemed likely to yield large profits to the club members, though possibly creating a new competitor.

Banking clubs reappeared in the 1990s in a new guise. Instead of the generalist banking clubs of the 1970s and 1980s, these clubs were narrowly focused associations specializing in areas such as cash management.[8] Faced by competition from global banks, notably Citibank, Chase and Bank of America, domestic and regional banks formed club arrangements to provide their corporate clients with improved cash management services.

Two such clubs were IBOS and Connector, established, respectively, in 1991 and 1996, with pan-European memberships and links to banks around the world. Besides the day-to-day activities of their operating sections, they held regular board meetings to discuss strategy and an annual get-together of all the chief executives, set-ups distinctly similar to Orion and other consortium banks. In the case of IBOS, several of the Inter-Alpha member banks provided an example of how one of the wide-ranging clubs of the 1970s could continue to engage in practical co-operation in the twenty-first century. They envisaged that in time the relationship between members would go beyond just cash management.

When the wide-ranging ABECOR club was disbanded in 1997, after nearly a quarter of a century, one of its members, Barclays, formed a much more specialized club. This was a 'virtual network' of partner banks across Europe to supplement its own extensive corporate banking coverage; the partners were described as 'a managed network of locally based banks with which quality assured service arrangements are being set in place to deliver a consistent experience for customers.'[9] There was no grand strategic co-operative vision, but strictly practical objectives and the beneficiaries limited to the corporate banking area. In a similar vein, Commerzbank, having abandoned the Europartners club, created a strategic alliance with several European banks to facilitate cross-border payments.

LIMITED-PURPOSE JOINT VENTURES

Limited-purpose joint ventures involve modest commitments of strategic resources by participants to accomplish a specific mutually beneficial purpose.[10] The insurance 'pooling' or 'funding' entity is an example. Sharing risk is the essence of insurance and consortia abound in the insurance industry. For instance, British Aviation Insurance Group (BAIG), formed in 1924, is one of several jointly owned ventures in aviation risks; similar joint ventures deal with nuclear and pharmaceutical risk. Another well-established business was Trade Indemnity, whose ownership included a group of mainline insurance companies; founded in 1918, it became the leading company in the esoteric field of credit insurance. In 1996, it began the process of becoming controlled by Allianz, the largest insurance company in Europe, but retained consortium features in its ownership through the inclusion of other insurance company shareholders; it changed its name to EULER Trade Indemnity. A common feature of these insurance ventures was that they specialized in hazardous and complex niches of the insurance market in which the risk-spreading advantage of the consortium approach had not been diluted and where competition with their shareholders or partners was unlikely to arise. This appears to account for their longevity.

Trade finance is a field in which limited-purpose joint ventures between public and private sector bodies are found in many countries. In France, Banque Française du Commerce Extérieur was established after the war to promote French exports, benefiting from special state subsidies and guarantees to fulfil this role. Owned initially by Banque de France and several nationalized commercial banks, private capital was introduced in the 1980s and the range of activities was extended. In 1996, it merged with Crédit National, which then became a part of Natexis Banques Populaires, a wholesale and investment subsidiary of a co-operative banking group; trade finance became just one of many activities conducted by one of the largest banks in France with a listing in Paris.

Austria's Österreichische Kontrollbank AG was somewhat similar, being established in 1946 to promote exports and to provide capital markets services for the financial sector. It was jointly owned by a consortium of banks, some private sector and others with majority state shareholdings.

FULL-BLOWN JOINT VENTURES

A full-blown joint venture is a free-standing entity with its own strategic objectives.[11] This is the highest form of strategic alliance. It is the form taken by the consortium banks of the 1960–90s, placing them towards the top end of the hierarchy of strategic alliance forms.

The world's more than 50 regional development banks generally have consortium form, often involving both private and public sector shareholders.[12] Many of them were formed in the 1960s and 1970s when the consortium bank approach was regarded as radical and innovative. By the late 1980s, the bloom was off the fruit and a proposal for the formation of a major new regional development bank, the Asian Finance and Investment Corp, on a consortium basis caused raised eyebrows, particularly after the failure a few years earlier of the somewhat similar Private Investment Company for Asia, which was overexposed to the Philippines at the end of the Marcos era.[13] The purpose of the new Singapore-based entity, in which the Asian Development Bank and private sector commercial banks were to be shareholders, was to take equity stakes in investments along the lines of the International Finance Corporation.[14] Some observers were sceptical about the proposal: 'consortium banks, fashionable during the 1970s, nearly all closed as a result of conflicts between partners,' commented the *Financial Times*. 'On the surface there is no reason why similar problems should not arise.'[15]

Public purpose consortia may be formed to address the problem of market failure, a situation in which for one reason or another the market mechanism does not deliver economic efficiency. The absence of appropriate financial institutions to undertake roles deemed economically or socially important is a form of market failure. There are many examples of politically inspired consortium solutions, often combining public and private sector participants, to such institutional gaps or shortcomings.

The takeover of Yorkshire Bank by a group of other banks in 1911 was an early instance of a consortium solution to market failure. Yorkshire Bank was formed in 1859 to provide banking facilities for working men, the motives of the eminent and worthy founders being more philanthropic than profit oriented.[16] A financial crisis in 1910, caused by a downturn in the UK government securities market in which most of its funds were invested rather than through bad lending or malfeasance, threatened to lead to failure, with dire consequences for depositors. To avert this potentially social and commercial calamity, after consultation with the Bank of England and leading City figures, Yorkshire Bank was taken over by a consortium comprising eleven leading London and regional banks, including forerunners of Barclays, Lloyds, Midland and Royal Bank of Scotland. At one stage, in order to highlight its social mission, the name was changed to the picturesque Yorkshire Penny Bank.

Yorkshire Bank prospered in the subsequent decades, providing deposit and loan facilities for customers of modest means and achieving a dominant share of the Yorkshire market – one in four current accounts. By sticking to its last, Yorkshire Bank was consistently one of Europe's most profitable banks. At the same time, some of its shareholders, by now reduced to four through mergers, were losing money hand over fist in foreign adventures, investment banking and Third World lending. 'For us, overseas lending means Lancashire,' quipped general manager Graham Sunderland. 'Where's Brazil?,' he replied when asked by a journalist why Yorkshire Bank wasn't joining in the LDC lending spree, 'is it some place up Barnsley way?'

Yorkshire Bank's client base among social classes C2 and D limited rivalry between itself and its shareholders, which were after richer pickings and corporate accounts. Thus, unlike the consortium banks of the Euromarkets, Yorkshire Bank co-existed more or less amiably with its shareholders for 80 years. But in the late 1980s, banks became keen to free up capital by divesting non-strategic minority interests such as Yorkshire Bank. Since none of the shareholders would have been happy to see Yorkshire Bank falling into another UK bank's hands, they sold out in 1990 to the acquisitive National Australia Bank, which paid £1 billion, three times book value; it was a very full price and very timely for the shareholders, which had just had to make substantial provisions on their LDC loans.

3i came into being in 1945 as a pair of consortium entities, ICFC and FCI, which merged in 1974.[17] They were a solution to the problem of the so-called 'Macmillan gap' – the perceived failure of the capital market to provide finance for small to medium-sized British businesses. The founding shareholders were the Bank of England and the British clearing banks, the latter being dragged in screaming and kicking; Westminster Bank's general manager, Sir Charles Lidbury, called it 'an indirect levy' on the banks' resources for subsidising 'adventures in the interests of the "full employment" campaign,' while the National Provincial's general manager 'nearly had a fit.'[18] In the early years, there was little overlap between ICFC and FCI and the shareholders, and if there were tensions the Bank of England kept the peace.

Competition with the shareholders developed in the late 1960s as both sides spread their wings; when Glyn Mills[19] undertook the first flotation by a clearing bank in 1967, ICFC was its competitor for the mandate through its corporate finance operation. The development of merchant banking capabilities by Midland, NatWest and Barclays in the early 1970s, and the formation of their own venture capital arms later in the decade, found ICFC and its shareholders operating in the same markets with no clear rationale for the clearing bank minority shareholdings. As competition between 3i and its shareholders intensified, the ownership structure became more and more unsatisfactory. 3i was floated in June 1994, providing large profits for the shareholders and allowing 3i's management freedom to develop the business. As 3i joined the FTSE 100, Lidbury would have been astonished at the outcome.

State involvement tends to sustain the life expectancy of financial consortia; partial state ownership was a feature of all six surviving London consortium banks (see page 195) and of several outside the UK, such as Arab Banking Corporation and Gulf International Bank – in some cases because the economic or social requirements that led to their establishment remain a priority or because it is politically problematic to shut them down. Private sector financial consortia, on the other hand, come and go like private sector companies. But how does their life expectancy compare with other firms?

THE RISE AND FALL OF CONSORTIA AND STRATEGIC ALLIANCES

Few businesses are, like Monte dei Paschi di Siena (see page 35), able to trace their history over half a millennium. Longevity is the exception rather than the rule among business corporations, particularly among strategic alliances. Estimates of the average life expectancy of Fortune 500 mega-corporations are 40–50 years.[20] Among smaller companies, average life expectancy is considerably shorter. A study in the Netherlands of the average life expectancy of firms in Japan and Europe, regardless of size, produced a figure of just 12.5 years.[21]

The average life span of the 29 London consortium banks that were formed and demised between 1964 and 1992 was 14.7 years. Orion lasted 10.5 years as a consortium bank and 18 years as a stand-alone entity, straddling the average longevity of companies in the Netherlands study. Among Orion's peer group, MAIBL managed 20 years and EBC 12 years. By the standards of the banking industry, whose highly regulated institutions have longer life expectancies than other businesses, the consortium banks were relatively short-lived.[22]

Yet even in finance, there is a high rate of institutional attrition. The tombstone for the 1956 initial public offering conducted by Goldman Sachs on behalf of Ford Motor Company listed no less than 722 underwriters, virtually a catalogue of the significant Wall Street firms of the day. John

Whitehead, who became the Goldman Sachs senior partner, had a framed copy of that tombstone on the wall of his office. Every time one of the firms ceased to exist – either by going out of business, adopting corporate status, merging with a competitor or being absorbed by a conglomerate – he crossed off the name in red pen.[23] By the time that the Goldman Sachs partners voted to sell a part of the firm to the public in 1998, 42 years later, it was the last surviving partnership.

Yet some strategic alliances among financial institutions have been relatively long-lived. Probably the most important factor has been public sector involvement, which may provide protection by shielding such institutions from the full rigour of commercial pressures and making their demise a political issue. The other long-term survivors tend to be providers of technical or back-office functions far away from competition for clients and directly money-making activities.

Consortia are by no means a phenomenon of the past. 'We can read almost daily about strategic alliances being formed between firms on a national or international basis,' observe the authors of a leading study of the subject.[24] Indeed, globalization makes global strategic alliances more important and topical than ever. 'Globalization mandates alliances,' declares Kenichi Ohmae, head of McKinsey's Tokyo office, 'makes them absolutely essential to strategy.'[25] Yet , as the history of Orion and the consortium banking demonstrate above all, strategic alliances are a form of business organization that is particularly prone to pitfalls. Perhaps their experiences hold lessons for present and future practitioners.

The legacy of Orion

Orion is no more. But it survives in the memories of people who worked in the Euromarkets in the 1970s and 1980s.

Naturally, the recollections are most vivid among those employed at the bank, the Orion alumni numbering several hundred. By them it is recalled with an unusual degree of affection, many of those interviewed in the preparation of this book describing their time at Orion as the happiest period of their career.

Orion is also remembered by people who worked for other Euromarket banks, particularly the other investment and consortium banks. They speak of it with respect, citing the drive and ingenuity that created a thriving Euromarket business from a standing start. It is generally perceived as the most successful of the consortium banks; the lesson is widely drawn that if Orion couldn't make the consortium concept work, then nobody could.

Orion's legacy to the consortium concept is a set of cautionary lessons. It provides a case study, Harvard Business School style, of the tensions and contradictions inherent to consortium undertakings that would repay attention by any future group of banks or other organizations contemplating a consortium enterprise. But to regard the rise and fall of Orion simply as a tale of corporate failure, is to see the cup half empty not half full. Orion also got many things right and provides plenty of guidance as to how to make a consortium approach work. In Orion's heyday, the cup overflowed.

The acquisition of Orion by Royal Bank of Canada reinforced the international side of Royal Bank's business. It was also a major step in the development of Royal Bank's investment banking capabilities, in many ways paving the way for the acquisition of Dominion Securities half-a-dozen years later. Orion's demise as an independent entity was a logical, if ironic, outcome of Royal Bank's decision to make a wholehearted commitment to investment banking. Thus Orion's legacy to Royal Bank was a significant contribution to making it the most outward-looking and most investment banking oriented of the Canadian banks.

Orion also has a living legacy. It served as a training ground for an uncommonly able group of executives, many of whom became high-flyers in one of the shareholder banks or elsewhere. It was they, the Orion diaspora, who came together to make this book possible a decade after the disappearance of the bank at which they worked together, an almost unprecedented initiative. That enduring *esprit de corps* is itself testament that there really was something special about Orion.

Chronology, 1963–89

This chronology covers key political and economic developments in the quarter century that saw the transformation of the Euromarkets into the world's foremost financial markets. It also identifies milestones in the evolution of Orion; transactions mentioned are those which were the first or the largest of their type or otherwise noteworthy. The tables and graphs present key financial and economic data of the era. Details of Orion's financial history are to be found in Appendix IV.

Abbreviations: Chase (Chase Manhattan Bank), Royal (Royal Bank of Canada), NatPro (National Provincial Bank), Westminster (Westminster Bank), NatWest (National Westminster Bank), WestLB (Westdeutsche Landesbank Girozentrale), Mitsubishi (Mitsubishi Bank) and Orion (for Orion Bank, Orion Termbank, Orion Royal Bank and subsidiaries).

Under *Orion financings*: 'loans' are syndicated loans, NIFs, RUFs etc.; 'bonds' are public issues, private placements, FRNs, FRCDs and other securities, lead managed, co-managed, managed or advised by Orion. *New loan transactions* and *new bond transactions* are intended to show the range of Orion's client base and refer to clients not previously mentioned. The word '*subsequently*' in brackets indicates subsequent transactions of the same type and for the same client. Transaction amounts expressed in US dollars sometimes include non-dollar transactions, converted at the prevailing rates of exchange.

1963

Global events *Feb* Canadian Conservative government falls. *Apr* Lester Pearson Premier. *Mar* China and Pakistan settle border dispute. *May* Jomo Kenyatta Premier of Kenya. Organization of African Unity formed, after widespread decolonization. *Jun* Election of Pope Paul VI. *Aug* Test Ban

Treaty. *Oct* Harold Macmillan succeeded as UK Premier by Sir Alec Douglas-Home. Ludwig Erhard succeeds Konrad Adenauer as German Chancellor. *Nov* President Kennedy assassinated, succeeded by Lyndon Johnson.

> **International finance**   The Eurobond launch year. *Jan* Midland Bank, Deutsche, Amsterdamsche and SocGen of Belgium form European Advisory Committee (nucleus of EBIC club, Appendix III). *Feb* DM81 million Neckermann Euroequity issue (Morgan & Cie). *Apr* $20 million private placement for Belgium (Samuel Montagu). *Jul* US Interest Equalization Tax proposed (lasted until 1974). $15 million Autostrade Eurobond issue (Warburg). *Oct* G-10 countries launch study of international monetary system, under Robert Roosa. SF60 million Copenhagen Eurobond criticized by Swiss authorities for unauthorized use of SF (Morgan Grenfell). *Dec* First Japanese convertibles: $15 million Takeda Chemical (Morgan & Cie) and $5 million Canon Camera (Loeb Rhoades & M. Samuel).

Orion antecedents   Royal's European joint venture with Westminster aborted after President de Gaulle's first veto of UK membership of the EEC. Stung by Citibank buying into Mercantile Bank of Canada, Chase seeks to buy 25 per cent shareholding in Toronto Dominion Bank (approval not obtained).

1964

Global events   *Jan* Palestine Liberation Organisation (PLO) established. *Apr* Military takes power in Brazil. Introduction of 360 series enables IBM to maintain leadership in computer industry. *May* First publication of *Quotations of Chairman Mao*; 350 million copies printed in next four years. Death of Pandit Nehru, Indian Premier. *Jun* Nelson Mandela sentenced to life imprisonment for opposing apartheid in South Africa. *Jul* US Civil Rights Act. *Aug* Tonkin Gulf incident escalates US commitment to Vietnam War. Singapore secures independence from Malaysia. *Oct* Harold Wilson, Labour, elected UK Premier; speculation against £ sterling offset by concerted help from G-10 countries. Leonid Brezhnev replaces Nikita Khrushchev as Soviet leader. *Nov* King Faisal succeeds to Saudi throne.

> **International finance**   Eurobond issue volume up 360 per cent. Midland and International Banks created as first Euromarket consortium bank in London by Midland and three other banks, followed by 34 such banks by 1984 (Appendix II). *Feb* Fiduciary Trust opens London office, with United Nations Pension Fund as largest Eurobond institutional investor under a single manager. *Mar* German 25 per cent coupon tax on domestic issues

triggers DM Eurobond market. *May* $25 million Eurobond for Norway (Hambros). *Jun* $25 million IRI, Italy, Eurobond with Finsider warrants (Loeb Rhoades & M. Samuel). First straight corporate Eurobond, Kesko Oy (White Weld). *Oct* £/DM5 million City of Turin issue (Warburg). £ crisis causes 15 per cent import surcharge to be introduced.

1965

Global events *Jan* Death of Sir Winston Churchill. *Mar* Nicolae Ceausescu becomes leader of Romania; develops policy of independence from Soviet Union, financial self-sufficiency and internal suppression. *Jun* Army takes power in Algeria, under Houari Boumédienne. *Nov* Unilateral Declaration of Independence by Rhodesia; sanctions and 15 years of instability. Sese Seko Mobutu takes power in Congo (Zaire). *Dec* Ferdinand Marcos Philippine President.

International finance *Feb* US Voluntary Foreign Credit Restraint Program (lasted until 1974); 12 US corporates issued Eurobonds in 1965, first of many hundreds. *Jun* First corporate £/DM issues, for Mobil (Warburg) & Uniroyal (Hambros). *Jul* ENEL, Italy, does simultaneous issues in six EEC currencies under the Abs Plan (named after Hermann Abs of Deutsche Bank). *Oct* $25 million Monsanto convertible Eurobond (Dillon Read). First Euro–Guilder bond issue (no more until 1969).

Orion antecedents Royal and Westminster, with others, form RoyWest Corporation in Nassau to do trust and mortgage business.

1966

Global events *Jan* Second Indo–Pakistani War ended through Soviet good offices; Indira Gandhi becomes Indian Premier. Military takes power in Nigeria. *Mar* General Suharto takes effective power from President Sukarno in Indonesia. *May* UK economy 'blown off course' by seamen's strike. *Sep* Fed and other central banks help UK. *Jun* Military takes power in Argentina. *Aug* Cultural Revolution in China strengthens Mao Tse-Tung; Deng Xiao-Ping stripped of power for 'taking the capitalist road'. *Sep* President Hendrik Verwoerd, architect of apartheid in South Africa, assassinated. *Nov* Ludwig Erhard replaced as German Chancellor by Kurt Kiesinger. Bank of America licenses other banks to use its credit card; rise of VISA and Master Charge.

International finance Sir Charles Hambro warns that Eurobonds likely to be a 'temporary phenomenon'. *Mar* $27.5 million Transalpine Finance Holdings, the first Eurobond secured on throughput agreements

(Rothschild). *May* Citibank issues first negotiable Eurodollar CDs in London, with White Weld as market-maker. *Jun* First zero coupon Eurobond, $6 million for BP Tankers (Rothschild & Svenska Handelsbanken). *Dec* First DM Eurobonds convertible into US equity, Texaco and ITT. First Arab consortium bank formed, United Bank of Kuwait.

Orion antecedents Chase tries to form merchant bank in London with Rothschild and allies. NatPro and NM Rothschild & Sons form the first clearing/merchant banking joint venture in UK, National Provincial & Rothschild (NatWest sold its stake in 1969).

1967

Global events *Apr* Colonels take power in Greece. Death of Konrad Adenauer. *May* Secession of Biafra; civil war in Nigeria. *Jun* Six Day War in the Middle East; brief oil embargo and many Palestinians flee to Jordan. President de Gaulle cuts short state visit to Canada after exclaiming '*Vive Québec libre*' and *Dec* vetoes UK membership of the EEC for a second time. Dr Christiaan Barnard performs first heart transplant in Cape Town.

International finance Société Financière Européenne formed, as a consortium banking group, by five European banks (nucleus of ABECOR club; Appendix III) and Bank of America. Bondtrade set up by Kuhn Loeb & four others as Eurobond market-maker. Crown Agents, representing overseas governments in UK, becomes major Eurobond buyer. *Aug* KD15 million loan (Kuwait Investment Company) for World Bank marks start of Kuwaiti Dinar bond market; public issues followed in 1974. *Sep* Midland Bank acquires 33 per cent of London merchant bank, Samuel Montagu. *Nov* £ is devalued from $2.80 to $2.40, after record balance-of-payments monthly deficit. *Dec* First Euro–Franc issue, FF60 million for Roussel Uclaf (Crédit Commercial de France). Milton Friedman urges, in *Newsweek* articles, floating exchange rates and freedom to trade in foreign currencies.

Orion antecedents Westminster forms consortium bank, International Commercial Bank, with four others (NatWest sold its stake in 1971). 10 per cent mutual share exchange with Royal informally proposed by Chase (not carried out); subsequently, Chase and Royal presidents discuss joint venture in international banking. Report by Prices & Income Board suggests scope for UK bank mergers.

1968

Global events *Apr* Pierre Trudeau succeeds Lester Pearson as Premier of Canada. Assassination of Rev. Martin Luther King. *Jun* Assassination of

Senator Robert Kennedy. *Jul* Ba'athists take power in Iraq; rise of Saddam Hussein. *Aug* 'Prague Spring' reforms in Czechoslovakia crushed by Soviet Union; end of 'socialism with a human face'.

International finance   Convertible Eurobond issues up seven times; numerous speculative issues appear, e.g. LTV, King Resources, Gulf & Western and Robert Vesco's ICC International. *Jan* US Mandatory Foreign Investment Program (lasted until 1974). *Mar* Loss of confidence in US$, £ and other currencies creates gold rush; official gold pool arrangements collapse and dual market in gold established. *May* Student riots and subsequent strikes in France (*événements de mai*) defer further Euro–Franc issues until 1972. *Jun* First Euromarket syndicated loans, $15 million for Hungarian Aluminium (Bank of London and South America), $100 million for Austria (Bankers Trust International & Lehman Brothers). *Oct* Start of Asian Dollar market in Singapore (Bank of America). *Nov* Large capital inflows into Germany; proposal to devalue FF called 'worst form of absurdity' by President de Gaulle. *Dec* JP Morgan forms Euroclear, to facilitate Eurobond settlements.

Orion antecedents   *Jan* Merger of NatPro & Westminster announced, to create NatWest, stimulating *Feb* proposed merger of three other UK banks, Barclays, Lloyds and Martins, which was blocked on competition grounds. *Nov* Barclays alone bought Martins.

1969

Global events   *Jan* Richard Nixon President of the USA; intensifies negotiations to end Vietnam War. *Mar* Death of Dwight Eisenhower. Maiden flight of *Concorde*, Anglo–French supersonic airliner. *Apr* Charles de Gaulle resigns as President of France, succeeded by Georges Pompidou. *Jul* Juan Carlos nominated future King by Francisco Franco, Spanish head of state. *Apollo 11* lands two men on the moon. *Sep* Muammar Gaddafi takes power in Libya, after overthrow of King Idris. *Oct* Willy Brandt succeeds Kurt Kiesinger as German Chancellor. US–Soviet negotiations to limit arms (SALT).

International finance   Crédit Lyonnais launches UBAF in Paris, the first of three consortia, with Arab banks, led by a French public sector bank. Warburg and Paribas exchange shares and form US investment bank, Warburg Paribas Becker (dissolved in 1982–83). *Jan* Manufacturers Hanover Ltd opens in London and soon manages large syndicated loans, e.g. $80 million for Iran and $200 million for IMI (Italy). *Feb* Formation of Association of International Bond Dealers (later International Securities Market Association), to improve dealing procedures, after two years of settlements chaos. *Jun* IMF introduces Special Drawing Rights; SDR used for

three Eurobond issues, but not thereafter for several years. Launch of
Euromoney magazine. *Aug* FF devalued 11 per cent. *Sep* $56 million
Euroequity issue for mutual fund group, Investors Overseas Services, of
Bernie Cornfeld ('do you sincerely want to be rich?'); heavy losses for
investors in 1970. US banks Eurodollar borrowings subject to reserve
requirement (Regulation M), initially 10 per cent. *Sep* British banks agree
to disclose true profits in future and cease creating hidden reserves. *Oct*
DM revalued 9 per cent.

Orion antecedents   WestLB formed from merger of Landesbank für
Westfalen Girozentrale, Münster and Rheinische Girozentrale und
Provinzialbank, Düsseldorf. NatWest and Chase try to buy Standard Bank
(which merged with Chartered Bank instead); Chase participates in forming
Australian investment bank.

1970

Global events   *Jan* End of Nigerian civil war. *Jun* Conservatives win elec-
tion in UK; Edward Heath Premier. *Sep* Crisis in Jordan ('Black September');
expulsion of Palestinian fighters, many to Lebanon and Syria. Salvador
Allende elected President of Chile, launches Marxist programme. *Oct* Anwar
Sadat President of Egypt, after President Nasser's death. *Nov* Death of
Charles de Gaulle. Hafez Assad takes power in Syria.

International finance   Europartners and EBIC banking clubs formed;
major EEC banks plan wide co-operation, contemplating even full mergers
(Appendix III). First ECP issue: $15 million for Alcoa of Australia
(Schroders & White Weld). *Mar* Pirelli/Dunlop union announced, poten-
tial European cross-border merger (later dissolved). *May* $125 million
FRN for ENEL of Italy (Bankers Trust International & Warburg).
Canadian $ floats. *May* Werner Report points the way to EEC economic
and monetary union.

Orion   *Apr* Chase, NatWest and Royal, later joined by WestLB, conduct
studies about a new multinational bank. Unsuccessful efforts to acquire a
London merchant bank. *Oct* Three entities launched: Orion Termbank
(medium-term lending), Orion Bank (investment/merchant banking) and
Orion Multinational Services (planning and shareholder co-ordination).

1971

Global events   *Jan* Aswan High Dam completed in Egypt, with Soviet
help. Idi Amin takes power in Uganda. *Feb* Confrontation in Teheran;
OPEC extracts significant concessions from the international oil companies.

May Erich Honecker leader of East Germany. *Jul* United Arab Emirates proclaimed; British withdrawal from the Gulf. *Sep* Death of Nikita Khrushchev. *Oct* China joins United Nations, in lieu of Taiwan. *Nov* Third Indo–Pakistani War results in secession of East Pakistan and creation of Bangladesh; Zulfikar Ali Bhutto President of Pakistan.

International finance Turbulent year for currencies. *Jan* Cedel, formed by 71 banks as an alternative to Euroclear. *Mar* First $100 million Eurobond (Morgan Stanley for ESSO). *Apr* Inter-Alpha club formed by medium-sized EEC banks (Appendix III). *May* Germany and the Netherlands free exchange rates; SF and OS revalued. Japanese proposals to reduce balance of payments surplus. *Aug* President Nixon suspends US$ convertibility into gold and imposes 10 per cent import tax. *Sep* New UK 'Competition and Credit Control' policy stimulates inflation and imprudent lending. *Nov* $12 million First US corporate Euroequity issue, Baxter–Travenol. First Asian $ bond issue, $10 million for Development Bank of Singapore. *Dec* G-10 countries meet at Smithsonian Institution, Washington, and repeg exchange rates (US$ devalued 8 per cent generally, 17 per cent against Yen); Can$ continued to float. Gold price up from $35 to $38. Milton Friedman's article 'The Need for Futures Markets in Currencies'.

Orion Credito Italiano becomes shareholder. Unsuccessful search for French partner. NatWest sets up 100 per cent owned merchant bank, County Bank, initially for domestic business. Negotiations with Mitsubishi, which founds Japan International Bank in London with four other Japanese banks. *Orion financings* $363 million loans, $159 million bonds. *New loan transactions* $110 million, 8 yrs, Denmark (*subsequently* $4.9 billion). *New bond transactions* $42 million Hydro-Quebec (*subsequently* $1.1 billion). $42 million Denmark (*subsequently* $4.3 billion).

1972

Global events *Jan* Strikes, power cuts and inflation in UK; state of emergency declared. 'Bloody Sunday' in Northern Ireland leads to direct British rule. *Feb* President Nixon visits China. *Jun* Watergate break-in. *Aug* President Amin of Uganda launches mass expulsion of British Asians. *Sep* Bobby Fischer defeats Boris Spassky for the world chess championship in Iceland. Norway withdraws application to join EEC.

International finance Average Euroloan spread 1.01 per cent. *Mar* 'Snake' established to stabilize European exchange rates. *Apr* £10 million Eurosterling bond for AMOCO; this market not used again until 1977. *May* Chicago Mercantile Exchange introduces currency futures contracts, dismissed as insignificant at the time. *Jun* Under severe pressure, £ leaves the 'snake'. *Jul* *Euromoney* speculates on the demise of Euromarkets when US controls end.

Negative interest rate on non-resident SF deposits. French Franc Eurobond market re-opens, with 22 issues by end of 1972. *Sep* Japanese banks authorized to issue CDs in London. *Oct* $41 million Euroequity issue for Trade Development Bank (Manufacturers Hanover & Rothschild). Morgan Guaranty opens Euroclear membership to other banks, while continuing to manage it.

Orion   Starts multinational leasing. Mitsubishi becomes shareholder. WestLB opens London branch. Libra Bank set up as merchant bank for Latin America by Orion's six shareholders and four other banks. *Orion financings* $122 million loans, $311 million bonds. *New loan transactions* $23 million, 7 yrs, J. Lyons & Co. (plus $5 million Euroequity). $15 million Chrysler Corporation (*subsequently* $1.7 billion). $70 million, 10 yrs, Bank of Greece (*subsequently* $2 billion). $150 million, 3 yrs, Istituto Mobiliare Italiano (*subsequently* $725 million). *New bond transactions* First A$/DM Eurobond, $36 million Rural and Industries Bank of Western Australia (*subsequently* $50 million). $42 million bond Province of Quebec (*subsequently* $1.5 billion).

1973

Global events   *Jan* UK, Denmark and Ireland join EEC. Nixon re-elected US President. Paris agreement to end Vietnam War (not achieved until 1975). Death of Lyndon Johnson. *Mar* Iran nationalizes foreign oil companies. *Apr* Death of Pablo Picasso, the artist. *Jun–Sep* OPEC, concerned about falling $ value of oil receipts, threatens use of the 'oil weapon'. *Oct* Yom Kippur War between Arab states and Israel. Turbulent foreign exchange markets, rise in interest rates, four-fold oil price rise and oil embargo (first 'oil shock'). *Sep* Juan Peron returns from exile to resume Argentina's Presidency. General Pinochet takes power in Chile; 'Chicago boys', disciples of Milton Friedman, introduce market economy.

International finance   Euroloans increase, especially to LDCs, with longer maturities. Eurobond issues down by a third; market price-falls lead to carrying and trading losses. Euro$ financings for UK local authorities. *Feb* 10 per cent devaluation of $; EEC currencies and Yen float. *Apr* Midland Bank increases its stake in Samuel Montagu to 100 per cent. $1 billion syndicated loan for UK's Electricity Council. *May* Black–Scholes paper published, setting out method of valuing options. *Jul* Gordon Richardson succeeds Leslie O'Brien as Bank of England Governor. *Sep* Leb£50 million Eurobond for European Investment Bank, tapping Middle East funds. Collapse of National Bank of San Diego and *Nov* UK 'secondary' bank, London and County Securities. Bank of England launches 'lifeboat' for banks in difficulties, mainly due to property and shipping loans.

Orion   Rapid growth in all areas; following losses, Eurobond trading curtailed. Orion Shipping Holdings formed. *Apr* Chase Manhattan Ltd launched ('centrepiece' of Chase's syndicated loan activities; similar aim for Chase Manhattan Asia). *Orion financings* $1.1 billion loans, $243 million bonds. *New loan transactions* $500 million, 10 yrs, Italian merchant bank, Mediobanca, affiliate of Credito Italiano. Governmental borrowers: $140 million, 14 yrs, Brazil *(subsequently* $3 billion), $150 million, 15 yrs, Algeria *(subsequently* $1.5 billion), $40 million, 10 yrs, Nicaragua. $21 million, 9 yrs, OKG, Sweden *(subsequently* $310 million) *New bond transactions* $42 million bond for NatWest *(subsequently* $3.5 billion). Four UK local authority issues (Bristol, Coventry, Nottingham and Teesside).

1974

Global events   *Feb* UK Chancellor of the Exchequer speaks of 'gravest situation since the end of the war'; Conservative government falls and Harold Wilson is again Premier. *Apr* President Pompidou of France dies, succeeded by Valéry Giscard d'Estaing. Military takes power in Portugal. *May* Helmut Schmidt succeeds Willy Brandt as German Chancellor. *Jul* Turks invade Cyprus, leading to partition. Civilian rule restored in Greece; Konstantinos Karamanlis Premier. *Aug* Watergate scandal forces resignation of President Nixon, succeeded by Gerald Ford. *Sep* Haile Selassie deposed in Ethiopia; Marxists take over.

International finance   Petrodollar recycling to OECD and LDC economies, alongside increased IMF facilities. Oil prices rise modestly until 1978. Formation of Credit Suisse White Weld (CSWW). *Jan* US Interest Equalization Tax and other capital controls abolished; fears for the future of the Eurobond markets not fulfilled, although 1974 saw further losses and 48 per cent reduction in new issues. *May* Franklin National Bank collapses; business taken over by European American (EBIC club, Appendix III). First Can$ issues, $15 million for British Columbia (Crédit Commercial de France). *Jun* Foreign exchange losses bring down Bankhaus ID Herstatt and damage several leading banks, including Lloyds and WestLB. Rise in interest rates; Italian, Japanese and some consortium banks suffer from 'tiering' in interbank funding. *Jul* Sale of 25 per cent of Krupp Steel Corp. to Iran. *Sep* Bank of England requires comfort letters from consortium bank owners. *Oct* Launch of *AGEFI* magazine (later *IFR*). Penalty on SF deposits drives investors to DM securities.

Orion   David Montagu, Chairman, simplifies corporate structure; one entity, Orion Bank, replaces three. Orion Pacific co-founds Amanah–Chase Merchant Bank in Malaysia. Representative office opened in New York. Unsuccessful attempt to buy merchant bank, Hill Samuel. Strategic alliance with Goldman Sachs discussed, but not achieved. *Orion financings* $1.3 billion loans, $192 million bonds. *New loan transactions* Orion and its shareholders play leading role in $2.5 billion loan to UK Treasury and $500 million, 10 yrs, loan to Greater London Council. $420 million, 10 yrs, Burmah Oil, to acquire Signal Oil and Gas. $45 million, 12 yrs, Banco Nacional de Obras y Servicios Públicos, Mexico (*subsequently* $1 billion). $10 million, 10 yrs, Trinidad & Tobago (*subsequently* $341 million). $400 million, 5 yrs, New Zealand (*subsequently* $2.8 billion). $50 million, 10 yrs, ENI, Italy (*subsequently* $1.8 billion). *New bond transactions* First OS and KD Eurobonds Österreichische Kontrollbank (*subsequently* 15 issues for $1.1 billion). KD5 million bond Ireland (*subsequently* $2.1 billion).

1975

Global events   *Feb* Margaret Thatcher replaces Edward Heath as Conservative leader in UK. *Mar* King Faisal of Saudi Arabia assassinated by deranged nephew. *Apr* Fall of Saigon leads to reunification of Vietnam under Communist rule. Lebanon's 15-year civil war begins; much outside interference. Microsoft founded by Bill Gates (aged 19) and Paul Allen (22) to develop microcomputer operating systems. *Jun* State of emergency declared in India. *Aug* Helsinki agreement signed by 35 countries, including USA and Soviet Union, to promote detente in Europe. *Oct* Dr Andrei Sakharov awarded Nobel Peace Prize. *Nov* Death of Francisco Franco; Juan Carlos becomes King of Spain. *Dec* Indonesia invades East Timor.

International finance   Eurobond market recovers; new issues up nearly four times. Mean Euroloan spreads at highest level, 1.56 per cent, followed by steady decline; further rise in LDC borrowing. Banks become active issuers of FRNs. *Feb* Burmah Oil unable to service its debts; Bank of England provides a guarantee and takes over Burmah's 21 per cent shareholding in BP. *May* Deregulation of US stock market leads to consolidation in US securities firms. Bank of England reclassifies UK consortium banks, initially with 29 constituents; Association of London Consortium Banks formed. *Jun* UK commences North Sea oil production, which helps the £. *Aug* Co-operation between central banks on cross-border supervision of banks (Basle Concordat). *Sep* First to abandon consortium banking status in London, Rothschild Intercontinental Bank is bought by American Express. *Oct* $50 million pre-priced Eurobond issue, New Zealand (Kidder Peabody). *Nov* New York City financing crisis weakens US$. Chicago Board of Trade introduces financial futures.

Orion   Fifth annual report states that the consortium concept of banking was now established and Orion considered a leading multinational bank. Orion particularly active in Canadian $ issues and business with OPEC countries. County Bank expands into fund management and Euromarket activities; NatWest aims to support both Orion and County. *Aug* Negotiates sale of Deutsche Babcock stake to Iranian government. *Orion financings* $1.2

billion loans, $391 million bonds. *New loan transactions* $75 million, 5 yrs, Malaysia (*subsequently* $3.5 billion). $400 million, 7 yrs, Hong Kong Mass Transit Railway Corp. (*subsequently* $1.3 billion). $55 million, 5 yrs, Indonesia (*subsequently* $4.2 billion). $150 million, 7 yrs, Frigg Gas Field. *New bond transactions* $30 million, Province of Manitoba (*subsequently* $833 million). KD7 million, Pekema Oy, Finland. KD6 million, TVO, Finland (*subsequently* $83 million).

1976

Global events *Jan* Death of Chou En-Lai, Chinese Premier. *Mar* Military takes power in Argentina. *Apr* First democratic elections in Portugal for over 50 years; Mario Soares Premier. James Callaghan replaces Harold Wilson as UK Premier. Morocco and Mauritania annex phosphate-rich Spanish Sahara. Apple Computer founded by Stephen Wozniak (aged 26) and Steven Jobs (21); launches the first personal computer. *Jun* Wang Laboratories introduces advanced word processors. *Sep* Death of Mao Tse-Tung.

International finance First international edition of *Institutional Investor*. *FRN* issues up five times; mostly for banks. 1 per cent spread on $500 million, Electricité de France Euroloan. Deutsche Bank launches $300 million and $500 million Eurobonds for EEC. *Aug* Mexico devalues peso, after 22 years' linkage to US$. *Sep* UK economic crisis; applies to IMF for support. *Nov* EEC loans to support UK and Italy. First pure A$ Eurobond issue for Australian Industrial Development Corporation (Schroders). *Dec* 9.1 per cent stake in FIAT acquired by Libyan Arab Foreign Bank for $415 million. IMF $3.9 billion support for UK.

Orion After 3 years of good profits, Orion pays first dividend. Increase in leasing and corporate finance activity. Orion's shareholders subscribe $18 million Subordinated Loan. *Orion financings* $1.7 billion loans, $1.4 billion bonds. *New loan transactions* US$300 million, 5 yrs, UK National Water Council. Lead manages, with European Banking Company, first Euroloan European Economic Community ($300 million, 5 yrs). $300 million, 5 yrs, Petróleos Mexicanos (*subsequently* $2 billion). $150 million, 5 yrs, National Bank of Hungary (*subsequently* $600 million). *New bond transactions* $70 million, Royal Bank of Canada (*subsequently* $1.9 billion). $40 million, Creditanstalt-Bankverein (*subsequently* $874 million). $75 million, Saskatchewan (*subsequently* $700 million).

1977

Global events *Jan* Jimmy Carter President of USA. *Jun* Black-out in New York emphasizes seriousness of energy crisis. First general election in Spain for over 40 years; Adolfo Suarez Premier. *Jul* 'Gang of Four' disgraced in China; Deng Xiao-Ping resumes leadership role and plans reforms. Pakistan Premier Zulfikar Ali Bhutto deposed by Mohammed Zia Ul-Haq, who imposes military rule. *Sep* Laker Airways launches cut-price transatlantic service, *Skytrain*. *Nov* President Sadat of Egypt visits Israel on peace mission.

International finance Unico club formed by European co-operative banks (Appendix III). Eurosterling bond market reopens. *Jan* $3 billion loan from Bank of International Settlements to UK. First Eurobond 'bought deal'; $200 million for Mobil (UBS). *Feb* UK $1.5 billion Euroloan breaks 1 per cent spread. *Apr* $10 million Floating-Rate CD for Dai-ichi Kangyo Bank in London (CSWW), first of many FRCDs for Japanese banks. Fraudulent losses of SF1.5 billion uncovered at Crédit Suisse. *May* First Euro–Yen issue, Y10 billion for European Investment Bank. *Dec* Largest corporate Eurobond to date, $500 million for Shell (UBS). Critical report on Crown Agents of UK, which lost £200 million; it had been active in Eurobonds. Germany and Japan attempt to ward off hot money.

Orion Lower margins and competitive pressures caused Orion to be a cautious lender, while increasing its syndication activities. Multiple tranche issue for Österreichische Kontrollbank. *Orion financings* $2.6 billion loans, $2 billion bonds. *New loan transactions* $150 million, 6 yrs, Deutsche Aussenhandelsbank (*subsequently* $1.4 billion). $600 million, 8 yrs, Electricité de France (*subsequently* $2.2 billion). $300 million, 7 yrs, Province of Quebec (*subsequently* $2.5 billion). $130 million, 7 yrs, RENFE, Spain (*subsequently* $311 million). *New bond transactions* $30 million Mitsubishi Bank (*subsequently* $592 million). $45 million National Bank of Hungary (*subsequently* $102 million). $45 million, SNCF, France (*subsequently* $250 million).

1978

Global events *May* Italian Premier, Aldo Moro, found killed after kidnapping by terrorists. *Aug* Death of Jomo Kenyatta, Kenyan President; succeeded by Daniel Arap Moi. *Sep* Camp David agreement, sponsored by President Carter, between Israeli Premier, Menachem Begin and Egyptian President, Anwar Sadat; 'framework for peace' in the Middle East. *Sep* Election of Polish Pope, John Paul II, after deaths of Paul VI and John Paul I, who reigned for only 33 days. Change encouraged in East Europe, especially Poland. *Dec* USA and China resume diplomatic relations, after 30 years. *Sep–Dec* Widespread demonstrations against the Shah in Iran, leading to oil prices being more than doubled by the end of 1980 (second 'oil shock').

International finance Inflationary fears and interest rate rises; value of DM new Eurobond issues up 45 per cent, US$ issues down 30 per cent. *Jan* 1 per cent spread on $1 billion Nigeria Euroloan. *Apr* Stanley Ross & Partners formed to operate 'grey market' in Eurobonds. *Jul* Credit Suisse First Boston (CSFB) formed, successor to CSWW. *Nov* DM3 billion and SF2 billion 'Carter' bonds issued to strengthen US$. *Dec* First Euronote issue, $30 million for New Zealand Shipping Company (Citibank). ½ per cent spread on $250 million British Gas Euroloan.

Orion Increased activity in syndicated loans; 14 loans each over $100 million handled. International bond management service set up. David Montagu, Chairman, questions Orion's future as a consortium bank, but shareholders prefer no change. *Orion financings* $6.9 billion loans, $1.9 billion bonds. *New loan transactions* $200 million, 7 yrs, Finlands Bank (*subsequently* $150 million). $1.25 billion, 8 yrs, Hydro-Quebec (*subsequently* $1.25 billion). $600 million, 5 yrs, Banco Nacional de Crédito Rural, Mexico. $200 million, 8–9 yrs, Morocco. $250 million, 8 yrs, Kombinat Gornizco–Hutriczy, Poland. $100 million, 5 yrs, Romanian Foreign Trade Bank. *New bond transactions* $150 million, Chase Manhattan (*subsequently* $825 million). $46 million, European Investment Bank (*subsequently* $2.8 billion).

1979

Global events *Jan* The Shah leaves Iran. *Feb* Ayatollah Khomeini proclaims an Islamic republic. *Mar* Israel and Egypt sign peace treaty. *Apr* President Amin deposed as President of Uganda. *May* After 'winter of discontent', Margaret Thatcher becomes UK Premier. *Jun* Oil import restrictions agreed at Toyko summit; talk of oil reaching $100 per barrel. SONY Walkman launched (200 million sold over next 20 years). *Jul* Saddam Hussein President of Iraq. *Aug* Elections in Nigeria; military gives way to civilian government. *Oct* USA hands over canal to Panama. *Nov* 52 US diplomats taken hostage for 444 days in Teheran; Iranian assets frozen. *Dec* Soviet invasion of Afghanistan (stay for nearly ten years). US rescue of Chrysler Corp. from bankruptcy.

International finance Rise in US$ interest rates causes Eurobond trading losses; the market adapted with a 77 per cent increase in FRNs, less vulnerable than fixed-rate bonds to interest rates rises. Citibank and others develop interest rate swaps in London. *Mar* European Monetary System and Exchange Rate Mechanism formally introduced, without UK participation; hopes of a 'zone of monetary stability'. *Apr* First drop-lock bond, $30 million for TVO Power (CSFB). *Jun* First auction issue in the Eurobond market, for European Investment Bank. *Aug* Paul Volcker Chairman of the

Federal Reserve Board. *Oct* UK foreign exchange controls ended. First Volcker package to curb inflation (running at 13.3 per cent, highest since 1946) and protect US$; Fed's plan to target monetary aggregates hits markets ('Saturday Night Massacre') and helps the growth of derivatives. 0.4 per cent spread on Electricité de France $1 billion Euroloan, but changing Japanese bank attitudes help arrest the slide in spreads.

Orion Loans virtually unchanged over previous year, as result of conservative posture; US$ depreciation, lower margins and UK cost inflation reduce profits. *Sep* Crisis as Chairman, David Montagu, resigns; several top people leave for Swiss Bank Corp. *Orion financings* $6.6 billion loans, $2.6 billion bonds. *New loan transactions* $140 million, 7 yrs, Cyprus. $185 million, 8 yrs, Dominican Republic. $800 million, 10 yrs, Sweden (*subsequently* $13 billion). $100 million, 9 yrs, Caixa Geral, Portugal (*subsequently* $1.1 billion). *New bond transactions* First currency-swapped Eurobond issue, DM 60 million, Roylease, subsidiary of Royal. $100 million, Electricité de France (*subsequently* $1.9 million). SDR20 million, Nordic Investment Bank (*subsequently* $324 million). $100 million, Finland (*subsequently* $230 million). $100 million, Sweden (*subsequently* $6.1 billion).

1980

Global events *Mar* Robert Mugabe President of Zimbabwe, formerly Rhodesia. *Apr* Failed attempt to rescue US hostages in Teheran. *May* Death of President Tito of Yugoslavia; fears of a power vacuum. Referendum fails to support Quebec's secession from Canada. *Jun* Cable News Network (CNN) launched by Ted Turner. *Aug* Liberalization in Poland; free trade unions permitted, with the right to strike. *Sep* Following border dispute, Iraq invades Iran; loss of OPEC cohesion and disruption of supplies.

International finance Oil price rises brings middle-ranking energy companies to Eurobond markets. Turbulent markets lead to Eurobond losses, but new issue volume again up. Fewer fixed-interest issues; innovations abound, e.g. Eurocommercial paper programmes, perpetual putable FRNs, partly paid bonds, bonds with option to buy additional bonds and bonds linked to commodities. *Jan* Gold reaches high of $850 per ounce (cold war and currency anxieties), but falls to $481 within 2 months. *Mar* The Hunt brothers fail to corner silver, which collapses from a high of $50 per ounce. Second Volcker package to protect US$. *Jun* Midland Bank announces intention to buy control of Crocker Bank in the USA; the ensuing problems led to Midland's loss of independence. *Sep* National Bank of Kuwait arranges $250 million for Yugoslavia soon after President Tito's death. *Nov* Spot oil price reaches $41. *Dec* US prime rate reaches a high of 21.5 per cent.

Orion   Further reduction in profits. *Orion financings* $15.3 billion loans, $2.4 billion bonds. *New loan transactions* $400 million, 8 yrs, Electrobras, Brazil. $1.8 billion, 7 yrs, Venezuela (*subsequently* $1.4 billion). $2.3 billion, 7–9 yrs, Belgium (*subsequently* $925 million). $25 million, 8 yrs, Peru (*subsequently* $327 million). $275 million, 7 yrs, Ceskoslovenska Obchodni Banka. $170 million, 8 yrs, Trust Houses Forte. $50 million, 10 yrs, Ardal og Sundal Verke, Norway. *New bond transactions* First equity linked Eurobond issue for a Canadian borrower, $40 million for Bow Valley. $50 million, Banco Central de Costa Rica. DM150 million, Venezuela.

1981

Global events   *Jan* Ronald Reagan President of USA. Following the Algiers Accords, the US hostages released by Iran, which pays off its bank debt and recovers its frozen assets. *Feb* Failed *coup d'état* attempt in Spain. *May* François Mitterand President of France. *Jul* Marriage of Prince Charles and Lady Diana Spencer. *Aug* President Reagan announces lower taxes, higher defence and lower social expenditure. First IBM personal computer, with Microsoft operating system. *Sep* First TGV train in France. *Oct* President Sadat of Egypt assassinated, succeeded by Hosni Mubarak. *Dec* Martial law in Poland; arrests include Lech Walesa, leader of Solidarity trade union. Jerry Rawlings takes power in Ghana.

International finance   Global recession and energy efficiency reduce demand for oil; price begins to fall steadily, putting pressure on oil producers, with large borrowings, such as Mexico, also affected by highest US$ interest rates since the Civil War. *Feb* $51.9 million Eurobond for Refinement, backed by gold (Drexel Burnham Lambert). *May* Saudi Arabian Monetary Agency agrees SDR8 billion loan to IMF. *Jun* $75 million Pepsico zero coupon Eurobond (CSFB). US banks allowed 'International Banking Facilities' by the Federal Reserve, facilitating their Eurocurrency business. *Aug* IBM and the World Bank swap entire bond issues. *Sep* Poland's debt rescheduled. FF devalued (twice again in 1982–83). *Oct* $500 million note issuance facility (NIF) for New Zealand (Citibank).

Orion   Record year for financings; profits affected by difficult markets. *Feb* shareholders subscribe a further $32 million Subordinated Loan. *Jun* Royal bought out the other five shareholders; name changed to Orion Royal Bank; combined Royal/Orion ranked 5th in Euroloans. *Orion financings* $16.2 billion loans, $6.4 billion bonds. *New loan transactions* $131 million, 10 yrs, Laker Airways. $680 million, 10 yrs, Orissa National Aluminium Company, India. $300 million, 8 yrs, Bank of Thailand (*subsequently* $300 million). $535 million, 3 yrs, Saudi Oger. $700 million, 8 yrs, Korea Exchange Bank (*subsequently* $4.1 billion to Korean banks). $50 million, 8 yrs, Banco

del Estado de Chile (*subsequently* $260 million). *New bond transactions*
$200 million, Colombia. $130 million, World Bank (*subsequently* $5.1 billion).
$25 million, European Economic Community (*subsequently* $4.5 billion).
$100 million, Banque Française pour le Commerce Extérieur (*subsequently* $1.8
billion). $225 million, Banque Nationale de Paris (*subsequently* $1.5 billion).

1982

Global events   *Jan* Break-up of AT&T agreed with US government, after
law suits on competition grounds. Argentina cancels treaty with Chile over
Beagle Channel. *Feb* Nationalization of leading banks and other companies
in France. *Apr* UK freezes Argentine assets in London, after invasion of
Falkland Islands, later repulsed. *Jun* Israeli invasion of Lebanon; PLO
expelled from Beirut. *Aug* King Fahad succeeds to Saudi throne. *Oct* Helmut
Kohl German Chancellor. Felipe Gonzalez Socialist Premier of Spain. Trade
unions disbanded in Poland. *Nov* Soviet leader, Leonid Brezhnev, dies; successor, Yuri Andropov, delegates functions to youngest Politburo member,
Mikhail Gorbachev.

International finance   *Jan* $50 million Eurobond with warrants for
Mitsubishi Chemical (Morgan Stanley); over $130 billion such issues for
Japanese companies by end of 1989. *Feb* Devaluation of Mexican peso;
balance-of-payments crisis, due to lower oil prices, flight of capital and
higher debt service costs. *Jun* Security Pacific buys 29.9 per cent of Hoare
Govett, London stockbrokers; first of many such deals. Bank of America
arranges $2.5 billion loan to Mexico, 85 per cent left with underwriters.
Collapse of Banco Ambrosiano (fraud) and *July* of Penn Square Bank
(energy loans). *Jul* Fed begins to relax tight monetary policy, leading to
lower interest rates. *Aug* Mexico unable to meet its commitments; Latin
American debt crisis. Souk Al-Manakh stock market collapse in Kuwait,
with $92 billion post-dated cheques outstanding. *Sep* London
International Financial Futures Exchange (LIFFE) opens. *Dec* IMF agrees
rescue package for Mexico, including rescheduling and 'new money' facilities. Currency options introduced on the Philadelphia Stock Exchange.

Orion   Profits recovery; Orion ranked 12th among Eurobond managers.
Orion financings $16.8 billion loans, $14.5 billion bonds. *New loan transactions.* $450 million, 8 yrs, YPF and $107 million, 10 yrs, Aerolineas
Argentinas. $4 billion, 10 yrs, France (*subsequently* $3.6 billion). SDR200
million, 8 yrs, African Development Bank. $300 million, Ireland (*subsequent-
ly* $616 million). *New bond transactions* $305 million, Mexico (average rate 18
per cent). $750 million, Canada (*subsequently* $1.5 billion). $250 million,
Crédit Lyonnais (*subsequently* $1.3 billion). $100 million, Bank of Tokyo (*subsequently* $900 million), similar deals for other Japanese banks. Yen15 million,

Commonwealth of Australia (*subsequently* $1.1 billion). $100 million, Commerzbank (*subsequently* $841 million). $300 million, Deutsche Bank (*subsequently* $632 million). $150 million, Austria (*subsequently* $577 million).

1983

Global events *Feb* US–Soviet negotiations to reduce arms (START). *Mar* President Reagan proposes Strategic Defense Initiative ('Star Wars'). *Jun* The Pope visits his homeland, Poland. *Jul* Martial law lifted in Poland. *Aug* Bettino Craxi first socialist Premier of Italy. *Sep* South Korean airliner, erroneously thought to be spying, shot down over USSR; all aboard killed. *Oct* Military resumes power in Nigeria. US invasion of Grenada. *Nov* Rauf Denktesh declares independent state in Northern Cyprus. *Dec* Raul Alfonsin first democratically elected president of Argentina for eight years.

International finance IMF arranges debt rescheduling for 24 countries in 1982–83. *Jan* First $1 billion Eurobond, for Sweden (CSFB). Robin Leigh-Pemberton succeeds Gordon Richardson as Governor of Bank of England. *May* Basle Concordat of 1975 revised. *Jun* $1.8 billion FRN for EEC (CSFB). *Jul* Deregulation of London Stock Exchange agreed with UK government. *Aug* Quadrex Securities fails to issue EuroTreasury warrants for Transamerica; the idea was taken up by others. *Nov* Michael Milken (of Drexel Burnham Lambert) proposes issuing 'junk bonds' for takeover deals; Mesa Petroleum uses junk bonds to bid for Gulf Oil Corporation, 30 times its size.

Orion Profits 50 per cent up. Lower loan business offset by record Eurobond year. Orion in management group of about 40 per cent of all new Eurobond issues and listed 7th in league table. Significantly higher volume of Eurobond trading. New York presence to build up international investment banking business in the USA. *Orion financings* $11.9 billion loans, $19.8 billion bonds. *New loan transactions* $500 million, Australian Wheat Board (*subsequently* $500 million). $300 million, 7 yrs, Sultanate of Oman (*subsequently* $400 million). $325 million, 10 yrs, Central Bank of the Philippines. *New bond transactions* $100 million, Allied Irish Banks (*subsequently* $100 million). $400 million, Belgium (*subsequently* $2.1 billion). $200 million, Spain (*subsequently* $1.3 billion).

1984

Global events *Jan* AT&T divests itself of 22 'Baby Bells'; increased competition in the telecom sector. *Feb* Death of Soviet leader, Yuri Andropov, succeeded by Konstantin Chernenko, with Mikhail Gorbachev effectively his deputy. *Mar* UK miners strike. *Jun* Pierre Trudeau resigns, after 16 years (with one brief interruption) as Canadian Premier. *Aug* Amnesty for political prisoners in Poland. *Sep* UK agrees to return Hong Kong to China in 1997. *Oct* Indira Gandhi, Indian Premier, assassinated; succeeded by her son, Rajiv. Bomb attack by IRA on Mrs Thatcher and other UK politicians in Brighton.

International finance International Primary Market Association formed by new issue managers. Commissions continue to fall on FRN issues (from 1.5 per cent average in 1980–83 to 0.5 per cent average in 1983–86). *Mar* $1 billion convertible Eurobond for Texaco (CSFB). *May* Continental Illinois, eighth largest US bank, rescued by US government, having suffered from real estate, energy and LDC loan losses. *Oct* Johnson Matthey Bankers rescued by Bank of England. *Nov* £3.9 billion privatization of British Telecom in UK (Kleinwort Benson); other privatizations follow, in UK and many other countries.

Orion Profits down by a third; pre-payments reduced loan portfolio and securities markets were difficult. Representative offices opened in Toronto and Tokyo. Orion forms merchant banking joint venture with China International Trust and Investment Corporation in Hong Kong. *Orion financings* $20.6 billion loans, $39.4 billion bonds. *New loan transactions* $130 million, 8 yrs, Tunisia. *New bond transactions* $200 million, National Commercial Bank, Saudi Arabia. $57 million, Banque Indosuez (*subsequently* $425 million). $100 million, KLM. $557 million, six Norwegian borrowers. $300 million, Banca Commerciale Italiana.

1985

Global events *Jan* Tancredo Nieves first civilian President in Brazil since 1964. *Mar* Mikhail Gorbachev comes to power in the Soviet Union, on the death of Konstantin Chernenko; inaugurates new policies based on *perestroika* (change and development) and *glasnost* (openness). Large hole in the ozone layer identified. *Nov* Cordial first Gorbachev–Reagan summit in Geneva. Anglo–Irish Agreement on the future of Northern Ireland.

International finance Mean Euroloan spreads over LIBOR 0.65 per cent. Commercial banks build up capital funds through issue of perpetual FRNs, largely bought by other banks; FRN issues represent over 40 per cent of Eurobond market. CSFB first to handle over 100 Euromarket issues in a year. *Feb* Central banks act to depress the 'grossly overvalued' US$. *Mar* International Swap Dealers Association formed. *Sep* Plaza Accord by the USA, the UK, France, Germany and Japan to depress US$. The Yen rises rapidly; accelerating Japanese speculation in securities, art and land, and major acquisitions of overseas companies and real estate.

Collapse of oil prices makes problems for many US banks and S&L Associations. *Oct* US Treasury Secretary James Baker proposes plan to help heavily indebted LDC countries, through additional loans, debt-equity swaps and other market techniques. *Nov* Tokyo futures market opens.

Orion Record profits. Orion in 54 per cent of Eurobond management groups, particularly in bank FRNs; dominant position in Australian and Canadian $ bond issues. Lead manages $1 billion undated FRN for NatWest. Begins to distribute Canadian equities offshore. Following London Stock Exchange deregulation, acquires 29.9 per cent of equity stockbroker, Kitcat & Aitken, but fails to buy bond stockbroker. *Orion financings* $22.4 billion loans, $76.4 billion bonds, including $23.4 billion for banks. *New loan transactions* $3.6 billion, 7 yrs, France. $1.3 billion, 5 yrs, John Deere Credit Company. $110 million, 5 yrs, National Bank of Iceland. $60 million, 8 yrs, Gabon. *New bond transactions* $61 million, Bank of China. $600 million, Student Loan Marketing. $2.5 billion, United Kingdom.

1986

Global events *Jan* Spain and Portugal join the EEC. UK and France agree to build tunnel under the Channel. Yoweri Musseveni takes power in Uganda. *Feb* Ferdinand Marcos gives way to Corazon Aquino as Philippine President. Olaf Palme, Swedish Premier, assassinated. *Apr* Chernobyl reactor explodes. US air strike on Libya. *Jul* Spot oil price falls to $7.20 a barrel; *Oct* Sheikh Ahmed Zaki Yamani replaced as Saudi Oil Minister, after 24 years. *Oct* Second Reagan–Gorbachev summit at Reykjavik; disagreement on 'Star Wars' and other matters.

International finance *Feb* Repeal of Securities Laws in Canada. Marché à Terme des Instruments Financiers (MATIF) set up in Paris. Midland Bank sells its interest in Crocker Bank; estimated loss £1 billion. *Sep* $2.1 billion Euroequity issue for FIAT on behalf of Libyan Arab Foreign Bank, largely left with underwriters (Deutsche Bank and Mediobanca). *Aug* Sumitomo Bank 12.5 per cent stake in Goldman Sachs for $500 million announced. *Oct* Deregulation completed on London Stock Exchange ('Big Bang'), removing barriers between financial institutions; stockbrokers and market-makers sold to UK and international banks. *Nov* Liquidity crisis in the FRN market; perpetuals become virtually unsellable, falling 4 per cent on average in a week and leading to 67 per cent reduction in FRN issues in 1987. *Dec* Canadian government announces that banks will be able to buy securities houses.

Orion Increases stake in Kitcat & Aitken to 100 per cent. Lower levels of loan and bond financings arranged by Orion than for previous year.

Profitability eroded by intense competition, falling margins and FRN crisis; Orion records small loss. The market moves into areas where Orion weaker, e.g. Yen, US$ and Euroequities. RBC Gilts Ltd formed to deal in UK government bonds (one of 27 competitor firms in this market). *Orion financings* $1.1 billion loans, $58.2 billion bonds.

1987

Global events   *Feb* Bettino Craxi, longest serving ($3\frac{1}{2}$ years) Italian Premier, resigns. *Apr* Quebec recognized as a 'distinct society' by provincial premiers in Canada. Portugal agrees handover of Macao to China in 1999. *Nov* Tunisian President-for-Life, Habib Bourgiba deposed, aged 84. Boris Yeltsin dismissed as Moscow's Communist party leader. *Dec* Reagan–Gorbachev agreement in Washington on large-scale US and Soviet destruction of missiles. Infitada; uprising of Palestinians in West Bank and Gaza.

International finance   *Feb* Louvre Accord; G-7 finance ministers agree to co-ordinate policies so as to arrest fall of US$ and stabilize currencies. Brazil unilaterally suspends debt servicing payments. *Mar* Scandinavian Bank issues multi-currency shares in London, to mirror its business mix. *Apr* Litigation after buying Getty Oil forces Texaco into bankruptcy (largest to date). UK company, Ferranti International, forced into liquidation after paying £421 million for US acquisition. *May* Citibank's $3 billion reserve against its LDC debt portfolio causes other banks to follow suit and triggers steady fall of LDC loans in secondary market. *Jun* Alan Greenspan succeeds Paul Volcker as Federal Reserve Chairman. Lowest coupon for Japanese warrants issue; 0.875 per cent on $150 million issue for Tokyu (Yamaichi). *Aug* Bank of England guidelines to UK banks on provisioning ('matrix'); heavy losses for many banks, as some consortium banks go out of business. *Oct* Stock market crash in the midst of equity offer of £7.3 billion of BP shares for UK government (advised by Rothschilds); Kuwait buys 21.7 per cent stake, later reduced to 10 per cent. Japan liquidates foreign assets to participate in *Nov* $35 billion privatization issue of Nippon Telegraph & Telephone; Nomura ranked first among Eurobond managers.

Orion   Makes substantial provisions against Third World debt, leading to loss; overall reduction in lending business. *Nov* Drops out of the Eurobond and UK gilts businesses. *Dec* Royal agrees to acquire 75 per cent of Dominion Securities, a leading investment bank in Canada, following deregulation. *Orion financings* $823 million loans, $25.9 billion bonds.

1988

Global events *Jan* US–Canadian free trade agreement. *Feb* Dispute between Azeris and Armenians in USSR over Nagorno–Karabakh. *Mar* Soviet withdrawal from Afghanistan announced. President Ceausescu of Romania plans destruction of 8000 rural villages and relocation of inhabitants to towns. *Jul* Ayatollah Khomeini accepts cease-fire to end Iran–Iraq war ('worse than taking poison'); huge human and economic losses, with no gain for either side. *Aug* President Zia Ul-Haq killed in air crash. *Nov* Benazir Bhutto becomes Premier of Pakistan. *Oct* Baltic republics begin attempts to secede from the USSR. *Dec* 270 killed by terrorists in Lockerbie air crash.

International finance *Jul* Basle Capital Accord sets 8 per cent capital adequacy ratio for banks. *Sep* Silverado Savings & Loan Association collapses with $1 billion loss; US S&Ls lose $13 billion in a single year. *Oct* BCCI and ten employees indicted in Florida for money laundering. *Dec* CSFB restructured into CS First Boston. $25 billion acquisition of RJR Nabisco, using junk bonds, with help of Drexel Burnham Lambert, which is fined $650 million for its securities activities and goes into bankruptcy 14 months later.

Orion Ceases investment banking activities. Further significant provisions, in accordance with Bank of England matrix, leads to third year of loss. Retirement of some directors; transfer of others to Royal, which scales back Orion business and integrates it with RBC Dominion Securities International. *Orion financings* $920 million loans, $668 million bonds.

1989

Global events *Jan* George Bush President of the USA. *Feb* Last Soviet troops leave Afghanistan (1 million estimated killed in the war). *Feb* Fatwa against Salman Rushdie by Ayatollah Khomeini. *Jun* Khomeini dies, succeeded as President of Iran by Hashemi Rafsanjani. Demonstrations crushed in Tiananmen Square, Beijing. *Jul* South African President P.W. Botha meets imprisoned Nelson Mandela; he is succeeded as President by F.W. de Klerk. *Aug* Ethnic unrest at the fringes of the Soviet Union. General breakdown of Communist regimes in East Europe and moves towards democracy. *Sep* Lebanese reconciliation agreed in Taif. *Sep* Hungary opens its borders with Austria, permitting many East Germans to escape. *Nov* Berlin Wall comes down. *Dec* Chile and Brazil elect civilian presidents. USA ousts General Noriega, Panamanian leader.

International finance International banks make further heavy provision on LDC debt. Equity linked issues, mainly Japanese, account for one-third of Eurobond market. *Feb* London Borough of Hammersmith & Fulham dealt in swaps, beyond its legal powers, up to principal amount of £3.3 billion, large losses for banks. *Mar* US Treasury Secretary Nicholas Brady proposes using IMF funds to reduce debt load for heavily indebted countries. *Apr* Delors Report recommends three-stage approach to Economic & Monetary Union in Europe. *May* Mexico, Philippines and Costa Rica sign first debt reduction agreements with banks, under the Brady Plan. *Jul* Leveraged buy-out attempt on BAT. *Aug* $500 million Eurobond for New Zealand (Morgan Stanley); fees 0.375 per cent, compared to 2.5 per cent a quarter of a century earlier for such transactions. *Nov* High-profile Japanese acquisitions in USA, Rockefeller Center ($846 million) and Columbia Pictures ($3.4 billion). *Dec* Bank of Japan raises interest rates, triggering a 48 per cent fall in stock market over next 9 months, after it reaches all-time high at year's end.

Orion Restoration of profits. *Nov* ORB's name is changed to Royal Bank of Canada Europe Limited. The end of Orion as a trading name in international financial markets; the company remains a prime banking subsidiary of Royal Bank of Canada.

TABLES AND GRAPHS

Sources for tables and graphs on pages 236–239: Capital DATA and Bondware, *Euromoney*, for Euromarket volumes. Gold prices from the World Gold Council.

TABLES AND GRAPHS 1963–76

	1963	1964	1965	1966	1967	1968	1969	1970	1971	1972	1973	1974	1975	1976
Global GNP (recession encircled)														
GNP per caput ($)	2 928	3 058	3 138	3 254	3 332	3 464	3 597	3 688	3 754	3 887	4 056	(4 035)	(3 994)	4 107
Inflation (per cent)	2.7	3.5	3.9	4.3	1.7	2.6	3.8	4.8	4.2	5.4	13.7	22.3	10.5	10.2
Euromarket volumes (billion)														
Total Eurodeposits ($)	12	14	17	21	25	34	50	65	85	110	175	230	265	340
Total Eurobonds ($)	0.1	0.7	0.8	1.3	1.8	3.1	2.9	2.7	3.5	5.3	3.5	1.6	6.6	13
Total Euroloans ($)								4.9	4.0	6.8	21.9	29.2	21.9	28.9
LDC Euroloans ($)								0.5	1.3	2.4	7.3	7.3	11.1	15.0
IMF loans to LDCs (SDR)	1.0	0.9	1.1	1.1	1.3	1.4	1.3	0.8	0.8	1.1	1.0	2.2	4.0	6.5
Exchange rates (year end)														
US$/£	2.80	2.79	2.80	2.79	2.41	2.38	2.40	2.42	2.55	2.35	2.32	2.35	2.02	1.70
DM/US$	3.98	3.97	4.01	3.98	4.00	4.00	3.69	3.63	3.27	3.20	2.70	2.41	2.62	2.36
Yen/US$	362	360	361	363	362	358	358	354	315	302	280	300	305	293

Eurodollar 3-Month Deposit Rates and Euroloan spread over LIBOR (basis points)

	1963	1964	1965	1966	1967	1968	1969	1970	1971	1972	1973	1974	1975	1976
Oil and gold prices (year end)														
Oil official price ($ per barrel)	1.33	1.33	1.33	1.33	1.30	1.28	1.35	1.75	1.90	2.10	9.60	10.46	11.51	12.09
Gold ($ per ounce)	35	35	35	35	35	42	35	37	44	65	112	187	140	135
Financial derivatives (million contracts)														
Chicago Board of Trade														0.1
Chicago Mercantile Exchange										0.1	0.3	0.1	0.2	0.3
Stock markets (year end)														
New York				786	905	943	800	838	889	1020	851	616	852	1000
London				94	121	174	147	136	194	218	150	67	158	152
Tokyo				1452	1281	1715	2358	1987	2713	5207	4306	3817	4359	4987

Nov 63 – President Kennedy assassinated
Jul 63 – Interest Equalization Tax and first Eurobonds
Jun 63 – Origins of future EBIC banking club
Aug 64 – Escalation of Vietnam War
64/65 – First Consortium banks in London
May 66 – First Eurodollar CDs
Oct 67 – £ devaluation
Jun 68 – First Eurobonds
Dec 68 – Euroclear formed for settling Eurobonds
Jun 69 – Launch of Euromoney magazine
May 70 – Werner Report points to EEC union
Oct 70 – First Eurodollar FRN
Aug 71 – Orion formed
Dec 71 – First US$ devaluation; end of link to gold
May 72 – CME introduces financial futures
Feb 73 – Second US$ devaluation
Oct 73 – Middle East War/First 'Oil Shock'
Nov 73 – Banking crisis in London
Jun 74 – Herstatt failure
May 75 – Vietnam under Communist rule
Jun 75 – UK oil production commences
Nov 76 – IMF bails out UK and Italy

TABLES AND GRAPHS 1977–89

	1977	1978	1979	1980	1981	1982	1983	1984	1985	1986	1987	1988	1989
Global GNP (recession encircled)													
GNP per caput ($)	4194	4297	4393	4390	4377	4315	4349	4461	4535	4607	4694	4820	4916
Inflation (per cent)	10.0	7.7	14.2	17.3	13.2	11.1	11.3	10.0	7.9	2.3	7.5	12.7	18.8
Euromarket volumes (billion)													
Total Eurodeposits ($)	435	530	665	810	945	1020	1085	1265	1485	1775	2220	2545	2920
Total Eurobonds ($)	16.1	12.3	14.9	19.8	27.1	48.1	48.0	86.4	133.3	184.8	143.9	182.4	223.0
Total Euroloans ($)	41.8	70.2	82.8	69.5	78.7	61.1	41.0	68.4	91.3	85.0	122.3	205.3	185.2
LDC Euroloans ($)	21.0	37.3	48.0	36.6	37.7	30.8	15.0	21.3	17.8	25.2	12.0	25.1	27.9
IMF loans to LDCs (SDR)	6.4	6.6	7.4	9.9	15.8	22.2	32.5	37.1	37.1	34.8	30.2	26.5	24.7
Exchange rates (year end)													
US$/£	1.92	2.04	2.22	2.39	1.91	1.62	1.45	1.16	1.45	1.49	1.88	1.81	1.61
DM/US$	2.10	1.82	1.73	1.95	2.25	2.38	2.72	3.15	2.45	1.92	1.58	1.77	1.69
Yen/US$	240	194	240	203	220	235	232	252	200	158	121	125	144

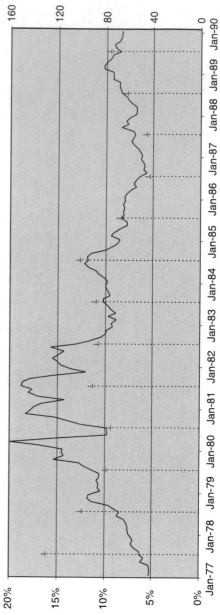

Eurodollar 3-Month Deposit Rates and Euroloan spread over LIBOR (basis points)

	1977	1978	1979	1980	1981	1982	1983	1984	1985	1986	1987	1988	1989
Oil and gold prices (year end)													
Oil official price ($ per barrel)	12.70	13.34	26.00	32.00	34.00	34.00	29.00	29.00	28.00	15.15	17.52	13.15	18.40
Gold ($ per ounce)	165	226	512	590	398	457	382	308	327	391	484	410	401
Financial derivatives (million contracts)													
Chicago Board of Trade	0.5	1.5	3.6	8.8	16.4	19.9	23.7	39.2	55.8	76.3	97.0	98.0	101.4
Chicago Mercantile Exchange	0.9	2.3	4.1	9.8	14.7	18.5	24.8	41.0	47.3	59.3	73.2	66.9	95.1
LIFFE & MATIF combined						0.2	1.4	2.6	3.6	8.7	25.6	31.9	49.5
Swaps outstanding ($ billion)											867	1328	1952
Stock markets (year end)													
New York	831	805	839	964	875	1027	1259	1212	1547	1896	1939	2169	2753
London	215	220	230	292	313	382	470	593	683	835	870	927	1205
Tokyo	4866	6001	6570	7063	7682	8017	9894	11543	13083	18820	21564	30159	38916

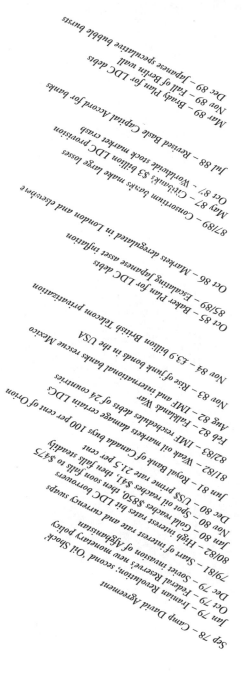

Sep 78 – Camp David Agreement

Jan 79 – Iranian Revolution: second 'Oil Shock'

Oct 79 – Federal Reserve's new monetary policy

Dec 79 – Soviet invasion of Afghanistan

79/81 – Start of interest rate and currency swaps

Jan 80 – High interest rates hit LDC borrowers

Nov 80 – Gold reaches $850, then soon falls to $475

Dec 80 – Spot oil reaches $41, then falls steadily; US$ prime rate 21.5 per cent

Jun 81 – Royal Bank of Canada buys 100 per cent of Orion

81/82 – Weak oil markets damage certain LDC

Feb 82 – IMF reschedules debts of 24 countries

Aug 82 – Falklands War

Nov 82 – IMF and international banks rescue Mexico

Nov 83 – Rise of junk bonds in the USA

Nov 84 – £3.9 billion British Telecom privatization

Oct 85 – Baker Plan for LDC debts

85/89 – Escalating Japanese asset inflation

Oct 86 – Markets deregulated in London and elsewhere

8/7/89

May 87 – Citibank's $3 billion LDC losses

Oct 87 – Worldwide stock market crash

Jul 88 – Revised Basle Capital Accord for banks

Mar 89 – Brady Plan for LDC debts

Nov 89 – Fall of Berlin wall

Dec 89 – Japanese speculative bubble bursts

Euromarket consortium banks

S1/27 ORION BANK
S1/28 PK CHRISTIANIA BANK (UK)
S1/29 ROTHSCHILD INTERCONTINENTAL BANK
S1/30 SAUDI INTERNATIONAL BANK
S1/31 SCANDINAVIAN BANK
S1/32 UBAF BANK
S1/33 UNITED BANK OF KUWAIT
S1/34 UNITED INTERNATIONAL BANK
S1/35 WESTERN AMERICAN BANK (EUROPE)

Section 2. 20 Other Consortium Bank Groups

S2/1 ALLIED BANK INTERNATIONAL
S2/2 ARAB BANKING CORPORATION & ARLABANK
    INTERNATIONAL
S2/3 JULIUS BAER INTERNATIONAL
S2/4 BAII HOLDINGS
S2/5 BANKERS TRUST INTERNATIONAL LTD
S2/6 BANK OF AMERICA LTD & BANQUE AMERIBAS
S2/7 BANQUE DE PARIS ET DES PAYS BAS LTD
S2/8 BANQUE DE SUEZ (UK)
S2/9 BANQUE EUROPÉENNE DE CRÉDIT
S2/10 BANQUE EUROPÉENNE DE TOKYO
S2/11 BURSTON AND TEXAS COMMERCE BANK
S2/12 CREDIT SUISSE WHITE WELD
S2/13 EUROPEAN ARAB HOLDING
S2/14 FRAB HOLDING
S2/15 GULF INTERNATIONAL BANK
S2/16 INTERCONTINENTAL BANKING SERVICES
S2/17 MANUFACTURERS HANOVER LTD
S2/18 MERRILL LYNCH–BROWN SHIPLEY BANK
S2/19 SOCIÉTÉ FINANCIERE EUROPÉENNE
S2/20 UNION DE BANQUES ARABES ET FRANÇAISES

Section 3. Consortium Bank Interests of the 50 Largest Banks
Section 4. Comparative Statistics for Consortium and Other Banks in the UK

Introduction

In May 1975, the Bank of England separately categorized UK consortium banks in a new way for reporting purposes.[1] In the same year, the Association of Consortium Banks was formed in London. By that time, the consortium

---

[1] See Section 4 of this Appendix: note on Bank of England statistics.

banks had become established City institutions, accounting for 10.7 per cent of British banks' foreign currency loans.

The listing of May 1975 comprised 29 consortium banks, to which 10 were added in the following 10 years, while some dropped out; thus, a total of 39 were so categorized. The Bank of England defined consortium banks as banks owned by other banks, in which no other bank had over 50 per cent ownership and in which at least one shareholder was an overseas bank. The first, Midland and International Banks, was formed in 1964.

The separate categorization of consortium banks by the Bank of England was suspended in July 1987; by that time, their share of British banks' foreign currency loans had fallen to 4.0 per cent. Their position in London continued to decline, as they went out of business or were taken over, usually by one of their shareholders. The Association of Consortium Banks was absorbed by Foreign Banks and Securities Houses Association.

Among the 39 consortium banks, 16 were multinational in character, while 23 were regional, of which 14 had a one-country focus. Their business mix varied greatly from bank to bank, in line with varying aspirations of their founders. The core activities were:

(1) extending and managing Eurocurrency loans, particularly for medium- and long-term maturities, mostly cross-border; from the mid-1980s onwards, some banks began trading in such debt;

(2) treasury and foreign exchange trading, especially in currencies related to their ownership; finding deposits in the inter-bank market, in order to fund their loans, was a major activity, while derivatives business grew greatly towards the end of the period;

(3) issuing, marketing and trading Eurobonds, public and private, with or without equity content, Floating Rate Notes, Floating Rate Deposits and other securities.

Some consortium banks also undertook mergers and acquisitions, Euroequities, corporate finance, country advice, trade promotion, private banking, fund management, venture capital, real estate, leasing and other activities.

Section 1. 35 UK Consortium Banks (as defined by Bank of England, 1975 to 1987): profiles the ownership, business and finances of 35 of the 39 consortium banks as defined by the Bank of England. All based in London, make up the bulk of the consortium bank movement of the 1970s and 1980s. Four are excluded; three were subsidiaries, whose figures are included in those of their parent banks; one was a small Jersey bank, of short duration.[2] The ultimate fate of the 35 consortium banks in Section 1 was:

Control acquired by one of the shareholding banks	20
Control acquired by an unconnected bank	2

---

[2] The four excluded are: Italian International Bank (Channel Islands), Orion Bank (Guernsey), Orion Termbank and Standard & Chase Bank C.I.

Liquidated	8
Surviving in January 1999, as consortium banks	5

The five survivors all had a regional focus; they were British Arab Commercial Bank (formerly UBAF Bank), Iran Overseas Investment Bank, Jordan International Bank, Saudi International Bank and United Bank of Kuwait. Note on definitions and sources appears at the end of Section 1 (page 285).

Section 2. 20 Other Consortium Bank Groups: profiles 20 other significant Euromarket consortium bank groups, which were outside the Bank of England's 1975 categorization of consortium banks, but active in London's time zone.

Section 3. Consortium Banking Interests of the 50 Largest Banks: shows the prevalence among the world's biggest banks of using consortium bank structures as part of their international strategy.

Section 4. Comparative Statistics for Consortium and Other Banks in the UK:
Table 1 UK Consortium Banks' Foreign Currency Loans
Table 2 UK Consortium Banks' Use of the Inter-bank Market for Foreign Currency Funding
Table 3 Profitability of UK Consortium Banks.

Section 1. 35 UK Consortium Banks (as defined by Bank of England, 1975 to 1987)
S1/1 ANGLO–ROMANIAN BANK
Founded 1973; consortium status to 1997. CH 01110826.

Ownership Romanian Bank for Foreign Trade (later renamed Bancorex SA) 50 per cent, Barclays Bank International 30 per cent, Manufacturers Hanover Trust 20 per cent. In 1997, Bancorex began buying out its two partners, completing the process in May 1998.

History & business The bank became the leading bank in London specializing in Romanian business. Its main activities were trade finance, direct lending, participation in syndicated loans and treasury; it was not engaged in Eurobonds, fund management or corporate finance. Its niche was the financing of Romania's international trade, particularly with the UK. Initially, the loan portfolio was mainly short-term, but maturities were extended and, by 1981, 50 per cent of loans had maturities of between 3 and 9 years. In the mid-1980s, under President Ceausescu's policy of independence, Romania's foreign debt was largely repaid, at the expense of economic development. As much of the bank's lending was to Romania, its assets inevitably declined in size. In the late 1980s and early 1990s, the bank made substantial provisions against non-performing sovereign debt; however, it continued to receive support from its shareholders through subordinated loans and new capital. Some of the provisions were written back in 1993 and the rest of the sovereign debt was sold in 1994. Trade financing opportunities increased, as Romania gradually adopted a market economy, after the overthrow of President Ceausescu in 1989. The acquisition in 1997–98 of 100 per cent of the bank's capital by Bancorex, Romania's leading bank, enabled it to develop its UK business with those in Germany, France, Italy and Egypt more effectively.

Personnel *Chairmen* Sir L. Glass, 1973–81, C.P. Lunn, 1981–86, P.S. Ardron, 1986–98. *Managing Directors* F. Radu, 1973–81, T. Giurgiu, 1981–86, F. Lungoci, 1986–91, M. Radui, 1991–98.

Finances (£ million)

YE 31/12	1974	1975	1976	1977	1978	1979
Total assets	33.1	62.7	88.8	109.4	122.2	123.1
Cap. & reserves	1.6	3.3	3.5	4.7	4.9	5.2
Pre-tax profit	0.4	0.9	1.3	1.2	1.2	1.3
Dividend	0.1	0.2	0.4	0.4	0.4	0.4
YE 31/12	**1980**	**1981**	**1982**	**1983**	**1984**	**1985**
Total assets	127.8	117.8	118.9	127.3	140.2	121.7
Cap. & reserves	6.3	6.6	7.0	7.4	8.0	8.7
Pre-tax profit	1.1	0.8	1.5	1.1	1.6	1.5
Dividend	0.5	0.0	0.0	0.0	0.0	0.3
YE 31/12	**1986**	**1987**	**1988**	**1989**	**1990**	**1991**
Total assets	109.1	75.0	56.9	50.6	40.5	54.5
Cap. & reserves	9.4	1.7	3.1	−0.5	6.5	6.5
Pre-tax profit	1.0	−8.3	1.4	−7.0	0.0	0.0
Dividend	0.0	0.0	0.0	0.0	0.0	0.0
YE 31/12	**1992**	**1993**	**1994**	**1995**	**1996**	**1997**
Total assets	48.6	65.3	66.5	73.7	81.2	89.6
Cap. & reserves	8.5	15.8	16.3	17.7	23.0	24.1
Pre-tax profit	−4.4	7.3	0.5	1.3	1.2	1.1
Dividend	0.0	0.0	0.0	0.0	0.0	0.0

NOTE: 20 months to 31/12/74.

S1/2 ANGLO–YUGOSLAV BANK
AY BANK
Founded 1980; consortium status to 1989. CH 01483013.

Ownership Initially, Barclays Bank International, Manufacturers Hanover Trust (25 per cent each) and a group of Yugoslav banks, Beogradska Banka, Investiciona Banka, Jugobanka, Ljubljanska Banka, Privredna Banka, Stopanska Banka, Vojvodjanska Banka and Zagrebacka Banka (6.25 per cent each). In 1987–89, there were changes in ownership, including the sale by Barclays and Manufacturers of their stakes. It then became, and remains, just over 50 per cent owned by Beogradska Banka, the leading Serbian bank; several banks from the current and former Yugoslav states have minority stakes.

History & business The bank was set up to encourage and finance trade between Yugoslavia, the UK, the USA and other countries. During the 1980s, this trade expanded significantly as the Yugoslav economy gradually opened to market forces. Among its important customers were the six largest Yugoslav exporters to the UK, which it provided with a complete financial service. In 1987, the bank made provisions against its Third World debt, in accordance with the Bank of England's requirements. The turmoil in Yugoslavia and the June 1992 UN Sanctions had a marked effect on the bank. However, it continued its traditional business in London under a new name, AY Bank, which was adopted to reflect that some of the shareholders came from new independent states, such as Croatia and Slovenia, that were no longer part of Yugoslavia.

Personnel *Chairmen* N. Barac, 1980–82, Mrs B. Vucic, 1982–89. *Chief Executives* B. Bartlett, 1980–83, D.E. Waple, 1983–89. *Deputy Chief Executives* M. Drulovic, 1980–85, M. Radosavljevic, 1985–89.

Finances (£ million)

YE 30/6	1981	1982	1983	1984	1985	1986
Total assets	76.6	65.3	56.3	62.0	78.6	79.1
Cap. & reserves	5.1	5.3	5.5	5.8	6.2	6.5
Pre-tax profit	0.3	0.6	0.7	0.6	0.9	0.7
Dividend	0.0	0.1	0.1	0.1	0.1	0.1

YE 30/6	1987	1988	1989
Total assets	71.3	52.5	55.9
Cap. & reserves	5.2	5.7	6.9
Pre-tax profit	−1.6	0.6	0.3
Dividend	0.0	0.0	0.0

NOTE: 16 months to 30/6/81.

S1/3 ASSOCIATED JAPANESE BANK (INTERNATIONAL)
Founded 1970; consortium status to 1990. CH 00996788.

Ownership Founded by the Japanese investment bank, Nomura Securities, and four Japanese commercial banks, Sanwa Bank, Mitsui Bank, Dai-Ichi Bank and Nippon Kangyo Bank; after the latter two merged to form Dai-Ichi Kangyo Bank in 1971, there were four shareholders, each with 25 per cent. In 1990, Sanwa Bank bought out its fellow shareholders.

History & business In its first annual report, it announced its aim to offer a complete range of banking services, but in practice it came to specialize mainly in medium-term sovereign lending activities. By the mid-1970s, its share-holders had established their own Euromarket operations in London and had invested in other consortium banks, so that there were few opportunities for referrals from them. The bank made its decisions independently of its shareholders and most of its loans arose from invitations by leading US and European banks to participate in their syndicates. Long-term advances became an important business for the bank, reaching a peak of £414 million in February 1985, or 58 per cent of total assets. Part of the lending was to Third World countries; although much of this exposure was assigned to the bank's shareholders in 1988, significant provisions were still required. After the bank's acquisition by one of its shareholders, Sanwa Bank, it was amalgamated with the latter bank's own UK investment bank, Sanwa International.

Personnel *Chairmen* G. Suzuki, 1970–79, Y. Emori, 1979–83. *General Managers* Y. Emori, 1970–79, Y. Hemmi, 1979–83. *Managing Directors* K. Yoshioka, 1983–89, T. Iwabuchi, 1989–90.

Finances (£ million)

YE 28/2	1972	1973	1974	1975	1976
Total assets	77.6	171.1	292.3	295.9	338.1
Cap. & reserves	3.6	4.0	8.0	8.5	9.1
Pre-tax profit	0.3	0.6	1.2	1.6	1.7
Dividend	0.0	0.0	0.1	0.2	0.2
YE 28/2	**1977**	**1978**	**1979**	**1980**	**1981**
Total assets	431.4	439.4	458.6	465.4	544.3
Cap. & reserves	10.2	11.3	12.5	16.5	17.4
Pre-tax profit	3.1	3.2	3.6	3.5	4.1
Dividend	0.3	0.4	0.4	0.4	1.0
YE 28/2	**1982**	**1983**	**1984**	**1985**	**1986**
Total assets	558.8	588.8	595.8	715.5	603.1
Cap. & reserves	19.7	22.2	24.3	26.9	29.7
Pre-tax profit	4.1	3.2	3.3	4.0	4.0
Dividend	0.0	0.0	0.0	0.0	0.0
YE 28/2	**1987**	**1988**	**1989**	**1990**	
Total assets	587.9	520.0	431.1	291.7	
Cap. & reserves	33.3	29.3	29.7	14.0	
Pre-tax profit	3.7	−3.8	0.9	−15.9	
Dividend	0.0	0.0	0.0	0.0	

NOTE: 14 months to 28/2/72.

S1/4 ATLANTIC INTERNATIONAL BANK
Founded 1969; consortium status to 1988. CH 00941055.

Ownership Originally four US and four European banks, each with 12.5 per cent; however, by 1974, three of them, Banque de Neuflize, Schlumberger, Mallet, France, First Pennsylvania Bank and United California Bank had dropped out. The shareholders were then Manufacturers National Bank of Detroit 25 per cent, National Shawmut Bank of Boston 25 per cent, F. van Lanschot Bankiers, Netherlands 16.7 per cent, Charterhouse Japhet, UK

16.7 per cent and Banco di Napoli 16.7 per cent; the latter three banks sold out in 1977, 1982 and 1986, respectively. The remaining two US banks, Manufacturers and Shawmut, each with a 50 per cent share at the time, wound up the bank in March 1988.

History & business The bank was primarily a medium-term lending institution. Initially, its exposure was mainly to the USA, particularly in 1969–71, when there was much demand for medium-term proposals from US borrowers; its 1975 results were affected by provisions against its US real estate investment trust lending. In the mid-1970s, the bank diversified its lending to other countries; by 1981, it had loan commitments in 38 countries, mainly European and Latin American. The bank provided a wide range of financing facilities and was also active in treasury/foreign exchange business; it was not involved significantly in the securities business. The bank was seriously affected by the Third World debt crisis; earnings were substantially reduced by the need to make provisions, which amounted to £34.8 million in 1987, a figure in excess of the bank's capital funds, leading to the closure of the bank.

Personnel *Chairmen* L.H. Martin, 1970–72, J.C. van Lanschot, 1972, W.P. Davis III, 1973, H.S. Clarke, 1974–86. *Managing Directors* R.E. Rowton, 1972–74, C.R. Saunders, 1974–77, J.T. Cannis, 1977, L.F. Swift, 1977–82, J.J. Buttigieg, 1982–84, R.C. Davis, 1984–87.

Finances (£ million)

YE 30/6	1970	1971	1972	1973	1974	1975
Total assets	29.8	44.1	56.0	66.6	72.3	69.3
Cap. & reserves	1.1	1.2	1.3	1.5	2.7	2.6
Pre-tax profit	0.1	0.1	0.3	0.3	0.4	0.2
Dividend	0.0	0.0	0.0	0.0	0.0	0.0
YE 30/6	1976	1977	1978	1979	1980	1981
Total assets	93.7	122.0	135.1	136.6	142.6	170.7
Cap. & reserves	2.8	3.0	3.4	3.9	4.4	5.9
Pre-tax profit	0.5	0.7	0.9	1.1	1.0	1.1
Dividend	0.0	0.0	0.0	0.0	0.0	0.0
YE 30/6	1982	1983	1984	1985	1986	1987
Total assets	202.8	216.1	249.1	255.5	191.0	127.5
Cap. & reserves	7.9	8.6	9.4	11.1	11.5	−23.5
Pre-tax profit	1.0	1.4	1.6	1.2	0.8	−35.0
Dividend	0.0	0.0	0.0	0.0	0.0	0.0

S1/5 BAII plc
Founded 1865; consortium status 1983 to 1990. CH 00502560.

Ownership Gray Dawes & Co, a banking subsidiary of the Far Eastern trading group, Inchcape, adopted consortium bank status in July 1983 and changed its name to BAII plc, when it was acquired by the consortium banking group,

Compagnie Arabe et Internationale d'Investissement, Luxembourg, which was later renamed BAII Holdings (S2/4); in 1990, over 90 per cent of its capital was bought by Banque Nationale de Paris.

History & business In 1983, BAII plc became the principal London banking subsidiary of BAII Holdings, an investment and commercial banking group with emphasis on the Arab world. After the deregulation of the Stock Exchange in London, BAII Holdings acquired control of Sheppards and Chase, stockbrokers; it also had a fund management arm in London. In 1987, BAII plc was affected by the Third World debt crisis and transferred sovereign loans of £15 million to another BAII company. In 1988, the decision was made to transfer the banking and investment business of BAII plc to a London branch of its sister bank, Banque Arabe et Internationale d'Investissement, Paris; BAII plc then surrendered its banking licence and became a specialist in leasing and asset based finance, particularly in the UK and France, which together represented half the fast growing European leasing market.

Personnel *Chairman* Y.C. Lamarche, 1983–89. *Deputy Chairman* G.L. Tedder, 1984–89 (Managing Director 1983–84). *Managing Directors* N. Danville, 1984–86, L. Rutherford, 1986–87, S. Udale, 1987–89.

Finances (£ million)

YE 31/12	1983	1984	1985	1986	1987	1988
Total assets	220.7	249.3	335.4	451.1	430.7	144.4
Cap. & reserves	12.1	13.2	14.4	30.4	32.3	31.8
Pre-tax profit	0.7	0.8	1.2	2.2	1.6	1.3
Dividend	3.8	0.0	0.0	0.0	0.0	3.0

S1/6 BANCO URQUIJO HISPANO AMERICANO
Founded 1973; consortium status 1976 to 1983. CH 01108417.

Ownership Initially, a subsidiary of Banco Urquijo, Spain. From 1976, it was owned equally by Banco Urquijo and Banco Hispano Americano, Spain; the latter bought control of the former in 1983.

History & business Established in 1973 as a wholly owned subsidiary of Banco Urquijo, the predominant industrial and merchant bank in Spain in the decades after the end of the Civil War (1936–39); it launched a number of leading industrial companies in Spain, in which it was a shareholder as well as banker. In 1976, Banco Hispano Americano, a leading Spanish commercial bank and shareholder of Banco Urquijo, acquired a 50 per cent stake in the bank (which became known as BUHAL). Its activities spanned treasury and foreign exchange, commercial lending in Eurocurrencies and sterling, trade finance, leasing, Eurobond issues and fund management. It held leading positions in London as market-maker in the peseta, adviser on the

Spanish stock market and lender to Spanish borrowers; it led 34 syndicated loans for Spanish borrowers between 1976 and 1983. Its chairman, George Moore, was a former chairman of Citibank; among its directors was a former deputy prime minister of Spain, Antonio Barrera de Irimo, and a future minister of industry, Alberto Oliart Sussol. Banco Urquijo ran into severe difficulties in 1983 because of its industrial and property holdings in Spain and its rapid expansion abroad; it was taken over by Banco Hispano Americano, which thus took full control of this bank.

Personnel *Chairman* G.S. Moore, 1976–83. *Managing Director* W.K. Mendenhall, 1976–83. *Deputy Managing Directors* G. de las Heras, 1976, F. Navarro Chazarra, 1976–77, L. Caballero Arcon, 1978–82, F. Pascual Garcia, 1978–82, L.A. Robert Gonzalez, 1982–83, E. Sanmarti da Silva, 1982–83.

Finances (£ million)

YE 31/12	1976	1977	1978	1979	1980	1981	1982
Total assets	61.7	90.0	103.9	141.6	160.8	210.5	324.2
Cap. & reserves	5.0	5.6	6.4	10.9	11.6	12.6	13.7
Pre-tax profit	1.3	1.5	1.7	0.7	1.2	2.0	2.3
Dividend	0.0	0.0	0.0	0.0	0.0	0.0	0.0

S1/7 BROWN HARRIMAN & INTERNATIONAL BANKS
FLEMING SUEZ BROWN BROTHERS
BANQUE FRANÇAISE DE CRÉDIT INTERNATIONAL
Founded 1968; consortium status to 1983. CH 00931897.

Ownership The bank's history as a consortium bank was in three stages:

(1) In 1968, it was founded by Cie Financière de Suez, a Paris-based international holding company, Robert Fleming & Co., London merchant bankers, and Brown Brothers Harriman & Co (BBH), New York, the largest private bank in the USA, which also did brokerage business and was a member of the New York Stock Exchange. It was first named Fleming Suez, then Fleming Suez Brown Brothers.

(2) In 1972, Fleming and Suez dropped out and it became owned by BBH under the name Brown Harriman International, but the ownership was soon widened by the inclusion of First National Bank of Minneapolis and Pittsburg National Bank (10 per cent each), Prudential Assurance Company, London (18 per cent) and six Inter-Alpha Group member banks (40 per cent, see Appendix III), Banco Ambrosiano, BHF Bank, Crédit Commercial de France (CCF), Kredietbank, Nederlandsche Middenstandsbank and Williams & Glyn's Bank; BBH retained 22 per cent, providing the new name, Brown Harriman & International Banks,

and the management. Privatbanken, an Inter-Alpha member bank, later joined, resulting in small changes in the shareholdings.

(3) In 1977, CCF and Banque Internationale pour l'Afrique Occidentale (BIAO) acquired 100 per cent of the capital and the name was changed to Banque Française de Crédit International. The bank was liquidated in 1983.

History & business Its business was that of an international merchant bank; its activities included loans, current and deposit accounts in sterling and Eurocurrencies, foreign exchange, leasing, trade finance, Eurobonds and corporate financial advice. Robert Fleming became a participant because it wanted a banking licence, while Suez wanted a stronger presence in London (although it had a stake in another UK bank, S2/8). They withdrew in 1972 because the bank seemed likely to compete with their own operations. It was reorganized by the third founder, BBH, which was motivated by the opportunity to enter the international underwriting banking business, from which it was excluded at home because of the Glass–Steagall Act. Thereafter, its shareholders provided a wide geographic coverage, especially in Europe and North America; it provided a London presence for two major US regional banks. One of the non-executive Directors was Robert Roosa; as Under Secretary of State at the US Treasury, he had helped create the Interest Equalization Tax in 1963 and devised the 'Roosa Bonds' to soak up international liquidity. After being acquired by two French banks in 1977, the bank developed a focus on French business; in 1980, it acquired BIAO's Piraeus branch and expanded into trade financing with African countries. In the following year, the African dimension was enhanced; BIAO created a holding company in which International Bank for West Africa took shares. However, CCF and BIAO were banks with very different profiles; each of them wanted its own London presence and more capital was needed for growth and provisions. Therefore, the decision was made to put the bank into voluntary liquidation in 1983, its business being then taken over by a BIAO branch in London.

Personnel *Chairmen* M.J. Babington-Smith, 1969–72, Sir J. Hogg, 1972–81. *Managing Directors* Hon J.C. Loder (Lord Wakehurst), 1969–73, P.G. Vance, 1973–80, A. de Montigny, 1980–81. *General Manager* E.P. Jaggard, 1969–73. *Senior General Manager* P. Delbruck, 1980–81. *Executive Directors* G.B. de la Presle, 1970, F.M. Greene Jr, 1971–73, A.T. Enders, 1973–76, L.F.B. Vale, 1973–78.

Finances (£ million)

YE 31/3	1970	1971	1972	1973	1974	1975
Total assets	24.4	35.0	38.5	67.3	70.0	70.3
Cap. & reserves	2.0	2.1	2.1	3.9	4.0	4.6

Pre-tax profit	0.1	0.0	0.1	0.0	0.3	0.4
Dividend	0.0	0.0	0.0	0.0	0.0	0.0
YE 31/3 & 31/12	**1976**	**1977**	**1977**	**1978**	**1979**	**1980**
Total assets	79.8	87.5	81.1	80.1	94.1	106.2
Cap. & reserves	4.8	4.9	5.1	5.3	5.5	6.7
Pre-tax profit	0.5	0.5	0.4	0.5	0.8	1.3
Dividend	0.1	0.0	0.0	0.0	0.2	0.3

YE 31/12	**1981**
Total assets	153.9
Cap. & reserves	5.9
Pre-tax profit	1.0
Dividend	0.0

NOTES: (1) 12 months to 31/3/77. (2) 9 months to 31/12/77; thereafter, 12 months to 31/12.

S1/8 EURO–LATINAMERICAN BANK
Founded 1974; consortium status to 1990. CH 01179379.

Ownership *50 per cent European*: Algemene Bank Nederland, Banca Nazionale del Lavoro, Banque Bruxelles Lambert, Banque Nationale de Paris, Barclays Bank International, Bayerische Hypotheken- und Wechsel-Bank, Dresdner Bank, Österreichische Länderbank (ABECOR member banks; see Appendix III), Banco Central, Spain, Union Bank of Switzerland and Deutsche Südamerikanische Bank (each less than 5 per cent).

50 per cent Latin American: Banca Serfin, Mexico, Banco de Colombia, Banco de la Nación, Peru, Banco de la Nación Argentina, Banco de la República Oriental del Uruguay, Banco del Estado de Chile, Banco do Brasil, Banco Industrial de Venezuela, Banco del Pichincha, Ecuador, Banco Mercantil de São Paulo, Brazil and, from 1979, Banco del Estado de Bolivia (each with less than 6 per cent).

History & business The bank (EULABANK) was set up as a multi-bank joint venture to strengthen the economic ties between Latin America and Europe. Its first Chairman, Dr Jaime Michelsen, described its creation as a 'long-term investment to meet the growing demand in Latin America for finance and investment from Europe rather than as a means of merely capitalizing upon the rapid development of the Eurocurrency markets.' The Chairmanship, Deputy Chairmanship and Executive Committee composition rotated between the continents. Its business was medium- and long-term Eurocurrency loans, a forfait finance, project finance, Latin American trade finance, treasury, foreign exchange, leasing and advice on European investment in Latin America and vice versa. The principal activity was the arrangement of and participation in Eurocurrency lending to the Latin American public and private sectors. By the end of 1982, the inability of Mexico, Argentina and Brazil, soon followed by other countries, to meet their debt obligations put an end to the search for new medium-term lending. Thereafter, the bank concentrated on trade finance, particularly for its shareholder banks, as well as participating in 'new money' arrangements to help sovereign borrowers. In view of the uncertain outlook, the bank paid no dividends after 1982, to build up the capital base, which had already benefited from a $25 million subordinated note issue in 1981. By 1986, while sovereign exposure had reached 96 per cent, the scale of provisions recommended by the Bank of England in 1987 proved to be too large for the bank's capital resources and foreseeable profits. In November 1988, the shareholders subscribed to £121 million Non-Cumulative Irredeemable Preferred Stock, but the financial condition of most of the borrowers continued to deteriorate; early in 1990, a voluntary liquidation took place, with all the shareholder banks purchasing loans, in proportion to their shareholdings.

Personnel *Chairmen* Dr J. Michelsen, 1974–76, Prof. A. Ferrari, 1976–78, Dr K. Rischbieter, 1979, Dr O.R. Colin, 1979–80, C.P. Lunn, 1980–82, Dr J.J. de Olloqui, 1982–84, G. Hanselmann, 1984–86, F.A. Slinger, 1986–88, L. de Bievre, 1988–90. *General Managers* A.C. Campos, 1974–78, G.M. Gunson, 1978–90 (Managing Director from 1986). *Deputy General Managers* A.C. Raedecke, 1974–78, H.A. Heinig, 1978–90.

Finances (£ million)

YE 30/9	1975	1976	1977	1978	1979	1980	1981
Total assets	42.3	103.7	160.0	237.1	355.3	413.1	648.0
Cap. & reserves	8.8	10.2	13.2	16.5	19.2	22.1	25.8
Pre-tax profit	0.7	1.8	3.1	4.0	6.9	7.6	9.8
Dividend	0.0	0.0	0.0	0.4	0.7	0.8	1.0
YE 30/9	1982	1983	1984	1985	1986	1987	1988
Total assets	692.6	689.0	921.2	894.8	795.2	754.9	591.9
Cap. & reserves	28.8	33.4	38.0	42.9	48.0	48.1	50.6
Pre-tax profit	8.3	7.2	8.8	8.9	8.7	3.3	5.5
Dividend	0.0	0.0	0.0	0.0	0.0	0.0	0.0

S1/9 EUROPEAN ARAB BANK

Founded 1976; consortium status to 1989. CH 01285555.

Ownership Subsidiary of European Arab Holding, Luxembourg (S2/13).

History & business The bank was set up as the London arm of the European Arab Holding consortium banking group, which brought together a considerable number of the most powerful private and public sector institutions of the Arab countries, Europe and Japan. The bank's first Board of Directors (26 strong) included the Chairmen or senior Executives of some of the largest European and Arab banks and public sector institutions, demonstrating a high level of commitment to this consortium group. The results, however, were unsatisfactory and European Arab Holding, the parent, was reluctant to continue making the regular injections of capital which were needed. So, in December 1985, the decision was made to run down this bank's activities, which took place over the following three years; in the process, it had to make significant provisions on its Third World debt, before activity ceased in January 1989.

Personnel *Chairmen* Dr A.M. Kaissouni, 1976–85, A.A.H. Al-Sagar, 1985–89. *Managing Directors/General Managers* R.B. Botcherby, 1976–80, B. Elsadek, 1977–84, W. Major, 1980–83, K. Hammer, 1983–87, N. El-Sahhar, 1984–87, J. Suidan, 1986–87, S. Munro, 1987–89.

Finances (£ million)

YE 31/12	1977	1978	1979	1980	1981	1982
Total assets	85.3	110.9	133.0	147.3	270.3	437.2
Cap. & reserves	4.9	7.4	7.3	7.8	12.6	13.7
Pre-tax profit	0.1	0.2	−0.1	1.1	1.6	2.2
Dividend	0.0	0.0	0.0	0.0	0.0	0.0

YE 31/12	1983	1984	1985	1986	1987	1988
Total assets	355.9	433.7	314.1	229.1	140.0	108.6
Cap. & reserves	14.9	15.9	24.7	−4.7	0.0	−7.7
Pre-tax profit	1.8	2.2	0.4	−30.8	−0.6	−7.6
Dividend	0.0	0.0	0.0	0.0	0.0	0.0

NOTE: 13 months to 31/12/77.

S1/10 EUROPEAN BANKING COMPANY
Founded 1973; consortium status to 1985. CH 01053200.

Ownership Amsterdam–Rotterdam Bank, Banca Commerciale Italiana, Creditanstalt-Bankverein, Deutsche Bank, Midland Bank, Société Générale and Société Générale de Banque, each with an equal share (EBIC member banks; see Appendix III). Amsterdam–Rotterdam Bank bought out its fellow EBIC shareholders in 1985.

History & business European Banking Company (EBC) was set up as an international investment bank. It carried out the full range of Eurocurrency activities, with emphasis on Eurobond, FRN and FRCD issues, market-making and foreign exchange. It managed syndicated loans, using its shareholders as main participants in its deals, not seeking to build up a large loan portfolio of its own; it managed the first Eurocurrency syndicated loan financing for the EEC, in 1976, for $300 million, together with Orion Bank. It specialized in large shipping, mining and energy projects, particularly for clients of its shareholder banks. EBC managed or co-managed over $20 billion of financings between 1974 and 1981. Its first Managing Director, Stanislas Yassukovich, had been a pioneer of the Eurobond market at White Weld (S2/12). In 1982, it united managerially and operationally with its sister bank, Banque Européenne de Crédit, Brussels (S2/9), which did complementary activities and had the same shareholders, though EBC and BEC remained distinct legal entities. Loan and venture capital provisions affected the result for 1984.

Personnel *Chairmen* C.F. Karsten, 1974–79, P.-E. Janssen, 1979–84, G.N. Schmidt-Chiari, 1984. *Managing Director* S.M. Yassukovich, 1974–83 (Deputy Chairman & Group Chief Executive 1983–84). *Executive Director and Secretary* J.C. Chandler, 1974–81. *Deputy Managing Directors* I.T.H. Logie, 1975–80, W.R. Slee, 1979 (Managing Director & Group Chief Operating Officer 1983 84). *Managing Directors* W A Blackwell, R.C. Kahrmann, P.J.M. Bulters, D.R. Mitchem (1984).

Finances (£ million)

YE 31/12	1974	1975	1976	1977	1978	1979
Total assets	171.4	227.4	257.3	318.0	308.7	337.1
Cap. & reserves	10.5	11.7	12.7	16.9	19.0	20.1
Pre-tax profit	1.2	2.1	3.2	1.8	2.1	2.2
Dividend	0.0	0.0	0.5	0.5	0.0	0.5

YE 31/12	1980	1981	1982	1983	1984
Total assets	359.7	458.6	522.7	553.1	614.7
Cap. & reserves	21.1	23.5	24.1	27.2	21.9
Pre-tax profit	2.8	3.0	2.1	4.2	−2.9
Dividend	0.5	0.5	0.5	0.0	0.0

NOTE: 17 months to 31/12/74.

S1/11 EUROPEAN BRAZILIAN BANK

Founded 1972; consortium status to 1988. CH 01040949.

Ownership Banco do Brasil and Bank of America (31.9 per cent each), Deutsche Bank, Union Bank of Switzerland (13.7 per cent each) and Dai-Ichi Kangyo Bank (8.8 per cent). Initially, the Bank of America stake was partly held by two affiliates in which Kleinwort Benson and Paribas were shareholders, Bank of America Ltd and Banque Ameribas (S2/6).

History & business The philosophy of the bank, known as Eurobraz, was described by its first Chairman, Dr Nestor Jost, as 'to operate as effectively as possible in the area of Latin American expansion, with special attention, initially, to the rapid development of the Brazilian economy.' The basic business was the organization and syndication of loans for major projects, institutions, companies and governmental agencies. The bank's loan portfolio came to be almost entirely of Latin American character, although, in its early history, Eurobraz made some loans to French real estate, which resulted in provisions in 1974–75. In order to secure diversification, a small proportion of the loans were to countries other than Brazil, but the Brazilian exposure was invariably over 80 per cent of the whole. The lending programme was supported by the bank's Treasury, whose main function was the raising of deposits in the inter-bank market. The bank entered the Eurobond market, through the co-management of Eurobond issues for Brazil; however, it did not aspire to be a major investment bank, given the preference of its two largest shareholders not to support the bank in this area. Eurobraz's Chairman was always the President, for the time being, of Banco do Brasil and the Deputy Chairman was a senior banker from Bank of America; management was organized by these two banks, the largest shareholders. In 1982, the bank suffered from the effects of the Latin American debt crisis and had to call on its shareholders for $500 million deposits, but succeeded in reducing this figure in the following years. However, the weight of provisions that had to be provided in 1987 on its loan portfolio caused a loss of £247 million in 1987; in the following year, the bank gave up its banking licence and liquidation was initiated, which was finally accomplished in 1997.

Personnel *Chairmen* Dr N. Jost, 1972–74, Dr A. Calmon de Sa, 1974–77, Dr K. Rischbieter, 1977–79, Dr O.R. Colin, 1979–85, Dr C.C. de Magalhaes, 1985–88. *Deputy Chairmen* P. Haas, 1972–75, W.H. Bolin, 1976–82, W.V. Young, 1982–87. *Managing Directors* R. Verhagen, 1972–74, F.W. Grol, 1974–83, Sir J. Hall, Bt, 1983–87, *Deputy Managing Directors* A.M. dos Reis, 1972–74, J.C.M. Serrano, 1974–78, H. Wimmer, 1978–85, M.F. de Nobrega, 1985–87, R. do R. Malheiros Franco, 1987. *Company Secretaries/General Managers/Administration Heads* M. Gibbs, 1973–74, P.R. Sandringham, 1974–86, P. Taylor, 1986–87.

Finances (£ million)

YE 31/12	1972	1973	1974	1975	1976	1977
Total assets	65.6	118.5	133.3	182.5	300.4	326.4
Cap. & reserves	2.2	5.0	5.9	10.4	12.7	14.2
Pre-tax profit	0.4	2.0	2.9	2.2	4.2	3.2
Dividend	0.1	0.1	0.1	0.1	0.1	0.0

YE 31/12	1978	1979	1980	1981	1982	1983
Total assets	386.8	441.4	415.0	816.8	766.0	812.9
Cap. & reserves	16.5	18.5	21.1	29.0	39.9	47.5
Pre-tax profit	5.5	6.7	6.6	16.1	25.3	19.3
Dividend	0.0	0.5	0.0	0.0	1.0	0.0

YE 31/12	1984	1985	1986	1987
Total assets	1104.7	891.8	862.2	495.7
Cap. & reserves	60.5	68.0	75.7	−175.2
Pre-tax profit	31.0	21.2	19.7	−247.8
Dividend	0.0	0.0	0.0	0.0

NOTE: 8 months to 31/12/72.

S1/12 FENNOSCANDIA BANK
Founded 1982; consortium status to 1990. CH 01686044.

Ownership Skopbank, Finland and Swedbank, Sweden. These banking groups acted as the central and foreign trade banks for the savings bank systems of their two countries. At the time of FennoScandia's formation, they had already had a successful investment and private banking venture in Luxembourg, Banque Nordeurope, which was established in 1973; it was acquired in its entirety by Swedbank in 1989. Skopbank bought Swedbank's 50 per cent share of FennoScandia Bank in 1990.

History & business Short-term and medium-term Eurocurrency facilities, treasury and foreign exchange (with a Nordic emphasis), guarantees, leasing and advice on UK opportunities for Nordic corporate customers. From 1985, it had a retail branch dedicated to dealing with visitors from Nordic countries in London. The decision by Skopbank to acquire the totality of FennoScandia Bank was dictated by Skopbank's growing international activities, making it desirable to have full control.

Personnel *Chairmen* J.N. Butterwick, 1983–86, C. Wegelius, 1986–89. *Managing Director* J. Ankarcrona, 1983–89.

Finances (£ million)

YE 31/12	1983	1984	1985	1986	1987	1988	1989
Total assets	72.2	129.2	156.0	258.6	379.1	475.1	532.8
Cap. & reserves	9.7	10.1	10.2	20.7	20.8	30.9	31.0
Pre-tax profit	−0.3	0.5	0.5	1.2	1.9	2.4	0.5
Dividend	0.0	0.0	0.0	0.0	0.8	1.0	0.0

S1/13 INTERNATIONAL COMMERCIAL BANK
Founded 1967; consortium status to 1990. CH 00911089.

Ownership Initially, Commerzbank, First National Bank of Chicago, Hong Kong & Shanghai Banking Corporation, Irving Trust, New York and Westminster Bank (20 per cent each). After helping to set up Orion, Westminster's successor, National Westminster Bank, sold its stake in 1971 and two other banks became shareholders in 1973, each with 11 per cent, Banco di Roma and Crédit Lyonnais, Commerzbank's share going down to 12 per cent; these three banks were associated through the Europartners club (see Appendix III). The share of the other three banks then went up to 22 per cent each.

History & business The main business was medium-term Eurocurrency lending. The customers covered a wide geographical spread; in 1979, borrowers were from 76 countries, a number of them from the Third World, and included both governments and companies. The leasing subsidiary was a steady contributor to profits. When the Third World debt problems became acute in the early 1980s, the bank's profitability enabled it to make significant provisions; the bank diversified its activities and entered the forfaiting business, switching its lending focus to short-term trade finance away from sovereign lending. A confirming house subsidiary was formed in 1986, as an adjunct to the forfaiting business, and a mortgage lending subsidiary was set up to develop Sterling lending opportunities. However, the provisions required on Third World debt by the Bank of England's 1987 guidelines and non-payment of interest by Brazil and other countries adversely affected results, with losses being made in 1987 and 1989. While the shareholders injected new capital and provided other support to maintain confidence in the bank, the decision was made to surrender its banking licence in June 1990 and run down the business in an orderly fashion.

Personnel *Chairmen* S.G. Gates, 1967–72, A.G. Boardman Jr, 1972, Sir J. Saunders, 1972–81, S.H. Wright, 1981–83, Dr W. Jahn, 1984–88, Sir M. Sandberg, 1988–90. *Managing Directors* D. Robson, 1967–76, K.F. Einfeld, 1976–83 (Acting Chairman, 1983–84), G.J. Stapstead, 1983–89, M.W. Wells, 1989–90.

Finances (£ million)

YE 31/12	1968	1969	1970	1971	1972	1973
Total assets	144.2	270.8	310.4	316.1	362.1	420.8
Cap. & reserves	3.9	5.1	6.2	7.2	9.4	10.7
Pre-tax profit	1.3	1.5	1.9	1.9	3.9	3.2
Dividend	0.0	0.1	0.1	0.1	0.1	0.2

YE 31/12	1974	1975	1976	1977	1978	1979
Total assets	387.7	422.7	505.0	487.8	505.7	521.4
Cap. & reserves	11.8	13.4	15.3	17.3	19.7	22.1
Pre-tax profit	3.1	4.0	4.6	6.1	6.7	6.7
Dividend	0.2	0.2	0.3	0.7	0.7	0.7

YE 31/12	1980	1981	1982	1983	1984	1985
Total assets	555.9	781.8	945.7	1053.5	1287.6	1040.0
Cap. & reserves	25.0	33.9	42.5	47.1	52.0	57.1
Pre-tax profit	7.5	8.5	9.4	10.9	10.9	11.8
Dividend	0.7	0.7	1.2	1.2	1.2	1.2

YE 31/12	1986	1987	1988	1989
Total assets	1019.6	881.3	813.9	566.6
Cap. & reserves	62.2	42.5	52.1	−47.6
Pre-tax profit	11.8	−33.6	3.9	−99.8
Dividend	1.2	0.0	0.0	0.0

NOTES: (1) 17 months to 31/12/68. (2) Pro-forma balance sheet as at 31/12/89 shows capital and reserves of £8.4 million after shareholder support.

S1/14 INTERNATIONAL ENERGY BANK
SFE BANK
Founded 1973; consortium status to 1989. CH 01136240.

Ownership Bank of Scotland, Barclays Bank International (15 per cent each), Canadian Imperial Bank of Commerce, Republic National Bank of Dallas, Société Financière Européenne, Luxembourg (S2/19) (20 per cent each) and Banque Worms, France (10 per cent). One shareholder, SFE, in July 1983, bought out four of its fellow shareholders and increased its stake to 85 per cent, Barclays retaining its 15 per cent stake; the bank was renamed SFE Bank in 1985. The bank thus remained indirectly a consortium bank, until it was acquired by Banca Popolare di Novara in December 1989.

History & business The concept of the bank was first discussed late in 1972. The oil price rises in the following year and the beginning of North Sea oil production coincided with the early history of the bank. The founding shareholders included two leading energy banks from the USA and Canada, which provided the first two presidents of the bank. Bank of Scotland, described in early annual reports as Scotland's 'senior bank', had a considerable interest and expertise in energy financing, North Sea oil being very significant to the Scottish economy; the French shareholder was part of the Worms group, which had large interests in shipping and oil. Initially, the bank devoted much of its effort to the new North Sea opportunities, being involved in financing the Claymore Field and Piper Field in 1974 and 1975. However, the mandate was gradually expanded by geography and business area; by the late 1970s, it covered the financing of oil, gas, nuclear power and uranium, coal, hydro-electric power, biomass, forestry and solar energy. The activities financed were not only production, but also refining, petrochemicals, shipping, transmission, pipelines, drilling rigs and recycling. The bank described itself as 'the specialized bank for financing energy requirements world-wide.' Financing facilities included multi-currency loans, export financing, acceptance credits, leasing and the arrangement of equity finance. The acquisition by Société Financière Européenne (SFE) in 1983 was intended to strengthen the bank, through the availability of resources and contacts of its shareholders, which were nine of the largest banks in the world, and of the other specialized units in the SFE Group. New capital and subordinated debt were provided by the shareholders in 1984, but the bank's results were adversely affected by its sovereign risk exposure and the problems of some of its customers in the energy sector. In 1988 it was decided to disband the entire SFE Group, resulting in the sale of SFE Bank in London.

Personnel *Chairmen* T.W. Walker, 1973–78, C.P. Lunn, 1978–88, J.A. Champion, 1988–89 (also Chief Executive). *Presidents/Chief Executives* E.E. Monteith Jr, 1973–76, V.R.B. Nordheimer, 1976–77, G.F. Ahalt, 1977–79, I.T.H. Logie, 1980–83, B. Guetin, 1983–86, B. Grimmond, 1986–88.

Finances (£ million)					
YE 31/12	**1974**	**1975**	**1976**	**1977**	**1978**
Total assets	41.1	83.5	125.2	151.8	224.1
Cap. & reserves	10.2	10.6	11.5	12.2	13.1
Pre-tax profit	0.7	1.0	1.9	2.1	2.5
Dividend	0.0	0.0	0.0	0.3	0.3

YE 31/12	1979	1980	1981	1982	1983
Total assets	246.0	290.7	351.3	361.1	383.7
Cap. & reserves	14.5	16.5	23.9	24.9	25.9
Pre-tax profit	3.4	3.8	3.1	0.9	1.8
Dividend	0.4	0.4	0.5	0.0	0.0
YE 31/12	1984	1985	1986	1987	1988
Total assets	557.9	506.0	576.5	501.7	544.8
Cap. & reserves	41.0	42.5	43.7	47.5	49.5
Pre-tax profit	2.4	2.8	1.8	−2.1	3.3
Dividend	0.0	0.0	0.0	0.0	0.0

NOTE: 15 months to 31/12/74.

S1/15 INTERNATIONAL MEXICAN BANK
Founded 1973; consortium status to 1992. CH 01144506.

Ownership Initially, Banco Nacional de México (BNM) (38 per cent), Inlat (DESC industrial group) (13 per cent), Bank of America (20 per cent), Paribas, Dai-Ichi Kangyo Bank, Deutsche Bank and Union Bank of Switzerland (7.25 per cent each). In 1977, Paribas dropped out, despite being one of the founding shareholders of BNM, as did Inlat; in 1979, Nacional Financiera and Banco Nacional de Comércio Exterior (both controlled by the Mexican Government) came in as shareholders, through Intermex Holding SA, which was set up to own the bank and a sister bank in Nassau. Deutsche, Union and Dai-Ichi Kangyo dropped out in 1989–90, while BNM and Bank of America remained the largest shareholders; BNM acquired 51 per cent of the bank in 1992 and 100 per cent in 1994.

History & business The consortium bank in London mostly specialized in Mexican business. At the time of its formation in 1973, the Mexican economy was growing very strongly and became a beneficiary of the double rise in oil prices and of a stable currency. Its main activities were short- and medium-term credits, managing loan syndications, particularly for Mexican borrowers, and treasury operations. Over the years, the bank broadened its activities to include managing Eurobond issues and extended its coverage to the rest of Latin America. The bank was seriously affected by the first Mexican crisis of August 1982, but was aided by the availability of stand-by lines from its shareholders of $526 million. New lines of business were introduced, such as trade finance, forfaiting and debt trading. A reorganization (including closure of its sister bank in Nassau) resulted in significant loan provisions between 1989 and 1990, after which the loan book (by then much reduced in size) was put right and capital ratios restored. The bank's take-over by its biggest shareholder, Banco Nacional de México, enabled it to become the latter's in-house investment bank.

Personnel *Chairmen* A.F. Legorreta, 1974–83, M.E. McMillen Jr, 1983–86, R.A. Saalfeld, 1986–89, G. Hanselmann, 1989–92. *Managing Director* G. Legrain, 1974–92. *Deputy Managing Directors* F. Willy, 1974–76, F. Carrera, 1977–79, J. Chico, 1979–83, J.M. Fabre, 1983–85, R. Mancera, 1985–89, I. Lara, 1990–92.

Finances (£ million)

YE 31/12	1974	1975	1976	1977	1978	1979
Total assets	19.6	59.3	149.1	145.4	166.4	214.7
Cap. & reserves	2.5	5.3	6.4	7.3	9.2	11.1
Pre-tax profit	0.1	0.7	2.2	2.1	2.0	1.9
Dividend	0.0	0.0	0.0	0.0	0.0	0.0
YE 31/12 & 31/3	**1980**	**1981**	**1983**	**1984**	**1985**	**1986**
Total assets	210.9	355.6	381.2	380.3	473.4	381.3
Cap. & reserves	12.2	16.1	20.4	23.5	27.7	29.8
Pre-tax profit	2.3	8.3	9.0	6.3	8.9	5.9
Dividend	0.0	0.0	0.0	0.0	0.0	0.0
YE 31/3	**1987**	**1988**	**1989**	**1990**	**1991**	**1992**
Total assets	341.6	247.1	287.6	239.5	177.7	222.2
Cap. & reserves	31.8	32.0	26.7	26.7	34.6	44.7
Pre-tax profit	5.2	2.6	−39.3	0.0	7.9	10.9
Dividend	0.0	0.0	0.0	0.0	0.0	0.0

NOTES: (1) 14 months to 31/12/74. (2) 15 months to 31/3/83; thereafter 12 months to 31/3.

S1/16 IRAN OVERSEAS INVESTMENT BANK
Founded 1973. CH 01126618.

Ownership Initially Bank Melli Iran, Industrial and Mining Development Bank of Iran (later Bank of Industry and Mine), Barclays Bank International, Midland Bank, Deutsche Bank, Société Générale, Bank of America, Manufacturers Hanover Trust, Bank of Tokyo and Industrial Bank of Japan (10 per cent each). After an increase in capital in 1975, the two Iranian banks increased their stakes to 25 per cent each, the international banks reducing theirs to 6.25 per cent each. In 1982, Bank Melli and Bank Saderat Iran bought out the international banks and the bank became owned equally by the four Iranian banks.

History & business The bank was set up to tap international financial markets for the development of Iran's economy and to give Iran significant expertise in those markets, which was then lacking in the indigenous banks. The international bank shareholders were chosen to give the new bank all necessary prestige and support. Its business was Eurocurrency loans, export credit, trade finance, project financing, foreign exchange and private placements. Its Chairmen were *ex officio* representatives of the Iranian shareholders and its first Managing Director, Darius Oskoui, had previously been

in charge of Iran's overseas borrowing programme, a key part of the bank's purpose. However, the bank diversified its lending activities and, by the end of
the 1970s, it had participated in, syndicated or managed over $3 billion of
loans to 26 countries, as well as extending significant credits to Iranian public and private sector borrowers. The bank faced difficulties after the Iranian
revolution of 1979; the Algiers Accords of 1981 resulted in the repayment of
Iran's international debts, in which the bank played an important role, but
it reduced the range of activities, loan portfolio and earnings for some years.
In the mid-1980s, the bank developed its trade finance activities and formed
a subsidiary for trading, mainly with Iran. It received significant deposits
from Iran and was a net provider of funds to the inter-bank market.

Personnel *Chairmen* A.G. Kheradjou, 1973–79, J. Shoraka, 1979, E.
Arabzadeh, 1980–82, H.Sh.H. Taleghani, 1982–84, A. Azizi, 1984–86,
M. Ghassemi, 1986, K. Najafi Elmi, 1986–90, M. Arami, 1990–93, V. Seif,
1993–97, M. Harati Nik, 1997–98, A. Amiralsami, 1998–present.
Managing Directors D.M. Oskoui, 1973–80, S.A. Taheri, 1980–84,
P. Gorjestani, 1984–87, S.S. Razavi, 1987–94, M. Khodabandehloo,
1994–present. *Deputy Managing Directors and General Managers* G.G. Bell,
1973–78, H. Sasson, 1980–83. *Assistant Managing Directors* G.R.M.
Cordiner, 1983–85, K.A. Gibbs, 1988–92, C.L.T. Jenkins, 1992–present.

Finances (£ million)

YE 30/9	1974	1975	1976	1977	1978	1979	1980
Total assets	27.3	67.6	112.8	129.4	150.2	117.4	104.7
Cap. & reserves	5.0	8.5	8.9	9.3	10.0	10.7	11.3
Pre-tax profit	0.1	1.0	2.0	1.8	2.3	1.6	1.2
Dividend	0.0	0.0	0.5	0.5	0.5	0.0	0.0
YE 30/9	**1981**	**1982**	**1983**	**1984**	**1985**	**1986**	**1987**
Total assets	112.0	141.1	166.9	206.2	209.3	181.7	103.0
Cap. & reserves	12.3	13.3	14.5	20.8	20.8	21.1	20.5
Pre-tax profit	1.3	1.6	1.7	0.5	2.1	0.3	−0.9
Dividend	0.0	0.0	0.0	0.0	1.4	0.0	0.0
YE 30/9	**1988**	**1989**	**1990**	**1991**	**1992**	**1993**	**1994**
Total assets	93.4	104.1	142.5	151.6	140.2	158.5	174.1
Cap. & reserves	21.3	21.3	24.5	28.2	32.5	49.2	50.7
Pre-tax profit	1.1	0.0	3.2	2.2	3.3	1.3	2.1
Dividend	0.0	0.0	0.0	0.0	0.0	0.0	0.0
YE 30/9	**1995**	**1996**	**1997**	**1998**			
Total assets	200.8	234.5	253.8	245.2			
Cap. & reserves	53.0	56.1	58.2	58.9			
Pre-tax profit	6.3	10.1	10.4	4.0			
Dividend	2.0	3.7	5.0	2.0			

S1/17 ITAB BANK
Founded 1983; consortium status to 1988. CH 01777359.

Ownership Istituto Mobiliare Italiano (28 per cent), Banca Popolare di Milano, Cassa di Risparmio di Torino and Credito Romagnolo (24 per cent each). Its name, ITAB, was an acronym of Italian Banking Group, the originally intended name. It was bought out by one of its shareholders, Banca CRT, Cassa di Risparmio di Torino, in June 1988, changing its name to London Italian Bank.

History & business When Istituto Mobiliare Italiano (IMI) planned a new merchant banking operation in London, it decided to go into partnership with a limited number of like-minded Italian banks; its partners were banks with strong market positions in prosperous regions of Northern Italy. IMI itself was an Italian public sector institution of national significance, which was dedicated to medium-term lending and merchant banking. The bank's initial focus was on trade-related business of its shareholders' customer base in Italy and on treasury activities; later, the plan was to develop a wider range of merchant banking services for an international clientele. In order to strengthen marketing efforts, each of the shareholders seconded an officer to the bank in London. Among its non-executive directors were Lord Christopher Soames, former UK Ambassador to France, and Minos Zombanakis, who had pioneered the syndicated loan business from 1969 onwards at Manufacturers Hanover Ltd (S2/17). The bank expanded its corporate finance activities, acting as lead manager or manager of several financings, mainly of an Italian character. In 1987 and 1988, the bank made significant provisions against its loan portfolio, in accordance with the Bank of England's guidelines, which led to the decision by one of the banks, CRT, to buy out its partners.

Personnel *Chairmen* M. Ercolani, 1983–88, M. Bortolussi, 1988. *General Managers* N. Dubini, 1983–87, A. Rossetti, 1987–88.

Finances (£ million)

YE 31/12	1984	1985	1986	1987	1988
Total assets	184.2	210.1	233.7	206.3	186.9
Cap. & reserves	10.1	15.3	15.6	15.6	15.1
Pre-tax profit	0.2	0.4	0.6	0.1	−0.4
Dividend	0.0	0.0	0.0	0.0	0.0

S1/18 ITALIAN INTERNATIONAL BANK
Founded 1972; consortium status to 1980. CH 01041119.

Ownership Anciennes Institutions de Crédit Italiennes Holding SA, Luxembourg (AICI), which was owned equally by Banco di Napoli, Banco di Sicilia, Istituto Bancario San Paolo di Torino and Monte dei Paschi di Siena, which bought out the other shareholders in July 1980.

History & business IIB was the first international consortium venture by four large Italian banks, which were among the oldest in the world. Their aim was to use AICI as a vehicle to create similar banks in the other major financial centres of the world. IIB's activities were inter-bank deposits, foreign exchange, CD issuance, commercial and syndicated lending in Sterling and Eurocurrencies, leasing, corporate advice, Eurobond and UK equity underwriting. IIB's Channel Islands subsidiary conducted trust and administration business and was a source of deposits from outside the money markets. There was an Anglo–Italian emphasis in the business. In 1976 and 1977, IIB required shareholder support, as a result of non-performance of certain UK loans undertaken at the time of the secondary banking crisis of 1973–74. Its first chairman was a former governor of the Bank of England, Lord Cobbold; he had spent his early career in Italy, where he played a notable part in reorganizing the banking venture, Compagnia Italo–Britannica. Among the other directors were James Callaghan, the former UK chancellor of the exchequer and future prime minister, and Sir Charles Forte, the hotelier.

Personnel *Chairmen* Lord Cobbold, 1972–75, R. Raw, 1975–78, Dr R. Paolucci, 1978–79, G.C. Nunziante, 1980–81. *Chief Executives/Managing Directors* R. Taylor, 1972–76, E. Varesio (acting), 1977, J. Baden, 1978–81.

Finances (£ million)

YE 30/6	1973	1974	1975	1976	1977
Total assets	107.0	147.0	151.0	179.0	164.0
Cap. & reserves	7.7	7.9	10.5	10.6	11.7
Pre-tax profit	0.3	0.4	0.2	0.2	−8.9
Dividend	0.0	0.0	0.0	0.0	0.0

YE 30/6	1978	1979	1980	1981
Total assets	165.0	187.0	234.0	351.0
Cap. & reserves	12.8	13.9	15.4	17.4
Pre-tax profit	1.1	1.1	1.6	2.1
Dividend	0.0	0.0	0.0	0.0

NOTE: 17 months to 31/12/73.

S1/19 JAPAN INTERNATIONAL BANK
Founded 1970; consortium status to 1991. CH 00997447.

Ownership Four Japanese commercial banks, Fuji Bank, Mitsubishi Bank, Sumitomo Bank and Tokai Bank (20 per cent each), and three Japanese investment banks, Daiwa Securities, Nikko Securities and Yamaichi Securities (6.7 per cent each). Tokai Bank bought out the other shareholders in October 1991.

History & business The bank's special emphasis was on medium-to longer-term Eurocurrency lending, as well as Eurocurrency deposits and underwriting issues of Eurosecurities. By the mid-1970s, its shareholders had established their own Euromarket operations in London, as commercial and investment bankers, so that the opportunities for referrals from them were lessened; Mitsubishi Bank had also acquired a stake in Orion Bank and Libra Bank in 1972. In 1988, the shareholders took over £107 million of the bank's sovereign risk loans, which, otherwise, in accordance with the Bank of England's guidelines, would have caused additional provisions of £28 million. After the 1991 acquisition by Tokai Bank, its activities were merged with those of Tokai's own UK investment bank, Tokai International.

Personnel *Directors/General Managers* T. Kawashima, 1971–73, Y. Imaizumi, 1973–77, Y. Kajiura, 1977–78, R. Kawashima, 1978–82, K. Naito, 1982–85, Y. Okomura, 1985–88, F. Iida, 1988–91.

Finances (£ million)

YE31/12	1971	1972	1973	1974	1975	1976	1977
Total assets	51.7	105.8	217.0	248.2	296.8	379.3	381.2
Cap. & reserves	3.6	3.9	7.8	11.8	12.3	13.3	14.2
Pre-tax profit	0.0	0.5	0.8	1.7	1.8	3.0	3.0
Dividend	0.0	0.0	0.1	0.3	0.3	0.4	0.5

YE 31/12	1978	1979	1980	1981	1982	1983	1984
Total assets	383.3	387.8	411.8	480.0	631.6	560.8	548.5
Cap. & reserves	15.1	16.0	17.2	20.6	22.1	25.7	26.5
Pre-tax profit	3.1	3.1	3.8	3.1	2.7	3.3	4.2
Dividend	0.5	0.5	0.6	0.6	0.6	0.9	0.0

YE 31/12	1985	1986	1987	1988	1989	1990	1991
Total assets	527.4	526.6	427.0	439.7	273.6	128.5	15.0
Cap. & reserves	29.6	31.9	33.3	31.2	21.7	6.2	3.5
Pre-tax profit	4.2	3.7	0.8	−2.0	−9.5	−15.5	−2.7
Dividend	0.0	0.0	0.0	0.0	0.0	0.0	0.0

S1/20 JORDAN INTERNATIONAL BANK
Founded 1984. CH 01814093.

Ownership The Government of the Hashemite Kingdom of Jordan (20 per cent) and the public sector Housing Bank (15 per cent) founded the bank, together with 14 Jordanian commercial banks and finance houses (none holding more than 6 per cent); most of the leading Jordanian banks participated, except Arab Bank, the largest, which was already represented in London. Over the years, there were some additions and removals in the shareholding group; at the end of 1997, the Government had 15 per cent and the now privatized Housing Bank 22 per cent. The next largest shareholder was Jordan National Bank, with 13.9 per cent, the other eight all having shareholdings below 10 per cent. All the shareholders were Jordanian institutions, some of them having non-Jordanian investors as minority shareholders.

History & business Several years of careful planning preceded its creation in 1984. The Central Bank of Jordan (whose Governor, Dr Mohamed Nabulsi, was the bank's first Chairman) and the country's commercial banks and finance houses wanted a greater presence for Jordan in some of the world's leading financial centres. Jordan was becoming an increasingly active sovereign borrower and a London bank could help the country to secure the best terms. A collective presence in London seemed the most economical way for the Jordanian banks to expand their international activities. In the early years, loan losses hampered progress, but, after 1988, the bank reduced its loan exposure, building up its correspondent banking, treasury and private banking business. It did a lot of business with its Jordanian bank shareholders, which provided the bulk of its deposits as well as an important outlet for its liquidity. In 1997, the bank acted as Co-Lead Manager for the first Eurobond for a Jordanian borrower and was authorized to conduct investment business in the UK. From 1991, investment holdings, mostly Eurobonds, Brady bonds and Floating Rate Notes, were an increasing part of the business and, at the end of 1998, represented about 54 per cent of total assets.

Personnel *Chairmen* Dr M.S. Nabulsi, 1984–85 and 1989–96, H.S. Kasim, 1985–89, Dr Z. Fariz, 1996–present. *Deputy Chairman* Z. Khouri, 1985–present. *General Managers* M.E. Constant, 1984–86, J. Bell, 1986 (Acting), T.A. Sharaf, 1987–90, T. Barnes, 1990 (Acting), T. Poland, 1990–94, M.I. Carter, 1996–present.

Finances (£ million)

YE 31/12	1985	1986	1987	1988	1989	1990	1991
Total assets	63.9	82.3	70.2	75.9	86.1	68.2	101.6
Cap. & reserves	9.8	9.3	8.6	8.7	8.7	7.6	12.5
Pre-tax profit	0.2	−0.5	−0.8	0.2	0.0	−1.1	−0.2
Dividend	0.0	0.0	0.0	0.0	0.0	0.0	0.0
YE 31/12	1992	1993	1994	1995	1996	1997	1998
Total assets	146.2	150.9	167.4	211.7	168.8	185.5	179.6
Cap. & reserves	14.1	20.2	20.4	20.6	21.8	22.2	22.5
Pre-tax profit	1.6	1.1	1.1	1.5	1.7	0.6	0.4
Dividend	0.0	0.0	0.5	0.8	0.0	0.0	0.0

S1/21 LIBRA BANK

Founded 1972; consortium status to 1990. CH 01076744.

Ownership *Orion Bank shareholders*: Chase Manhattan Bank (23.6 per cent), Mitsubishi Bank, Royal Bank of Canada, Westdeutsche Landesbank Girozentrale (10.6 per cent each), Credito Italiano (7.1 per cent) and National Westminster Bank (5 per cent). *Others*: Swiss Bank Corporation (10.6 per cent), Banco Itaú, Brazil, Banco de Comércio, Mexico (8 per cent each) and Banco Espirito Santo e Comercial de Lisboa (5.9 per cent).

History & business After the successful launch of Orion Bank, its six shareholders formed Libra Bank as a specialist bank for Latin American business;
they were joined by four other banks. Chase was the bank's biggest shareholder and provided the Managing Directors, on secondment. Libra's aim was
to be an institution combining the full services of an international merchant
bank with specialized knowledge of Latin America and the Caribbean. For its
first decade, one of uninterrupted growth in assets and profits, the principal
activity of the bank was making and managing loans to governmental, corporate and bank borrowers in Latin America. Business development and execution was facilitated by offices in five Latin American cities and New York.
In 1982, and thereafter, Mexico, Argentina, Brazil and other countries negotiated debt rescheduling programmes, in which the bank played its full part.
Loan growth, other than 'new money' facilities, was curtailed and, from
1984, investment banking activities grew rapidly and made a large contribution to earnings. Advice was offered on debt conversion schemes, capital
increases and acquisitions, mainly in Latin America. The bank was a pioneer
and became a market leader in trading developing country debt; in 1989,
volume reached $11.5 billion and fees from investment banking alone cov-
ered operating costs twice. Thereby, the bank was able to build up loan loss
reserves of £193 million out of profits. However, Latin American sovereign
debt constituted over 75 per cent of its assets and the Bank of England's provisioning recommendations, coupled with the weight of non-performing
loans in the run-up to the Brady reschedulings, caused the shareholders to put
up another £248.8 million, in fresh capital and perpetual loans/deposits; as a
result, the shareholders, early in 1990, decided to liquidate the bank, through
a repurchase of loans to cover in full Libra's liabilities.

Personnel *Chairmen* Dr A. Machado Gomez, 1972–78, Sir P. Macadam,
1984–89. *Managing Directors* T.F. Gaffney, 1972–85 (Non-Executive
Director, 1985–89), P.A. Belmont, 1985–89 (General Manager, 1974–85).
Executive Directors F.Z. Haller, K.B. Ramsay, C. Santistevan, 1985–89.

Finances (£ million)

YE 31/12	1973	1974	1975	1976	1977	1978
Total assets	110.6	142.6	172.5	273.9	306.9	449.4
Cap. & reserves	6.6	7.6	9.2	10.8	12.9	15.6
Pre-tax profit	0.6	2.0	3.0	4.2	5.1	7.7
Dividend	0.0	0.0	0.0	0.4	0.4	0.5

YE 31/12	1979	1980	1981	1982	1983	1984
Total assets	519.1	806.6	1245.5	1518.2	1771.4	2320.5
Cap. & reserves	19.3	40.4	51.4	65.3	77.6	92.2
Pre-tax profit	10.2	22.8	27.7	38.5	31.1	42.6
Dividend	0.5	1.1	1.6	1.6	1.5	1.6

YE 31/12	1985	1986	1987	1988	1989
Total assets	1967.3	1965.1	1672.9	1371.0	1241.1
Cap. & reserves	107.6	133.7	140.6	148.1	−203.4
Pre-tax profit	43.0	43.9	16.7	24.3	−559.8
Dividend	1.6	1.6	0.0	0.0	0.0

NOTES: (1) 14 months to 31/12/73. (2) 1980 profit includes £10 468 000 exceptional item. (3) Capital and reserves (1986–89) includes £10 million preference capital subscribed by non-bank institutions; dividend is on equity capital only.

S1/22 LONDON & CONTINENTAL BANKERS
Founded 1973; consortium status to 1990. CH 01722872.

Ownership Initially Deutsche Genossenschaftskasse (DG Bank, 50.2 per cent) and 10 others, none with more than 11 per cent: Andelsbanken, Denmark, Banca Nazionale dell'Agricoltura, Italy, Banque Fédérative du Crédit Mutuel, France, Centrale Rabobank, Netherlands, CERA, Belgium, Crédit Agricole, France, Genossenschaftliche Zentralbank, Austria, Jordbrukets Bank, Sweden, Osuuspankken Keskuspankki Oy, Finland and S.G. Warburg & Co., UK. In 1977, Crédit Agricole increased its stake to 17 per cent (to become the second largest shareholder), when Caisse Centrale des Banques Populaires, France also became a shareholder; at that time, DG Bank's stake was reduced to 35 per cent. S.G. Warburg sold out in 1979; Bondernes Bank, Norway (1980) and Caisse Centrale Desjardins du Québec, Canada (1982) became shareholders. In 1986, DG Bank began the process of buying out all the other shareholders, completing it early in 1990.

History & business The shareholders were predominantly co-operative banks, except S.G. Warburg, which contributed international merchant banking expertise in the formative years. In 1973, the co-operative banks had little international banking experience and they formed this bank to meet their Eurocurrency and international merchant banking needs; it represented a broad commitment of its owners and was not simply a commercial venture. The shareholding banks had millions of customers throughout Western Europe and around 40 000 banking offices, with a business deeply rooted in the trade, industry and agriculture of their countries. The early emphasis of the business was on loans, treasury, underwriting and corporate finance; later, the bank went into leasing, general and agricultural consulting and management buy-outs. The lending strategy was geared to the needs of the shareholders' customers, but the bank also developed significant exposure beyond the borders of Europe. In 1981, it had exposure on over 50 countries (57 per cent Europe and North America, 21 per cent Latin America and 22 per cent other parts of the world), 70 per cent of which had medium- or long-term maturities. Thereafter, merchant banking rather than lending activities was emphasized, but the bank had to make significant provisions on its loans in 1986–89 and reduced its exposure to sovereign debt.

In 1986, Crédit Agricole, the second largest shareholder and one of the largest banks in the world, withdrew because of a strategic change in business policy; subsequently, the other banks were also bought out, enabling DG Bank to recapitalize the bank and integrate it into its own operations, under a new name, DG Investment Bank. Despite the end of the consortium character of this bank, several of the shareholders continued to co-operate closely in the Unico Banking Group, founded in 1977 (see Appendix III).

Personnel *Chairmen* Lord Shawcross, 1974–80, H. Guthardt, 1980–86, G. Schmidt-Weyland, 1986–89, U. Flach, 1989. *Managing Directors* E. Clifton-Brown, 1973–75, B.D. Campbell, 1975–83, G.H. Hoffman, 1975–88 (Vice Chairman and CEO, 1986–88), M.J. Gibbs, 1986–89, Dr F.G. Leitner, 1987–89, F.C. Dietz, 1988–89, R.R. Garnham, 1988–89.

Finances (£ million)

YE 31/3	1974	1975	1976	1977	1978	1979
Total assets	110.0	152.2	184.8	250.3	267.7	278.6
Cap. & reserves	10.7	11.1	11.5	17.6	18.0	18.6
Pre-tax profit	0.6	0.8	1.0	1.3	2.0	2.2
Dividend	0.0	0.0	0.0	0.0	0.5	0.5
YE 31/3	**1980**	**1981**	**1982**	**1983**	**1984**	**1985**
Total assets	303.5	377.1	415.9	534.5	556.6	576.3
Cap. & reserves	24.3	24.4	25.4	25.8	26.5	28.9
Pre-tax profit	1.7	2.4	2.5	2.7	3.1	3.5
Dividend	0.5	1.0	1.0	1.0	0.3	0.5
YE 31/3 & 31/12	**1986**	**1986**	**1987**	**1988**	**1989**	
Total assets	544.0	383.2	292.5	240.1	291.8	
Cap. & reserves	30.6	30.7	31.2	30.3	29.6	
Pre-tax profit	4.0	0.3	−14.3	−0.3	−17.8	
Dividend	0.7	0.0	0.0	0.0	0.0	

NOTES: (1) 9 months to 31/3/74. (2) 12 months to 31/3/86, 9 months to 31/12/86; thereafter 12 months to 31/12.

S1/23 LONDON INTERSTATE BANK
Founded 1971; consortium status to 1984. CH 00992750.

Ownership Initially five US regional banks and one London merchant bank, each with 16.7 per cent: First National Bank of Atlanta, First Western Bank & Trust, Los Angeles, Indiana National Bank, Maryland National Bank, Mercantile Trust Company, St Louis, with Keyser Ullman. Of the founders, First National, First Western (after being acquired by Lloyds Bank), Mercantile and Keyser Ullman dropped out, while Hamburgische Landesbank Girozentrale bought and sold a holding during the 1970s. By 1982, the bank was owned equally by two of the founders, Indiana National and Maryland National, and by two Scandinavian banks, Götabanken, Sweden,

and Sparekassen SDS, Denmark, which bought out its three fellow shareholders in September 1984.

History & business The business was short- and medium-term lending,
mainly in Eurocurrencies, trade finance, deposits and foreign exchange; in
1980, leasing and hire purchase were added. At first, the bank had a clear
geographical focus in that over 80 per cent of the capital was owned by five
US regional banks, none of them with London branches; thus, the bank was
an 'important extension to their international capabilities.' Over the years,
the ownership changes affected the pattern of the bank's business, with more
emphasis on the UK, Germany and Scandinavia. Large syndicated loans
were avoided and the focus was on Eurocurrency services provided to the
bank's shareholders and their customers; maturities were kept short, 55 per
cent of the loan portfolio maturing in less than 12 months in 1981.
Although about 20 per cent of its exposure was to Latin America in
1982–83, the shareholders took over the doubtful debts and the bank continued to increase its profits after coming under single ownership in 1984.

Personnel *Chairmen* I.I. Stoutzker, 1971–75, B.S. Barnes, 1975–78,
W. Griffin Morrel, Jr, 1978–82, R.H. Kohrs, 1982–84. *Managing Directors*
J.A. Pell, 1971–78, R.N. Bee, 1978–84.

Finances (£ million)

YE 31/3	1972	1973	1974	1975	1976	1977	1978
Total assets	40.9	53.4	66.4	45.9	52.1	63.4	77.5
Cap. & reserves	2.6	2.7	2.9	3.0	6.3	6.0	6.1
Pre-tax profit	0.1	0.1	0.3	0.0	0.2	0.4	0.3
Dividend	0.0	0.0	0.0	0.0	0.0	0.0	0.0

YE 31/3	1979	1980	1981	1982	1983	1984
Total assets	85.9	92.1	104.5	134.3	155.0	171.0
Cap. & reserves	6.5	6.7	7.1	7.6	8.0	8.3
Pre-tax profit	0.4	0.5	0.6	0.7	0.9	0.9
Dividend	0.0	0.0	0.0	0.0	0.0	0.0

NOTE: 13 months to 31/3/72.

S1/24 LONDON MULTINATIONAL BANK
Founded 1970; consortium status to 1977. CH 00978945.

Ownership Chemical Bank, New York, Crédit Suisse (30 per cent each),
Northern Trust, Chicago and Baring Brothers & Co (20 per cent each). In
1977, Chemical bought out its fellow shareholders.

History & business Describing itself as 'the multinational merchant
bank' ('Multibank'), it engaged in short- and medium-term finance, private
placements, foreign exchange, Eurocurrency deposits, management, underwriting and distribution of public issues of securities. Its customers were

commercial companies, financial institutions, governments and governmental agencies. Multibank pioneered the concept of issuing Eurobonds on behalf of UK local authorities, managing issues for Bristol and several others in 1973. It established associated companies with operations in Hong Kong, Singapore and Kuala Lumpur, in conjunction with Sanwa Bank and others. Its first chairman, Lord Cromer, was a former governor of the Bank of England and, between 1971 and 1974, British Ambassador to the USA. Its managing director, John Hyde, was the first chairman of the Association of Consortium Banks when it was established in London, in 1975. In the mid-1970s, it became evident that more capital would be needed to develop the business; Chemical and Crédit Suisse were much larger than the other two shareholder banks and, in any event, each of them felt less need for this bank than at its foundation. Thus, Chemical Bank bought out the other three, with the aim that it might play a leading role in Chemical's worldwide merchant banking activities.

Personnel *Chairmen* Lord Cromer, 1970 and 1974–77, A. Carnwath, 1971–74. *Managing Director* J.B. Hyde, 1970–77.

Finances (£ million)

YE 31/10	1970	1971	1972	1973	1974	1975	1976	1977
Total assets	27.2	121.1	173.2	225.9	258.3	327.6	420.4	416.3
Cap. & reserves	2.0	4.3	4.9	5.5	6.1	7.0	8.2	7.7
Pre-tax profit	0.0	0.5	1.1	1.5	1.6	2.2	2.6	2.7
Dividend	0.0	0.0	0.1	0.1	0.2	0.2	0.2	1.8

NOTE: 6 months to 31/10/70.

S1/25 MIDLAND & INTERNATIONAL BANKS
Founded 1964; consortium status to 1983. CH 00791766.

Ownership Midland Bank (45 per cent), Toronto Dominion Bank (26 per cent), Commercial Bank of Australia (10 per cent) and Standard Bank (19 per cent), which bought out its partners in 1983.

History & business The bank, generally known as MAIBL, was set up by four British Commonwealth banks, so that 'wherever appropriate, they could jointly undertake international financial business.' It would 'provide finance for periods which would not suit the commercial banking system,' as Midland Bank described it in 1965. It became the first of the London-based consortium banks to participate in the Euromarkets. The main thrust of the business was in the area of medium-term loans in sterling and other currencies to borrowers all over the world; loans were commonly syndicated among the bank's shareholders. The bank was also active in the treasury area and in leasing. A notable activity was the ownership, since early in its history, by MAIBL of shares in its own shareholders; these shares were sold very favourably in September 1978, the proceeds being added to inner reserves. Until 1979, MAIBL was able to build up undisclosed reserves, so that its profit & loss statements were not comparable to those of other consortium banks. The results for 1982–83 were affected by the need for provisions, in the light of world recession and liquidity problems for sovereign borrowers. The bank's first chief executive was a former Midland Bank manager and the bank's chairmen were all chairmen of Midland Bank; its deputy chairman from 1975 to 1983 was Lord Barber, UK chancellor of the exchequer (1970–74). In February 1983, MAIBL was acquired in its entirety by Standard Chartered Merchant Bank, a subsidiary of one of its shareholders; the latter planned to complement the lending strengths of MAIBL with its own fee-earning activities.

Personnel *Chairmen* Sir A. Forbes, 1964–76, Lord Armstrong of Sanderstead, 1976–80, Sir David Barran, 1980–82, Sir Donald Barron, 1982–83. *Chief Executives* H.J. Witheridge, General Manager, 1964–71 (Director, 1971), J.H. Jennings, General Manager & Director, 1972 (Managing Director, 1973–83, Vice Chairman, 1983).

Finances (£ million)

YE 31/3	1966	1967	1968	1969	1970	1971
Total assets	182.8	224.5	324.2	399.1	483.4	491.3
Cap. & reserves	*10.0*	*10.5*	*10.6*	*10.7*	*10.8*	*11.4*
Profit	*0.4*	*0.4*	*0.6*	*0.6*	*0.6*	*1.4*
Dividend	0.2	0.3	0.5	0.5	0.5	0.8
YE 31/3	**1972**	**1973**	**1974**	**1975**	**1976**	**1977**
Total assets	490.5	491.5	587.2	654.4	799.0	895.7
Cap. & reserves	*12.2*	*13.2*	*21.1*	*22.2*	*23.6*	*25.4*
Profit	*1.8*	*1.8*	*1.6*	*2.0*	*2.4*	*2.9*
Dividend	1.0	0.8	0.7	0.9	1.0	1.1
YE 31/3 & 6/2	**1978**	**1979**	**1980**	**1981**	**1982**	**1983**
Total assets	940.0	976.6	1118.1	1236.1	1396.3	1693.6
Cap. & reserves	*29.6*	*32.3*	39.8	45.0	49.9	45.7
Profit	*3.8*	*4.4*	10.6	11.3	6.9	7.9
Dividend	1.7	1.8	2.0	2.2	2.5	11.0

NOTES: (1) The use of *italics* for capital & reserves and profit for the periods to 31/3/79 indicates that they are stated after transfers to undisclosed contingency reserves; the UK Companies Acts allowed certain UK banks, formed before 1967, to use this practice, though disclosed profits were expected to reflect the actual trends. From 1980, profits are stated pre-tax and capital & reserves include minority interests. (2) Dividends were expressed net of tax in 1966–68. (3) 10 months to 6/2/83.

S1/26 NORDIC BANK
Founded 1971; consortium status to 1984. CH 01974499.

Ownership Initially, Den norske Creditbank, Norway, Kansallis–Osake–Pankki, Finland and Svenska Handelsbanken, Sweden (33.33 per cent each);

in 1977, Copenhagen Handelsbank subscribed to a 25 per cent share, and the share of the other three banks was reduced to 25 per cent each. Between December 1983 and February 1984, Den norske Creditbank acquired 100 per cent of the shares.

History & business Short- and medium-term Eurocurrency and sterling facilities, project and export finance, treasury and foreign exchange, corporate finance, investment banking and leasing. In 1978, its size was greatly increased through the acquisition of 60 per cent of Nordfinanz Bank, Zurich, one of the major foreign banks in Switzerland; 45 per cent of this stake was sold in 1983, reducing the balance sheet in that year, when the bank ceased to be a consortium bank. A lot of business was with Nordic customers and currencies. Special expertise was developed in oil, forestry and, also, shipping, which necessitated provisions, in 1983, because of low cargo rates. It became active in derivatives and was the only consortium bank to be listed as doing more than 2 per cent of LIFFE's turnover in 1983. The bank had significant operations and representation in the Asia–Pacific area. Den norske Creditbank bought out its partners, because they all had developed their own international banking operations. Moreover, as the largest bank in Norway, it needed its own presence in London, a major centre for oil and shipping business; these were central sectors of the Norwegian economy and constituted a significant part of the bank's client base.

Personnel *Chairmen* J. Melander, 1971–73, M. Virkkunen, 1973–75, J. Wallander, 1975–77, J. Melander, 1977–79, H.E. Johansen, 1979–81, V. Makkonen, 1981–83, J. Ekman, 1983, L.T. Loddesol, 1983–84. *Managing Directors* D.W.C. Allen, 1971–76 (Vice Chairman, 1976–83), J.R. Sclater, 1976–84. *Deputy Managing Directors* J. Ankarcrona, 1976–83, B.P. Hudson, 1981–84, J.N. Simpson, 1981–84, W.H. Main, 1981–82, S. Wessel-Aas, 1983–84.

Finances (£ million)

YE 31/12	1971	1972	1973	1974	1975	1976	1977
Total assets	51.2	99.1	166.9	209.2	253.1	333.7	457.9
Cap. & reserves	3.0	3.3	6.8	8.6	9.3	9.7	13.7
Pre-tax profit	0.1	0.5	1.0	1.7	1.6	0.9	2.2
Dividend	0.0	0.0	0.0	0.0	0.0	0.0	0.3

YE 31/12	1978	1979	1980	1981	1982	1983
Total assets	1069.1	1227.1	1441.2	1941.6	2167.1	1405.7
Cap. & reserves	66.9	70.0	73.7	95.4	102.2	72.2
Pre-tax profit	3.3	10.0	12.0	12.4	9.5	6.1
Dividend	0.5	1.8	2.1	2.8	0.0	0.0

NOTE: 10 months to 31/12/71.

S1/27 ORION BANK
Founded 1970; consortium status to 1981. CH 00995939.

Ownership Chase Manhattan Bank, National Westminster Bank, Royal Bank of Canada, Westdeutsche Landesbank Girozentrale (initially 23.25 per cent, later 20 per cent each), Credito Italiano (initially 7 per cent, later 10 per cent) and Mitsubishi Bank, which joined the shareholding group in 1972 (10 per cent). The other shareholders were bought out by Royal Bank of Canada in June 1981, which injected its London Eurocurrency lending business and changed the name to Orion Royal Bank.

History, business & personnel International investment banking, as described elsewhere in this book.

Finances (£ million)

YE 31/12	1971	1972	1973	1974	1975	1976
Total assets	174.4	338.5	547.3	550.0	717.2	998.3
Cap. & reserves	10.9	12.8	16.7	23.7	27.3	35.9
Pre-tax profit	0.8	1.5	1.6	4.9	7.4	9.7
Dividend	0.0	0.0	0.0	0.0	0.0	0.8
YE 31/12 & 30/9	1977	1978	1979	1980	1981	
Total assets	1025.6	1115.3	1231.9	1283.2	1939.2	
Cap. & reserves	39.9	46.8	52.9	57.6	60.8	
Pre-tax profit	10.2	10.1	8.5	7.2	4.2	
Dividend	0.8	0.8	0.8	0.8	3.0	

NOTES: (1) 9 months to 30/9/81. (2) There were two operating entities, Orion Bank and Orion Termbank in 1971–73; their figures are combined here. Fuller financial information is given in Appendix III, also for the period after 1981, when it was a subsidiary of Royal Bank of Canada.

S1/28 PK CHRISTIANIA BANK (UK)
Founded 1978; consortium status 1982–86. CH 01150715.

Ownership Initially 100 per cent subsidiary of PKbanken, Sweden; in April 1982, Christiania Bank og Kreditkasse, Norway took a 50 per cent stake, with PKbanken retaining 50 per cent. It became a wholly owned subsidiary of Christiania Bank in 1986.

History & business In December 1981, PKbanken and Christiania Bank og Kreditkasse decided to merge their overseas subsidiaries, to provide a strong international banking force with a Scandinavian accent. Between them, they then had a presence in the USA, Germany, France, Luxembourg, Hong Kong, Singapore, Brazil and, through this consortium bank, the UK. PKbanken was then the largest Swedish bank, measured by deposits, and was 84 per cent owned by the Kingdom of Sweden; on the other hand, Christiania Bank, the only bank with offices in all of Norway's counties, was entirely privately owned. PK Christiania Bank (UK) was created as a consortium bank from PKbanken's UK existing licensed deposit taker and securities firm, PKB Investments. By the end of 1983, it could claim to be conducting a 'full investment and commercial banking activity' in London; the client base was mainly, though not exclusively, Scandinavian in character. The two shareholders supported a rapid growth in the bank, subscribing to capital increases in 1984 and 1986, as well as subordinated loans. In the treasury area, the bank became very active in swaps and futures, joining LIFFE in 1985. The two shareholders had decided, in their co-operative agreement, to devolve their various capital markets activities to the bank, which became very active in that area; for example, in 1985, it was in the management group of 106 Eurobond issues and began trading in Scandinavian equities. In the same year, so as to support the capital markets business, the bank opened a representative office in Tokyo. Its financing business included specialization in shipping and project finance, export finance, counter trade services, forfaiting (mainly with Eastern Europe), guarantees and leasing. The rapid growth in the bank's business, coupled with the need for more capital and the need for loan loss provisions, caused the shareholders to review the ownership structure. In July 1986, it was taken over by Christiania Bank, and, in 1987, it was placed into members' voluntary liquidation, in order to be transformed into a Christiania Bank branch. An indemnity against potential losses on loans with a net book value of £24 million was given by the bank.

Personnel *Chairmen* B. Danielsson, 1982–83 and 1985–86, T. Moursond, 1984–85. *Managing Directors* N. Vitelli, 1982–84, G. Ljungdahl, 1984–86.

Finances (£ million)

YE 31/12	1982	1983	1984	1985	1986
Total assets	233.8	321.4	428.9	517.4	486.7
Cap. & reserves	13.5	14.4	20.0	20.8	12.8
Pre-tax profit	1.2	1.9	1.0	1.4	−11.6
Dividend	0.0	0.8	0.0	0.0	0.0

S1/29 ROTHSCHILD INTERCONTINENTAL BANK
Founded 1966; consortium status to 1975. CH 00883476.

Ownership Initially, a 50/50 joint venture between National Provincial Bank and London merchant bankers, N.M. Rothschild & Sons. In 1968, Rothschilds brought in as shareholders fellow members of the 'Five Arrows' group, Banque Privée, Switzerland, Pierson Heldring & Pierson, the Netherlands, Banque Lambert, Belgium and Banque Rothschild, France. In October 1969, National Provincial's successor, National Westminster Bank, sold its shares and the bank was renamed Rothschild Intercontinental Bank; then, First City National Bank of Houston, Seattle First National Bank and National City Bank of Cleveland each acquired stakes of 12.5 per cent. Later, minority stakes were acquired by Industrial Bank of Japan, Sal Oppenheim Jr & Cie, Germany and Eagle Star Insurance Group, UK. The bank was effectively controlled by the 'Five Arrows' group until acquired by American Express Company in September 1975, when its name changed to Amex Bank Limited.

History & business Eurocurrency, sterling and DM banking. Its main activities were short- and medium-term lending, directly and through syndications, treasury, trusteeships, investment holding, underwriting and dealing; the bank had a relatively small role in the Eurobond market, in which its shareholders in the 'Five Arrows' group had a strong position. For Rothschilds, it provided possible access to investment banking opportunities from major commercial banks; after 1969, it provided London representation and access to the Eurocurrency market for its three US bank shareholders, which were the leading banks in their regions of the USA, and the intangible benefit of association with the house of Rothschild. The bank's lending operations were primarily directed to borrowers in the UK, continental Europe and the Far East; the bank specialized in loans to certain industries, such as shipping and natural resources. The bank depended on the inter-bank market less than some other consortium banks, having developed good relations with a number of central banks around the world.

Personnel *Chairmen* D.J. Robarts, 1968, L. de Rothschild 1969–75. *Deputy Chairman* M. Bucks, 1971–75. *Director and General Manager* Hon T. Stonor (Lord Camoys), 1968–75 (Managing Director, 1970–75). *Deputy Managing Directors* N.D. Peers, 1971–74, P.L. Macdougall, 1971–75.

Finances (£ million)

YE 30/9	1968	1969	1970	1971	1972	1973	1974	1975
Total assets	107.8	135.4	131.8	185.8	240.0	347.9	384.0	358.4
Cap. & reserves	1.8	2.0	2.2	4.7	6.3	8.8	11.3	13.5
Pre-tax profit	0.3	0.4	0.6	1.0	1.5	2.3	1.4	2.3
Dividend	0.0	0.0	0.0	0.1	0.1	0.1	0.1	0.0

NOTE: 15 months to 31/12/75.

S1/30 SAUDI INTERNATIONAL BANK
Founded 1975. CH 01223938.

Ownership Saudi Arabian Monetary Agency (SAMA) (50 per cent), Riyad Bank and National Commercial Bank, Saudi Arabia (2.5 per cent each), Morgan Guaranty Trust Company of New York (JP Morgan, 20 per cent), Bank of Tokyo, Banque Nationale de Paris, Deutsche Bank, National Westminster Bank and Union Bank of Switzerland (5 per cent each). Ownership was unchanged until 1999, when the bank merged with Gulf International Bank (S2/15); the merged bank was then 72.5 per cent owned by GIB's owner, Gulf Investment Corporation, a consortium investment company, owned by the six GCC countries, 22.2 per cent by SAMA and 5.3 per cent by JP Morgan.

History & business Al-Bank Al-Saudi Al-Alami Limited (the legal name for the generally known Saudi International Bank) was established in London to be the international bank with special expertise in Saudi Arabia; its activities spanned capital markets, corporate finance, fund management, treasury and banking. It was a major manager of Saudi-owned investments and of loans for Saudi energy projects; it was a leading market-maker in the Saudi Riyal. Its top management was supplied by JP Morgan. In 1983, the bank subscribed to 10 per cent of a new bank, United Saudi Commercial Bank, Riyadh, and provided technical assistance to it; in 1994, this holding was sold. In the late 1980s, significant loan loss provisions were made and shareholder support provided, through new capital, perpetual loans and the purchase of non-performing loans. Thereafter, the focus of the bank moved more towards fee-earning business, while the loan portfolio was reduced. Its main shareholder, SAMA, was the Saudi central banking organization, and its first chairman was the then minister of finance, Sheikh Mohammed Abalkhail, who resigned in 1987, but became chairman again in 1996; the chairman for the intervening period was Sheikh Abdul Aziz Al-Quraishi, former governor of SAMA. Also on the board, successively, were former governors of the Bank of England, Lord O'Brien and Lord Richardson. The bank had a presence in New York and Tokyo. Of the merger with GIB, the chairman said 'the opportunities afforded by the merger of our investment banking business with Gulf International Bank's wholesale lending business are exciting.'

Personnel *Chairmen* M. Abalkhail, 1975–87 and 1996–99, A. Al-Quraishi, 1987–96. *Executive Directors and Chief Executive Officers* E.C. Felton, 1975–80, A. Prindl, 1980–82, P.J. de Roos, 1982–95, R.J. McGinn, 1995–99.

Finances (£ million)

YE 31/12	1975	1976	1977	1978	1979	1980
Total assets	13.1	227.6	416.5	487.7	785.2	1228.2
Cap. & reserves	12.5	13.3	26.3	27.8	41.6	55.7
Pre-tax profit	0.4	1.8	1.4	3.1	5.5	7.4
Dividend	0.0	0.0	0.0	0.0	0.8	1.3

YE 31/12	1981	1982	1983	1984	1985	1986
Total assets	2021.7	2531.7	2772.8	3044.8	3064.8	3226.9
Cap. & reserves	60.9	77.3	99.9	109.0	135.6	141.8
Pre-tax profit	9.9	15.3	20.3	23.3	19.1	17.8
Dividend	2.0	3.0	3.8	4.5	4.5	4.0

YE 31/12	1987	1988	1989	1990	1991	1992
Total assets	2350.0	2553.2	2562.5	2229.7	2413.6	2725.4
Cap. & reserves	138.3	143.8	132.1	134.3	140.4	147.7
Pre-tax profit	−44.5	11.0	−10.9	2.5	3.1	14.0
Dividend	0.0	2.6	0.0	0.0	0.0	2.0

YE 31/12	1993	1994	1995	1996	1997	1998
Total assets	3069.9	3231.7	3236.4	3094.6	3095.1	2989.6
Cap. & reserves	158.6	172.4	188.5	203.9	219.0	227.9
Pre-tax profit	23.9	72.1	35.2	35.3	32.2	14.6
Dividend	5.0	6.0	7.0	8.0	8.0	4.0

NOTES: (1) 3 months to 31/12/75. (2) 1994 profit includes £44 million gain on sale of holding in United Saudi Commercial Bank.

S1/31 SCANDINAVIAN BANK
Founded 1969; consortium status to 1990. CH 02041441.

Ownership Initially, Skandinaviska Enskilda Banken, Sweden, Bergens Privatbank (later Bergen Bank), Nordiska Foreningsbanken (later Union Bank of Finland), Den Danske Landmansbank and Den Danske Provinsbank, Landsbanki Islands, Iceland (in 1971) and Skånska Banken, Sweden (in 1972) became shareholders, with less than 5 per cent each. From 1969 to 1987, Skandinaviska's stake varied between 33 per cent and 46 per cent, those of Bergen and Union between 19 per cent and 27 per cent each. In 1983, the two Danish banks and, in 1985, Skånska sold out; in 1985, Privatbanken, Denmark bought a 10 per cent stake. In March 1987, the bank offered 36 per cent of its capital on the International Stock Exchange, London; in February 1990, the bank shareholders (Skandinaviska, Bergen, Union, Privatbanken and Landsbanki) bought back the publicly held shares; later, in the same year, Skandinaviska bought out its partners.

History & business Trade and medium-term finance, foreign exchange and treasury, securities underwriting, dealing and advice, fund management and trust business. Business connected with the Nordic countries was of particular importance. It opened its first overseas offices, in Hong Kong and Bahrain, in 1974 and established a presence in 11 other countries. Its size was greatly increased, in 1982, by the acquisition of 66 per cent (later 76 per cent) of Banque Scandinave en Suisse. By the late 1980s, it could claim to be one of the top 20 international banking groups in London; it was providing a wide range of financial, investment and merchant banking services to private and institutional customers in the UK and overseas, without loss of its Scandinavian emphasis. At the same time, traditional commercial banking activities were de-emphasized, £52 million having to be provided for in 1987 and 1989, mainly for Latin American and other non-performing loans. For the 1987 flotation, which raised £28 million for expansion from 10 000 investors, a unique structure was established; the bank's Sterling capital was divided into units of four currencies, to reflect the overall mix of its business. The shares were issued at 210 pence and soon rose to 288, but were hit by 'the double whammy of the October 1987 crash and third world debt write-off,' as the *Investors Chronicle* put it. By December 1989, the shares had fallen to 133, when the five shareholding banks offered to buy them for 225, which they did early in 1990. It was at first announced that the bank would continue as an autonomous bank, but major mergers among Scandinavian banks (including Bergen Bank and Privatbanken), in anticipation of the single market in Europe, influenced the decision for one bank, Skandinaviska, to buy out the others later in 1990.

Personnel *Chairmen* L.E. Thunholm, 1969–84, C.G. Olsson, 1984–87, E.G. Greve, 1987–89. *Managing Directors* S.G. Malmberg, 1969–71, J.S. Gadd, 1971–80 (also Chief Executive), G.F. Bouton (also Group Chief Executive), 1980–89, D.J. Hughes, 1973–80, D.M. Johnson, 1976–87.

Finances (£ million)

YE 31/12	1969	1970	1971	1972	1973	1974
Total assets	66.6	114.8	149.4	219.4	296.8	344.0
Cap. & reserves	2.0	3.5	6.2	6.8	11.0	18.2
Pre-tax profit	0.1	0.7	1.3	1.6	2.2	3.2
Dividend	0.0	0.0	0.0	0.3	0.4	0.4

YE 31/12	1975	1976	1977	1978	1979	1980
Total assets	501.5	729.8	851.9	1026.3	1121.5	1271.9
Cap. & reserves	25.9	28.3	30.8	33.4	46.3	49.0
Pre-tax profit	4.8	6.5	7.3	8.3	9.3	10.3
Dividend	0.6	0.8	1.2	1.6	1.6	2.4

YE 31/12	1981	1982	1983	1984	1985	1986
Total assets	1397.3	2002.4	2496.1	3000.8	3267.9	3512.8
Cap. & reserves	59.7	113.7	119.2	124.8	128.5	147.9
Pre-tax profit	11.4	13.2	10.2	12.1	14.2	26.4
Dividend	2.4	3.1	3.1	3.3	3.9	3.9

YE 31/12	1987	1988	1989
Total assets	3255.6	3139.0	3128.5
Cap & reserves	148.8	143.7	148.6
Pre-tax profit	−0.6	23.6	−3.2
Dividend	6.4	6.8	2.4

NOTE: 6 months to 31/12/69.

S1/32 UBAF BANK
BRITISH ARAB COMMERCIAL BANK
Founded 1972. CH 02139145.

Ownership Initially Union de Banques Arabes et Françaises, France (UBAF) 50 per cent, Central Bank of Libya 25 per cent and Midland Bank 25 per cent; early in the bank's history, UBAF and the Central Bank of Libya were replaced by Ubic Nederland, a holding company for the Arab shareholders of UBAF, and Libyan Arab Foreign Bank (LAFB). Between 1990 and 1995, Ubic sold its 50 per cent shareholding in stages; four of Ubic's banks became direct shareholders, namely Bank Al-Maghrib, Banque Extérieure d'Algérie, Central Bank of Egypt and Rafidain Bank, Iraq, while the HSBC Group increased its holding to 46.5 per cent (Midland Bank, 41.5 per cent, and British Bank of the Middle East, 5 per cent). The name was changed, in 1996, to British Arab Commercial Bank.

History & business UBAF Bank was founded as the London arm of the UBAF consortium group (S2/20); its business was commercial banking, medium-term financing and treasury activities, with special emphasis on financing trade between the Arab world, the UK and Europe. In the late 1980s, the bank made large provisions against sovereign debt exposure and was recapitalized by its shareholders. New activities were developed in the 1990s, such as leasing and property finance; a trade finance agency product was launched in 1998, together with other new marketing initiatives.

Personnel *Chairmen* M.M. Abushadi, 1972–93, R.A. Misellati, 1993–95, J.A.P. Hill, 1995–present. *Executive Directors* A. Saudi, 1972–81, A. Al-Sherif, 1981–87. *General Manager* W. Cronk, 1972–76. *Chief Executives* C. Burkin, 1977–84, P.J.W. Taplin, 1984–97, R. Shaw, 1997–present. *Deputy Chief Executive and General Manager* M. Fezzani, 1984–present.

Finances (£ million)

YE 31/12	1972	1973	1974	1975	1976	1977
Total assets	60.7	161.0	208.3	256.0	373.1	431.4
Cap. & reserves	2.0	5.2	5.8	5.9	11.7	12.4
Pre-tax profit	0.0	0.5	1.1	0.9	2.3	2.8
Dividend	0.0	0.0	0.0	0.3	0.3	0.6

YE 31/12	1978	1979	1980	1981	1982	1983
Total assets	471.9	473.1	550.1	687.0	860.7	1170.5
Cap. & reserves	13.2	20.4	21.5	28.4	35.0	51.1
Pre-tax profit	3.1	4.8	5.0	7.5	9.2	12.1
Dividend	0.7	1.0	1.4	1.7	2.6	2.9

YE 31/12	1984	1985	1986	1987	1988	1989
Total assets	1204.7	1181.4	1060.1	930.6	937.0	1012.1
Cap. & reserves	53.3	61.1	67.2	2.6	54.8	11.6
Pre-tax profit	14.3	11.4	10.4	−84.5	4.5	−51.2
Dividend	3.4	3.9	0.0	0.0	0.0	0.0

YE 31/12	1990	1991	1992	1993	1994	1995
Total assets	665.9	644.3	837.1	784.8	893.1	972.8
Cap. & reserves	59.4	61.7	87.5	100.8	108.4	116.1
Pre-tax profit	2.8	6.4	17.4	27.2	28.6	36.7
Dividend	0.0	0.0	0.0	5.0	10.0	15.0

YE 31/12	1996	1997	1998
Total assets	1267.0	1309.1	1274.6
Cap. & reserves	117.7	118.5	118.9
Pre-tax profit	17.8	17.9	20.4
Dividend	10.0	12.0	14.1

NOTE: 9 months to 31/12/72.

S1/33 UNITED BANK OF KUWAIT
Founded 1966. CH 00877859.

Ownership Initially five Kuwaiti financial institutions, one of which, National Bank of Kuwait, dropped out when it opened a London branch. Over the years, there have been other changes in ownership, which has remained exclusively Kuwaiti; at the end of 1998, UBK's principal shareholders were The Public Institution for Social Security, an agency of the State of Kuwait, Gulf Projects Investment Company, The Gulf Bank, The Commercial Bank of Kuwait, Alahli Bank of Kuwait and Kuwait Real Estate Bank.

History and business UBK was established to serve the overseas banking, treasury and investment needs of Kuwaiti institutions (of both the public and private sectors) and individuals. Its first Chairman, Abdlatif Al-Hamad, had served as Director General of the Kuwait Fund for Arab Development and as Kuwait's Minister of Finance; Fahad Al-Rajaan is Director General of The Public Institute for Social Security, a major governmental institution in Kuwait. In 1982, it was a founder member of the London International Financial Futures Exchange. In 1990, UBK played a major role in supporting the Kuwaiti community during Iraq's occupation of Kuwait. Its main business areas have been commercial and private banking, asset management, Islamic investment banking and property finance; while most of it had a Kuwaiti character, there has also been a significant amount of non-Kuwaiti business, such as UK commercial and residential property finance. The 1998 results were affected adversely by the volatility in global markets. The bank had representation in New York, Dubai and Kuwait; in March 1999, UBK announced the acquisition of 22.7 per cent of Alahli Commercial Bank, Bahrain.

Personnel *Chairmen* A.Y. Al-Hamad, 1966–81, S.F. Al-Marzouk, 1981–83, F.M. Al-Rajaan, 1983–present. *General Managers/CEOs* T.M. Tagg, 1966–72, D.J. West, 1972–86, C. Keen 1986–98, David Witham (Acting) 1998, Adel El Labban, 1999–present.

Finances (£ million)

YE 31/12	1966	1967	1968	1969	1970	1971
Total assets	2.1	42.1	116.8	149.0	204.7	222.9
Cap. & reserves	1.0	1.0	1.3	1.4	1.6	1.7
Pre-tax profit	0.0	0.1	0.1	0.2	0.3	0.3
Dividend	0.0	0.0	0.0	0.0	0.0	0.0

YE 31/12	1972	1973	1974	1975	1976	1977
Total assets	212.4	239.4	265.7	321.8	400.6	401.4
Cap. & reserves	2.0	2.3	2.5	4.8	7.3	7.5
Pre-tax profit	0.3	0.4	0.6	1.2	1.4	1.3
Dividend	0.0	0.0	0.0	0.3	0.3	0.3

YE 31/12	1978	1979	1980	1981	1982	1983
Total assets	396.4	450.5	478.9	642.5	1232.3	1611.0
Cap. & reserves	7.5	17.0	21.1	24.0	46.7	61.3
Pre-tax profit	−0.2	2.7	4.4	4.9	10.9	10.1
Dividend	0.3	0.0	0.7	0.0	0.0	0.0

YE 31/12	1984	1985	1986	1987	1988	1989
Total assets	1899.9	2266.2	2316.8	2001.6	2321.0	2272.5
Cap. & reserves	69.2	74.6	95.7	115.6	117.2	120.3
Pre-tax profit	10.8	12.4	15.3	1.1	2.1	4.1
Dividend	0.0	5.8	7.1	0.0	0.0	0.0

YE 31/12	1990	1991	1992	1993	1994	1995
Total assets	1959.6	1723.3	1923.1	1903.6	1843.4	1840.0
Cap. & reserves	110.4	121.0	128.5	131.0	131.8	132.1
Pre-tax profit	5.5	10.1	10.3	14.6	15.1	12.1
Dividend	0.0	0.0	0.0	7.7	10.4	7.7

YE 31/12	1996	1997	1998
Total assets	1754.0	1798.0	1467.8
Cap. & reserves	132.6	133.3	134.5
Pre-tax profit	15.7	19.4	−9.0
Dividend	10.7	13.1	0.0

NOTE: 8 months to 31/12/66.

S1/34 UNITED INTERNATIONAL BANK

Founded 1970; consortium status to 1979. CH 00984871.

Ownership Banco de Bilbao (which acquired the shareholding of one of the founders, Banco di Roma, in 1972), Bank Mees & Hope, Netherlands, Bank of Nova Scotia, Banque Française du Commerce Extérieur, Bayerische Hypotheken- und Wechsel-Bank, Crédit du Nord, France, Crocker National Bank, USA, Sveriges Kreditbank, Williams & Glyn's Bank and Privatbanken, Denmark (10 per cent each); the latter bought out its fellow shareholders in 1979.

History & business The main areas of business were medium- and short-term Eurocurrency loans and treasury; Eurobonds, corporate finance and private placements were other areas of business. In the bank's early years, natural resources lending and shipping were important parts of its exposure. In 1974, soon after the oil price rises, the bank opened a representative office in the United Arab Emirates. Its main aims were to generate infrastructural loans to public and private sector Gulf borrowers and to gain access to Gulf surpluses. In 1977, it set up a Jersey subsidiary and launched the United International Bond Fund, aimed particularly at investors in the OPEC countries. Sir Norman Biggs, a past Chairman of Esso Petroleum, was Chairman of the bank and its UK shareholder, Williams & Glyn's Bank; the other shareholders were also represented on the board at Chairman or CEO level. The Chief Executive, Alberto Weissmüller, was well known as an authority on consortium banks, later becoming an adviser to the Bank of England. By 1977, lending margins were being reduced and the bank held back the growth of its loan portfolio in the light of the extended maturities then becoming prevalent in the Eurocurrency loan market; thus the bank's profitability was diminished. Moreover, the shareholders were becoming involved in the same areas as the bank. Privatbanken's acquisition of the bank in 1979 enabled the Danish bank to extend the range of its services and improve co-ordination between its offices in Copenhagen, New York, Luxembourg and London. It was the only Nordic bank at the time to have a wholly owned subsidiary in London and could promote itself as 'the Danish Bank in London'.

Personnel *Chairmen* Sir N.P. Biggs, 1971–79, A. Schmiegelow, 1979. *Chief Executive and Managing Director* A.A. Weissmüller, 1971–79.

Finances (£ million)

YE 31/12	1971	1972	1973	1974	1975
Total assets	45.3	127.7	162.3	163.5	181.2
Cap. & reserves	4.0	4.3	4.4	6.5	6.8
Pre-tax profit	0.2	0.4	0.7	1.0	1.2
Dividend	0.0	0.0	0.1	0.2	0.2

YE 31/12	1976	1977	1978	1979
Total assets	216.0	222.5	239.8	260.0
Cap. & reserves	7.3	7.8	8.7	9.1
Pre-tax profit	1.7	1.6	1.6	0.8
Dividend	0.3	0.3	0.3	0.0

NOTE: 15 months to 31/12/71.

S1/35 WESTERN AMERICAN BANK (EUROPE)
BANK OF TOKYO AND DETROIT (INTERNATIONAL)
Founded 1967, consortium status to 1980. CH 00924205.

Ownership The bank was founded by Security Pacific National Bank, Los Angeles, Wells Fargo Bank, San Francisco, National Bank of Detroit (24 per cent each) and Hambros Bank, UK (28 per cent); in 1972, Bank of Tokyo became a 22.5 per cent shareholder, the US banks reducing their stakes to 22.5 per cent each and Hambros to 10 per cent. In 1975, Hambros sold its remaining shares in equal proportions to the other shareholders. In 1978, the bank was taken over by Bank of Tokyo (75 per cent) and National

Bank of Detroit (25 per cent) and renamed Bank of Tokyo and Detroit (International) and, in 1980, by Bank of Tokyo alone and renamed Bank of Tokyo International (see S2/10 for its sister bank in Paris).

History & business The bank grew rapidly in the first five years of its existence and became an early leader among London consortium banks. In 1968–70, the emphasis was on arranging Eurocurrency loans, but treasury activities and dealing in securities also became very significant. By the end of 1972, it was London's largest consortium bank; it could claim to have arranged $3 billion of loans since its incorporation and to have a daily trading volume of $750 million in foreign exchange, deposits, CDs, equities, convertible and straight bonds. The bank had become one of the largest market makers in Eurobonds and had a 5–10 per cent share of CD trading in London; it was an early participant in floating rate notes, which became a very large part of the Eurobond market. In the spring of 1973, the bank led and took a big position in a $75 million 8.25 per cent bond issue for the City of Glasgow, the largest local authority issue till then, not long before interest rates rose markedly; it was also, by then, heavily exposed to the UK property market. Both these areas of business proved very costly to the bank. Thereafter, the bank faced considerable difficulties; its deposit base was substantially reduced and the shareholders purchased loans of £191 million from the bank, without recourse. Bond trading ceased in September 1974, after losses caused by rising interest rates; foreign exchange and several other activities were curtailed or eliminated. Overheads were reduced and profitability recovered on a much reduced balance sheet, until the bank came under the control of Bank of Tokyo.

Personnel *Chairmen* R.M. Cook, 1967–69, J.O. Hambro, 1969–1976, F.G. Larkin Jr, 1976–78, Y. Kashiwagi, 1978–80. *Managing Directors* J. Pryor (also Vice Chairman), 1967–74, J.E. Baird, 1969–73, J. Appelmans, 1970–74, R.D. Siff, 1970–72, G.E. Rothell, 1972–77, H.P. Pirquet, 1973–75, E. Donnell, 1977–78, M.A. Oka, 1978–80.

Finances (£ million)

YE 31/1	1969	1970	1971	1972	1973	1974
Total assets	104.2	204.9	315.0	396.7	660.9	565.0
Cap. & reserves	5.4	5.6	6.1	15.7	18.8	18.8
Pre-tax profit	0.7	1.0	1.4	2.9	3.3	0.9
Dividend	0.0	0.3	0.3	0.3	0.6	0.0
YE 31/1 & 31/12	**1975**	**1976**	**1977**	**1978**	**1978**	**1979**
Total assets	133.3	137.8	158.9	155.7	175.5	191.8
Cap. & reserves	19.1	18.4	18.7	10.0	11.7	12.6
Pre-tax profit	0.9	1.5	1.5	2.1	3.4	2.0
Dividend	0.0	1.5	0.8	1.3	0.0	0.0

NOTES: (1) 13 months to 31/1/69. (2) 12 months to 31/1/78. (3) 11 months to 31/12/78. (4) 12 months to 31/12/79.

NOTE ON SOURCES: The information in Section 1 is derived from UK Companies House returns, annual reports and former employees of the banks, the press and the recollections of contemporary observers. CH, followed by a number, identifies the Companies House file. The annual reports may not give the entire picture of the business, since some consortium banks were supported by their shareholders or taken over by one of them in circumstances not apparent from the annual reports; shareholder support could take the form of purchasing non-performing loans, supplying deposits on easy terms and subscribing to subordinated loan stock. Information about banks before or after they had consortium status (as defined by the Bank of England's 1975 formula) is not included. Capital and reserves includes minority interests. Dividends are those paid on equity capital in cash; stock and preference dividends are excluded. Consolidated figures are used, where available. Shareholding banks are usually described by their contemporary names; many of them later acquired new names or ownerships. In the case of most US bank shareholders, the holding was normally taken by an associated company of the main operating bank, which is listed as the shareholder. Some of the banks began life as Licensed Deposit Takers, being recognized as banks only after a few years of operation.

Section 2. 20 Other Consortium Bank Groups

The consortium banks described in Section 1 were banks defined as such in 1975 by the Bank of England. Many other consortia were established in the 1970s and 1980s, both in London and in other financial centres around the world. There were numerous alliances between European and Middle East or Japanese banks, to help them gain experience of the Euromarkets. There were 'Yankee merchant banks', the investment banking subsidiaries of US commercial banks, some of which at first had minority shareholding partners, but later became 100 per cent owned. Consortia were set up to penetrate the Australian market, to make industrial loans in Spain, to finance Eastern Europe and to participate in the 'tiger' economies of the Far East. There was and is a huge variety of consortia with particular regional or industrial aims.

Most of these banks gave up their consortium status, usually through absorption by one of the shareholders or liquidation. The following 20 consortium groups active in London's time zone (of which only four survive as consortia) were noteworthy and illustrate the strategy of the founders.

S2/1 Allied Bank International, New York, was formed, in 1969, by 18 regional US banks to act as their international arm; US banking laws prevented out-of-state branches and Allied was established as an 'Edge Act' institution, which precluded domestic business. In order to exploit the Euromarkets, a London branch was opened in 1970. Allied had a diverse range of international activities, but eventually encountered stiff competition from its own shareholders and diminishing support. The bank suffered losses from Latin American exposure, the shipping market and Nigerian trade finance. It ceased operations in 1986–87.

S2/2 Arab Banking Corporation, Bahrain (ABC) was formed in 1980 by Kuwait, Libyan and Abu Dhabi government agencies. Its Chief Executive from foundation until 1994 was Abdulla Saudi, previously of the Libyan Arab Foreign Bank. One of ABC's affiliates was **Arlabank International,** Bahrain set up in 1977 as a specialist in Latin America, with Arab and Latin American shareholders; it grew rapidly, with a Peruvian subsidiary and a London representative office, but it was liquidated after heavy provisions on Latin American loans, suffering a similar fate to that of other banks with similar orientation (S1/8, S1/11, S1/15 and S1/21). In 1990, part of ABC's capital was taken up by private and institutional shareholders; its shares became quoted in Bahrain and Paris. Activities spanned investment, corporate, treasury and retail banking activities in the Arab world, Europe, the Americas and the Far East, including a big operation in London. Total assets at the end of 1998 were $26.1 billion.

S2/3 Julius Baer International was a 51 per cent owned London subsidiary of a leading Swiss private bank, 49 per cent being owned by a leading UK finance company, United Dominions Trust. Later, it was absorbed *in toto* by its parent.

S2/4 BAII Holdings, Luxembourg, was set up in 1973 as an international investment and commercial banking group, with a strong Arab emphasis and French influence. Initial ownership: *50 per cent Arab*, 12 institutional investors from eight Arab countries, and *50 per cent Western*, of which 25 per cent Société Financière Européenne (S2/19) and 25 per cent six international banks, headed by Banque Nationale de Paris; later, Bank of China became a shareholder. Its main operating subsidiary was Banque Arabe et Internationale d'Investissement, Paris; it had affiliates in London (S1/5), Bahrain, New York and Hong Kong. After LDC debt problems, over 90 per cent of the capital was acquired by Banque Nationale de Paris, in 1990.

S2/5 Bankers Trust International Ltd (originally P.P. Rodoconachi, a London private bank, established in 1860) was the UK consortium banking subsidiary of Bankers Trust, New York, with the leading UK chemical company, ICI, as a shareholder in it, but it became wholly owned by Bankers Trust. In April 1970, the first Floating-Rate Note in the Euromarkets for an industrial borrower, ENEL, was launched by BTI, whose Evan Galbraith was credited with the innovation.

S2/6 Bank of America Ltd was formed in 1971 in London to do medium-term lending and Eurobond business. Its shareholders were Bank of America, then the largest commercial bank in the world, 75 per cent, and Kleinwort Benson, the London merchant bank, 25 per cent. It became a 100 per cent subsidiary of Bank of America in 1974. Bank of America's strength was based on the relatively unrestricted market of California; it used joint ventures extensively to make progress and catch up overseas with its main US competitors, such as Chase and Citibank. Its partners included Paribas, through **Banque Ameribas**, and Kleinwort Benson in the Far East; its joint ventures in the Middle East included BCCI, from 1972 to 1980. It had stakes in five other consortia covered here (S1/11, S1/15, S1/16, S2/4 and S2/19).

S2/7 Banque de Paris et des Pays Bas Ltd was formed in London in 1964 by Paribas as a partly owned merchant banking subsidiary; its partners included S.G. Warburg and Lehman Brothers; it also bought a UK securities house. In 1969, it was converted to a branch, partly because of Bank of England regulations. The bank's historian wrote: '... the bank's first encounter with the Anglo-Saxon world had proved to be quite disappointing in outcome, although full of lessons for the future.' In the early 1970s, Paribas had 40 per cent of a joint venture with Bank of America, Banque Ameribas (S2/6); it had small stakes at the foundation of two London consortium banks (S1/11 and S1/15), which were soon sold. In 1974, Paribas and S.G. Warburg formed Warburg Paribas Becker as a US investment bank; it was dissolved in 1982–83.

S2/8 Banque de Suez (UK) was, in the early 1970s, an affiliate of Compagnie Financière de Suez, which also had a consortium banking interest in UK through Fleming Suez Brown Brothers (S1/7). This bank was integrated into the London branch of another Suez subsidiary, Banque de l'Indochine et de Suez, in 1977.

S2/9 Banque Européenne de Crédit, Brussels, was established in 1967 and became owned by the seven EBIC banks (Appendix III); Crédit Lyonnais was briefly a shareholder at the start, but dropped out because of conflict of interest, in view of its Europartners association (Appendix III). Its prime business was medium-term lending. Between 1982 and 1985, it was united operationally with European Banking Company in London (S1/10). It was liquidated in 1986, because of losses arising from the international debt crisis and because of potential shareholder competition.

S2/10 Banque Européenne de Tokyo, Paris, was founded in 1968 as a wholly owned subsidiary by Bank of Tokyo; between 1970 and 1974, seven other Japanese banks became shareholders. Its business was mainly medium-term lending, similar to that of the Japanese consortium banks in London (S1/3 and S1/19). In the late 1980s, it became a wholly owned subsidiary of Bank of Tokyo, which had already acquired Western American Bank in London (S1/35).

S2/11 Burston and Texas Commerce Bank was founded as a family bank in 1955, under the name of N. Burston & Co. Texas Commerce Bank acquired a 35 per cent stake in 1968 and a new name was adopted; however, the secondary banking crisis caused problems for the Burston business and the Texas bank acquired the rest of the shares in 1975.

S2/12 Credit Suisse White Weld, 1974, **Credit Suisse First Boston**, 1978 and **CS First Boston**, 1988 were successive joint ventures between US investment banks, White Weld & Co, First Boston Corporation and the Swiss universal bank, Crédit Suisse. The predominant business was international investment banking. On its own, the US investment bank, White Weld & Co had been a key participant in the Eurobond market from 1963 onwards, through its European offices, with particular strengths in trading and distribution. Many Euromarket innovations had their origins there and its successor firms. Despite occasional friction between London, New York and Zurich, the firm is a rare and successful example of commercial and investment banking under one roof.

S2/13 European Arab Holding, Luxembourg, was founded in 1972. The ownership was divided equally between international and Arab interests, as follows: *45 per cent non-Arab* – seven EBIC member banks (Appendix III) together with Midland and International Banks (S1/25), two Japanese and one Swiss bank; *45 per cent Arab* – 16 public and private sector institutional investors; *10 per cent mixed Arab/non-Arab* – Frab Holding, Luxembourg (S2/14). The main business was commercial and investment banking, with an Arab emphasis. Its banking subsidiaries were in London (S1/9), Frankfurt, Brussels and Bahrain; it also had a representative office in Cairo. The group had to make heavy provisions, mainly because of the Latin American debt crisis, and its shareholders, because of their widely differing strengths, were not all equally in a position to subscribe the capital needed to maintain the ownership balance. Therefore, its operating banks were gradually liquidated between 1985 and 1991, the holding company being finally liquidated in 1992.

S2/14 Frab Holding, Luxembourg, was set up in 1969 as a consortium banking group, owned as 50 per cent by Arab banks, companies and individuals, 25 per cent by Société Générale, France, and 25 per cent by seven other European and Japanese shareholders. The acronym 'Frab' was intended to indicate a Franco–Arab emphasis in the venture; its principal operating bank was in Paris. 51 per cent of the capital was acquired by one of its shareholders, National Bank of Kuwait, the largest Kuwaiti commercial bank, in 1981; it became a wholly owned subsidiary of NBK in 1989.

S2/15 Gulf International Bank, Bahrain, was founded in 1975 by Bahrain, Kuwait, Oman, Qatar, Saudi Arabia and the United Arab Emirates, currently the Gulf Co-operation Council (GCC) countries, and Iraq. In 1990, substantial losses led to a reorganization under which the bank became a 100 per cent subsidiary of Gulf Investment Corporation, Kuwait, owned by the six GCC countries. The GIC group's activities span investment banking, corporate banking and global markets; its customer base is the public and private sector of the Gulf and multinationals active in the Gulf. Its principal overseas offices are in London, New York and Singapore. Total assets at the end of 1998 were $10.2 billion. In 1999, GIB merged with Saudi International Bank (S1/30), leaving the merged bank 72.5 per cent owned by GIC.

S2/16 Intercontinental Banking Services Ltd was launched in 1967 by Barclays Bank, Lloyds Bank and five British overseas banks, which had 3000 branches outside the UK. Its aim was to exchange information and provide advice about overseas markets and to manage syndicated loans. Its distinguished first board, including the Chairmen and Chief Executives of its shareholders, suggested a greater aspiration than its initial objectives, perhaps the creation of a large British overseas bank. Soon after the launch of the newly merged National Westminster Bank in January 1968, Barclays, Lloyds and Martins proposed their own merger, which was banned on competition grounds (see page 317). Barclays and Lloyds, which had differing views of the value of consortia, then resumed their competitive relationship; another shareholder, ANZ Bank, was ceasing to feel like a British overseas bank and planning its move to Australia. So, the company was effectively closed down, with no loans having been syndicated and little else achieved.

S2/17 Manufacturers Hanover Ltd was set up in London in 1969 as the investment banking arm of the US commercial bank, Manufacturers Hanover Trust, which held 75 per cent of the capital, the balance being held by N.M. Rothschild & Sons, Riunione Adriatica di Sicurta and Long Term Credit Bank of Japan. The first two of many loans arranged by this bank were $80 million for Iran and $200 million for Istituto Mobiliare Italiano in 1969. The chief executive was Minos Zombanakis, a leading architect and initiator of the Eurocurrency syndicated loan business; in 1972, he became Vice Chairman of First Boston in Europe (for FB's later international history, see S2/12) and pioneered the entry of US investment banks into the syndicated loan business. Later, banks tended to do syndicated loan business directly and, in 1980, Manufacturers Hanover Ltd became a wholly owned subsidiary of its parent. MHT had stakes in three other consortium banks in London (S1/1, S1/2 and S1/16).

S2/18 Merrill Lynch–Brown Shipley Bank was set up in London in 1972, as a joint venture between Merrill Lynch, the world's largest securities firm at the time, and Brown Shipley, a well-established small merchant bank, where Montagu Norman, governor of the Bank of England in the 1920s and

1930s, and Edward Heath, later British prime minister, had worked. The bank's aim was to do short- and medium-term financing in sterling and Eurocurrencies; ML also took a 2 per cent stake in BS itself. The two shareholders were widely divergent in size and character; the joint venture was ended when ML acquired 100 per cent of the bank in 1976 and developed it as an adjunct of its securities and investment banking business.

S2/19 Société Financière Européenne was set up in Luxembourg in 1967 by Bank of America and five European banks which became part of the ABECOR group (Appendix III); later, three more banks joined. Its business was international investment and commercial banking; conducted through affiliates and subsidiaries in London (International Energy Bank, S1/14), Paris, New York, Nassau and Curacao; it held a 25 per cent interest in BAII (S2/4). However, the results were disappointing and it was wound up between 1988 and 1992.

S2/20 UBAF (Union de Banques Arabes et Françaises) was initiated by the Arab League, through banks or institutions representing every Arab country at the time, and Crédit Lyonnais, France, in 1969. The UBAF group, chaired for its first 20 years by Mohammed Abushadi, brought together more than 50 banks and other institutions, from 19 Arab and 7 other countries, in a network of affiliated banks. It described itself as 'a banking system for Arab and international co-operation.' The largest of the UBAF banks was in France; there were others in Bahrain, the USA, Germany, Luxembourg, Italy, Hong Kong, Tunisia and the UK. The normal pattern was for each affiliated bank to be controlled by UBAF's Arab shareholders, with a minority interest taken by major banks native to the country concerned. The predominant activities were commercial banking, international payments and syndicated loans, including several 'jumbo' loans for major Arab infrastructural projects. During the 1970s, the group grew rapidly and was ranked 147 in size in the world bank listings of *The Banker* in 1983. However, the overall returns were inadequate and the corporate structure unduly complicated; the affiliates have acquired a life of their own, with new shareholders and names, or been liquidated. UBAF Bank, renamed British Arab Commercial Bank (S1/32), became independent of UBAF, though with some commonality of shareholders; it was 46.5 per cent owned by HSBC. UBAF, Paris, continued to be a joint venture between 24 Arab banks, together owning 56 per cent of the capital, and Crédit Lyonnais, 44 per cent.

Section 3. Consortium Banking Interests of the 50 Largest Banks
The following table shows the widespread participation of the 50 largest banks in consortium banks as part of their international strategy. The banks are listed in order of their size in 1980 (in *The Banker*), although some of the interests had been realized before and others acquired after 1980. The names

of the banks are as they were at the time of the investment being made. Only the banks listed in Sections 1 and 2 are included, but several of the 50 banks had interests in other consortium bank and financial industry joint ventures. The table also shows their participation in the European banking clubs described in Appendix III.

Shareholding bank	Interest in consortium banking groups listed in Sections 1 and 2 *Interest in European banking clubs (in italics)*
Crédit Agricole	London and Continental Bankers *UNICO*
Bank of America	BAII, Bank of America Ltd, Banque Ameribas, European Brazilian Bank, International Energy Bank, International Mexican Bank, Iran Overseas Investment Bank, Société Financière Européenne
Citibank	NONE
Banque Nationale de Paris	BAII, Euro–Latinamerican Bank, International Energy Bank, Saudi International Bank, Société Financière Européenne *ABECOR*
Deutsche Bank	Banque Européenne de Crédit, European Arab, European Banking Company, European Brazilian Bank, Iran Overseas Investment Bank, International Mexican Bank, Saudi International Bank *EBIC*
Crédit Lyonnais	International Commercial Bank, UBAF, Banque Européenne de Crédit *Europartners*
Société Générale	Banque Européenne de Crédit, European Arab, European Banking Company, Frab, Iran Overseas Investment Bank *EBIC*
Dresdner Bank	BAII, Euro–Latinamerican Bank, International Energy Bank, Société Financière Européenne *ABECOR*
Barclays Bank Group	Anglo–Romanian Bank, Anglo–Yugoslav Bank, BAII, Euro–Latinamerican Bank, Intercontinental Banking Services, International Energy Bank, Iran Overseas Investment Bank, Société Financière Européenne *ABECOR*
Dai-Ichi Kangyo Bank	Associated Japanese Bank (International), European Brazilian Bank, International Mexican Bank

(continued)

Shareholding bank	Interest in consortium banking groups listed in Sections 1 and 2 *Interest in European banking clubs (in italics)*
National Westminster Bank	International Commercial Bank, Libra Bank, Orion Bank, Saudi International Bank
Chase Manhattan	Libra Bank, Orion Bank
Westdeutsche Landesbank	Libra Bank, Orion Bank, UBAF affiliate
Fuji Bank	European Arab, Japan International Bank
Commerzbank	International Commercial Bank, UBAF affiliate *Europartners*
Sumitomo Bank	Japan International Bank, Société Financière Européenne
Mitsubishi Bank	Japan International Bank, Libra Bank, Orion Bank
Sanwa Bank	Associated Japanese Bank (International), UBAF affiliate
Norinchukin Bank	NONE
Banco do Brasil	BAII, European Brazilian Bank, Euro–Latinamerican Bank
Bayersiche Vereinsbank	UBAF affiliate
Industrial Bank of Japan	Banque Européenne de Tokyo, European Arab, Iran Overseas Investment Bank, Frab, Rothschild Intercontinental Bank
Banca Nazionale del Lavoro	BAII, Euro–Latinamerican Bank, International Energy Bank, Société Financière Européenne, UBAF affiliate *ABECOR*
Manufacturers Hanover	Anglo–Romanian Bank, Anglo–Yugoslav Bank, Iran Overseas Investment Bank, Manufacturers Hanover Ltd
Rabobank	London and Continental Bankers *UNICO*
Midland Bank	Banque Européenne de Crédit, European Arab, European Banking Company, UBAF Bank, Iran Overseas Investment Bank, Midland and International Banks *EBIC*
Amsterdam–Rotterdam Bank	Banque Européenne de Crédit, European Arab, European Banking Company, Frab *EBIC*
Swiss Bank Corporation	Frab, Libra Bank, European Arab
JP Morgan & Co	Saudi International Bank
Bayerische Landesbank	NONE

(continued)

Shareholding bank	Interest in consortium banking groups listed in Sections 1 and 2 *Interest in European banking clubs (in italics)*
Union Bank of Switzerland	BAII, European Brazilian Bank, Euro–Latinamerican Bank, International Mexican Bank, Saudi International Bank, Société Financière Européenne
Bayerische Hypotheken und Wechsel-Bank	BAII, Euro–Latinamerican Bank, International Energy Bank, United International Bank *ABECOR*
Algemene Bank Nederland	BAII, Euro–Latinamerican Bank, International Energy Bank, Société Financière Européenne *ABECOR*
Royal Bank of Canada	Libra Bank, Orion Bank
Tokai Bank	Japan International Bank
Mitsui Bank	Associated Japanese Bank (International), UBAF affiliate
Lloyds Bank	Intercontinental Banking Services
Banca Commerciale Italiana	Banque Européenne de Crédit, European Arab, European Banking Company *EBIC*
Long Term Credit Bank of Japan	Banque Européenne de Tokyo, Manufacturers Hanover Ltd, UBAF affiliate
Chemical Bank	London Multinational Bank
Canadian Imperial Bank of Commerce	BAII, International Energy Bank
Taiyo Kobe Bank	Banque Européenne de Tokyo
Bank of Tokyo	Banque Européenne de Tokyo, Iran Overseas Investment Bank, Saudi International Bank, Western American Bank (Europe), UBAF affiliate
Banco di Roma	International Commercial Bank, UBAF affiliate, United International Bank *Europartners*
Société Générale de Banque	Banque Européenne de Crédit, European Arab, European Banking Company, Frab *EBIC*
Crédit Suisse	European Arab, London Multinational Bank, Credit Suisse White Weld
Continental Illinois	NONE
DG Bank	London and Continental Bankers *UNICO*
Daiwa Bank	NONE
Paribas	Banque Ameribas, Banque de Paris et des Pays Bas Ltd, European Brazilian Bank, International Mexican Bank

Section 4. Comparative Statistics for Consortium and Other Banks in the UK

Tables (1) and (2) below show the lending volumes and use of the inter-bank market in the foreign currency business of banks in the UK; the data source is the *Quarterly Bulletin* of the Bank of England. Table (3) below shows the overall profitability of the 35 consortium banks that appear in Section 1; the statistics are calculated from the annual reports of the banks.

The consortium banks first appeared as a separate category in Bank of England banking statistics in October 1971; they included a number of banks where more than 50 per cent of the capital was owned by another bank. These banks were excluded from the consortium banking category in May 1975, when the Bank made a major reclassification of banks in the UK. Thereafter, consortium banks were more narrowly defined as banks owned by other banks, in which no other bank had more than 50 per cent owner-ship and in which at least one shareholder was an overseas bank. Information about their assets and liabilities was published each month until July 1987, when consortium banks ceased to be classified as such by the Bank; there-after, they were included in the category 'other overseas banks'.

(1) UK Consortium Banks' Foreign Currency Loans

This table shows the foreign currency loans of banks in the UK, between 1975 and 1987. The number of consortium banks in the table varied between 23 and 29, as banks came and went. In 1987, there were still 23; by 1991, there remained only six, the others having come under single control or been liquidated.

£ billion

Date 31 May	1975	1976	1977	1978	1979	1980	1981
British banks	5.9	7.9	9.0	10.1	10.4	12.2	15.3
American banks	6.4	7.8	9.2	11.1	10.2	11.2	13.3
Japanese banks	1.6	2.3	2.8	3.9	5.1	6.1	7.9
Other overseas banks	3.5	5.2	7.1	8.2	8.4	9.5	12.4
Consortium banks	2.1	3.0	3.6	4.0	3.9	4.0	5.3
Total	**19.5**	**26.2**	**31.7**	**37.3**	**38.0**	**43.0**	**54.2**
Consortium banks' share (per cent)	*10.7*	*11.4*	*11.4*	*10.7*	*10.3*	*9.3*	*9.8*

Date 31 May	1982	1983	1984	1985	1986	1987
British banks	21.4	27.9	32.5	33.8	28.7	30.2
American banks	17.6	20.9	22.8	26.8	23.0	25.6
Japanese banks	12.4	17.0	21.1	24.5	26.1	33.1
Other overseas banks	18.9	25.6	31.0	38.9	36.0	37.7
Consortium banks	5.7	6.4	7.2	6.7	5.6	5.3
Total	**76.0**	**97.8**	**114.6**	**130.7**	**119.4**	**131.9**
Consortium banks' share (per cent)	*7.5*	*6.5*	*6.3*	*5.1*	*4.6*	*4.0*

(2) UK Consortium Banks' Use of the Inter-bank Market for Foreign Currency Funding

In September 1981, the Bank of England published a detailed survey of the inter-bank market. Central monetary institutions were excluded from this analysis of the market. American banks were the main suppliers to the inter-bank market, while consortium banks had the most dependence on it. Although the tables cover only three years, the dependence of consortium banks on the inter-bank market was a constant feature of their funding throughout the 1970s and 1980s. In 1978–80, on 30 June, the proportion of foreign currency liabilities of UK banks due to the inter-bank market was as follows:

per cent	1978	1979	1980
British banks	57	59	59
American banks	49	46	43
Japanese banks	65	69	75
Other overseas banks	68	64	64
Consortium banks	81	82	79

In the same years, the degree to which different categories of banks were net foreign currency lenders or borrowers in the inter-bank market was as follows:

£ billion	1978	1979	1980
British banks	1.3	0.7	4.5
American banks	21.6	30.4	40.3
Japanese banks	1.5	1.7	3.3
Other overseas banks	4.3	10.4	15.8
Consortium banks	(4.8)	(5.2)	(5.7)

(3) Profitability of UK Consortium Banks

This table shows the combined profitability, from 1966 to 1990, of all 35 banks described in Section 1; not all of them were extant for the whole period. Pre-tax profit is used as the measure of return, because of the distorting effect of leasing on after-tax profit; capital allowances arising from leasing activities enabled banks to defer tax. Profits between 1982 and 1986 were boosted by higher spreads and fees on rescheduled LDC debt, with modest loan loss provisions being made in those years. In August 1987 and, again, at the end of 1989, the Bank of England required a stricter provisioning policy, which resulted in large losses for many consortium banks in those two years and the need for much increased shareholder support. Some of the support took the form of shareholders acquiring doubtful loans in

such a way as to avoid heavy provisioning in the consortium banks' profit
and loss accounts; to that extent, the table may overstate their profits or
understate their losses.

£ million	1966	1967	1968	1969	1970
Total assets	184.9	266.6	693.2	1 125.1	1 531.3
Total cap. & reserves	11.0	11.5	17.6	26.6	35.0
Total pre-tax profit	0.4	0.5	2.3	3.5	5.3
Return on cap. & reserves	3.6%	4.3%	13.1%	13.2%	15.2%
Number of banks	*2*	*2*	*4*	*6*	*9*

	1971	1972	1973	1974	1975
Total assets	2 203.3	3 104.7	4 632.1	5 497.5	6 119.5
Total cap. & reserves	66.4	95.4	142.4	225.6	288.3
Total pre-tax profit	8.9	17.1	23.3	33.4	45.7
Return on cap. & reserves	13.4%	18.0%	16.4%	14.8%	15.9%
Number of banks	*13*	*17*	*19*	*25*	*27*

	1976	1977	1978	1979	1980
Total assets	7 921.0	9 088.3	10 215.7	11 496.4	12 719.7
Total cap. & reserves	317.6	364.3	452.9	536.6	603.7
Total pre-tax profit	64.3	62.1	82.6	102.0	128.3
Return on cap. & reserves	20.2%	17.0%	18.2%	19.0%	21.3%
Number of banks	*27*	*28*	*27*	*27*	*25*

	1981	1982	1983	1984	1985
Total assets	17 491.5	18 641.9	20 169.5	20 200.7	19 332.6
Total cap. & reserves	723.9	819.8	900.4	878.5	959.8
Total pre-tax profit	158.6	179.0	166.7	182.6	171.7
Return on cap. & reserves	21.9%	21.8%	18.5%	20.8%	17.9%
Number of banks	*26*	*24*	*25*	*24*	*23*

	1986	1987	1988	1989	1990
Total assets	19 419.2	15 886.3	14 812.1	12 797.1	5 996.1
Total cap. & reserves	1 057.1	703.7	973.3	337.6	427.5
Total pre-tax profit	136.0	−419.1	20.6	−735.9	−28.3
Return on cap. & reserves	12.9%	−59.6%	2.1%	−218.0%	−6.6%
Number of banks	*23*	*23*	*22*	*20*	*15*

European banking clubs
EBIC – Europartners – Inter-Alpha – ABECOR – Unico

Following the Treaty of Rome in 1957 and the establishment of the European Economic Community, many of the larger commercial banks in Europe felt the need for stronger cross-border co-operation. The Werner Report of 1970, presaging a common European currency, spurred this inclination. To this end, five far-ranging associations, club-like in character, were formed between similar banks of different nationalities; the association was, on occasion, cemented by a modest exchange of shares. They were EBIC, Europartners, Inter-Alpha, ABECOR and Unico. The clubs were driven at Chairman and Board level, backed by working parties and initiatives at all levels in the banks; each club had a secretariat and some had a management or holding company as well.

THE RISE AND FALL OF THE EUROPEAN BANKING CLUBS

The reasons for forming these banking clubs, which were at their zenith in the 1970s and early 1980s, were to:

- share experiences and information over a wide front;
- meet the needs of their customers throughout Europe, particularly in each others' home markets;
- finance large projects and conduct other mutually beneficial business together;
- establish special-purpose joint ventures, such as consortium or investment banks;
- share the costs and risks of representation outside Europe;
- exchange personnel and improve cross-border training opportunities;

- seek cost-effective co-operation in technology, research and marketing;
- meet the challenge of the US bank invasion of European markets.

For some, a key aim was to lay the groundwork for a potential merged bank, able to operate throughout Europe as a single entity. For others, the clubs were seen as loose associations, with no realistic expectation of merger. The predecessor of one of these clubs, EBIC, was known as the 'club des céli-bataires'; it was formed by three banks in 1958, its name indicating Platonic friendship, with marriage seen as but a distant possibility.

The club strategy depended on member banks not competing directly with each other. At the time of their creation, most of the members had large retail networks and substantial market shares at home; they had minimal presence in each others' countries, but some had significant activities outside Europe. When, in the mid-1970s, member banks decided to expand through direct presence in each others' home markets, the clubs became something of an inconvenience; however, attempts were made to adopt a 'two-tier approach' and keep the clubs alive, while simultaneously building overseas branches and subsidiaries. Although many club members maintained close bilateral relations, most member banks had second thoughts about club strategies; three clubs ceased altogether, while two remain in a modified way. Club strategies continue to be used for specific purposes, among smaller banks and in the investment banking world.

Among the reasons why the clubs went out of fashion were:

- competition between members;
- the slow advent of European integration, complicated by tax, legal and regulatory factors;
- loss of idealistic fervour, as the founders of these clubs retired;
- unrewarding, if not disastrous, results from their jointly owned consortium banks;
- domestic preoccupations, which reduced the management enthusiasm for international adventures;
- unquantifiable revenue gains in what critics saw as expensive talking shops;
- complications in admitting new members, as with the European Economic Community itself;
- industry-wide technology co-operation being more important than intra-club co-operation (for example, Eurocheque and SWIFT);
- widely different performances among the members, which unbalanced the clubs.

WHAT BECAME OF THE EUROPEAN BANKING CLUBS?

The three that have ceased were originally the largest – EBIC, Europartners and ABECOR. EBIC's epitaph, as expressed by the historians of Deutsche

Bank, might have wider application: '... if one assumes a further motive in addition to co-operation, namely to merge into a Europe bank, then EBIC failed completely ... however, the EBIC co-operation was not a mistake, but a sensible interim step in [the bank's] institutional development.'

Two clubs, Inter-Alpha and Unico, were still active in 2000. Inter-Alpha took on a new lease of life in 1986, continuing with an increased number of members, but lower intensity of contact than in its early days. Some of the members derived significant benefit from their shareholdings in each other; for example, Royal Bank of Scotland's Spanish partner, BSCH, played a significant role in Royal's acquisition of NatWest in 2000. The Unico Banking Group, consisting of 10 co-operative banks, continued to flourish; their predominantly mutual ownership limited share exchange possibilities or merger aspirations.

The club strategy seems to be most successful in specific activities or in bilateral operations between members. For example, one former ABECOR member, Barclays, showed a commitment to club strategy, when it announced, in June 1998, a 'virtual network' of partner banks to serve the corporate sector throughout Europe; the partners were chosen for their abilities to carry out specific functions rather than on account of any grand design. Clubs were set up to enable banks to provide joint cash management services, such as IBOS, in which several Inter-Alpha banks are involved, and Connector. Unico launched a cash management product to coincide with the new euro in 1999. Smaller banks could derive benefit from club strategies; for example, in 1998, Fokus Bank of Trondheim, Norway, helped form a nine-country regional banking club as a discussion forum to meet the challenge of a fast-moving banking environment.

PROFILES OF FIVE EUROPEAN BANKING CLUBS

The five European banking clubs, together with their members, dates of joining, subsequent (or parent group) names and sizes in 1977, are described below (consortium banking groups, prefixed S1/ or S2/, are described in Appendix II).

European Banks International Company (EBIC)

Combined assets $188 billion in 1977 (ceased 1992)

Amsterdamsche Bank,
  Netherlands (1958) (AMRO)
Deutsche Bank, Germany (1958)
Société Générale de Banque
  de Belgique (1958)

Midland Bank, UK (1963)
Creditanstalt-Bankverein, Austria (1971)
Société Générale, France (1971)
Banca Commerciale Italiana (1973)

In 1958, Deutsche Bank, Amsterdamsche Bank and Société Générale de Banque de Belgique formed the 'club des célibataires'; the aim was to co-operate in a number of areas, the arrangement to be secret, so as not to upset correspondent relationships. In December 1962, Hermann Abs, Chairman of Deutsche Bank, approached Tony Hellmuth, Assistant General Manager of Midland Bank, with a view to Midland joining the club. As a result, Midland Bank joined the other three banks to form the European Advisory Committee (EAC), as part of its 'grand design' for international banking, which involved relying on correspondent banking relationships rather than direct representation overseas. At this time, the existence of the EAC was announced publicly. An ultimate merger of the four banks was considered a possibility, if European integration made it practicable or desirable.

In 1967, Banque Européenne de Crédit à Moyen Terme (BEC, S2/9) was formed in Brussels by the four EAC banks, together with Samuel Montagu & Co., Midland's associated merchant bank in London; Crédit Lyonnais' brief involvement in BEC is described in the next section 'Europartners'. BEC soon became a leading Eurocurrency consortium bank, specializing in medium- and long-term loans. In 1968, European American Banking Corporation and European American Bank and Trust Company were formed from the New York subsidiary of Société Générale de Banque de Belgique; in 1974, after the failure of Franklin National Bank, a significant part of that bank's business, including 100 branches in metropolitan New York, was bought by European American, which put it among the 20 largest banking organizations in the USA.

In 1970, European Banks International Company (EBIC), Brussels, was set up as a management company for the group, which came to be known as EBIC. Three more banks joined the EBIC club – Société Générale (1971), Creditanstalt-Bankverein (1971) and Banca Commerciale Italiana (1973); all three were state-controlled banks, a potential complication in any future merger plans, since the other four belonged to the private sector.

Consortium banks were an important part of EBIC's club strategy; in addition to BEC and European American, four other consortium banking groups were formed by EBIC. Two of them had some non-EBIC shareholders: Euro–Pacific Finance Corporation, Melbourne (1970), with Australian, Japanese and US banks, and European Arab Holding (1972, S2/13), with Arab institutions and some other non-EBIC banks. Two others – European Asian Bank (formed from a Deutsche Bank subsidiary in 1972) and European Banking Company, London (1973, S1/10) – were exclusively owned by the EBIC banks at their inception. The latter became a successful international investment bank, under the leadership of Stanislas Yassukovich.

At the era of its highest profile, in the late 1970s, the EBIC members were financing many large projects together and were present, through their six consortium banking groups, in many different markets and businesses. They had a network of over 10 000 branches in Europe and, in European American, the largest European-owned bank in America. The structure was in place for closer co-operation. However, as the EBIC banks expanded overseas in their own names and into each others' home markets, the EBIC strategy became increasingly complicated to maintain. One by one, from the mid-1980s onwards, EBIC's consortium banks, some of them having made large losses on Third World lending, were wound up or sold to one of the member banks; AMRO's purchase of both European Banking Company and European American gave the Netherlands bank a big step forward in its international business. By the time that EBIC was formally terminated at the end of 1992, it had been effectively inoperative for several years.

Europartners

Combined assets $109 billion in 1977 (ceased 1991–93)

Commerzbank, Germany (1970)   Banco di Roma, Italy (1971)
Crédit Lyonnais, France (1970)   Banco Hispano Americano,
                                 Spain (1973)

In October 1970, Crédit Lyonnais and Commerzbank signed a wide-ranging co-operative agreement in Düsseldorf; these two banks were joined by Banco di Roma in January 1971. The equity capital of Crédit Lyonnais was entirely owned by the French state and that of Banco di Roma was owned over 90 per cent by Istituto per la Ricostruzione Industriale, the balance being owned by a large number of mostly small shareholders. Commerzbank was a private sector bank. These three banks were the first members of what came to be called the Europartners group.

The origins of this group can be traced to 1962 and 1966, when Crédit Lyonnais twice tried to form a special association with Deutsche Bank; however, Deutsche was already developing the ties which led to the creation of the EBIC club. During the 1960s, potential EBIC members did not want to include a state-owned bank; one Midland banker said that 'we don't want de Gaulle in our club,' President de Gaulle having twice vetoed UK membership of the EEC. In 1967, Deutsche and its allies formed Banque Européenne de Crédit (S2/9), without Crédit Lyonnais, though inviting it in later. This event ('une cruelle déception') led Crédit Lyonnais to seek another association in Germany.

Commerzbank was an ideal choice for this purpose. A close working relationship had been forged between Maurice Schlogel, Directeur Général of Crédit Lyonnais, and Paul Lichtenberg, Speaker of the Board of Managing Directors of Commerzbank, in the late 1960s, which resulted in some significant areas of co-operation. At that time, Italian banks were tightly controlled at home by the authorities and the Europartners club opened up

new opportunities for Banco di Roma. At about the same time, two associations were created involving leading Italian and foreign companies, between
Fiat and Citroën in vehicles and Pirelli and Dunlop in tyres; these unions did
not survive.

The aim of the association between the three banks was 'progressive operational integration as a stage towards the creation of a unified banking combine.' Dr Danilo Ciulli of Banco di Roma called it a 'ideale fusione' and
Jürgen Reimnitz of Commerzbank 'a family, not a club.' Full unification
might be difficult for legal and political reasons, in view of the public sector
interest in two of the banks, but there was a definite aspiration in that direction; the association was described as a 'quasi-merger.' This feature distinguished Europartners from the other European banking clubs, which were
looser in character. In the group's first full year, 14 working parties were set up
to cover all aspects of the member banks' business. A one-third interest was
taken by the three banks in the London consortium bank, International
Commercial Bank, in 1973 (S1/13), and they were also associated through
parts of the UBAF group (S2/20); Europartners Securities Corporation was
set up as an investment bank in New York and several other joint ventures (for
example, in Amsterdam, Saarbrücken and Cairo) and representative offices
were established around the world. In October 1973, a leading Spanish
private sector bank, Banco Hispano Americano, became a member;
Commerzbank became a 10 per cent shareholder in the Spanish bank in 1984.

An early issue was the choice of a British banking partner; the logical candidate was Lloyds Bank, the other members of the 'Big Four' being committed elsewhere. However, as its Chairman, Eric Faulkner, explained in his
1972 annual statement: 'consortium-owned banking operations, the bankers
clubs so frequently referred to in the press, were not the right answer for
Lloyds Bank;' in fact, Lloyds was intent on disposing of its affiliated interests
at the time. Lloyds Bank did, however, enter into an 'informal agreement,
falling short of any investment or formal association' with Crédit Lyonnais
and Commerzbank under which the three banks would provide reciprocal
credit facilities in each others' currencies to customers; Mitsui Bank made a
similar agreement with the group. NatWest and Williams & Glyn's Bank had
also been sounded out as a potential UK member, without success.

Throughout the 1970s and early 1980s, Europartners promoted itself
as a group; the main areas for co-operation were reciprocal credits, large
international financings, advice on direct investment, personnel exchanges,
marketing and tourist assistance. The group had 5000 branches and other
forms of presence in over 50 countries, being particularly strong in their
home countries of Europe. However, little progress towards a merger was
made and the enthusiasm was already waning by 1975. The joint ventures
ceased, with large losses in the case of International Commercial Bank, or
were taken over by one of the member banks. In 1988, Jean-Yves Haberer

became Chairman of Crédit Lyonnais and, under his leadership, the bank expanded its loan book and international presence aggressively; it made acquisitions in Spain, Italy and Germany which were potentially serious competitors of Europartner banks in those countries. This headlong expansion eventually resulted in the bank having to be rescued by the French government.

Meanwhile, in the early 1990s, both Banco di Roma and Banco Hispano Americano were involved in domestic mergers, while Commerzbank was actively expanding at home and abroad; the fall of the Berlin Wall had presented a major opportunity and challenge. Commerzbank and Banco Central Hispanoamericano (successor to Banco Hispano Americano) held 4–5 per cent stakes in each other and had close bilateral relations. Between 1991 and 1993, the Europartners association was dissolved by mutual agreement; however, when the privatization of Crédit Lyonnais was announced in June 1999, Commerzbank appeared as a 4 per cent shareholder in the core ownership group.

Inter-Alpha Group of Banks

Combined assets $36 billion in 1977

(Phase 1)

Banco Ambrosiano,
  Italy (1971, left 1982)
Crédit Commercial de
  France (1971)
Kredietbank, Belgium (1971)
Nederlandsche Middenstandsbank
  (1971) (ING)

Williams & Glyn's Bank,
  UK (1971) (RBS)
BHF Bank, Germany (1972)
Privatbanken, Denmark (1973)

(Phase 2)

Banco de Bilbao,
  Spain (1986, left 1997)
Istituto Bancario San Paolo di Torino,
  Italy (1986)
Banco Espirito Santo e
  Comercial de Lisboa (1988)

AIB Group, Ireland (1989)
National Bank of Greece (1990)
Nordbanken, Sweden (1995)
Merita Bank, Finland (1997)
Banco Santander, Spain (1998)
  (BSCH)

Note: The Finnish and Swedish members merged in 1998 to form MeritaNordbanken Group.

The history of the Inter-Alpha Group of Banks can be traced back to a joint shareholding of four friendly banks in a fifth, Kredietbank SA Luxembourgoise; this bank, an affiliate of Kredietbank of Belgium, was also partly owned by

Banco Ambrosiano, Crédit Commercial de France (CCF) and Nederlandsche Middenstandsbank. Around the boardroom table of the Luxembourg bank, the idea of a new banking group began to emerge. Luc Wauters, an active proponent of European unity and a future Chairman of Kredietbank, was the prime mover of the group. In 1971, Williams & Glyn's Bank (part of the same group as the Royal Bank of Scotland (RBS), with which it was fully merged in 1985) joined the club, followed by BHF Bank in 1972 and Privatbanken in 1973. The group consisted of these seven banks until 1982.

Inter-Alpha was an association of medium-sized banks, which were significantly smaller than members of the other clubs at their formation; they had a reasonable branch presence at home (over 1800 branches, though quite unevenly distributed). They also had a strong commitment to corporate and investment banking. Kredietbank and its Luxembourg affiliate had been pioneers of the Eurobond market; its Chairman, Fernand Collin, and younger colleague, André Coussement, are credited with pioneering the European unit of account, which became a significant currency for new issues. CCF was a leader in French Franc Eurobond issues and Williams & Glyn's was the first UK clearing bank to launch an offer for sale of corporate equity on the London Stock Exchange since the end of the Second World War.

The aim of Inter-Alpha was to 'provide a world-wide corporate financial service second to none.' The service, which covered both finance and advice, was designed to meet the needs of major multinationals, medium-sized and smaller companies, where the banks had a strong market share at home. Companies could obtain 'reciprocal' credit at the branch of the local Inter-Alpha bank, by arrangement of the company's own branch; this service was particularly useful for medium-sized companies expanding abroad for the first time. For larger borrowers, Inter-Alpha members organized Eurobond and syndicated loan facilities, often inviting one another as co-managers.

Development was driven at regular meetings of a Steering Committee, consisting of Chairmen or Managing Directors, and a Permanent Co-ordinating Committee, to 'ensure decisive co-operation at the working level.' They were supported by a Secretariat in Paris, between 1973 and 1985, run by François Garelli, who later wrote a history of the group. In addition, there were regular *ad hoc* meetings, conferences and working parties, not necessarily involving all the members. Secondments and training initiatives were arranged. The possibility of a full-scale merger of the members was never high on the agenda, but several members took modest shareholdings in each other, in addition to the shares held in Kredietbank SA Luxembourgoise. The group took a 40 per cent share in the London consortium bank, Brown Harriman & International Banks (S1/7) in 1972 and launched a Far Eastern investment banking group, Inter-Alpha Asia, in 1974; both of these joint ventures were bought out by one of the Inter-Alpha member banks, in 1977 and 1984, respectively. Joint representative offices were opened in São Paulo, Singapore, New York, Tokyo and Teheran.

In 1982, CCF was nationalized, together with several other leading French banks, following President Mitterand's election victory of 1981. The bank's Chairman, Jean-Maxime Lévêque, a leading proponent of Inter-Alpha, made outspoken criticisms of nationalization and resigned; however, CCF remained in the group. Also in 1982, Banco Ambrosiano was bankrupted through massive frauds and the Bank of Italy established a successor bank, Nuovo Banco Ambrosiano, with support from leading Italian banks; the new bank did not join Inter-Alpha. For the next four years, the group consisted of six members.

In 1986, the group took on a new lease of life, with the adhesion of Istituto Bancario San Paolo di Torino and Banco de Bilbao. CCF was returned to the private sector in 1987 and, thereafter, Inter-Alpha was considerably enlarged, though with a lower profile than it had in the 1970s. Partly as a result of mergers, several of the members had become among the largest banks in their home markets. It remained a loose and informal federation of like-minded banks, which sought avenues of co-operation among themselves; members also engaged in significant bilateral activities. For example, Charterhouse, a UK merchant bank, was owned by three of them, RBS, BHF and CCF between 1993 and 1996, when RBS sold its stake to the other two banks. RBS and BSCH had a wide-ranging association, cemented by mutual stakes in each other below 10 per cent, but BSCH increased its stake to 10 per cent in support of RBS's acquisition of NatWest in 2000. The link between some members and Kredietbank SA Luxembourgoise continues. ING and Kredietbank were each 20 per cent shareholders in CCF, though they both had to give up acquisition aspirations in the face of HSBC's successful bid for control in 2000; ING was also a major shareholder in BHF Bank, eventually acquiring control. There was an Inter-Alpha Banking School and an international training programme for selected staff of the member banks, in conjunction with INSEAD.

The chief executives and others met regularly to discuss opportunities and exchange information, through the Steering Committee and the Permanent Co-ordinating Committee; each member bank had an Inter-Alpha Desk to maximize relevant contacts and encourage co-operation. Top management considered that Inter-Alpha was an invaluable mechanism for preparing their banks for a single currency Europe.

Associated Banks of Europe Corporation (ABECOR)

Combined assets $202 billion in 1977 (ceased 1997)

Algemene Bank Nederland
 (1971, left 1991)
Banque de Bruxelles,
 Belgium (1971)

Banca Nazionale del Lavoro,
 Italy (1974)
Banque Nationale de Paris,
 France (1974)

Bayerische Hypotheken- und   Banque Internationale à
  Wechsel-Bank, Germany (1971)   Luxembourg (1974)
Dresdner Bank,   Barclays Bank, UK (1974)
  Germany (1971)   Österreichische Länderbank,
                                       Austria (1974)

ABECOR was established in 1974 by nine banks; initially, two of the smaller banks were associate members, becoming full members later on. ABECOR's roots go back to April 1967 with the formation of Société Financière Européenne (SFE) by five of the future ABECOR members together with the Bank of America. SFE was an international medium-term lending and investment banking group, based in Luxembourg and Paris, which became a 'special associated member' of ABECOR. In the following years, further avenues of co-operation were explored. In 1971, ABECOR was formed as a legal entity by Algemene Bank Nederland (ABN), Dresdner Bank, Banque de Bruxelles and Bayerische Hypotheken- und Wechsel-Bank (Hypo-Bank), through which these four banks set up a US investment bank. In 1972, a training institute was set up in Bad Homburg by six of the ABECOR banks. In April 1974, ABECOR was reorganized, with its full complement of banks, and launched.

Pierre Ledoux, Chairman of Banque Nationale de Paris (BNP) and, in the first instance, of the ABECOR Steering Committee, said that the group's aim was to 'explore in a creative spirit' all possible avenues of mutual co-operation. The intention was that it should remain a loose and informal association, with no apparent aspiration towards a merger. Its loose character enabled it to accommodate as many as nine full members, including two large banks, Dresdner and Hypo-Bank, from the same country. The association was dedicated to co-operation in Europe. The members were free to operate independently outside Europe, where some of them, such as ABN, BNP and Barclays, already had extensive activities. This feature distinguished ABECOR from the other clubs, where the establishment of joint investments overseas tended to be part of the strategy.

For corporate borrowers, a reciprocal credit system, ABECORCREDIT, was created; it allowed speedy access to working capital for subsidiary companies in another country, with the support of parent company guarantees. ABECOR members participated in consortium banks such as SFE (S2/19), BAII (Appendix II, S2/4), Euro–Latinamerican Bank (S1/8), International Energy Bank (S1/14) and International Nuclear Credit Bank. These banks ceased operations, sometimes with large losses, or came under single control in the late 1980s and early 1990s.

ABECOR marketed itself in a series of advertisements as 'the biggest banking association of its kind in the world.' It had over 12 000 branches in the early 1980s. The Secretariat in Brussels was responsible for group liaison. A major part of the enterprise was devoted to making the member banks more effective through co-operation in such areas as economic, company and country analysis, sovereign debt rescheduling, computers, cash management, marketing, prevention of fraud and training. It took on a direct lobbying role for its members with the European Commission in Brussels.

The benefits had proved insufficient, for some time, to justify the continuation of ABECOR and, in September 1997, the Steering Committee decided to dissolve it. ABIN, its training institute, continued after the end of ABECOR itself; the Spanish bank, Banco Bilbao Vizcaya, joined ABIN, as did ABN–AMRO Bank, successor to ABN, which had dropped out of ABECOR in 1991, but resumed its involvement in ABIN in 1996. In addition to the training of member banks' employees, ABIN made an exceptional arrangement to assist in the training of Russian bankers in 1996.

Unico Banking Group

Combined assets $94 billion in 1977

Andelsbanken, Denmark (1977, left 1990)
Crédit Agricole, France (1977)
DG Bank, Germany (1977)
OKOBANK, Finland (1977)
Rabobank Nederland (1977)
RZB-Austria (1977)

CERA Bank, Belgium (1987)
Foreningsbanken, Sweden (1991, left 1999)
ICCREA, Italy (1991)
Union of Swiss Raiffesen Banks (1997)
Banco Cooperativo Espãnol (1998)
Banca Intesa, Italy (1999)
La Caixa, Spain (1999)

The Unico Banking Group was established in 1977 by a group of six European co-operative banks that had deep roots in the trade, industry and agriculture of their countries, particularly at the smaller end of the spectrum; they also had a large retail business. However, despite having nearly 40 000 outlets in their home markets, their international scope was relatively limited; the formation of Unico was designed to meet this deficiency. Each of the founders had a mutual ownership structure, other than Andelsbanken, which left the group in 1990, when it merged with another Danish bank.

Subsequently, the group was enlarged and consists of 11 members, of which three are associated member banks. There is no UK member, in the absence of a comparable co-operative banking movement in the UK and the propensity of UK mutual financial institutions to adopt shareholding status. However, a presence in London was achieved through participation in a consortium bank, London & Continental Bankers, by certain of the Unico members. This bank (S1/22) was founded in 1973, before the creation of Unico, and absorbed by DG Bank in 1990, by which time some Unico members had their own representation in the UK.

In 1991, the group extended its scope beyond the borders of Europe, by establishing its International Platform, to which were invited Japan's Norinchukin Bank, Canada's Caisse Centrale Desjardins and Chile's Banco del Desarrollo. The International Platform met once a year at the time of the annual meetings of the World Bank.

Unico sought ways for the member banks to work together, primarily in Europe, in corporate, international and retail banking. The organization was headed by a Steering Committee and was backed by a Secretariat in Amsterdam; there were working groups developing new products and services, as well as promoting technological co-operation. The Unico Banking Institute, established for training purposes in 1982, ran conferences, workshops and seminars. Although the banks were co-operative and mutual in character, they had greatly extended the range of their activities and, in some cases, a part of the share capital was quoted on the stock market. They competed with the large universal banks across a wide front, as well as maintaining their dominant role in the small industrial, trading, personal and agricultural sectors. The launch of its cash management system, UniCash, at the same time as the euro, in 1999, was considered an important development by Unico; this product has some non-Unico members as participants, such as Lloyds TSB Bank.

Unico's strategy was summed up by its Secretary General, Rémy Lasne, in 1998: 'Unico member banks realize that they are extremely powerful as a group. First, given their common co-operative roots, they share the same values and concerns. Secondly, they all have a long history of serving their clients' and members' needs first and foremost. And last but not least, their combined market share of around 15 per cent means their significant weight in the single currency bloc cannot be matched by any other player in Europe.'

Sources

Annual reports of shareholder banks.
Brochures of the five banking clubs.

Bussière, Eric, 'Paribas, le Crédit Lyonnais et leur stratégie européenne depuis les années 1960: entre anticipations et choix de la raison', in Y. Cassis and S. Battilossi (eds), *European Banking and the European Challenge, 1950s–1970s* (Oxford: Oxford University Press, forthcoming).
Gall, Lothar, Gerald D. Feldman, Harold James, Carl-Ludwig Holtferich and Hans E. Buschgen, *The Deutsche Bank 1870–1995* (London: Weidenfeld & Nicolson, 1995).
Garelli, François, *The Inter-Alpha Group* (Edinburgh: Royal Bank of Scotland, 1987).
Green, Michael, 'New model multinational bank', *The Banker*, vol. 121 (May 1971), pp. 480–487.
Holmes A.R. and E. Green, *Midland: 150 years of banking business* (London: Batsford, 1986).
Jones, Geoffrey, *British Multinational Banking 1830–1990* (Oxford: Clarendon Press, 1993).
Ross, Duncan, 'European banking clubs in the 1960s: a flawed strategy', *Business and Economic History*, vol. 27, no. 2 (Winter 1998), pp. 353–366.

Orion directors and financial statistics

Listed below are: Chairmen and Chief Executives of Orion Bank, 1971–81, Orion Termbank, 1970–74, Orion Multinational Services, 1970–74 and Orion Royal Bank, 1981–88; Vice and Deputy Chairmen of Orion Bank, 1979–81 and Orion Royal Bank, 1981–88; Managing, Executive and Non-Executive Directors of Orion Bank, 1971–81, Orion Termbank, 1970–74, Orion Multinational Services, 1970–74 and Orion Royal Bank, 1981–88.

DIR = Date appointed as Director; NED = Non-Executive Director, other than shareholder representatives.

Chairmen and Chief Executives		Deputy and Vice Chairmen and Executive Vice Presidents	
Abell, J.N.	1982–85	Chataway, C.J., (DIR 1974)	1979–88
Caccia, Lord (DIR 1971)	1973–74	Cravero, A. (DIR 1979)	1981–85
Cunningham, T.J. III (DIR 1970)	1979–81	De Gelsey, W.H.M. (DIR 1973)	1979–88
		Hubbard, P.M. (DIR 1974)	1979–86
Dibbs, A.H.A.	1970–73	Paterson, R.C. (DIR 1980)	1981–82
Finlayson, J.F. (DIR 1973)	1981–82	Pritchard, D. (DIR 1986)	1986–89
Grierson, R.H.	1971–73	Taylor, P.A.	1986–88
Haley, J.C.	1970–73		
Hardinge, Lord	1981–82		
Kelly, B.V.	1973–74		
Montagu, Hon. David	1974–79		
Sanders, J.R.	1986–89		
Sandon, Lord	1979–81		
Styles, R.G.P. (DIR 1971)	1985–86		
Wilkinson, P.W.	1972–73		

Managing Directors, Executive and Non-Executive Directors

Achen, N.C.	Baker-Bates, R.P.	Barnett, D.J.
Beale, D.G.	Bergel, N.S.	Betley, T.I.
Bobba, F. (NED)	Bonsor, M.C.	Bowbyes, A.A.
Brand, C.C.	Brennan, M.A.	Broughton, A.W.
Browning, P.J.	Bunting, J.M.	Burgun, G.I.
Burnett, D.H.	Canning, S.	Chamberlain, R.A.
Cohen, J.N.	Cook, J.P.	Crookston, S.A.
Cruickshank, A.A.C.	D'Alessandro, D.	Detrie, A.P.M.P.J.
Dukes, L.D.C.	Fane, J.P. MC	Fetzer, R.W.
Fisher, C.J.H.	Fisher III, F.C.	Fraser, I.H.
Fujita, K.	Gager, S.D.	Geddes, A.J.C
Gilday, R.A.	Girle, P.A.	Goldman, Sir Samuel
Grothgar, V.K.E.	Gurry, W.P.	Hall, G.E.
Hall, R.C.	Hasskamp, P.	Hesson, P.J.
Hitchcock, H.A.	Hofmann, P.H.	Hooft, P.C.
Horack III, F.E.	Jackman, T.J.	Jalving, D.L.
Johnson, N.G.	Kelly, B.V.	Kerr, J.E.
Kikano, K.N.	Klingsick, M.G.	Knight, R.B.
Knul, A.	Koehrer, R.W.	Kollar, A.
Konomos, G.J.	Kuhlmann, P.	Kunisch, H.A.
Lallier, A.M.S.	Langton, J.L.	Large, A.M.B.
Lipfert, Prof. Dr H.	Logie, I.T.H.	Loudon, J.H. (NED)
Lubran, J.F.	Mackay, W.C.C.	Malvezzi, G.
Marengo, P.C.	Marple, A.C.	Marshall, A.J.
Martinuzzi, L.S.	McFadyen, W.N.	McGill, B.J.
McLaughlin, W. Earle	Meir, N.P.H.	Melchett, Lord (NED)
Mills, S.J.	Molendi, A.	Monnet, F.-M.
Morgan, I.J.	Mutkin, H.G.	Nakamura, T.
Nezzo, A.	Norton, P.J.	Oddie, H.E.T.
Ogden, W.S.	Okada, S.	Opiat, R.J.
Palmer, D.C.	Perry, M.J.	Petts, L.
Pook, J.R.	Poullain, Dr L.	Raetting, L.R.

Raikes, A.F.
Rivosecchi, M.
Ross, M.S.
Schoeppler, O.
Sippel, Dr H.
Sturgeon, C.L.
Tatrallyay, G.P.Z.
Thiel, G.
Utting, R.A.
Vere-Hodge, N.M.
Watson, M.A.
Whitehead, D.
Wong, E.Y.H.
Wright, A.J.
Youssef, G.

Reid, D.S.
Robertson, D.L.
Rossi, G.
Seipp, W.
Stanley, R.E.
Sugiyama, N.
Taylor, A.R.
Tibbles, C.I.
Vaile, D.W.
Villas-Boas, M.
Webb, A.A.
Wilkinson, Sir Graham
Woods, G.D.
Wynne, G.L.

Reilly, F.R.
Romines, J.C.
Scammell, S.G.A.
Seliwoniuk, J.
Stokes, W.F.
Taneda, K.
Terenghi, M.
Townley, J.A.B.
Van der Beugel, T.M.
Villiers, N.C.H.
Webber, M.O.
Wilson, T.M.
Wraw, C.G.
Yamamuro, Y.

Orion financial statistics

The following key financial statistics are derived from Orion's annual reports; there are three distinct phases. From 1970 to 1974, there were two trading entities, Orion Bank (OB), a merchant bank, and Orion Termbank (OTB), a medium-term lending bank, with group co-ordination provided by a non-trading company, Orion Multinational Services (OMS). These three companies were separately owned by the shareholders. The shareholding consortium took shape over a two-year period; by the end of 1972, 20 per cent each was owned by Chase Manhattan Bank, Royal Bank of Canada, National Westminster Bank and Westdeutsche Landesbank Girozentrale and 10 per cent each by Credito Italiano and Mitsubishi Bank.

On 30 December 1974, a reorganization took effect: OTB acquired OB and changed its name to OB, which became the prime trading entity. In June 1981, Royal Bank of Canada bought out the other five shareholders and merged OB with another UK subsidiary, changing OB's name to Orion Royal Bank (ORB). Its name was changed in November 1989 to Royal Bank of Canada Europe Limited (RBCE), and it remains a major trading unit of Royal Bank of Canada. All figures are in £ million, unless otherwise stated.

Year	Total footings	Loans	Leased assets	Liquid assets	Other assets	Deposits	Capital & reserves	Sub-ordinated loan	Other liabilities	Pre-tax profit	Pre-tax return (per cent)	Net income	Dividend paid
1971 OB	17.8	12.6	nil	5.1	nil	12.8	5.0	nil	nil	nil	–	nil	nil
1971 OTB	156.6	60.1	nil	96.4	0.1	150.4	5.9	nil	0.3	0.8	13.5	0.5	nil
1972 OB	59.4	36.2	nil	20.5	2.7	54.2	5.2	nil	nil	0.4	7.7	0.2	nil
1972 OTB	278.1	115.9	nil	162.0	0.2	270.1	7.6	nil	0.4	1.1	14.5	0.7	nil
1973 OB	139.3	58.0	nil	79.1	6.7	134.4	4.9	nil	nil	(0.4)	–	(0.3)	nil
1973 OTB	408.0	174.9	nil	233.1	nil	395.5	11.8	nil	0.5	2.0	16.9	1.1	nil
1974 OB	550.0	489.4	nil	34.1	8.1	524.2	23.7	nil	2.1	4.9	20.7	2.4	nil
1975 OB	717.2	593.0	nil	101.1	23.1	684.3	27.3	nil	3.6	7.4	27.1	3.6	nil
1976 OB	998.3	793.8	5.5	166.8	32.2	946.4	35.9	10.6	5.5	9.7	27.0	5.1	0.8
1977 OB	1025.6	824.6	16.3	144.2	40.4	969.0	39.9	9.4	7.2	10.2	25.6	5.4	0.8
1978 OB	1115.3	897.2	28.8	154.4	34.9	1051.1	46.8	8.8	8.6	10.1	21.6	8.0	0.8
1979 OB	1231.9	931.5	33.9	221.6	44.9	1163.0	52.9	8.1	7.9	8.5	16.1	7.5	0.8
1980 OB	1283.2	783.8	38.7	410.3	50.4	1209.9	57.6	7.5	8.2	7.2	13.0	5.9	0.8
1981 ORB	1939.2	1208.9	59.2	549.0	122.1	1828.5	60.8	31.6	18.3	4.2	9.2	4.3	3.0
1982 ORB	2050.5	1213.8	60.3	616.7	159.7	1933.0	73.0	35.4	7.1	10.2	13.4	7.1	3.5
1983 ORB	1993.7	1144.4	53.3	635.8	160.2	1867.0	79.8	40.1	6.8	15.5	20.6	13.7	9.5

1984 ORB	2606.2	1270.0	40.2	823.4	472.6	2119.6	85.0	48.5	353.1	10.5	*12.4*	8.5	nil
1985 ORB	2577.4	911.0	86.7	820.4	759.3	2006.2	93.6	42.7	434.9	17.7	*19.0*	17.2	5.4
1986 ORB	2746.3	520.2	120.2	852.5	1253.4	1853.5	84.3	79.6	728.9	(3.4)	–	(0.2)	nil
1987 ORB	2941.2	152.9	129.9	1835.1	823.3	2234.1	48.5	70.7	587.9	(16.7)	–	(16.8)	17.2
1988 ORB	726.4	92.1	nil	269.3	365.0	486.9	33.4	64.6	141.5	(14.2)	–	(14.2)	nil
1989 ORB	556.9	57.0	nil	171.2	328.7	377.1	55.6	72.9	51.3	8.9	*16.9*	8.9	nil

Source: Orion annual reports.

NOTES

(1) Accounting dates are 31 December 1971–80, 30 September 1981–87 and 30 October 1988–89; periods are 12 months, except for 1971 (OB 4 months), 1981 (9 months) and 1988 (13 months).

(2) Return is the pre-tax profits expressed as a percentage of year-end capital & reserves, annualized in 1981; figures in brackets indicate losses.

(3) Amounts of less than £50 000 appear as nil.

(4) Figures are consolidated for 1974–87, unconsolidated for 1971–73 and 1988–89.

(5) Capital & reserves includes minority interests.

(6) The figures for loan outstandings fell in 1980 because of the reclassification of certain loans to other banks.

(7) Leasing activity resulted in low levels of current taxation, because of deferral of tax; leasing was commenced in 1973, but its volume was insufficient to be segregated until 1976.

(8) The increase in footings in 1981 was mainly due to the merger of OB and RBCE, after Royal Bank of Canada acquired 100 per cent control.

(9) The rise in other assets and other liabilities, from 1984, was primarily due to increased securities trading; most of this activity (Eurobonds and UK gilts) was terminated at the end of 1987.

The Orion shareholders in 1970

This appendix profiles the Orion shareholders as they were in 1970.

Chase Manhattan Bank, New York (Chase) was ranked number 3 by size both in the USA and world bank listings, behind Bank of America and First National City Bank (now Citibank). Its assets were $22.2 billion at the end of 1969. The bank's origins can be traced back to the creation of The Manhattan Company in 1799 by Aaron Burr (later Vice President of the United States, who killed a rival banker, Alexander Hamilton, in a duel in 1804) and others, in order ostensibly to provide clean water to the people of New York. Its charter enabled it to carry out other activities and, in the same year, Bank of The Manhattan Company opened its doors at 40 Wall Street. In 1808, the water operation was sold and the company concentrated on banking. The bank prospered throughout the nineteenth century, even maintaining its dividend in the 1873 panic.

Chase National Bank was established in 1877 in New York; it developed rapidly in the early part of the twentieth century through merger and acquisition. In 1917, it set up The Chase Securities Corporation, but its activities were halted by the Glass–Steagall Act (1933), which separated commercial from investment banking. The Equitable Trust Company, controlled by the Rockefeller family, became part of Chase National in 1930. In 1955, Chase National Bank and Bank of The Manhattan Company were merged.

In the 1960s, under the leadership of David Rockefeller, Chase Manhattan Bank, already very strong at home, undertook a major expansion overseas. At the start of the decade, Chase was represented in 18 territories outside the USA; ten years later, Chase was present in 73 overseas territories, more often than not through joint ventures or strategic stakes. Among the countries where Chase was particularly keen to expand was Canada; in 1963, Chase endeavoured to buy 25 per cent of the capital of Toronto Dominion Bank, but the move was not approved by the Canadian authorities.

However, Chase's great rival, Citibank, succeeded in acquiring control of a smaller bank, Mercantile Bank of Canada. In 1967, Chase made a similar, though more modest, proposal to Royal Bank of Canada (see below), which helped set the scene for the negotiations leading to Orion's formation.

In 1969, to facilitate diversification outside traditional commercial banking, the bank became a subsidiary of a one bank holding company. Despite the Glass–Steagall Act, Chase was able to participate in certain investment banking ventures outside the USA, making its investments through specialized group companies rather than the bank itself; Chase participated in setting up an investment bank in Australia in 1969, as well as Orion in 1970 and several others in the 1970s.

Royal Bank of Canada, Montreal (Royal Bank) was ranked number 12 in the world bank listings and first in Canada, with assets of $9.5 billion at the end of 1969. Its origins go back to 1864, when a group of merchants in Halifax, Nova Scotia, formed the Merchants Bank, which was incorporated in 1869, under a federal charter, as the Merchants Bank of Halifax. Its initial focus was international rather than domestic; its Bermuda branch (1882) was opened before its Montreal branch (1887). Among its earliest correspondent relationships were those established with forerunners of future Orion partners, Chase and NatWest, in 1888 and 1889. In 1901, with the growth of its domestic activities, the bank adopted its present name. The head office was moved from Halifax to Montreal in 1907. The bank grew through branching and acquisitions and by the mid-1920s it had become the largest bank in Canada.

Overseas, branches were established in New York (1899), London (1910), Barcelona (1918), Paris (1919) and Vladivostok, which both opened and closed in 1919. There was also significant expansion in the Caribbean and Latin America, notably Cuba, where, in the early 1920s, the bank had 65 branches. In 1925, the Bank of Central and South America was acquired, providing the basis of the bank's Latin American business, although much of the bank's network there was closed or nationalized.

After the Second World War, Royal Bank maintained its leadership in the Canadian banking market, serving the personal, institutional and corporate sectors. It played a major role in financing Canada's energy and mineral industries. In the late 1950s, it was an early participant in the Eurocurrency market, taking US$ deposits from Moscow Narodny Bank; this London-based Soviet bank wished, for political reasons, to avoid New York banks, which were also subject to the Federal Reserve's Regulation Q (restricting the rate paid on deposits). In 1962, Royal Bank and Westminster Bank discussed a possible joint venture in Europe; it did not come to fruition, because President de Gaulle vetoed UK membership of the EEC in the following year. In 1965, a joint venture, RoyWest Banking Corporation, was set up by

Royal Bank, Westminster Bank and others in Nassau, Bahamas, to do medium-term lending and trustee business.

A revision of Canadian bank regulation in 1967 stimulated competition although investment banking was still not permitted; Royal Bank maintained its all-round growth, achieving a particularly strong position in residential mortgages. In the same year, Chase informally proposed a 10 per cent exchange of shares with Royal Bank, which never happened. Soon afterwards, discussions took place between the presidents of the two banks about forming a major consortium bank together; these talks culminated in the formation, with its partners, of Orion in 1970, which opened up new activities and markets for Royal Bank.

National Westminster Bank, London (NatWest) was ranked number 7 in the world bank listings, with assets of $10.6 billion at the end of 1969, and second in the UK, after Barclays. The bank was created in 1968–1970, although its forerunners can be traced back to the middle of the seventeenth century. A report of the Prices and Income Board, a UK governmental agency, in 1967 had envisaged rationalization within the UK banking industry, although probably not among the 'Big Five' – Barclays, Lloyds, Midland, National Provincial and Westminster. Thus, the announcement, in January 1968, that two of them, National Provincial Bank and Westminster Bank, planned to merge, was a great surprise. It prompted two of the other 'Big Five', Barclays and Lloyds, to propose a three-way merger between them and Martins Bank, which was blocked on monopoly grounds; later, Martins was bought by Barclays alone. It took nearly two years to accomplish the operational and regulatory requirements, before the new National Westminster Bank opened its doors on 1 January 1970.

The NatWest, as it soon came to be known, grew out of dozens of earlier mergers, acquisitions and name changes. Banking legislation in England in the early nineteenth century encouraged the spread of joint stock banks in competition with private banking partnerships. The NatWest's main components were three joint stock banks: (1) District Bank, founded in 1829, which, in 1962, became an autonomous subsidiary of (2) National Provincial Bank, founded in 1833, and (3) Westminster Bank, founded in 1834. The joint stock system enabled these three banks to set up a network of branches covering most of England and Wales. In addition, numerous private banks came into their ownership, notably Smiths of Nottingham (founded in 1658) and Coutts & Co (1692), traditional bankers to British royalty and nobility.

Although the new NatWest had some 3600 branches in the UK and a major share of the domestic market, its international business was much smaller than that of its three main competitors, Barclays, Lloyds and Midland; this was seen to be NatWest's most promising area of potential growth.

NatWest's predecessors had created overseas joint ventures, mainly in Europe, one such being the (ultimately unsuccessful) Compagnia Italo–Britannica, with its future Orion partner, Credito Italiano. In 1962 and 1965, substantial discussions about co-operation between Royal Bank of Canada and Westminster resulted in the formation of RoyWest (see above). In 1966, National Provincial and London merchant bankers, N.M. Rothschild & Sons, formed a joint venture, National Provincial & Rothschild (London), later renamed Rothschild Intercontinental Bank. In the following year, Westminster formed International Commercial Bank, a consortium bank set up primarily for making medium-term Eurocurrency loans, with four other international banks; NatWest sold its interests in these two joint ventures in 1969 and 1971 (described in Appendix II, S1/29 and S1/13). Orion's creation opened up new avenues for NatWest in international investment banking and medium- and long-term lending. Although these activities were not formally barred to NatWest, they were regarded at the time as unsuitable for UK clearing banks; attitudes soon changed.

Westdeutsche Landesbank Girozentrale, Düsseldorf (WestLB) was ranked number 14 in the world listings at the end of 1969 and first in West Germany, with assets of \$9.35 billion. As the largest bank in West Germany's most populous state, North Rhine–Westphalia, and as its banker, WestLB was a major force in the economy. WestLB was owned by the state government, local authorities and regional savings banks, for all of which it provided banking services.

WestLB's history as a public sector bank goes back to 1818, when the Swedish government offered 160 000 taler to the province of Westphalia, as reparation for damage caused by Swedish and Danish soldiers in the Napoleonic Wars. These funds were used to form the Provinzialbank–Hülfskasse of Westphalia in 1832; a similar bank was created in neighbouring Rhineland in 1854. They became important contributors to the development of Prussia and, later, Germany in the 19th century.

These two banks became landesbanks at the end of the 19th century, under the names Landesbank für Westfalen Girozentrale and Rheinische Girozentrale und Provinzialbank; their head offices were, respectively, in Münster and Düsseldorf. Surviving difficult times during and between two World Wars, with the advent of the Marshall Plan and the currency reforms of 1948, they participated actively in the recovery of West Germany.

In 1969, the two landesbanks were merged into a single entity, Westdeutsche Landesbank Girozentrale, with head offices in Düsseldorf and Münster, becoming the largest public sector bank in West Germany. Until that time, the leading private sector universal banks, such as Deutsche Bank, Dresdner Bank and Commerzbank, had a dominant position in West German industry and trade. The creation of WestLB represented a significant competitor for these three banks domestically; its new strength and size meant that it could also become a strong competitor on the international scene as well, in its own name and through its association with Orion.

Credito Italiano, Milan (Credito) was ranked number 40 in the world listings and 4 in Italy at the end of 1969, with assets of $6.1 billion. It was founded as Banca di Genova in 1870, soon after the unification of Italy; initially, it operated as a regional institution in Liguria, from which it expanded into the industrial North and other parts of Italy. In 1895, a financial crisis struck the Italian banking sector and the bank was reorganized, with the participation of some foreign banks; among them were two German banks, R. Warschauer & C., a merchant bank, and Nationalbank für Deutschland, an antecedent of Dresdner Bank; the name was then changed to Credito Italiano.

For the next two decades, Credito expanded rapidly, both domestically and internationally; it acquired additional shareholders from France, Belgium and Switzerland. Its activities were those of a *banca mista*, spanning both commercial and merchant banking; it developed strong ties with Italian industry and acquired a significant portfolio of industrial equities. In 1911, Credito Italiano opened an affiliate in Brazil, in partnership with a Belgian company, and a branch in London. By 1914, the bank had over 60 branches and offices. During the First World War, its international connections enabled it to finance essential imports into Italy. In 1916, with a NatWest forerunner and others, it formed Compagnia Italo–Britannica to promote Anglo–Italian trade and investment. In the 1920s, the bank resumed its international development, participating in joint ventures in China, Egypt and several European countries; it was increasingly engaged in merchant banking activities, participating in capital raising for many leading Italian companies.

The stock market crash in 1929 greatly reduced the value of the bank's equity investments and many of its industrial customers could not meet their commitments. In 1933, the government rescued the banking system by creating a state holding company, Istituto per la Ricostruzione Industriale (IRI). IRI then acquired most of Credito Italiano's equity portfolio and a 78 per cent stake in the bank itself (later increased to 82 per cent), as well as control of Banca Commerciale Italiana and Banco di Roma; although these three IRI banks retained many private shareholders, mostly with very small holdings, they were declared *banche di interesse nazionale* and came under strong governmental influence. Thereafter, for some years, Italian banks became confined to short-term commercial banking activities, mainly of a domestic character. The Banking Act of 1936 prevented banks from being industrial shareholders.

As the Italian economy prospered after the Second World War, so did the bank and it began to resume its international expansion. In 1946, Credito was a co-founder of Mediobanca, which became the leading merchant bank in Italy. Credito continued its policy of building up close contacts with the leading industrial groups; among its board members were leading industrialists, such as Giovanni Agnelli, head of FIAT, the vehicles and engineering group. In 1969, the first steps towards privatization took place when the IRI banks offered an increase of capital to private shareholders and Credito Italiano's shares were listed on the Milan Stock Exchange, thus raising the private sector's share of the bank from 18 per cent to 23 per cent. The investment in Orion enabled Credito to carry out financial operations in the Euromarkets for Italian public and private sector entities, activities that were otherwise difficult to carry out due to the Bank of Italy's strict controls.

Mitsubishi Bank, Tokyo was ranked number 16 in the world listings and second in Japan at the end of 1969, with assets of $9.27 billion. The bank traced its origins to a shipping company, Tsukumo Shokai, founded in 1870 by Yataro Iwasaki; he also founded a number of other businesses, which were to form the nucleus of the widely diversified Mitsubishi group of trading and industrial companies. One of them was a financial exchange house that also engaged in warehousing, Mitsubishi Kawasi-ten. This company, the forerunner of Mitsubishi Bank, began to do foreign currency transactions in 1890. As the Mitsubishi group grew, its financing needs also grew and, in 1919, the exchange office became independent and was incorporated as Mitsubishi Bank.

During the 1920s, as Japanese industry and trade expanded, Mitsubishi Bank built up its activities, deriving strength from co-operating with many other Mitsubishi companies under the *zaibatsu* system; by the 1930s, Mitsubishi was the second largest group in Japan. Under the US occupation after the Second World War, Japan's *zaibatsu* groups were dissolved and the Mitsubishi group was split into smaller companies. However, the bank, renamed Chiyoda Bank and chartered as a city bank, remained intact. In 1953, it re-assumed the name Mitsubishi Bank.

During the 1950s and 1960s, the bank became a major participant in the rapid growth of the Japanese economy. Much of its financing activities was directed to the Mitsubishi industrial and trading companies, for which it acted as 'house bank'; it also did extensive business outside the Mitsubishi group. As a city bank, Mitsubishi Bank was prohibited from certain foreign exchange, long-term lending and securities underwriting activities. Partly to mitigate the effect of these restrictions, the bank formed a London consortium bank, Japan International Bank (see Appendix II, S1/19), in 1970, with six other Japanese institutions, three of which were commercial banks and three securities houses. The opportunity to join Orion in 1972 gave Mitsubishi another vehicle for participating in the international commercial and investment banking market.

Sources

Bank annual reports and brochures.
Press and interviews.

Bankers Almanac.
Credito Italiano, Cento Anni, 1870–1970 (privately published by the bank, 1970).
Ince, C.H., *The Royal Bank of Canada: A Chronology, 1864–1969* (privately published by the bank, 1970).
McDowall, Duncan, *Quick to the Frontier: Canada's Royal Bank* (Toronto: McLelland & Stewart, 1993).
MITSUBISHI STORY, History, Now and Future (privately published by Mitsubishi Center).
Reed, Richard, *National Westminster Bank: A Short History* (privately published by the bank, 1989).
St James's Press, Encyclopedia of Company Histories (various volumes).
Wilson, J.D., *The Chase, 1945–85* (Cambridge MA: Harvard Business School Press, 1986).

To pp. 1–9

Prologue

[1] *New York Times*, 30 April 1970.
[2] NatWest Group Archives, NWB Dibbs Papers 6956. Multi-International Meeting at Chase Manhattan Bank, Wednesday 29 April 1970.

1 Origins of the Euromarkets

[1] Samuel L. Hayes and Philip M. Hubbard, *Investment Banking: A Tale of Three Cities* (Boston MA: Harvard Business School Press, 1990), p.34.
[2] Daniel R. Kane, *The Eurodollar Market and the Years of Crisis* (London: Croom Helm, 1983), p.2.
[3] R.B. Johnston, *The Economics of the Euro-Market: History, Theory and Policy* (London: Macmillan, 1983), p.33.
[4] 'The Euro-dollar market: What it means for London', *The Banker*, vol. 119 (August 1969), p.778.
[5] Paul Bareau, 'The international money and capital markets', in E. Victor Morgan, R.A. Brealy, B.S. Yamey and Paul Bareau (eds.), *City Lights: Essays on Financial Institutions and Markets in the City of London* (London: IEA, 1979) p.28.
[6] Kane, *The Eurodollar Market*, p.7.
[7] Johnston, *The Economics of the Euro-Market*, p.16.
[8] 'The Euro-dollar market: What it means for London', p.779.
[9] Paul Bareau, 'The international money and capital markets', p.59.
[10] R.B. Johnston, *The Economics of the Euro-Market*, p.11.
[11] 'The Euro-dollar market: What it means for London', p.779.
[12] Hayes and Hubbard, *Investment Banking*, p.31.
[13] Peter Shearlock and William Ellington, *The Eurobond Diaries* (Brussels: Euroclear, 1994), p.9.
[14] Shearlock and Ellington, *The Eurobond Diaries*, p.3.
[15] Ian M. Kerr, *A History of the Eurobond Market: The First 21 Years* (London: Euromoney Publications, 1984), p.16; Shearlock and Ellington, *The Eurobond Diaries*, p.4.
[16] Hayes and Hubbard, *Investment Banking*, p.30.
[17] Appendix II, S2/12.
[18] Kerr, *A History of the Eurobond Market*, p.14.
[19] Kerr, *A History of the Eurobond Market*, p.11.
[20] Kerr, *A History of the Eurobond Market*, p.15; Ian Fraser, *The High Road to England* (London: Michael Russell, 1999), p.260.
[21] Hayes and Hubbard, *Investment Banking*, p.30.
[22] Speech by Governor Lord Cromer, October 1962, quoted by Hayes and Hubbard, *Investment Banking*, p.30.

23 Ron Chernow, *The House of Morgan: An American Banking Dynasty and the Rise of Modern Finance* (New York: Atlantic Monthly Press, 1990), p.544.
24 Hayes and Hubbard, *Investment Banking*, Table 2.3, p.36.
25 Kerr, *A History of the Eurobond Market*, p.29.
26 Hayes and Hubbard, *Investment Banking*, p.35.
27 M.S. Mendelsohn, *Money on the Move: The Modern International Capital Market* (New York: McGraw-Hill, 1980), p.183.
28 Hayes and Hubbard, *Investment Banking*, p.45.
29 See Table 7.8.
30 Kerr, *A History of the Eurobond Market*, p.34; Hayes and Hubbard, *Investment Banking*, p.52.
31 Shearlock and Ellington, *The Eurobond Diaries*, p.12; Kerr, *A History of the Eurobond Market*, p.35.
32 Michael von Clemm, 'The rise of consortium banking', *Harvard Business Review*, vol. 49 (May–June 1971), p.128.
33 R.B. Johnston, *The Economics of the Euro-Market*, p.17.
34 Eugene Sarver, *The Eurocurrency Market Handbook* (New York: NYIF, 1988), p.22; Appendix II, S2/12.
35 Kane, *The Eurodollar Market*, p.12.
36 Robert, P. McDonald, *International Syndicated Loans* (London: Euromoney, 1982), p.31; on Bankers Trust International, see Appendix II, S2/5.
37 Appendix II, S2/17.
38 McDonald, *International Syndicated Loans*, Table 2, p.32.
39 Bank of England, *Quarterly Bulletin* – various issues.
40 Russell Taylor, *Going for Broke: Confessions of a Merchant Banker* (London: Simon & Schuster, 1993), p.139.
41 John Plender and Paul Wallace, *The Square Mile: A Guide to the New City of London* (London: Century Publishing, 1985), p.32.
42 'Foreign banks in London', *The Banker*, vol. 130 (November 1980), p.87.
43 Paul Bareau, 'The American bank invasion', *Euromoney* (May 1971), p.14.
44 R.B. Johnston, *The Economics of the Euro-Market*, p.13.

2 Rise of consortium banking

1 Bank of England, *Quarterly Bulletin* (June 1975). The 35 UK consortium banks discussed in this chapter are those fitting this definition, although there were also consortium banks which were partly owned subsidiaries of other banks or without a non-UK bank shareholder. They are profiled in Appendix II.
2 'Walter Wriston: Interview', *The Banker*, vol. 124 (July 1974), p.745.
3 Steven I. Davis, *The Euro-Bank* (London: Macmillan, 1976), pp.18–19.
4 Shearlock and Ellington, *The Eurobond Diaries*, p.14.
5 Anthony Sampson, *The Money Lenders* (London: Hodder & Stoughton, 1981), p.204.
6 Taylor, *Going for Broke*, p.133.
7 von Clemm, 'The rise of consortium banking', p.129. See Appendix II, S2/12.
8 Taylor, *Going for Broke*, p.133.

⁹ Alberto A. Weissmüller, 'London consortium banks', *Journal of the Institute of Bankers*, vol. 95 (August 1974), p.205.

¹⁰ *Wall Street Journal*, 25 May 1973.

¹¹ Appendix II, S2/20.

¹² Appendix II, S2/14.

¹³ Appendix II, S2/4.

¹⁴ Appendix II, S2/15.

¹⁵ Appendix II, S2/2.

¹⁶ Taylor, *Going for Broke*, p.133.

¹⁷ Interview with Peter Cooke, former Bank of England executive and chairman of the Banking Regulations and Supervisory Committee of the Bank for International Settlements – the 'Cooke Committee'.

¹⁸ John Brooks in *The New Yorker*, quoted in Sampson, *The Money Lenders*, p.80.

¹⁹ Appendix II, S2/16.

²⁰ Interview with the second Lord Cobbold of Bank of London and South America, son of the first Lord Cobbold who was chairman of Italian International Bank.

²¹ 23 May 1975, London Interstate Bank, Chairman's statement. See Appendix II, S1/23.

²² Appendix II, S1/25.

²³ Appendix II, S1/7, S1/29 and S2/17.

²⁴ Appendix II, S2/3 and S2/5; von Clemm, 'The rise of consortium banking', p.127.

²⁵ Appendix II, S2/14.

²⁶ Interview with Peter Cooke.

²⁷ See page 184.

²⁸ Michel Develle, 'Les Banques Multinationales de Financement à Moyen Terme et Leur Avenir', *Banque* (December 1972), p.1104.

²⁹ See page 43.

³⁰ von Clemm, 'The rise of consortium banking', p.128.

³¹ von Clemm, 'The rise of consortium banking', p.126.

³² Weissmüller, 'London consortium banks', p.210.

³³ Weissmüller, 'London consortium banks', p.217.

³⁴ Taylor, *Going for Broke*, p.133.

³⁵ von Clemm, 'The rise of consortium banking', p.130.

³⁶ See Appendix II for a description of three such banks: S2/5, S2/6 and S2/17.

³⁷ 'The record of the past 12 months', *The Banker*, vol. 123 (November 1973), p.1319.

³⁸ von Clemm, 'The rise of consortium banking', p.130.

³⁹ Appendix II, S4/2.

⁴⁰ Interview with William de Gelsey.

⁴¹ The five European banking clubs are described in Appendix III.

⁴² Servan-Schreiber, Jean-Jacques, *The American Challenge* (English edition – Melbourne: Penguin, 1968).

⁴³ 'Banking across frontiers', *The Economist*, 21 November 1964, p.851.

⁴⁴ Appendix II, S2/9.

⁴⁵ Eric Bussière, 'Paribas, le Crédit Lyonnais et leur stratégie européenne depuis les années 1960: entre anticipations et choix de la raison', in Y. Cassis and S. Battilossi (eds), *European Banking and the European Challenge, 1950s–1970s* (Oxford: Oxford University Press, forthcoming).

[46] Appendix II, S1/10.

[47] 'New model multinational bank', *The Banker*, vol. 121 (April 1971), pp.480–487. A bilateral alliance between Crédit Lyonnais and Commerzbank was signed in October 1970.

[48] Appendix II, S1/13.

[49] Appendix II, S2/20.

[50] Lloyds Bank annual report and accounts 1972, Chairman's statement.

[51] Lloyds Bank annual report and accounts 1972, Chairman's statement.

[52] Appendix II, S1/17.

[53] Appendix II, S2/19.

[54] Appendix II, S2/4.

[55] Appendix II, S/22.

[56] Source: Appendix II.

[57] Appendix II, S1/25.

[58] A.R. Holmes and E. Green, *Midland: 150 Years of Banking Business* (London: Batsford, 1986), p.252.

[59] Geoffrey Jones, *British Multinational Banking 1830–1990* (Oxford: Clarendon, 1993), pp.327–335.

[60] von Clemm, 'The rise of consortium banking', p.128.

[61] Derek F. Channon, *British Banking Strategy and the International Challenge* (London: Macmillan, 1977), p.169.

[62] von Clemm, 'The rise of consortium banking', p.126.

[63] Appendix II, S1/29.

[64] There were two earlier notable US commercial bank participations in London merchant banks: in 1910, JP Morgan & Co. (later Morgan Guaranty Trust) took a one-third stake in the forerunner of Morgan Grenfell; and in 1963, Citibank acquired a short-lived 14.5 per cent interest in M. Samuel (Hill Samuel).

[65] Edmund de Rothschild, *A Gilt-Edged Life* (London: John Murray, 1998), p.203. Interview with Leopold de Rothschild.

[66] Appendix II, S1/35.

[67] Appendix II, S1/13.

[68] Appendix III.

[69] Appendix II, S1/7.

[70] Appendix II, S1/4.

[71] Appendix II, S1/27.

[72] Appendix II, S1/30

[73] Appendix II, S1/23

[74] Appendix II, S1/22.

[75] London & Continental Bankers, annual reports for 1975 and 1981.

[76] Appendix III.

[77] Appendix II, S1/24

[78] Appendix II, S1/10.

[79] Appendix II, S2/12.

[80] Appendix II, S1/14.

[81] Appendix II, S1/33

[82] Appendix II, S1/16.

[83] Appendix II, S1/32 and S2/20.

[84] Appendix II, S1/31.

85 Appendix II, S1/26.
86 Taylor, *Going for Broke*, p.132.
87 Appendix II, S1/18.
88 Mikhail Gorbachev, *Memoirs* (New York: Doubleday, 1995), p.473.
89 Appendix II, S1/1.
90 Appendix II, S1/6.
91 Appendix II, S1/11.
92 Appendix II, S1/15.
93 Appendix II, S1/21.
94 Appendix II, S1/8.
95 Interview with Alan Peachey.
96 Alfredo Moutinho do Reis, 'Why a Brazilian bank joined a consortium', *Euromoney* (September 1972), p.26.
97 Appendix II, S1/3.
98 Appendix II, S1/19.
99 Appendix II, S1/11, S1/15, S1/16, S1/21, S1/29, S1/30, S1/35, S2/13, S2/14, S2/17, S2/19 and S2/20.
100 Appendix II, S1/5 and S1/9.
101 Appendix II, S1/30; Chernow, *The House of Morgan*, p.608.
102 Chernow, *The House of Morgan*, p.608.
103 Appendix II, S1/20.
104 Appendix II, S1/9 and S2/13.
105 Appendix II, S2/14.
106 See Appendix III.
107 Appendix II, S1/5 and S2/4.
108 Appendix II, S1/12 and S1/28.
109 Appendix II, S1/17.
110 Appendix II, S1/2.
111 What next for consortia?', *The Economist*, 14 February 1976.
112 Source: Appendix II.
113 *Wall Street Journal*, 25 May 1973.

3 Formation of Orion

1 Interview with David Montagu.
2 von Clemm, 'The rise of consortium banking', p.125.
3 McLaughlin, quoted in Duncan McDowall, *Quick to the Frontier: Canada's Royal Bank* (Toronto: McClelland & Stewart, 1993), p.408.
4 Interview with David Rockefeller.
5 The development of Chase Manhattan Bank up to 1970 is described in Appendix V.
6 John Donald Wilson, *The Chase: Chase Manhattan Bank, N.A., 1945–1985* (Boston MA: Harvard Business School Press, 1986), p.162.
7 Wilson, *The Chase*, p.172.
8 The development of Royal Bank of Canada up to 1970 is described in Appendix V.
9 McLaughlin, quoted in McDowall, *Quick to the Frontier*, p.443.
10 Harold van B. Cleveland and Thomas F. Huertas, *Citibank 1812–1970* (Cambridge MA: Harvard University Press, 1985), pp.434–435, note 16.

[11] The development of National Westminster Bank up to 1970 is described in Appendix V.

[12] Interview with Paul Taylor.

[13] NatWest Group Archives, NWB Dibbs Papers 6956. June 1969, 'Summary of Report: Rationalising and Extending the International Business on 28 January 1969', p.8.

[14] NatWest Group Archives, NWB Dibbs Papers 6956. 4 September 1969, 'Multi-International Bank Project', p.5.

[15] NatWest Group Archives, NWB Dibbs Papers 6956. June 1969, 'International Bank: Preliminary Report', p.13.

[16] NatWest Group Archives, NWB Dibbs Papers 6956. June 1969, 'International Bank: Preliminary Report', p.17.

[17] NatWest Group Archives, NWB Dibbs Papers 6956. 4 September 1969, 'Multi-International Bank Project', p.4.

[18] Interview with Jeff Cunningham.

[19] NatWest Group Archives, NWB Dibbs Papers 6956. 20 April 1970, 'International Banking', p.4.

[20] The development of Westdeutsche Landesbank Girozentrale up to 1970 is described in Appendix V.

[21] Appendix III.

[22] NatWest Group Archives, NWB Dibbs Papers 6956. 1 October 1970, 'Multi-International Bank Project', p.1.

[23] NatWest Group Archives, NWB Dibbs Papers 6956. 1 October 1970, 'Notes prepared by Mr Haley for Copenhagen Meeting, September 21/22 1970'.

[24] NatWest Group Archives, NWB Dibbs Papers 6956. 29 October 1970, Press Release: 'Four Leading World Banks Undertake New Joint Activities'.

[25] NatWest Group Archives, NWB Dibbs Papers 6959. 19 April 1971, Ronald Grierson, 'Memo on New Partners for Orion'.

[26] NatWest Group Archives, NWB Dibbs Papers 6872. September 1971, 'Orion Project No. 7 – Japan', p.i.

[27] NatWest Group Archives, NWB Dibbs Papers 6952. 17 June 1971, 'Potential Members of the Orion Group', p.4.

[28] NatWest Group Archives, NWB Dibbs Papers 6959. 19 April 1971, Ronald Grierson, 'Memo on New Partners for Orion'.

[29] The development of Credito Italiano up to 1970 is described in Appendix V.

[30] NatWest Group Archives, NWB Dibbs Papers 6952. 20 September 1971, Press Release 6957/12, 23 June 1971: 'Credito Italiano'.

[31] NatWest Group Archives, NWB Dibbs Papers 6957. 'Credito Italiano Factsheet', p.3.

[32] Orion papers provided by Alvaro Holgoin; John Haley, Report on Meeting with Credito Italiano, 8 April 1971.

[33] NatWest Group Archives, NWB Dibbs Papers 6957. 8 July 1971, 'Orion Project No. 5 – Italy', pp.3 and 7.

[34] NatWest Group Archives, NWB Dibbs Papers 6957. 8 July 1971, 'Orion Project No. 5 – Italy', pp.9–14.

[35] 'Fall of Italy's high priest of banking', *The Independent*, 14 April 1999. Dr Cuccia, a key figure in post-war Italian finance, was managing director of Mediobanca from 1946 to 1982.

36 NatWest Group Archives, NWB Dibbs Papers 6952. 17 June 1971, 'Potential Members of the Orion Group', p.4.
37 The development of Mitsubishi Bank up to 1970 is described in Appendix V.
38 NatWest Group Archives, NWB Dibbs Papers 6956. 29 April 1970, 'Multi-International Meeting at Chase Manhattan Bank', p.3.
39 NatWest Group Archives, NWB Dibbs Papers 6872. September 1971, 'Orion Project – No. 7', p.9.
40 NatWest Group Archives, NWB Dibbs Papers 6872. September 1971, 'Orion Project – No. 7', p.7.
41 Appendix II, S1/3 and S1/19.
42 Interview with William de Gelsey.
43 NatWest Group Archives, NWB Dibbs Papers 6872. September 1971, 'Orion Project – No. 7', Appendix, p.6.
44 NatWest Group Archives, NWB Dibbs Papers 6872. September 1971, 'Orion Project – No. 7', p.4.
45 NatWest Group Archives, NWB Dibbs Papers 6872. September 1971, 'Orion Project – No. 7', p.2.
46 NatWest Group Archives, NWB Dibbs Papers 6872. 'Memorandum from H.A. Hitchcock to A. Dibbs'.
47 NatWest Group Archives, NWB Dibbs Papers 6952. 17 June 1971, 'Potential Members of the Orion Group', p.4.
48 NatWest Group Archives, NWB Dibbs Papers 6951. 19 July 1971, OMS Board Minutes, p.3.
49 NatWest Group Archives, NWB Dibbs Papers 6872. 'Memorandum from H.A. Hitchcock to A. Dibbs'.
50 NatWest Group Archives, NWB Dibbs Papers 6872. 'Memorandum from H.A. Hitchcock to A. Dibbs'.
51 'Opening up Japan', *The Banker*, vol. 122 (April 1972), p.590.
52 NatWest Group Archives, NWB Dibbs Papers 6952. 17 June 1971, 'Potential Members of the Orion Group', p.4.
53 Interview with William de Gelsey.
54 Orion papers provided by Alvaro Holguin; Alvaro Holguin, Report on Orion Marketing in France, October 1976.
55 Orion papers provided by Alvaro Holguin; French Project Group Report, February 1970, p.16.
56 See Appendix III.
57 NatWest Group Archives, NWB Dibbs Papers 6956. 30 July 1970, 'Memo of Interview by H.A. Hitchcock with Crédit Lyonnais executives and Tanneguy de Feuilhade de Chauvin'.
58 Orion papers provided by Alvaro Holguin; Orion Multilateral Services, Report on France, February 1971.
59 NatWest Group Archives, NWB Dibbs Papers 6952. 18 February 1971, 'Memo from John Haley to Alex Dibbs. France'.
60 NatWest Group Archives, NWB Dibbs Papers 6952. 22 February 1971, 'Note from A. Dibbs to H.A. Hitchcock'.
61 Orion papers provided by Alvaro Holguin; John Haley, Report on Meetings with Société Générale, 6 April 1971.

62 Appendix III.
63 NatWest Group Archives, NWB Dibbs Papers 6957. 17 May 1971, 'New Partners for Orion'.
64 Appendix III.
65 Orion papers provided by Alvaro Holguin; Report of Meetings with Suez Banking Group, 25–30 January 1973.
66 Orion papers provided by Alvaro Holguin, Aide Memoire re Consideration by Shareholders of Possibility of Suez Association with the Orion Group, 22 January 1973.
67 NatWest Group Archives, NWB Dibbs Papers 6952. 17 June 1971, 'Potential Members of the Orion Group', p.4.
68 NatWest Group Archives, NWB Dibbs Papers 6873. 15 October 1971, 'Memorandum. From T.A. Green to H.A. Hitchcock re Orion Bank/Termbank/Services'.
69 Interview with Richard Knight.
70 NatWest Group Archives, NWB Dibbs Papers 6959. 1 May 1972, 'The Orion Banking Group', *NatWest Intelligence Bulletin*.
71 NatWest Group Archives, NWB Dibbs Papers 6956. 20 April 1970, 'International Banking', p.8.
72 NatWest Group Archives, NWB Dibbs Papers 6956. 4 September 1969, 'Multi-International Bank Project', p.6.
73 NatWest Group Archives, NWB Dibbs Papers 6956. 29 April 1970, 'Multi-International Bank Project Meeting at Chase Manhattan Bank', p.2.
74 NatWest Group Archives, NWB Dibbs Papers 6956. 29 April 1970, 'Multi-International Bank Project Meeting at Chase Manhattan Bank', p.2.
75 NatWest Group Archives, NWB Dibbs Papers 6956. 5 March 1970, 'Multi-International Bank Project Banking: UK Study Group Report', p.v.
76 NatWest Group Archives, NWB Dibbs Papers 6956. 29 April 1970, 'Multi-International Meeting at Chase Manhattan Bank', p.1.
77 NatWest Group Archives, NWB Dibbs Papers 6956. 30 April 1970, 'Note from W.B. Davidson to H.A. Hitchcock'.
78 NatWest Group Archives, NWB Dibbs Papers 6956. 15 June 1970, 'Memorandum of Meeting with Lord Poole'.
79 NatWest Group Archives, NWB Dibbs Papers 6956. 13 July 1970, 'Note on Meeting'.
80 NatWest Group Archives, NWB Dibbs Papers 6959. February 1971, John Haley, 'What Makes Orion Different?'
81 *Wall Street Journal*, 25 May 1973.
82 NatWest Group Archives, NWB Dibbs Papers 6873. Report by B.V. Kelly on Orion Multinational Services and the Orion Group Structure, 1 April 1976, p.3.
83 NatWest Group Archives, NWB Dibbs Papers 6873. Report by B.V. Kelly on Orion Multinational Services and the Orion Group Structure, 1 April 1976, p.4.
84 NatWest Group Archives, NWB Dibbs Papers 6956. 29 October 1970, Press Release: 'Four Leading World Banks Undertake New Joint Activities'.
85 Interview with Tony Cravero.
86 NatWest Group Archives, NWB Dibbs Papers 6952. March 1971, 'Twelve Questions on Orion'.

4   Orion gets going

1   Quoted in Mendelsohn, *Money on the Move*, p.13.
2   Paul A. Volcker and Toyoo Gyohten, *Changing Fortunes: the World's Money and the Threat to American Leadership* (New York: Times Books, 1992), p.101.
3   NatWest Group Archives, NWB Dibbs Papers 6960. Orion Multinational Services, Board Meeting, 14 December 1970, 'Premises'.
4   *Wall Street Journal*, 25 May 1973.
5   *NatWest Bankground*, No. 24, June 1972, p.1.
6   NatWest Group Archives, NWB Dibbs Papers 6960. Orion Multinational Services, Board Meeting, 14 December 1970.
7   NatWest Group Archives, NWB Dibbs Papers 6960. Orion Termbank, Board Meeting, 15 May 1971.
8   NatWest Group Archives, NWB Dibbs Papers 6955. Orion Termbank, Board Meeting, 15 February 1971.
9   NatWest Group Archives, NWB Dibbs Papers 6960. Orion Termbank, Board Meeting, 15 May 1971.
10 NatWest Group Archives, NWB Dibbs Papers 6960. Orion Termbank, Board Meeting, 15 May 1971.
11 NatWest Group Archives, NWB Dibbs Papers 6960. Orion Termbank, Board Meeting, 8 February 1972.
12 Sources: Orion – Orion Financings, May 1975; Market – Appendix I. 'Market share' means the proportion of syndicated loans in which Orion was either lead manager, co-lead manager or co-manager.
13 NatWest Group Archives, NWB Dibbs Papers 6958. Orion Bank, Board Meeting, 22 October 1973.
14 NatWest Group Archives, NWB Dibbs Papers 6958. Orion Bank, Board Meeting, 22 October 1973.
15 Sources: Loans – Appendix IV. Staff – NatWest Group Archives, NWB Dibbs Papers 6960. Orion Termbank, Board Papers, Assets and Staff at 31 December.
16 NatWest Group Archives, NWB Dibbs Papers 6960. Orion Termbank, Board Meeting, 8 February 1972.
17 Source: NatWest Group Archives, NWB Dibbs Papers 6960. Orion Termbank, Board Meeting, 13 February 1973.
18 Interview with Martin Klingsick.
19 Rae Weston, *Domestic and Multinational Banking* (London: Croom Helm, 1980), p.308.
20 Interview with Rod Chamberlain.
21 NatWest Group Archives, NWB Dibbs Papers 6955. Orion Termbank, Board Meeting, 23 October 1973, Item 8.
22 Source: Appendix IV.
23 NatWest Group Archives, NWB Dibbs Papers 6959. Orion Bank, Status Report re Managing Director, 22 December 1970. Meeting between head-hunter and NatWest chairman John Prideaux, Alex Dibbs and Senior Representatives Jeff Cunningham of Chase and Geoff Styles of Royal Bank.
24 Ian Fraser, *The High Road to England* (London: Michael Russell, 1999), p.323.
25 NatWest Group Archives, NWB Dibbs Papers 6959. Alex Dibbs, Note of conversation with Mr Haley, 13 January 1971.

[26] Peter Stormonth Darling, *City Cinderella: The Life and Times of Mercury Asset Management* (London: Weidenfeld & Nicolson, 1999), p.14.

[27] Fraser, *The High Road to England*, p.232.

[28] Ronald Grierson, *A Truant Disposition* (London: Weidenfeld & Nicolson, 1992).

[29] Fraser, *The High Road to England*, p.272.

[30] NatWest Group Archives, NWB Dibbs Papers 6959. Orion Bank, Progress Report No. 1, April 1971.

[31] NatWest Group Archives, NWB Dibbs Papers 6958. Orion Bank, Board Meeting, 17 May 1971.

[32] NatWest Group Archives, NWB Dibbs Papers 6958. Orion Bank, Board Meeting, 13 February 1973.

[33] NatWest Group Archives, NWB Dibbs Papers 6958. Orion Bank, Board Meeting, 18 October 1971.

[34] Interview with William de Gelsey.

[35] NatWest Group Archives, NWB Dibbs Papers 6959. Orion Bank, Progress Report No. 1, April 1971.

[36] NatWest Group Archives, NWB Dibbs Papers 6958. Orion Bank, Board Meeting, 13 February 1973.

[37] Interview with Sir Andrew Large.

[38] Interview with William de Gelsey.

[39] Interview with Sir Graham Wilkinson.

[40] Interview with Rod Chamberlain.

[41] NatWest Group Archives, NWB Dibbs Papers 6959. Orion Bank, Memo to staff from the Chairman, 28 December 1972.

[42] Interview with Rod Chamberlain.

[43] NatWest Group Archives, NWB Dibbs Papers 6958. Orion Bank, Chairman's Report to the Board, February 1973.

[44] NatWest Group Archives, NWB Dibbs Papers 6958. Orion Bank, Board Meeting, 17 May 1971.

[45] Interview with William de Gelsey.

[46] Interview with Sir Ronald Grierson.

[47] NatWest Group Archives, NWB Dibbs Papers 6959. Orion Bank, First Thoughts on Orion, 23 February 1971.

[48] NatWest Group Archives, NWB Dibbs Papers 6959. Orion Bank, First Thoughts on Orion, 23 February 1971.

[49] Sources: Orion – Orion Financings; Market – Hayes and Hubbard, *Investment Banking*, p.36. 'Market share' means the proportion of Eurobond new issues in which Orion was either lead manager, co-lead manager or co-manager.

[50] NatWest Group Archives, NWB Dibbs Papers 6958. Orion Bank, Chairman's Report to the Board, November 1972, p.4.

[51] NatWest Group Archives, NWB Dibbs Papers 6958. Orion Bank, Chairman's Report to the Board, November 1972, p.4.

[52] NatWest Group Archives, NWB Dibbs Papers 6958. Orion Bank, Report by the Joint Managing Directors to the Board, 22 October 1973.

[53] Appendix II, S1/35.

[54] NatWest Group Archives, NWB Dibbs Papers 6958. Orion Bank, Chairman's Report to the Board, July 1972.

55 NatWest Group Archives, NWB Dibbs Papers 6959. Memo, Ronald Grierson on Conversation with Leo Martinuzzi re Orion, 7 July 1972.

56 NatWest Group Archives, NWB Dibbs Papers 6959. Memo, Ronald Grierson on Conversation with Leo Martinuzzi re Orion, 7 July 1972.

57 NatWest Group Archives, NWB Dibbs Papers 6969. Letter from John Haley to Alex Dibbs, 17 July 1972; Interview with Jeff Cunningham.

58 *Wall Street Journal*, 23 May 1973.

59 Interview with Sir Graham Wilkinson.

60 NatWest Group Archives, NWB Dibbs Papers 6969. Letter from John Haley to Alex Dibbs, 17 July 1972.

61 NatWest Group Archives, NWB Dibbs Papers 6958. Orion Bank, Chairman's Report to the Board, July 1972.

62 NatWest Group Archives, NWB Dibbs Papers 6958. Orion Bank, Chairman's Report to the Board, July 1972.

63 NatWest Group Archives, NWB Dibbs Papers 6958. Orion Bank, Chairman's Report to the Board, February 1973.

64 NatWest Group Archives, NWB Dibbs Papers 6958. Orion Bank, Chairman's Report to the Board, February 1973.

65 NatWest Group Archives, NWB Dibbs Papers 6958. Orion Bank, Board Meeting, 8 May 1972.

66 NatWest Group Archives, NWB Dibbs Papers 6958. Orion Bank, Board Papers, Minutes of Meeting on 21 November 1972, p.3.

67 NatWest Group Archives, NWB Dibbs Papers 6958. Orion Bank, Board Papers, Minutes of Meeting on 21 November 1972, p.3.

68 Handelsbank was subsequently purchased by Orion shareholder NatWest and became part of Coutts & Co.

69 NatWest Group Archives, NWB Dibbs Papers 6958. Orion Bank, Minutes of Meeting on 7 February 1972.

70 Interview with Rod Chamberlain.

71 NatWest Group Archives, NWB Dibbs Papers 6958. Orion Bank, Chairman's Report to the Board, November 1972.

72 NatWest Group Archives, NWB Dibbs Papers 6958. Orion Bank, Chairman's Report to the Board, 8 May 1972.

73 NatWest Group Archives, NWB Dibbs Papers 6958. Orion Bank, Minutes of Board Meeting on 7 February 1972, p.2.

74 NatWest Group Archives, NWB Dibbs Papers 6958. List of Melchett's director-ships. *Who Was Who, 1971–1980*, p.536.

75 NatWest Group Archives, NWB Dibbs Papers 6958. Orion Bank, Minutes of Board Meeting on 7 February 1972, p.2.

76 'Orion Issue', *Financial Times*, 23 September 1972.

77 Interview with Rod Chamberlain.

78 NatWest Group Archives, NWB Dibbs Papers 6958. Orion Bank, Chairman's Report to the Board, November 1972.

79 NatWest Group Archives, NWB Dibbs Papers 6958. Orion Bank, Board Meeting, 22 October 1973.

80 NatWest Group Archives, NWB Dibbs Papers 6958. Orion Bank, Minutes of the Board Meeting on 8 May 1972.

81 *Who's Who 1974*, p.1263.
82 Interview with Sir Samuel Goldman.
83 Report of the Orion Bank Mission on Commonwealth Export Credit Finance (June 1973), p.1.
84 NatWest Group Archives, NWB Dibbs Papers 6958. Orion Bank, Chairman's Report to the Board, February 1973.
85 NatWest Group Archives, NWB Dibbs Papers 6958. Orion Bank, Board Meeting, 11 June 1973.
86 NatWest Group Archives, NWB Dibbs Papers 6958. Orion Bank, Board Papers, Chairman's Report to the Board, January 1972.
87 Source: Appendix IV.
88 NatWest Group Archives, NWB Dibbs Papers 6958. Orion Bank, Chairman's Report to the Board, May 1972.
89 NatWest Group Archives, NWB Dibbs Papers 6958. Orion Bank, Board Papers, Chairman's Report to the Board, November 1972, p.4.
90 NatWest Group Archives, NWB Dibbs Papers 6873. Proposed Merger of Orion Bank and Orion Termbank, July 1974.
91 NatWest Group Archives, NWB Dibbs Papers 6958. Orion Bank, Chairman's Report to the Board, May 1972.
92 NatWest Group Archives, NWB Dibbs Papers 6958. Orion Bank, Accounts, 31 December 1972.
93 NatWest Group Archives, NWB Dibbs Papers 6958. Orion Bank, Chairman's Report to the Board, May 1972.
94 NatWest Group Archives, NWB Dibbs Papers 6958. Orion Bank, Report by the Chairman, November 1972, p.5.
95 NatWest Group Archives, NWB Dibbs Papers 6958. Orion Bank, Chairman's Report to the Board, February 1973; Orion Bank, Report by the Joint Managing Directors to the Board, June 1973.
96 NatWest Group Archives, NWB Dibbs Papers 6958. Orion Bank, Minutes of Board Meeting, 11 June 1973.
97 Appendix II, S1/21.
98 Wilson, *The Chase*, p.233.
99 NatWest Group Archives, NWB Dibbs Papers 6960. Memorandum for Shareholders' Forum: Definition of Geographical Areas of Activities, 13 September 1974.
100 NatWest Group Archives, NWB Dibbs Papers 6960. Shareholders' Forum, Minutes of Meeting, 27 September 1974, 'Definition of Geographical Areas of Activities'.
101 Orion annual report & accounts 1972.
102 Nigel Lawson, *The View from Number 11* (London: Bantam Press, 1992), p.352.
103 NatWest Group Archives, NWB Dibbs Papers 6869. Orion Newsletter, June 1973.
104 NatWest Group Archives, NWB Dibbs Papers 6891. Orion Group of Companies, 1 April 1977.
105 NatWest Group Archives, NWB Dibbs Papers 6954. Orion Shareholders' Meeting, 12 February 1973.

[106] NatWest Group Archives, NWB Dibbs Papers 6957. Memo re Chairmen's Meeting in Washington, 26 September 1972.

[107] Grierson, *A Truant Disposition*, p.65.

[108] NatWest Group Archives, NWB Dibbs Papers 6958. Orion Bank, Minutes of Meeting, 13 February 1973.

[109] NatWest Group Archives, NWB Dibbs Papers 6954. Orion Shareholders' Forum, 12 February 1973.

[110] NatWest Group Archives, NWB Dibbs Papers 6958. Orion Bank, Chairman's Report, February 1973, p.1.

[111] Source: Appendix IV.

[112] NatWest Group Archives, NWB Dibbs Papers 6958. Report by the Joint Managing Directors to the Board, June 1973, p.1.

[113] NatWest Group Archives, NWB Dibbs Papers 6957. Letter from Philip Wilkinson to A. Dibbs, 18 October 1973.

[114] NatWest Group Archives, NWB Dibbs Papers 6957. Letter from Philip Wilkinson to A. Dibbs, 18 October 1973.

[115] 'Orion loses £1.2 million on Eurobond deals', *Financial Times*, 21 April 1974.

[116] Orion annual report & accounts 1972, p.4.

[117] Orion annual report & accounts 1973, p.4.

[118] Padraic Fallon, 'How David Montagu gave a lead to Orion Bank', *Euromoney* (May 1976), p.52.

5   Stormy weather: Montagu takes the helm

[1] John Littlewood, *The Stock Market* (London: Financial Times/Pitman, 1998), p.202.

[2] Appendix II, S1/30, and also Chapter 3.

[3] Appendix II, S1/23.

[4] Under English company law, companies cannot normally issue new shares below par value.

[5] Appendix III.

[6] Appendix II, S4/2.

[7] 'Consortium banks asked to give pledge on responsibility for rescue', *The Times*, 24 September 1974.

[8] *Euromoney* (November 1974), p.85.

[9] *Euromoney* (January 1975), p.77.

[10] Fallon, 'How David Montagu gave a lead to Orion bank', p.52.

[11] NatWest Group Archives, NWB Dibbs Papers 6954. Memo to the shareholders by John Haley, 17 August 1973.

[12] NatWest Group Archives, NWB Dibbs Papers 6954. Note for the Senior Representatives by Alex Dibbs, 12 November 1973.

[13] NatWest Group Archives, NWB Dibbs Papers 6954. Note for the Senior Representatives by Alex Dibbs, 12 November 1973.

[14] Clay Harris, 'Banking with a lucky lord', *Financial Times*, 20 May 1998.

[15] Harris, 'Banking with a lucky lord'.

[16] Interview with David Montagu.

[17] Interview with David Montagu.

[18] Interview with David Montagu.

[19] Interview with David Montagu.

[20] NatWest Group Archives, NWB Dibbs Papers 6954. David Montagu's Curriculum Vitae.

[21] Obituary of David Montagu, *Daily Telegraph*, 2 July 1998.

[22] Interview with David Montagu.

[23] NatWest Group Archives, NWB Dibbs Papers 6960. Orion Bank, Board Papers, Chief Executive's Report, 21 October 1974.

[24] See Chapter 6.

[25] NatWest Group Archives, NWB Dibbs Papers 6960. Orion Bank, Board Papers, Chief Executive's Report, 21 October 1974.

[26] NatWest Group Archives, NWB Dibbs Papers 6960. Orion Bank, Board Papers, Chief Executive's Report, 21 October 1974.

[27] NatWest Group Archives, NWB Dibbs Papers 6960. Orion Bank, Board Meeting, Chief Executive's Report, 21 October 1974.

[28] The New York office opened in July 1974.

[29] NatWest Group Archives, NWB Dibbs Papers 6960. Orion Bank, Minutes of Meeting of Shareholders' Representatives, 19 July 1974.

[30] Margaret Reid, *The Secondary Banking Crisis, 1973–75* (London: Macmillan, 1982), p.115; John Grady and Martin Weale, *British Banking, 1960–85* (London: Macmillan, 1986), p.113.

[31] NatWest Group Archives, NWB Dibbs Papers 6960. Minutes of Meeting of Shareholders' Representatives, 19 July 1974.

[32] NatWest Group Archives, NWB Dibbs Papers 6865. Letter from Alex Dibbs to Willard Butcher, 22 July 1974.

[33] NatWest Group Archives, NWB Dibbs Papers 6865. Note for the Chairman by Alex Dibbs, 22 July 1974.

[34] NatWest Group Archives, NWB Dibbs Papers 6865. Letter from Alex Dibbs to Willard Butcher, 22 July 1974.

[35] NatWest Group Archives, NWB Dibbs Papers 6873. Memorandum to John Haley from Alex Dibbs, 19 October 1971.

[36] NatWest Group Archives, NWB Dibbs Papers 6873. Memorandum to John Haley from Alex Dibbs, 19 October 1971.

[37] NatWest Group Archives, NWB Dibbs Papers 6873. Memorandum from Alex Dibbs to David Montagu, 8 October 1974.

[38] Interview with Sir George Blunden.

[39] NatWest Group Archives, NWB Dibbs Papers 6959. Note to J.C. Haley from R.H. Grierson re: Orion Bank & Orion Termbank, 24 September 1971.

[40] NatWest Group Archives, NWB Dibbs Papers 6958. Orion Bank, Board Meeting, Chairman's Report to the Board, 7 February 1972.

[41] NatWest Group Archives, NWB Dibbs Papers 6959. Note to all Orion Bank executives from R.H. Grierson, 28 December 1972.

[42] NatWest Group Archives, NWB Dibbs Papers 6873. Proposed Merger of Orion Bank Ltd and Orion Termbank Ltd, July 1974.

[43] Fallon, 'How David Montagu gave a lead to Orion Bank', p.52.

44 Interview with Spike Wright.
45 Interview with David Montagu.
46 NatWest Group Archives, NWB Dibbs Papers 6873. Future of the Orion Group, 4 March 1976.
47 NatWest Group Archives, NWB Dibbs Papers 6873. B.V. Kelly, Orion Multinational Services and The Orion Group Structure, 1 April 1976, p.5.
48 NatWest Group Archives, NWB Dibbs Papers 6873. Agreed Position of All Shareholders on the Proposed Structural Changes re OMS, 13 October 1976.
49 NatWest Group Archives, NWB Dibbs Papers 6873. Letter from Alex Dibbs to Harold Hitchcock, 13 October 1976.
50 Fallon, 'How David Montagu gave a lead to Orion Bank', p.52.
51 Harris, 'Banking with a lucky lord'.

6 Petrodollars

1 'When I am dead and opened, you shall find Calais lying in my heart.' *Holinshed's Chronicles*, quoted in the *Oxford Dictionary of Quotations*. Her declaration was prompted by the loss of Calais from the English throne in 1557.
2 Robert Lacey, *The Kingdom* (London: Hutchinson, 1981), p.323.
3 Michael Field, *A Hundred Million Dollars a Day* (London: Sedgwick & Jackson, 1975), p.25.
4 In some countries increased 'participation' took the form of higher takes, in others nationalization: Libya nationalized BP's interests in November 1971; Iraq nationalized the Western-owned Iraq Petroleum Company in June 1972; and Iran nationalized the foreign oil companies' interests in March 1973.
5 Source: *International Financial Statistics Yearbook* (Washington DC: IMF, 1999), p.130.
6 'Recent developments in British banking'. Speech to Cardiff Business Club, 25 October 1976, quoted in Reid, *The Secondary Banking Crisis*, p.113.
7 Source: IMF, *World Economic Outlook*, 1984.
8 Interview with Spike Wright.
9 Appendix II, Section 4(1).
10 IFR 25th Anniversary 1974–1999, *IFR* (August 1999), p.32.
11 Translation: 'It's my nephew who saved the pound'. Interview with Leonard Ingrams.
12 Interview with Euan Macdonald.
13 SAMA later moved to Riyadh.
14 William de Gelsey's address at his retirement dinner, 30 June 1988.
15 NatWest Group Archives, NWB Dibbs Papers 6960. Middle East, Status Report to the Shareholders' Forum, May 1974.
16 Wilson, *The Chase*, p.232.
17 NatWest Group Archives, NWB Dibbs Papers 6869. Orion Newsletter, June/July 1974.
18 The 1998 annual report of Daimler Chrysler showed Kuwait as the second largest shareholder, with a 7 per cent stake, after Deutsche Bank's 12 per cent stake.

[19] NatWest Group Archives, NWB Dibbs Papers 6960. Middle East, Status Report to the Shareholders' Forum, May 1974.

[20] Omar Kassem, 'The Gulf needs creative financial engineering', *Euromoney* (July 1981).

[21] Fida Darwiche, *The Gulf Stock Exchange Crash: The Rise and Fall of the Souq Al-Manakh* (London: Croom Helm, 1986), pp.6–7.

[22] Kerr, *A History of the Eurobond Market*, p.55.

[23] Appendix II, S1/33.

[24] Source: Frederick G. Fisher, *International Bonds* (London: Euromoney, 1981), p.137.

[25] NatWest Group Archives, NWB Dibbs Papers 6869. Orion Newsletter, August/September 1974.

[26] NatWest Group Archives, NWB Dibbs Papers 6869. Orion Newsletter, August/September 1974.

[27] William de Gelsey, 'A star of the early days', *IFR* (October 1993), p.xx.

[28] Interview with Philip Hubbard.

[29] Interview with Khodadad Farmanfarmaian.

[30] Interview with Sir Christopher Chataway.

[31] Appendix II, S1/16.

[32] Interview with Patrick Browning, NatWest Group Archives, NWB Dibbs Papers 6869. Orion Newsletter, June/July 1975.

[33] Later Lord King, chairman of British Airways.

[34] NatWest Group Archives, NWB Dibbs Papers 6869. Orion Newsletter, June/July 1975.

[35] NatWest Group Archives, NWB Dibbs Papers 6871. Shareholders' Forum, 8 February 1978.

[36] NatWest Group Archives, NWB Dibbs Papers 6874. Audit September 1977, Appendix D.

[37] NatWest Group Archives, NWB Dibbs Papers 6871. Shareholders' Forum, 8 February 1978.

[38] NatWest Group Archives, NWB Dibbs Papers 6871. Shareholders' Forum, 8 February 1978.

[39] Wilson, *The Chase*, p.298.

[40] Appendix II, S1/29.

[41] NatWest Group Archives, NWB Dibbs Papers 6869/29. Orion Newsletter, November 1973.

[42] Appendix II, S2/2.

[43] Appendix II, S1/30.

[44] Interview with Sir John Gray, later UK ambassador to Lebanon, OECD and Belgium.

[45] Philip L. Zweig, *Wriston: Walter Wriston, Citibank and the Rise and Fall of American Financial Supremacy* (New York: Crown Publishers, 1995), p.103. Wriston's provocative pronouncement was quoted in an article in the *New York Times*, 14 September 1982.

[46] Calculated from tables of Orion financings.

7   Competition and innovation

1   Volcker and Gyohten, *Changing Fortunes*, p.164.
2   Fisher, *International Bonds*, p.25.
3   Source: *The Banker*, vol. 136 (November 1986), p.69.
4   *Euromoney* (October 1980), p.17.
5   Source: I.D. Bond, *Syndicated Credits Market* (London: Bank of England, 1985), Table 13.
6   Philip Hubbard, 'Eurobond innovation', *IFR* (October 1993), p.liv.
7   Kerr, *A History of the Eurobond Market*, p.49.
8   Leo Melamed, *Leo Melamed on the Markets: Twenty Years of Financial History as Seen by the Man Who Revolutionised the Markets* (New York: John Wiley & Sons, 1993), p.x.
9   *Wall Street Journal*, 16 May 1972.
10 David Kynaston, *LIFFE: A Market and its Makers* (Cambridge: Granta Editions, 1997), p.8.
11 Peter L. Bernstein, *Against the Gods* (New York: John Wiley & Sons, 1996), pp.313–316.
12 Source: Chicago Mercantile Exchange and Chicago Board of Trade.
13 Hayes and Hubbard, *Investment Banking*, p.53.
14 IFR 25th Anniversary 1974–1999, *IFR* (August 1999), pp. 17 and 26.
15 Sources: Orion loans – Orion Financings, various years. Total syndicated loans – Bond, *Syndicated Loans*, Table 2: Value of syndicated loans announced. 'Market share' means the proportion of syndicated loans in which Orion was either lead manager, co-lead manager or co-manager.
16 Source: NatWest Group Archives, NWB Dibbs Papers 6915. Shareholders' Forum, October 1980, Review of Orion's business markets in the period 1976–1980, p.5.
17 NatWest Group Archives, NWB Dibbs Papers 6902. 'Review of the concept and objectives of Orion, 31 July 1978', p.8.
18 *The Economist*, 4 January 1975.
19 *The Times*, 28 January 1975.
20 Interviews with Neil Balfour, William Slee and John Nash.
21 Source: NatWest Group Archives, NWB Dibbs Papers 6902. 'Review of the concept and objectives of Orion, 31 July 1978', p.17.
22 Sources: Orion – Orion Financings, 1971–79. Total – Hayes and Hubbard, *Investment Banking*, p.36. 'Market share' means the proportion of Eurobond new issues in which Orion was either lead manager, co-lead manager or co-manager.
23 Hayes and Hubbard, *Investment Banking*, p.51.
24 Interview with William de Gelsey.
25 Source: Hayes and Hubbard, *Investment Banking*, p.51. The figures for Credit Suisse First Boston, formed in 1978, incorporate those of its predecessor, Credit Suisse White Weld.
26 William de Gelsey's address at his retirement dinner, 30 June 1988.
27 Interview with Rod Chamberlain.
28 NatWest Group Archives, NWB Dibbs Papers 6902. 'Review of the concept and objectives of Orion, 31 July 1978', p.19.

[29] First-time borrowers brought to the Eurobond market by Orion in the mid-1970s included British Columbia Telephone, Canadian Pacific, Consolidated Bathurst, Dominion Bridge, Great Lakes Paper, PanCanadian Petroleum, Société Nationale de Chemin de Fer Française, Walter E. Heller Canada and Babcock & Wilcox.

[30] Interview with Sir Andrew Large.

[31] Interview with Philip Hubbard.

[32] Other reports included: *The Coupon Curve*; *Warrant Exercise Patterns*; and *The Conversion Pattern of Convertible Eurobonds*.

[33] Hayes and Hubbard, *Investment Banking*, p.54.

[34] Hayes and Hubbard, *Investment Banking*, p.53; Philip Hubbard, 'Eurobond innovation', *IFR* (October 1993), p.liv.

[35] Philip Hubbard, 'Eurobond innovation', *IFR* (October 1993), p.liv.

[36] NatWest Group Archives, NWB Dibbs Papers 6902. 'Review of the concept and objectives of Orion, 31 July 1978', p.22; Philip Hubbard, *Euromoney* (November, 1975).

[37] NatWest Group Archives, NWB Dibbs Papers 6902. 'Review of the concept and objectives of Orion, 31 July 1978', p.25.

[38] NatWest Group Archives, NWB Dibbs Papers 6902. 'Review of the concept and objectives of Orion, 31 July 1978', p.25.

[39] Wilson, *The Chase*, pp.169–171.

[40] *Daily Telegraph*, 13 May 1975.

[41] Interview with Sir Christopher Chataway.

[42] NatWest Group Archives, NWB Dibbs Papers 6960. Shareholders' Forum, Minutes of meeting, 27 September 1974; 6960. Letter from Philip Girle, OMS, to shareholders' representatives, 29 January 1975.

[43] NatWest Group Archives, NWB Dibbs Papers 6960. Shareholders' Forum, 'Orion Pacific Funding', 19 May 1975.

[44] NatWest Group Archives, NWB Dibbs Papers 6902. 'Review of the concept and objectives of Orion, 31 July 1978', p.31.

[45] Orion report and accounts 1979.

[46] Orion report and accounts 1974.

[47] NatWest Group Archives, NWB Dibbs Papers 6869. Orion Newsletter, April 1974.

[48] NatWest Group Archives, NWB Dibbs Papers 6909. Shareholders' Forum, 'Memorandum of views and opinions of shareholders expressed at meetings ... on 30th October 1978'.

[49] NatWest Group Archives, NWB Dibbs Papers 6910. Shareholders' Forum, 5 February 1979.

[50] Orion report and accounts 1977.

[51] NatWest Group Archives, NWB Dibbs Papers 6902. 'Review of the concept and objectives of Orion, 31 July 1978', p.28.

[52] NatWest Group Archives, NWB Dibbs Papers 6902. 'Review of the concept and objectives of Orion, 31 July 1978', p.4.

[53] NatWest Group Archives, NWB Dibbs Papers 6909. Shareholders' Forum, 30 October 1978.

54 NatWest Group Archives, NWB Dibbs Papers 6869. Orion Newsletter, August 1973.

55 Source: Orion report and accounts – various years.

56 NatWest Group Archives, NWB Dibbs Papers 6915. Shareholders' Forum, October 1980, Review of Orion's business markets in the period 1976–1980.

57 NatWest Group Archives, NWB Dibbs Papers 6915. Shareholders' Forum, October 1980, Review of Orion's business markets in the period 1976–1980, p.10.

58 NatWest Group Archives, NWB Dibbs Papers 6912. Orion Bank Limited, Board Minutes, 1 December 1980.

59 NatWest Group Archives, NWB Dibbs Papers 6874. Orion inspection, 1977.

60 NatWest Group Archives, NWB Dibbs Papers 6915. OBL Policy Committee, 28 July 1980.

61 NatWest Group Archives, NWB Dibbs Papers 6910. Orion Shipping Holdings Limited, Financial Status Report, 31 December 1979.

62 NatWest Group Archives, NWB Dibbs Papers 6917. Orion Bank, Policy Committee Minutes, 27 April 1981.

63 Orion report and accounts 1978, p.5.

8   Shareholders and management

1 Interview with Rod Chamberlain.

2 See Appendix III.

3 NatWest Group Archives, NWB Dibbs Papers 6914. Harold Hitchcock, Comments on Aide-Memoire re: New Proposal for the Conduct of Business, 30 January 1980.

4 Fallon, 'How David Montagu gave a lead to Orion Bank', p.56.

5 Source: *Euromoney*, (September 1976), pp.24–26.

6 Wilson, *The Chase*, p.234; 'Chase's merchant bank', *The Banker*, vol. 123 (November 1973), p.958.

7 NatWest Group Archives, NWB Dibbs Papers 6957. Shareholders' Forum – Venice, 11 June 1973.

8 Padraic Fallon, 'The crisis at Orion Bank', *Euromoney* (December 1979), p.14.

9 NatWest Group Archives, NWB 20089. *NatWest Intelligence Bulletin*, November 1971.

10 NatWest Group Archives, NWB Dibbs Papers 6959. Orion, 1 April 1971.

11 Interview with John Padovan.

12 NatWest Group Archives, NWB Dibbs Papers 6918. David Montagu to Alex Dibbs, 18 July 1978.

13 NatWest Group Archives, NWB Dibbs Papers 6918. David Montagu to Alex Dibbs, 18 July 1978.

14 Fallon, 'The crisis at Orion Bank', p.15.

15 NatWest Group Archives, NWB Dibbs Papers 6913. Alex Dibbs' discussion with Jock Finlayson, 1979.

16 NatWest Group Archives, NWB Dibbs Papers 6918. Report by W.N. McFadyen, managing director of Orion, 14 August 1978.

[17] Source: NatWest Group Archives, NWB Dibbs Papers 6918. Report by W.N. McFadyen, managing director of Orion, 14 August 1978.

[18] NatWest Group Archives, NWB Dibbs Papers 6902. Review of the concept and objectives of Orion, 31 July 1978, p.5.

[19] Fallon, 'The crisis at Orion Bank', p.16.

[20] NatWest Group Archives, NWB Dibbs Papers 6910. Confidential Notes, Orion Shareholders' Forum, London, 5 February 1979.

[21] Fallon, 'The crisis at Orion Bank', p.19.

[22] Fallon, 'The crisis at Orion Bank', p.16.

[23] NatWest Group Archives, NWB Dibbs Papers 6909. Orion Bank Limited – Forum and Board Meetings – 30 October 1978.

[24] Fallon, 'The crisis at Orion Bank', p.16.

[25] Quoted in Anthony Sampson, *The Money Lenders: Bankers in a Dangerous World* (London: Hodder and Stoughton, 1981), p.18.

[26] Quoted in Sampson, *The Money Lenders*, p.18.

[27] Anthony Sampson, *The Money Lenders*, p.108.

[28] Fallon, 'The crisis at Orion Bank', p.16.

[29] NatWest Group Archives, NWB Dibbs Papers 6957. R.B. Knight, Proposed Orion twelve-year loan, 6 November 1973.

[30] NatWest Group Archives, NWB Dibbs Papers 6871. Shareholders' Forum, 15–18 October 1977.

[31] Fallon, 'The crisis at Orion Bank', p.16.

[32] Appendix II, S1/29.

[33] Appendix II, S1/24.

[34] NatWest Group Archives, NWB Dibbs Papers 6909. Letter from David Montagu to the chairmen of the shareholder banks, 7 September 1978.

[35] NatWest Group Archives, NWB Dibbs Papers 6902. Review of the concept and objectives of Orion, 31 July 1978.

[36] NatWest Group Archives, NWB Dibbs Papers 6909. Note for the Chairman, Orion Bank, 13 September 1978.

[37] NatWest Group Archives, NWB Dibbs Papers 6909. Notes of a meeting held in Washington on Tuesday, 26 September 1978.

[38] NatWest Group Archives, NWB Dibbs Papers 6902. Review of the concept and objectives of Orion, 31 July 1978, p.4.

[39] NatWest Group Archives, NWB Dibbs Papers 6960. Orion Shareholders' Forum – October 1978.

[40] NatWest Group Archives, NWB Dibbs Papers 6909. Memo from J.K. Finlayson to the chairman, Royal Bank of Canada. Orion Bank Limited – Forum and Board Meetings – 30 October 1978.

[41] NatWest Group Archives, NWB Dibbs Papers 6909. Orion Bank Limited – Forum and Board Meetings – 30 October 1978.

[42] NatWest Group Archives, NWB Dibbs Papers 6902. Review of the concept and objectives of Orion, 31 July 1978, p.6.

[43] NatWest Group Archives, NWB Dibbs Papers 6902. Orion Shareholders' Forum, Policy Paper, Comments, 30 October 1978.

[44] NatWest Group Archives, NWB Dibbs Papers 6960. Orion Shareholders' Forum – October 1978.

[45] See Chapter 7, Table 7.9.

[46] NatWest Group Archives, NWB Dibbs Papers 6909. Orion Bank Limited – Forum and Board Meetings – 30 October 1978.

[47] NatWest Group Archives, NWB Dibbs Papers 6909. Orion Bank Limited – Forum and Board Meetings – 30 October 1978.

[48] Fallon, 'The crisis at Orion Bank', p.19.

[49] NatWest Group Archives, NWB Dibbs Papers 6910. Shareholders' Forum – February 1979, 26 January 1979.

[50] NatWest Group Archives, NWB Dibbs Papers 6913. 26 July 1979, Note by Alex Dibbs re visit by David Montagu.

[51] Fallon, 'The crisis at Orion Bank', p.27.

[52] NatWest Group Archives, NWB Dibbs Papers 6913. Alex Dibbs to Robin Leigh-Pemberton, 19 September 1979.

[53] NatWest Group Archives, NWB Dibbs Papers 6913. Memorandum of Discussion re: Orion, August 1979.

[54] NatWest Group Archives, NWB Dibbs Papers 6913. Orion, 29 August 1979.

[55] Fallon, 'The crisis at Orion Bank', p.12.

[56] Fallon, 'The crisis at Orion Bank', p.24.

[57] *Daily Telegraph*, 11 October 1979.

[58] Fallon, 'The crisis at Orion Bank', p.14.

[59] Fallon, 'The crisis at Orion Bank', p.25.

[60] Interview with Philip Hubbard.

[61] Fallon, 'The crisis at Orion Bank', p.14.

---

9   Swimming against the tide

[1] Fallon, 'The crisis at Orion Bank', p.27.

[2] Fallon, 'The crisis at Orion Bank', p.22.

[3] Interview with Jeff Cunningham.

[4] Fallon, 'The crisis at Orion Bank', p.19.

[5] Fallon, 'The crisis at Orion Bank', p.21.

[6] '… a new head for Orion', *The Banker*, vol. 129 (December 1979), p.113.

[7] NatWest Group Archives, NWB 5803, 'Bank Profile 11: Viscount Sandon', *3 Crowns Magazine* (1967), pp.16–18.

[8] Fallon, 'The crisis at Orion Bank', p.21.

[9] Interview with Tony Cravero.

[10] 'Montagu departure marks watershed for Orion', *Financial Weekly*, 19 October 1979.

[11] Interview with Philip Hubbard.

[12] NatWest Group Archives, NWB Dibbs Papers 6897. Orion Bank Board Minutes, 30 October 1979.

[13] NatWest Group Archives, NWB Dibbs Papers 6897. Note by Alex Dibbs to Mr Hitchcock, 29 October 1979.

[14] NatWest Group Archives, NWB Dibbs Papers 6897. Orion Bank Limited, Board Minutes, 29 October 1979.

[15] Interview with Tony Cravero.

[16] Interview with Jeff Cunningham.
[17] NatWest Group Archives, NWB Dibbs Papers 6915. Orion Bank Limited, Minutes of the Policy Committee, 21 April 1980.
[18] NatWest Group Archives, NWB Dibbs Papers 6920. Letter from Alex Dibbs to Harold Hitchcock, 4 March 1980.
[19] NatWest Group Archives, NWB Dibbs Papers 6920. Letter from Jock Finlayson to Jeff Cunningham, 4 March 1980.
[20] NatWest Group Archives, NWB Dibbs Papers 6920. Telex from John Haley, Chase Manhattan Bank, New York, to Franz Lutolf, General Manager, Swiss Bank Corporation, Zurich, 4 March 1980.
[21] NatWest Group Archives, NWB Dibbs Papers 6920. Press Release, 8 February 1980.
[22] NatWest Group Archives, NWB Dibbs Papers 6914. T. J. Cunningham, New Proposals for the Conduct of Business, January 1980, p.1.
[23] NatWest Group Archives, NWB Dibbs Papers 6914. Viscount Sandon, Aide-Memoire re: New Proposals for the Conduct of Business, January 1980.
[24] NatWest Group Archives, NWB Dibbs Papers 6914. Harold Hitchcock, Comments on Aide-Memoire re: New Proposals for the Conduct of Business, 30 January 1980.
[25] NatWest Group Archives, NWB Dibbs Papers 6914. Viscount Sandon, Aide-Memoire re New Proposals for the Conduct of Business, January 1980.
[26] NatWest Group Archives, NWB Dibbs Papers 6914. T.J. Cunningham, New Proposals for the Conduct of Business, January 1980, p.4.
[27] NatWest Group Archives, NWB Dibbs Papers 6914. T.J. Cunningham, New Proposals for the Conduct of Business, January 1980, p.3.
[28] NatWest Group Archives, NWB Dibbs Papers 6914. T.J. Cunningham, New Proposals for the Conduct of Business, January 1980. pp.2–3.
[29] NatWest Group Archives, NWB Dibbs Papers 6914. Harold Hitchcock, Comments on Aide-Memoire re: New Proposals for the Conduct of Business, 30 January 1980.
[30] NatWest Group Archives, NWB Dibbs Papers 6914. Harold Hitchcock, Comments on Aide-Memoire re: New Proposals for the Conduct of Business, 30 January 1980.
[31] NatWest Group Archives, NWB Dibbs Papers 6914. Note to Mr H.A. Hitchcock from R.B. Knight, 6 February 1980.
[32] NatWest Group Archives, NWB Dibbs Papers 6910. Shareholders' Forum, Closed Session, 5 February 1979.
[33] NatWest Group Archives, NWB Dibbs Papers 6910. Meeting of Shareholders, 5 February 1980.
[34] Source: NatWest Group Archives, NWB Dibbs Papers 6910. Analysis of Income for 1979, 30 January 1980. This excludes £4.9 million interest on capital and the income of subsidiaries, notably Leasing and Guernsey.
[35] NatWest Group Archives, NWB Dibbs Papers 6910. Analysis of Income for 1979, 30 January 1980. This derived three-fifths from deposit dealing and two-fifths from foreign exchange transactions.
[36] NatWest Group Archives, NWB Dibbs Papers 6915. Orion Group Risk Analyis, 31 August 1980.

37 Sources: Market – 'Value of Syndicated Loans Announced', Bond, *Syndicated Credits Market*, Table 2; Orion – Orion Financings.

38 NatWest Group Archives, NWB Dibbs Papers 6915. OBL Policy Committee Minutes, 21 April 1980.

39 NatWest Group Archives, NWB Dibbs Papers 6915. OBL Policy Committee Minutes, 21 April 1980.

40 Interview with Patrick Browning.

41 NatWest Group Archives, NWB Dibbs Papers 6915. OBL Policy Committee Minutes, 21 April 1980.

42 Interview with Patrick Browning.

43 Fisher, *International Bonds*, p.25.

44 Kerr, *A History of the Eurobond Market*, p.59.

45 Kerr, *A History of the Eurobond Market*, p.63.

46 Kerr, *A History of the Eurobond Market*, p.107.

47 Sources: Market – Hayes and Hubbard, *Investment Banking*, p.36; Orion – Orion Financings.

48 Orion – Orion Financings, 1981; Hayes and Hubbard, *Investment Banking*, pp.51 and 55.

49 Orion report and accounts 1979.

50 NatWest Group Archives, NWB Dibbs Papers 6910. Analysis of Income for 1979, 30 January 1980.

51 Sources: Appendix IV.

52 NatWest Group Archives, NWB Dibbs Papers 6920. Orion Bank Limited, Request for Capital Increase, 3 November 1980.

53 NatWest Group Archives, NWB Dibbs Papers 6915. Review of Orion's Business Markets in the Period 1976–1980, Shareholders' Forum, October 1980, pp.2–3.

54 NatWest Group Archives, NWB Dibbs Papers 6915. Review of Orion's Business Markets in the Period 1976–1980, Shareholders' Forum, October 1980, p.14.

55 NatWest Group Archives, NWB Dibbs Papers 6915. Report of Secondary Market Activities, 3 October 1980.

56 NatWest Group Archives, NWB Dibbs Papers 6915. Report on Secondary Market Activities, 3 October 1980.

57 NatWest Group Archives, NWB Dibbs Papers 6920. Orion Bank Limited, Request for Capital Increase, 3 November 1980.

58 NatWest Group Archives, NWB Dibbs Papers 6920. Note from Dudley Sandon to Jeff Cunningham, no date.

59 Letter from Jeff Cunningham.

60 'The puzzling international approach of NatWest', *Euromoney* (July 1981), p.144.

61 'The puzzling international approach of NatWest', p.142.

62 NatWest Group Archives, NWB Dibbs Papers 6905. Note by Alex Dibbs to H.A. Hitchcock, 11 July 1978.

63 Interview with Philip Hubbard.

64 Interview with Jeff Cunningham.

65 'The puzzling international approach of NatWest', p.141.

66 Quoted in McDowell, *Quick to the Frontier*, p.414.

10   Orion Royal Bank

[1] McDowell, *Quick to the Frontier*, p.405.
[2] 'Royal Flush – or a bank in turmoil?', *Euromoney* (November 1987), p.54.
[3] Appendix IV.
[4] Interview with Jeff Cunningham.
[5] 'Consortium concern', *The Economist*, 25 October 1979.
[6] Interview with Rod Chamberlain.
[7] *Financial Times*, 2 September 1982.
[8] *Financial Times*, 2 September 1982.
[9] Hayes and Hubbard, *Investment Banking*, p.36.
[10] Sources: Orion – Orion Financings; Market – Capital DATA Ltd. 'Market share' means the proportion of Eurobond new issues in which Orion was either lead manager, co-lead manager or co-manager.
[11] Orion Financings, 1985.
[12] Orion Financings, 1985.
[13] William de Gelsey's address at his retirement dinner, 30 June 1988.
[14] Hayes and Hubbard, *Investment Banking*, p.361.
[15] Orion Financings, 1985.
[16] See Chapter 9.
[17] RBC Archive, Press release, 16 March 1987.
[18] Orion Royal Bank report and accounts, 1985.
[19] Interview with Henry Mutkin.
[20] Interview with Nicholas Villiers.
[21] Interview with Sir Christopher Chataway.
[22] Interview with Patrick Browning.
[23] *Financial Times*, 2 September 1982.
[24] Sources: Capital DATA Loanware. Data refers to lead/co-lead/co-agent participations with full amount apportionment. 'Market share' means the proportion of total market syndicated loans in which Royal Bank was either lead/co-lead/ co-agent.
[25] Source: *Euromoney* – 'Mean LIBOR pricing for facilities launched into Euro market. Data derived from public issue loans'.
[26] Orion Financings, 1985.
[27] Hayes and Hubbard, *Investment Banking*, p.54.
[28] Orion Financings, 1983.
[29] Orion Financings, 1985.
[30] Orion Financings, 1984.
[31] RBC Archive, *Insight* (May 1989), p.8.
[32] Interview with Alan Clifton.
[33] 'The sad tale of Orion Royal', *Euromoney* (January 1986), p.40.
[34] Source: Appendix IV.
[35] McDowell, *Quick to the Frontier*, p.422.
[36] 'The sad tale of Orion Royal', p.40.
[37] 'The sad tale of Orion Royal', p.38.
[38] 'The sad tale of Orion Royal', p.38.
[39] 'The Euromarket super-bank 1984 vintage', *IFR*, IFR 25th Anniversary, 1974–1999 (August 1999), p.48.

[40] 'The sad tale of Orion Royal', p.40.

[41] Samuel L. Hayes and Philip M. Hubbard, *Investment Banking: A Tale of Three Cities* (Boston MA: Harvard Business School, 1990).

[42] Interview with Philip Hubbard.

[43] 'The Euromarket super-bank 1984 vintage', p.48.

[44] *Financial Times*, 1 September 1986.

[45] Interview with John Sanders.

[46] Interview with David Pritchard.

[47] Source: Hayes and Hubbard, *Investment Banking*, p.77.

[48] Source: Troben Juul Andersen, *Euromarket Instruments: A Guide to the World's Largest Debt Market* (New York: New York Institute of Finance, 1990), p.115.

[49] Interview with David Pritchard.

[50] *IFR*, 6 December 1986.

[51] RBC Archive, Orion Royal Bank, Press Release, 16 March 1987, 'Floating rate note market making – March 1987'.

[52] Interview with John Sanders.

[53] Orion's withdrawal from the Eurobond market in 1987 allowed Hambros to increase its market share of the Australian dollar sector. In 1998 when Hambros was broken up, RBC Dominion Securities bought the business and re-entered a market that Orion Royal had quit a decade earlier.

[54] *Financial Times*, 3 November 1987.

[55] Source: Appendix IV.

[56] See page 191.

[57] Interview with Paul Taylor.

[58] Interview with Paul Taylor.

[59] RBC Archive, *Interest*, May 1989, p.6, Conversation with Michael Perry.

[60] RBC Archive, Letter from Bryce W. Douglas, vice president Dominion Securities Inc. to John Sanders, chairman and chief executive Orion Royal Bank, 2 March 1988.

[61] Interview with David Pritchard.

[62] Interview with David Pritchard.

[63] The name Orion is still owned by RBC.

---

11   Decline of consortium banking

[1] *Financial Times*, 31 August 1983.

[2] Source: Bank of England, *Quarterly Bulletin*. Appendix II, Section 4(1).

[3] Appendix II, S1/1.

[4] Source: Appendix II.

[5] Appendix II, S1/29.

[6] Appendix II, S1/24.

[7] Appendix II, S1/35.

[8] Appendix II, S1/4.

[9] Appendix II, S1/22.

[10] Appendix II, S1/23.

[11] Appendix II, S1/11.

12 Appendix II, S2/6.
13 Appendix II, S1/15.
14 Appendix II, S1/23.
15 Appendix II, S1/7.
16 Appendix II, S1/24.
17 London Multinational Bank, annual report 1977.
18 Appendix II, S1/31.
19 Appendix II, S2/1.
20 Interviews with Uli Pendl and Kevin Ruxton.
21 Interviews with Uli Pendl and Kevin Ruxton.
22 Appendix II, S1/4.
23 Appendix II, S1/19.
24 Appendix II, S1/10.
25 Appendix III.
26 Interview with Neil Balfour.
27 Interview with Neil Balfour.
28 Holmes and Green, *Midland*, p.44.
29 Source: Appendix II, Section 4(2).
30 Source: Bank of England, *Quarterly Bulletin*. Maturity transformation is the net foreign currency claims over one year as a percentage of total foreign currency claims, as at 31 May each year.
31 George S. Moore, *The Banker's Life* (New York: W.W. Norton & Co, 1987), p.211. He was referring to ADELA, a venture capital and leasing company for Latin America, of which he was a director.
32 Interview with George Gunson.
33 Appendix II, S1/31.
34 'Investors rush for bank shares: Scandinavian Bank', *The Guardian*, 5 March 1987.
35 *Investors Chronicle*, 8 December 1989.
36 London Multinational Bank, annual reports 1975, 1976 and 1977.
37 Appendix II, S1/24.
38 Richard B. Miller, *The Story of a Bank in Crisis* (New York: McGraw-Hill, 1993), p.108.
39 Zweig, *Wriston*, p.420.
40 IMF, *International Financial Statistics*.
41 Interview with Gérard Legrain.
42 Source: Appendix II.
43 Appendix II, S1/25.
44 Appendix II, S1/6.
45 Appendix II, S1/7.
46 *Financial Times*, 11 May 1985.
47 Appendix II, S1/23.
48 Appendix II, S1/31.
49 *Financial Times*, 23 August 1983.
50 *Financial Times*, 23 August 1983.

51 *Financial Times*, 31 August 1983.
52 *Financial Times*, 17 August 1983.
53 Volcker and Gyohten, *Changing Fortunes*, p.215.
54 'Citicorp comes clean on third-world debt', *The Economist*, 23 May 1987, p.65.
55 Volcker and Gyohten, *Changing Fortunes*, p.216.
56 Zweig, *Wriston*, p.851.
57 *Financial Times*, 10 January 1990.
58 *Financial Times*, 12 August 1987.
59 Appendix IV.
60 Source: Appendix II.
61 *Financial Times*, 5 December 1989.
62 *The Times*, 10 November 1989.
63 *Financial Times*, 10 January 1990.
64 *Financial Times*, 11 January 1989.
65 *Financial Times*, 13 March 1990.
66 *Financial Times*, 13 March 1990.
67 Interview with George Gunson.
68 *Financial Times*, 5 December 1989.
69 *Financial Times*, 8 September 1989.
70 *Financial Times*, 21 June 1991.
71 Appendix II, S1/3.
72 Appendix II, S1/31.
73 *Financial Times*, 13 December 1989.
74 *Financial Times*, 6 June 1990.
75 *Financial Times*, 27 September 1989.
76 *Financial Times*, 15 March 1990.
77 Source: Appendix II, Section 4(3).
78 Appendix III.
79 Bussière, 'Paribas, le Crédit Lyonnais et leur stratégie européenne depuis les années 1960: entre anticipations et choix de la raison'.
80 Appendix II, S1/33.
81 Appendix II, S1/32.
82 Appendix II, S1/20.
83 In 1999, Saudi International Bank merged with Gulf International Bank, as a result of which it remained indirectly in consortium ownership (Appendix II, S1/30).
84 Appendix II, S1/16.
85 Appendix II, S1/1.
86 Moore, *The Banker's Life*, p.211.
87 Interview with John Champion. Appendix II, S2/19.
88 Interview with George Gunson.
89 Lothar Gall, Gerald D. Feldman, Harold James, Carl-Ludwig Holtferich and Hans E. Buschgen, *The Deutsche Bank 1870–1995* (London: Weidenfeld & Nicolson, 1995), p.759.

12   Consortia and strategic alliances in finance

1 Gary Hamel, Yves L. Doz and C.K. Prahalad, 'Collaborate with your competitors – and win', *Harvard Business Review* (January–February 1989), p.133.
2 Peter Lorange and Johan Roos, *Strategic Alliances: Formation, Implementation, and Evolution* (Oxford: Blackwell, 1992), pp.3–12.
3 See Chapter 2; Richard Roberts, *Schroders: Merchants & Bankers* (London: Macmillan, 1992), pp.66–73.
4 Roberts, *Schroders*, p.364.
5 *Financial Times*, Global Stock Exchanges Supplement, p.II, 24 March 1998.
6 Interview with David Anthony, insurance sector analyst, Standard & Poors, London.
7 Eureko, annual report and accounts 1999, p.3.
8 'Cash service delivery: club or standalone?', *Corporate Finance*, March 1999, pp.28–32.
9 *Financial Times*, 26 June 1998. Barclays plc annual review 1998.
10 Lorange and Roos, *Strategic Alliances*, p.11.
11 Lorange and Roos, *Strategic Alliances*, p.12.
12 Richard Roberts, *Inside International Finance* (London: Orion, 1999), p.105.
13 George S. Moore, *The Banker's Life* (New York: W.W. Norton, 1987), p.212.
14 *Financial Times*, 24 April 1989.
15 *Financial Times*, 5 May 1989.
16 *A Profile: Yorkshire Bank*. Yorkshire Bank plc, Report and Accounts 1990.
17 ICFC: Industrial and Commercial Finance Corporation. FCI: Finance Corporation for Industry. See Richard Coopey and Donald Clarke, *3i: Fifty Years Investing in Industry* (Oxford: Oxford University Press, 1995).
18 David Kynaston, *The City of London: Illusions of Gold, 1914–1945* (Chatto & Windus, 1999), p.496.
19 Now part of Royal Bank of Scotland.
20 Arie de Geus, *The Living Company: Growth, Learning and Longevity in Business* (London: Nicholas Brearley, 1997), p.7.
21 de Geus, The Living Company, p.9.
22 Robert DeYoung, 'Birth, growth, and life or death of newly chartered banks', *Federal Reserve Bank of Chicago Economic Perspectives* (1999), iii, pp.18–35.
23 Lisa Endlich, *Goldman Sachs: The Culture of Success* (London: Little, Brown, 1999), p.ix.
24 Lorange and Roos, *Strategic Alliances*, p.3.
25 Kenichi Ohmae, 'Globalization makes alliances an essential tool for serving customers', *Harvard Business Review* (March–April 1989), p.143.

Index

NOTE: *Italic* script indicates a consortium banking group that is profiled in Appendix II; these names are followed by S1 or S2, plus number, which refers to Section 1 and Section 2 of the list of profiles on pages 241–2. Only banks that played a significant part in the narrative are indexed. Many banks have seen changes in their name and ownership in recent decades; new names or parentages of banks (as at June 2000) are shown in brackets. Banks operating through holding companies or subsidiaries are listed by their generally known name. P, plus numbers, indicates the page and plate in the plates section.